D1597834

ATLAS OF THE BIBLICAL WORLD

Joseph Rhymer

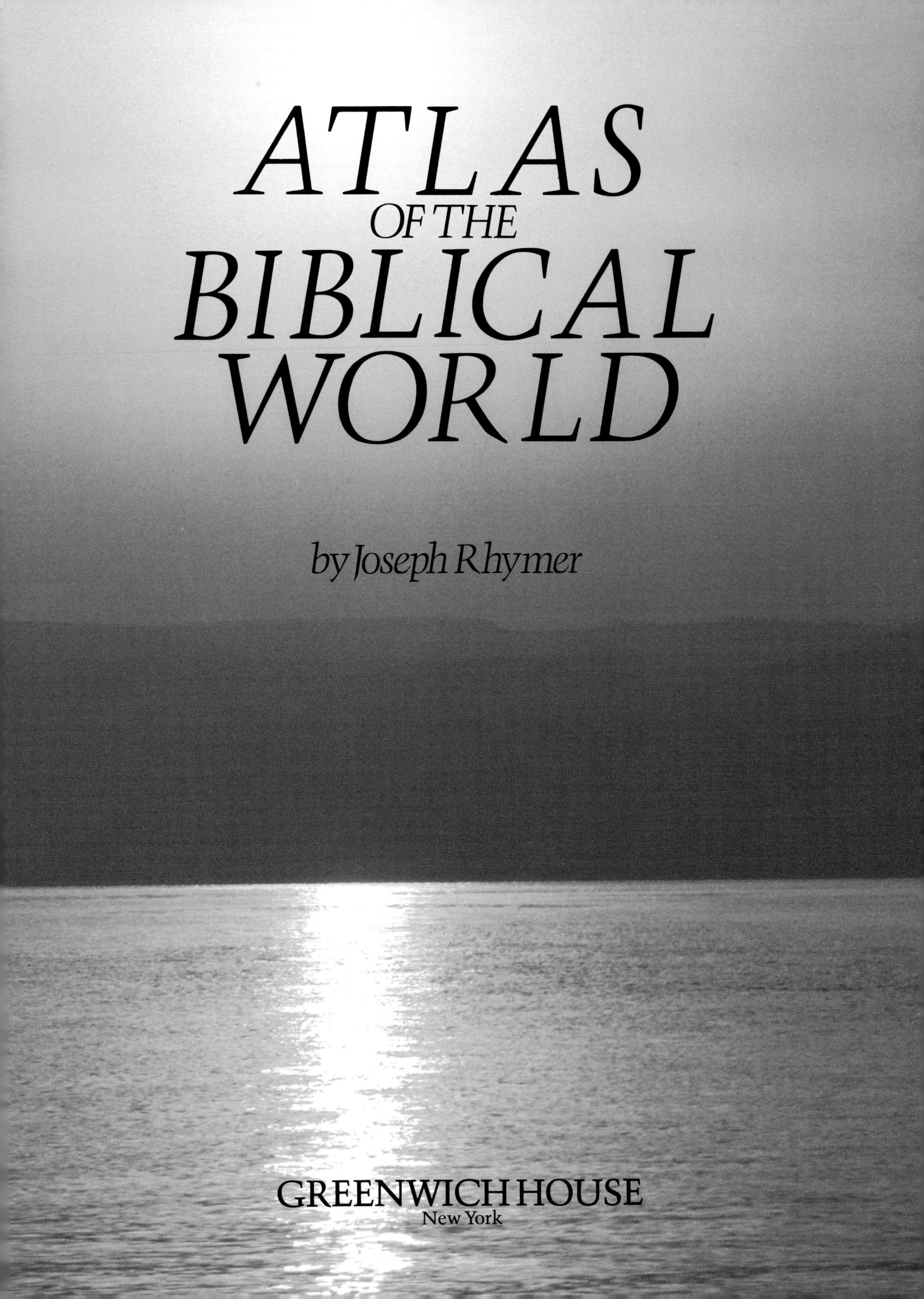

ATLAS OF THE BIBLICAL WORLD

by Joseph Rhymer

GREENWICH HOUSE
New York

For Jean

This 1982 edition is published by Greenwich House, a division of Arlington House, Inc., distributed by Crown Publishers, Inc.

Library of Congress Cataloging in Publication Data

Rhymer, Joseph, 1927-
Atlas of the biblical world.

Includes indexes.
1. Bible – Geography. 2. Bible – History of Biblical events. 3. Bible – History of contemporary events. 4. Bible – Antiquities. 5. Jews – History – To 70 A.D. 6. Church history – Primitive and early church, ca. 30-600. I. Title.
G2230.R47 1982 220.9'1 82-675195
ISBN 0-517-38357-8

h g f e d c b a

This book was designed and produced by QED Publishing Limited, 32 Kingly Court, London W1.

Art director Alastair Campbell
Production director Edward Kinsey
Editorial director Jeremy Harwood
Senior Editor Kathy Rooney
Editor Nicola Thompson
Editorial Hilary Arnold, Mary Trewby, Carol Cormack, Joanna Rait
Senior Designer Caroline Courtney
Design assistant Annie Collenette

Woodcuts Jonathan Heale
Illustrations Marion Appleton, Gerard Brown, Chris Forsey, Edwina Keene, Abdul Aziz Khan, David Mallott, Simon Roulstone, John Woodcock
Maps © Copyright 1982 QED Publishing Limited
Map Typography Line & Line

The photographs in this book were specially commissioned and were taken by Ian Howes

A limited edition of woodcuts by Jonathan Heale were specially commissioned for this book. Further details from QED Publishing Ltd, 32 Kingly Court, London W1, England.

QED would like to give special thanks to Fabian Russell-Cobb and Palle Bukdahl for their invaluable assistance.

Filmset in Great Britain by Text Filmsetters Ltd, Orpington, Kent and Flowery Typesetters, London.
Colour origination by Rodney Howe & Co Ltd, London and Hong Kong Graphic Arts Ltd, Hong Kong.
Printed in Hong Kong by Leefung Asco Printers Ltd.

Contents

Foreword

The Bible is one of the key source books in human history. Not only is it a foundation for two of the world's most influential religious faiths – Judaism and Christianity; it is also an enthralling account of human achievement at the time of the first civilizations.

To make full sense of this unique record, however, the reader needs to know as much as possible about the times in which it was written and, indeed, how the record came to be made. Only by placing the stories and events of the Bible in the broadest possible context and providing a modern explanation of what, on the surface, can appear archaic and difficult to understand, can today's readers gain a full appreciation of its message. The *Atlas of the Biblical World* provides a bridge between the world of the Bible and the world of the present day.

The author is deeply grateful to all who have helped in the creation of this book, particularly the principal consultant, John H. Fitzsimmons of St Peter's College, Glasgow; David S. M. Hamilton, Minister of New Kilpatrick Church of Scotland Parish, Bearsden; Noel S. Donnelly, and John A. McCarry. The author's original plans, textual material and suggestions became the book through the contributions and creative collaboration of Alastair Campbell, Ted Kinsey, Kathy Rooney, Nicola Thompson and Caroline Courtney of QED. John Todd, of Darton, Longman & Todd kindly gave permission for the text of *The Jerusalem Bible* to be used for the biblical quotations, and for its Chronological Table to be taken as a basis for the chronologies. The sequence followed for the biblical writings is adapted from the author's *The Bible in Order* (Darton, Longman & Todd/ Doubleday).

Joseph Rhymer
St Andrew's College,
Bearsden, Scotland.
August, 1982.

Editor's Note

Key to the chronologies

The chronologies throughout the book show the lives and reigns of people and when and where important events occurred. The dot to the left of each entry refers to the region affected.

A margin of error should be allowed for all dates before about 1000 BC as it is difficult to be precise about events and periods before this time. Dates given in brackets after the name of a ruler refer to the length of his reign; all other dates give the person's lifespan. For convenience, measurements are given in imperial with approximate metric equivalents afterwards.

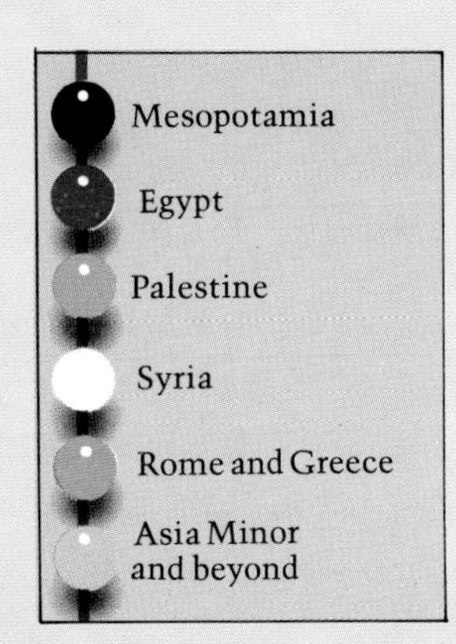

The following abbreviations of the books of the Bible are used in this book.

Old Testament

Genesis	Gen
Exodus	Exod
Leviticus	Lev
Numbers	Num
Deuteronomy	Deut
Joshua	Josh
Judges	Judg
Ruth	Ruth
1 Samuel	1 Sam
2 Samuel	2 Sam
1 Kings	1 Kgs
2 Kings	2 Kgs
1 Chronicles	1 Chr
2 Chronicles	2 Chr
Ezra	Ezr
Nehemiah	Neh
Tobit	Tobit
Judith	Judith
Esther	Esth
1 Maccabees	1 Macc
2 Maccabees	2 Macc
Job	Job
Psalms	Ps
Proverbs	Prov
Ecclesiastes	Eccles
Song of Songs	S. of Songs
Wisdom	Wis
Ecclesiasticus	Ecclus
Isaiah	Isa
Jeremiah	Jer
Lamentations	Lam
Baruch	Bar
Ezekiel	Ezek
Daniel	Dan
Hosea	Hos
Joel	Joel
Amos	Amos
Obadiah	Obad
Jonah	Jon
Micah	Mic
Nahum	Nah
Habakkuk	Hab
Zephaniah	Zeph
Haggai	Hag
Zechariah	Zech
Malachi	Mal

New Testament

Matthew	Matt
Mark	Mark
Luke	Luke
John	John
Act of the Apostles	Acts
Romans	Rom
1 Corinthians	1 Cor
2 Corinthians	2 Cor
Galatians	Gal
Ephesians	Eph
Philippians	Phil
Colossians	Col
1 Thessalonians	1 Thess
2 Thessalonians	2 Thess
1 Timothy	1 Tim
2 Timothy	2 Tim
Titus	Tit
Philemon	Philem
Hebrews	Heb
James	Jas
1 Peter	1 Pet
2 Peter	2 Pet
1 John	1 John
2 John	2 John
3 John	3 John
Jude	Jude
Revelation	Rev

1 · GOD'S CH

OSEN PEOPLE

Yahweh made Pharoah, king of Egypt, stubborn, and he gave chase to the sons of Israel as they made their triumphant escape. (Exod 14:8)

The Bible and its People

Although collated over nearly 2,000 years, the many fragments of material which make up the Bible – much of it evolved from an ancient oral tradition – are firmly linked by a common experience of God, who was an integral part of the people's history and lives.

The Bible is not the work of one person, one generation or even one nation. It is a collection of writings produced by many individuals over 2,000 years. Yet there is a firm link between the many fragments – they all express an experience of God. The Hebrew people who wrote the Old Testament and the early Christians who wrote the New Testament believed that God was making himself known to them and this was the central theme of their writings. Yet what they produced was not abstract religious philosophy. They wrote stories of ordinary, everyday life and detailed accounts of social and political history following the actual events that span those 2,000 years. God was an integral part of their history and daily existence and not a separate compartment of their lives.

It is impossible to say precisely how and when any single part of the Bible was written. Every book, every story and every incident it contains were related many times by many people. They were edited and amended in ancient times as the fragments were brought together. This long and complex process produced the Bible in its final form. The material was arranged not in the order in which it was written but in the order of religious importance.

Certain basic assumptions about the Bible can be made with confidence. It is in two parts and each part has a key. The escape from Egypt, the exodus, is the key to the Old Testament, and the crucifixion and resurrection of Jesus is the key to the New Testament. The exodus took place in *c*1250 BC and the crucifixion in *c*AD 30 but neither of these events was fully understood at those times. It was centuries before the significance of the escape from Egypt was seen and it took several generations to realize the full importance of the crucifixion.

Over the years, the stories of these events and their religious significance were passed on by word of mouth. They were part of the communal experience of history and worship and it was from these oral versions that the first written accounts were made. So the Bible, taking in these written accounts, traces the consequences of God's decisive acts through the lives of the people who were directly affected by them. There are other kinds of material in the Bible, including commentaries on the significance of the main events, but they were always written in ways that reflected the times and locations of those events. The writers were people trying to understand how their lives were affected by God. None of the material was merely speculative or written as abstract studies of religion.

In this atlas, the material which makes up the Bible has been arranged in the order in which it is believed it was written. There are disagreements between experts about details of timing and location of particular parts of the Bible, but, generally, it is possible to place the parts of the Bible in their historical context.

BELOW AND RIGHT The contents of the Bible are a combination of many experiences gathered together during a period of 2,000 years. Two historical events give form to the many different kinds of writing it contains – the Hebrew escape from Egypt in the thirteenth century BC, and the crucifixion of Jesus of Nazareth in the first century AD. In one way or another, all the biblical books reflect the religious meaning of these events on the lives of ordinary people. They believed that God had made himself known at such times, and that they could respond to such a God in their everyday lives. The Palestinian region today is still troubled by aggression and war, as it was in biblical times. People in all branches of society draw strength from their faith and belief.

BELOW The Hebrews adopted the farming techniques of the people of Palestine when they first settled in the region during the second millenium BC. But they jealously guarded their unique religious traditions, which had been confirmed for them by the escape from Egypt and the covenant with God. They came to see that their agricultural prosperity came from their God, just as he had met the needs of their shepherd ancestors. INSET LEFT Modern methods of irrigation have restored much of the old prosperity of Palestine, combined sometimes with simple but effective transportation. INSET RIGHT Routes through Palestine brought influences from powerful neighbours, and religious beliefs which the Hebrews adapted to their own needs.

The 'Fertile Crescent'

Palestine, which was settled by the 'Sea Peoples', was part of a 'fertile crescent' linking the vast rich valleys inhabited by two ancient civilizations – Egyptian and Mesopotamian. The Hebrews were one of the nomadic groups who grazed the sparse pastures between desert and fertile land.

'Fertile crescent'

Main trade routes

SETTLED AREAS **A long arc of agricultural land stretched from Egypt to Mesopotamia, through Palestine. Aptly called the 'fertile crescent', it supported the main settlements of the ancient Near and Middle East. Palestine was a narrow pass in the main land communications which each great power tried to control. The peoples of Palestine were often caught in confrontations between more powerful neighbours. Apart from the Egyptians, most of the inhabitants of the whole area originated in the region of the Arabian Desert before moving into the agricultural lands. Amorites and Aramaeans were nomadic pastoralists who established early kingdoms on the edge of the more prosperous parts. The Hebrews themselves were originally nomads who conquered Canaan.**

The two great civilizations of the Near and Middle East in ancient times grew up in two vast fertile valleys. The River Nile supported the ancient Egyptians while the Mesopotamians lived on the banks of the Tigris and Euphrates rivers. Between the two there is parched desert and the Dead Sea, and there is Palestine. This tiny corridor of land provides the only fertile strip from the Persian Gulf to the Nile Valley. Its position was vital. It linked the two abundant valleys forming a long stretch of fertile land from one end of the region to the other and known as the 'fertile crescent'. It also naturally became the major route for traders between the civilizations.

Rising in the complex of great African lakes which straddle the equator, the River Nile winds down through the Sudan and the eastern end of the Sahara Desert until it sprawls out into the fan-shaped swamp of river mouths and marshes which make up its delta. For most of its journey, it flows through desert, with minimal rainfall and no tributaries to feed it. The people who drained the marshes around the delta and learned to make use of the great river formed one of the oldest civilizations of the ancient world. The pyramids they built had been standing for more than 2,500 years when Jesus Christ was born.

The River Nile was the unifying factor for the peoples who lived along it. Its waters, and the mud it left behind after the annual floods from the mountains of Ethiopia, turned the desert into rich agricultural land and made Egypt the most dependable source of food in the eastern Mediterranean. Power shifted between the delta cities – Memphis in Lower Egypt, and Thebes, the capital of Upper Egypt, which ended where the First Cataract interrupted navigation from the coast. Beyond the First Cataract lay Nubia and, eventually, tropical Africa.

Beyond the desert to the east of Palestine was Mesopotamia, drained by both the Tigris and Euphrates which in ancient times entered the Persian Gulf separately, some 125 miles (200 km) north-west of the present coastline. To the east, the area is bordered by a long mountainous region stretching from India to Turkey. Between the mountains and the desert, Mesopotamia was peopled, like Egypt, by civilizations which had learned to control the river waters and use them for their agriculture. Power was located at several centres – Sumer and Babylonia near the Persian Gulf, straddling the River Euphrates, and Assyria about 435 miles (700 km) to the north on the River Tigris. Beyond Assyria was Mitanni. For all its apparent strength, Mesopotamia was frequently threatened by incursions from eastern mountain tribes, and no single power managed to dominate all Mesopotamia for long.

Beyond Syria to the north the Hittites inhabited the area which is now Turkey. The Hittites briefly extended their power into the 'fertile crescent', but their land had nothing comparable to the great rivers to give continuity, and they were overrun by migrants from the west.

Throughout the 'fertile crescent', from the Persian Gulf to the borders of Egypt, independent nomadic shepherds grazed the sparse areas of pasture between

RIGHT **The Near and Middle East is a region of great geographical contrasts, which have left their mark on the peoples of both ancient and modern times. Most dramatic is the deep cleft which contains the Dead Sea – the Salt Sea of the Bible – which has no outlet. Mineral deposits, formed by high evaporation rates, prevented farming, except where there were freshwater springs. Human settlements, such as Jericho, were only possible where these springs formed oases.**

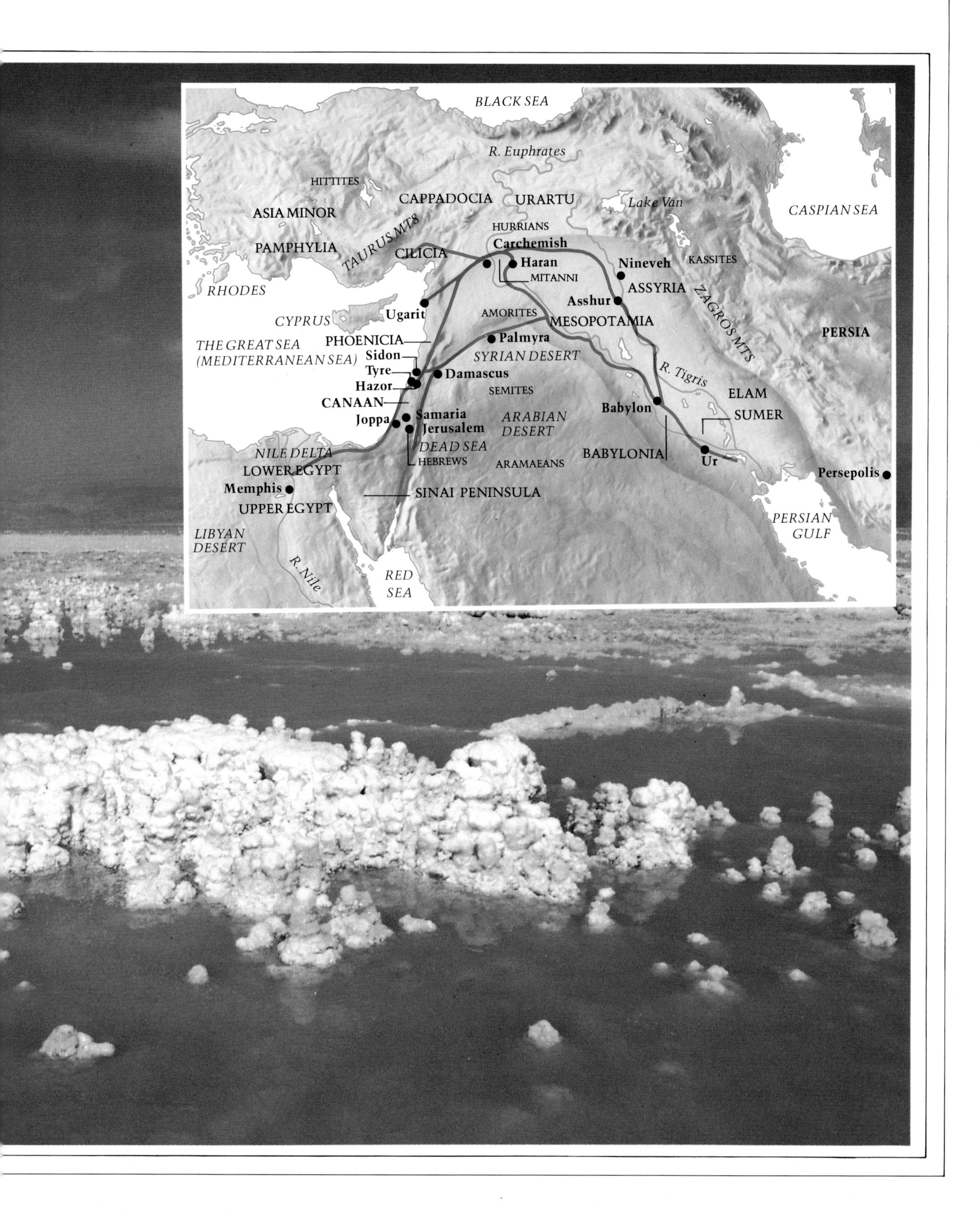
BLACK SEA
R. Euphrates
HITTITES
CAPPADOCIA
URARTU
Lake Van
CASPIAN SEA
ASIA MINOR
TAURUS MTS
HURRIANS
PAMPHYLIA
Carchemish
CILICIA
Haran
Nineveh
KASSITES
MITANNI
RHODES
ASSYRIA
Asshur
ZAGROS MTS
Ugarit
AMORITES
CYPRUS
MESOPOTAMIA
PERSIA
THE GREAT SEA
(MEDITERRANEAN SEA)
PHOENICIA
Palmyra
SYRIAN DESERT
Sidon
Tyre
Damascus
R. Tigris
Hazor
SEMITES
ELAM
CANAAN
Babylon
SUMER
Samaria
ARABIAN DESERT
Joppa
Jerusalem
DEAD SEA
NILE DELTA
BABYLONIA
HEBREWS
Ur
ARAMAEANS
LOWER EGYPT
Persepolis
Memphis
SINAI PENINSULA
UPPER EGYPT
PERSIAN GULF
LIBYAN DESERT
R. Nile
RED SEA

BELOW Within short distances Palestine shows dramatic changes in the level of the land. A deep rift valley slopes from east of Lebanon in the north to the Red Sea south of Palestine. In it, the Sea of Galilee is nearly 700 feet (210 metres) below sea level and the Dead Sea nearly 1300 feet (395 metres). As the Dead Sea has no outlet, its waters are heavily saturated with minerals. Westwards, Palestine slopes gently from desert to the fertile coastal plain.

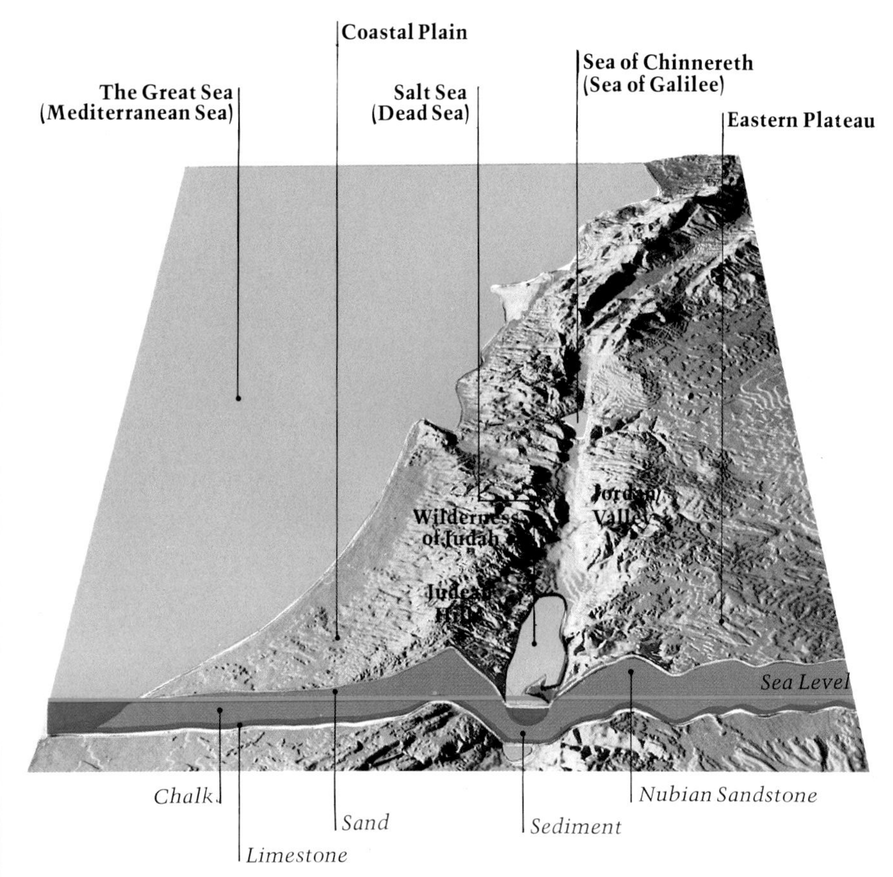

the desert and the fertile land. The Hebrews were originally such a group.

The name Palestine is derived from Philistine, the 'Sea Peoples' who arrived from the west at the end of the second millenium BC and briefly dominated the southern part of the land bridge from the Jordan Valley to the Mediterranean. Before the Philistines it was mainly occupied by Canaanites and is referred to as Canaan by the Hebrews. Its long desert frontier to the east exposed it to penetration from the nomadic desert peoples, including the Hebrews themselves, while its strategic position between Egypt to the south and the Mesopotamian and Hittite peoples of the east and north made it a politically sensitive area. It seldom enjoyed peace, but its peoples profited from the international trade routes which passed through it.

From the south, the route from Egypt passed into the coastal area. Here the shifting sands forced travellers inland for some 12 miles (20 km), to pass through the town of Aphek and northwards to the ridge of Mount Carmel. The Philistines settled in this coastal plain, establishing themselves at Gaza, Ashkelon and Ashdod near the coast, and at Gath and Ekron further inland to the south of Aphek. From this coastal plain minor roads led eastwards up through the lowland hills of the Shephelah, which was densely populated, to the hill country of Judah and the deep rift valley of the Salt Sea, today called the Dead Sea, 1285 feet (400 m) below sea level. Beyond the Salt Sea lie mountain ridges, with steep gullies running down into the rift valley, and

RIGHT The ruins of the ancient sanctuary at Dan, above the Sea of Galilee, marked the northern limits of Hebrew territory, after they had wrested the area from the Canaanites. The southern limit of habitable land in Palestine was at Beer-sheba, at the start of the desert area between Palestine and Egypt.

beyond these mountains the desert begins.

The Judean hills run northwards, parallel to the Jordan Valley, until they turn north-west to meet the Great Sea, as the Mediterranean Sea was called, at Mount Carmel and form the northern limits of the coastal plain. The major coastal route crosses the Carmel ridge to enter the Plain of Jezreel at the ancient fortress of Megiddo, where it splits. A western branch hugs the coast and an eastern branch goes on to Hazor and Damascus. Jezreel means 'God sows' in Hebrew, reflecting the fertility of this valley running from the Great Sea to the Jordan Valley, which is still more than 600 feet (180 m) below sea level where the River Jordan leaves the Sea of Galilee. This lake is called the Sea of Chinnereth in the Old Testament, and variously the Sea of Galilee, Lake of Gennesaret, and Sea of Tiberias in the New Testament.

Northwards again, between the upper Jordan Valley and the sea, the land rises steeply into Upper Galilee. Above the Sea of Galilee was Lake Huleh, a small expanse of water now only marshland, just about at sea level. At the eastern side of the very top of the Jordan Valley is Mount Hermon with its snow-covered peak which marked the northern limits of Palestine or Canaan. The road to Damascus and Mesopotamia passes south of Hermon. The King's Highway, a route used mainly by nomads, ran from Damascus southwards to Elath, situated on the Red Sea.

The towns which marked the traditional limits of the ancient land of Israel were Beer-sheba in the south and Dan in the north. That area contains extreme contrasts including mountain ridges and the lowest point on earth, and extremely fertile land and near desert. Such conditions led to many kinds of peoples with widely varied ways of life settling there. The international trading routes through the region remained its most important feature.

BELOW **The Hebrew nomads used the land in a regular pattern which gave the sparse pasture time to regrow.**
BOTTOM **Oases were essential features of the nomadic routes.**

Between the Rivers

The great Egyptian and Mesopotamian rivers support an agriculture otherwise impossible in the dry, hot climate. In Palestine rainfall varies but almost all the land is fertile if irrigated. Throughout the region cereals are a staple, and sheep and goats – either tended by nomads or farmed – the main livestock.

Scientists believe that in ancient times the climate of the Near and Middle East was wetter than in recent centuries. This is supported by evidence that in the central Sahara Desert plants were growing which are characteristic of the Mediterranean region and also that the area is cut by dry water courses which must once have carried water. There is other evidence, ranging from silt deposits to pollen analysis, but the question remains controversial since the caravan routes of ancient times passed through the same oases as now. Perhaps the best explanation is that there were fluctuations in climate with a general move towards arid conditions but with periods of wetter conditions. During wetter periods it would have been possible for certain areas to be occupied which today could not support a population of any number.

However, it was human occupation rather than climatic changes which had the most drastic effects on the region, effects which changed the conditions necessary for successful occupation. Human activity such as tree felling has had dramatic effects in terms of soil erosion and changes in the water-table.

Although the equator should in theory be the hottest area of the earth's surface, the hottest area in fact runs from the Sahara through central Arabia to the Punjab, only a little to the south of the Near and Middle East. This is due to the large land masses and their effects on heat radiation. Heat transfer is by air currents, particularly the jet streams. These are winds high in the atmosphere which blow at extremely high speeds. Major jet streams from the Mediterranean are responsible for bringing very warm air from the Sahara to the cold mountain ranges of western Asia. This warm air, combined with the melting of snow in the Taurus Mountains of Turkey and the Zagros Mountains of Persia, creates the conditions for the annual flooding of the Rivers Tigris and Euphrates. The agricultural cycle in Mesopotamia depended on this.

Similarly, the unique pattern of air currents over the north-west Indian Ocean creates the conditions for the annual flooding of the River Nile. During the summer months, an easterly air flow at high altitude creates turbulence at lower levels and carries moist air from the Indian Ocean to the mountains of Ethiopia and the Sudan in eastern Africa. The heavy rainfall of the monsoon flows into the Blue Nile, eventually to deposit silt in the enormously long, level stretch below the First Cataract where the Nile flows through Upper and Lower Egypt to the Mediterranean Sea. By contrast, westerly jet streams prevail from November to March,

C Copper
G Gold
I Iron
T Tin
Mediterranean Dense woodland; vines; wheat; olives
Steppe Grasslands; scorched in summer
Desert Thorny shrub; occasional grass
Savanna Grasslands; tall, isolated trees
Riverine Papyrus; lotus; reeds
Mixed Woodland
Fertile area
Isobars
Prevailing winds

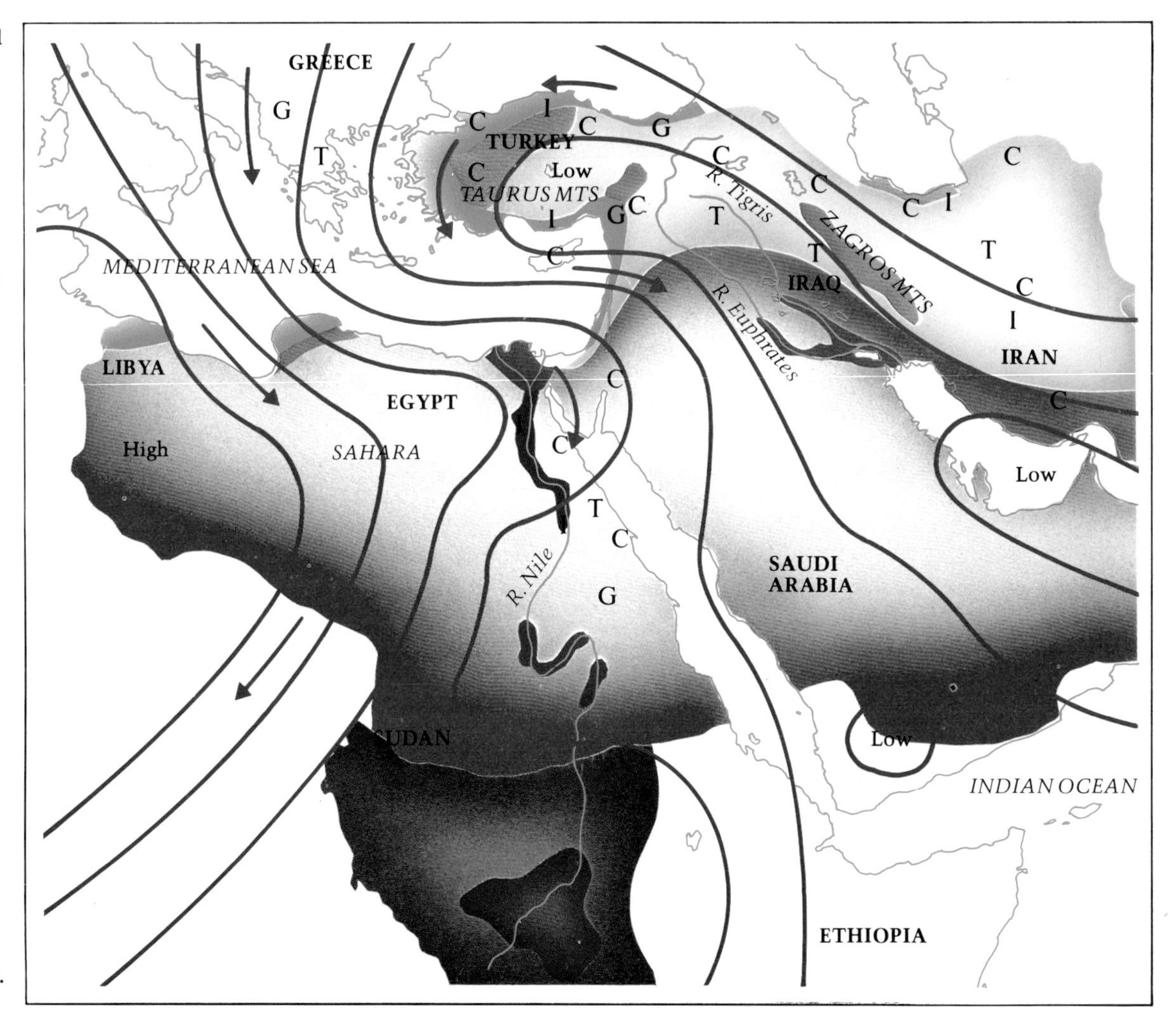

CLIMATE AND RESOURCES
Areas with Mediterranean or Riverine type climates and soil conditions which allowed the development of agriculture were able to support the largest populations. Here, surplus labour led to dramatic advances in civilization and large building programmes. But the desert regions also had a thriving number of nomadic pastoralists. The most important mineral resources were copper and tin, of which bronze is an alloy. There were also iron deposits, but iron did not replace bronze as the main material for tools and weapons until about 1200 BC.

BELOW **Water is the key to agriculture throughout the Near and Middle East, and where it is not available naturally it must be provided by irrigation. These fields of harvested wheat on the edge of the desert are watered by sprinklers.**

INSET **The date palm has been one of the most important staple foods from the earliest times, and it is still valued by the nomadic herdsmen. Natural pollination is uncertain, and this female tree has been pollinated by hand.**

in association with an air current which peters out by the time it reaches the coasts of southern Arabia, which are amongst the most arid in the world.

Whatever the minor changes in climate may have been, these very broad patterns have controlled the weather of the Near and Middle East during historical times. If anything, the area was rather more moist within the historical past, and able to support the size of population needed for the initial draining of the river marshes and the rise of civilizations in the two main river valleys.

Most of the Near and Middle East experiences a dry, hot climate, with large variations of temperature between day and night. But the great river systems of Egypt and Mesopotamia draw their waters from mountain ranges well beyond their main valleys and so can support agricultural economies which would otherwise be impossible. However, even in much of the desert, there are marginal areas which can support sheep and goats on sparse areas of pasture.

There are therefore two distinct types of livestock production – wandering herds led by nomadic herdsmen and shepherds, and the settled livestock farming with which the modern, developed world is more familiar. The two systems can exist happily side by side, for the shepherds are not competing with the farmers for land. A further factor in ancient times lay in the different social structures of nomadic tribes and farming communities. The latter often lived in fortified settlements, from which they farmed the surrounding agricultural lands, while the nomads travelled through the marginal lands and semi-desert areas without any close association with fixed settlements.

This accounts for tribal groups such as the Hebrews of patriarchal times (Gen 12 onwards) who travelled over large distances and across 'national' frontiers without much apparent hindrance from the settled peoples. The nomadic shepherds had to ensure that they were not competing with each other for routes to pasture lands, for it would have been fatal for one group to enter a marginal area where the ground had recently been grazed bare by another group. This explains why, in Genesis 13, Abraham and Lot agreed to take different parts of Palestine – they were nomads, rather than occupiers. Sheep and goats are still important and herded in large numbers in this area, for their milk and fleeces or skins, and because they are able to travel over fairly long distances.

Cereals were the main agricultural crops, as wheat and barley are indigenous to the region. Barley was a currency in Mesopotamia as early as 2000 BC. Modern bread wheat is a hybrid crop, but the ancient native *emmer* wheat is still grown widely because it is a much more hardy type.

When the flooded rivers of Mesopotamia and Egypt returned to their beds each year, they left a rich deposit of silt which formed the basis of the agricultural economy. As the ground dried, it was ploughed and irrigated by cutting water channels through the river banks. Unfortunately, this technique tended to divide the land into small squares which encouraged salt formation when the water evaporated. As the salt content of the land increased, harvest yields diminished – a proportion of 0.5 per cent salt prevents wheat growing, while 1 per cent prevents barley growing, and 2 per cent stops date palms from fruiting. Records from the second millenium BC show that this was a serious problem in Mesopotamia.

In addition to cereals and dates, other indigenous crops of the Near and Middle East include olives, grapes, apricots, figs, pomegranates, cherries and peaches. They were all cultivated together with vegetables such as lettuces and onions.

The Hebrew feast of Tabernacles or Booths was once the feast marking the end of one year and the beginning of a new one. By modern reckoning it falls in the autumn, in the months of September or October. It no longer marks the new year in Palestine, but its old significance lingers on. A keen watch is kept for rain during the eight days of its harvest festivities. The long dry summer of Palestine should be ending and the first rains falling to show that the agricultural year can start all over again.

The Mediterranean Sea is a small body of water compared with the Indian or Atlantic Oceans, so the weather in Palestine is influenced more by the great land masses of Asia and Africa than by the sea. Most of the rain which falls on Palestine comes from the Atlantic, carried on the predominantly westerly air flow, with support from the Mediterranean. Much of the moisture has been lost by the time the stream of Atlantic depressions reaches the eastern end of the Mediterranean. Seasonal weather patterns determine whether the moist winds will reach Palestine at all, and if they will release their moisture in the area.

In winter, the Mediterranean has its own distinctive

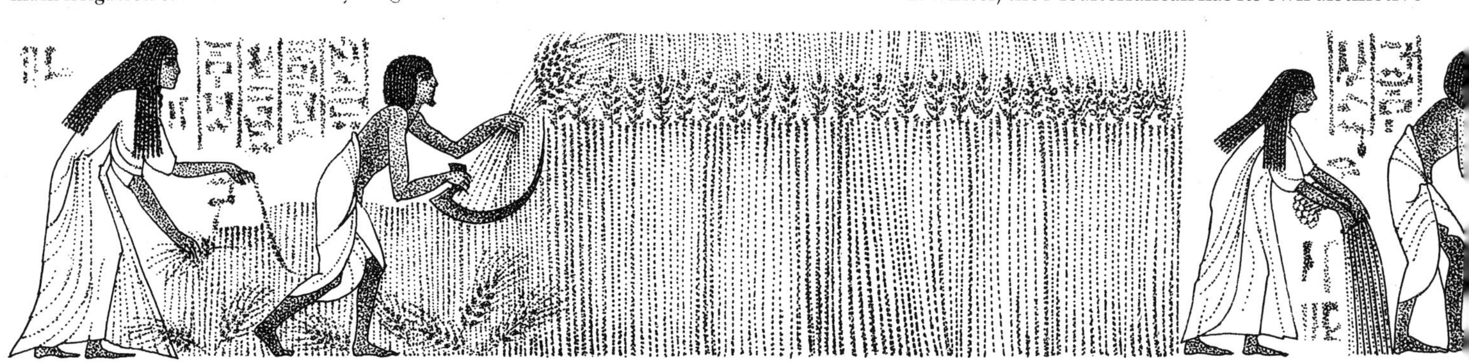

BELOW **Ancient illustrations of farming techniques show remarkably little difference from the methods in use in Europe and the United States until the agricultural revolution. Efficient hand sowing was essential for a good crop, which was then reaped by sickle and the straw harvested. Here, flax is being pulled as well, to be prepared for weaving into linen. A pair of oxen are being driven by this Egyptian ploughman, and date palms grow beside the main irrigation canal.**

LEFT **Although archaeologists have shown many parts farmed in biblical times are no longer productive, modern technology has made it possible to extend the land usage beyond the areas available to ancient farmers. Here, plastic cloches are being used to control weeds, protect plants during their early growth and ensure that the available water is used to maximum effect. With similar aims, farmers in biblical times directed water to the land over surprisingly long distances, particularly within Palestine, to cultivate such desert areas as the region south of the Dead Sea.**

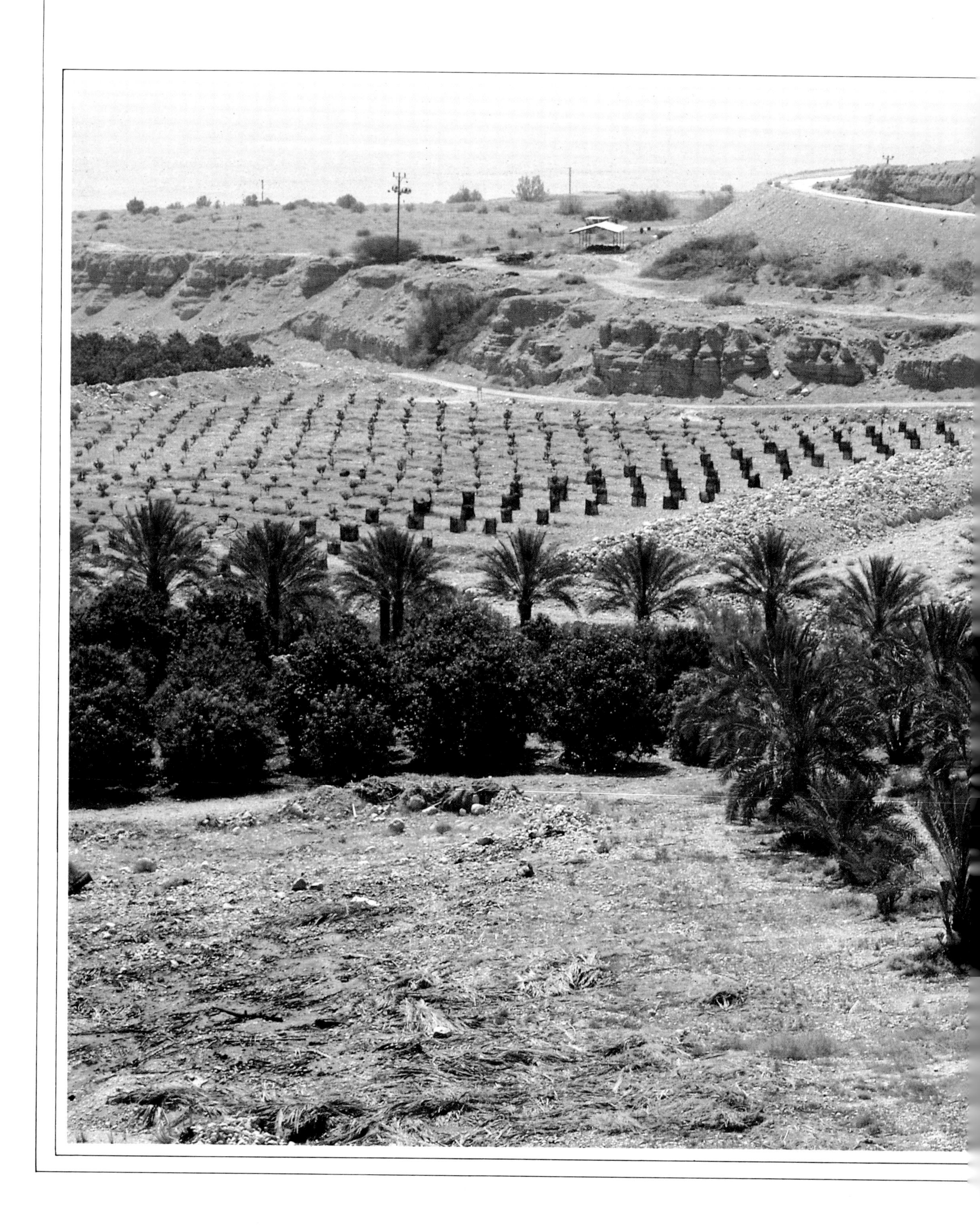

weather system. Atlantic depressions cross north-west Africa, Spain and Europe into the Mediterranean basin and on as far as Pakistan. On their way they become more constricted in area and more intense, even though they may not be as deep as the depressions with which northern Europe is so familiar. Rainfall results from warm, moisture-laden air hitting cooler air streams. This produces water vapour. The water vapour in the clouds then condenses into the droplets of rain. Very little of the moisture in the Atlantic depressions is released in Egypt because there is no high ground to force the air up to cooler levels. But the mountains of northern Palestine, and the ridge stretching from Mount Carmel down to Judea, will do so. Consequently there is a marked contrast in annual rainfall between the dry desert area south of Beer-sheba which receives little rain and the mountainous area of Upper Galilee where 55 in (140 cm) falls, mainly between the months of November and April.

In summer, a different pattern prevails. An area of high pressure, the 'Azores High', extends across north-west Africa as far as Libya and Egypt. There its edges meet a characteristic area of low pressure over Cyprus and southern Turkey. This blocks the Atlantic depressions or forces them further north, and the area of low pressure draws dry air from central Asia which reaches Palestine as hot, dry south-westerly winds. These seem to come from much the same direction as the wet, winter winds, but the air in them carries very little moisture and no rain falls.

In the wet months the rain usually takes the form of heavy cloudbursts, which produce the deep gullies in the steep sides of the Jordan Valley. Surprising notices by the roads there warn of flash floods. These occur because the ground, baked hard by the sun, cannot absorb the quantity of water which falls in a short period, and it floods across the surface for long distances.

LEFT **The shores of the Dead Sea form one of the most inhospitable places in the world, but remains of some of the world's oldest settlements have been discovered where freshwater springs break through the salt-laden soil. Here, at En-gedi, just north of Masada, a fertile oasis breaks the monotony of the bleak gullies and cliffs, as it has from the earliest times.**
BELOW **Modern technology serves an age-old purpose – bringing water to the crops.**

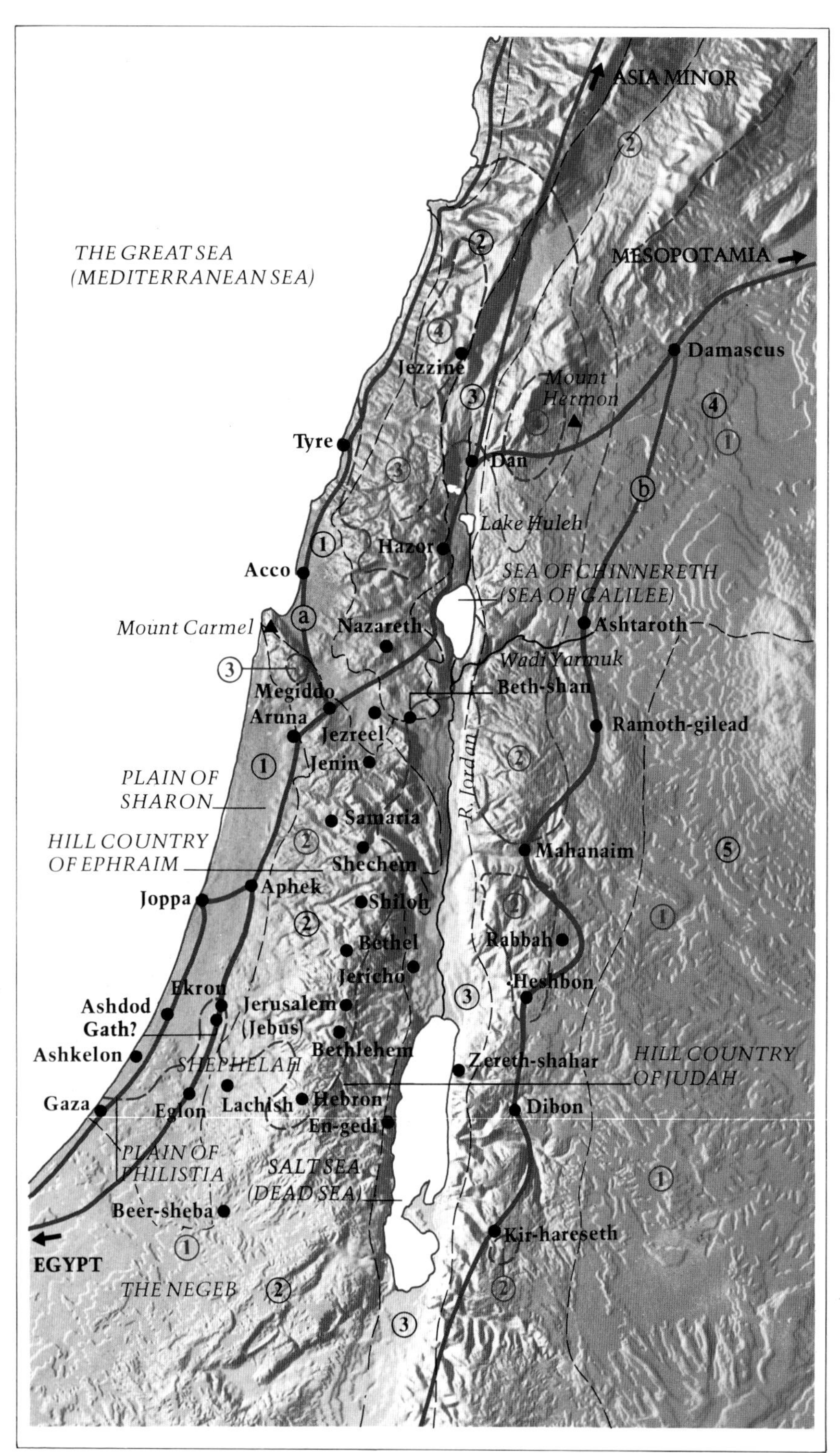

--- Rainfall:

① 0-15in/0-400mm

② 15-30in/400-800mm

③ 30-50in/800-1300mm

④ Above 50in/Above 1300mm

--- Natural regions:

① The Coastal Plain

② The Western Hills

③ The Rift Valley

④ The Eastern Hills

⑤ The Desert

ⓐ The Way of the Sea

ⓑ The King's Highway

PALESTINE'S CLIMATE
The northern mountains of Palestine bring rain from the moist westerly winds and feed the Jordan Valley. Further south, as the land falls away, Palestine becomes more arid.

Under such conditions, it is essential to dam gullies and direct the water into irrigation channels.

The significance of water for Palestinian agriculture is dramatically demonstrated by the effects of irrigation – crops grow to a sharp boundary where the irrigation ceases, to be replaced by brown, parched earth. Almost everywhere that water can be taken proves to be fertile land. An exception is the area around the Dead Sea, significantly named the Salt Sea in ancient times. It lies only some 50 miles (80 km) from the Mediterranean, but is 1285 ft (400 m) below sea level and has no exit for the waters of the river Jordan which flow in. Instead the water evaporates at a fast rate, causing high salt levels.

Yet even here the abundant freshwater springs of Jericho, only 9 miles (15 km) north in the same deep rift valley, provide luxuriant oasis conditions for one of the oldest of all settlements. Springs made occupation possible all down the western shores of the Salt Sea in biblical times, supplemented by dams in the deep gullies from the Judean hills. Such centres of population ranged from the great fortress of Masada, with its deep water cisterns on the top of the crag, to the Essene community at Qumran, where ritual bathing was an important part of the community's life.

Only the northern highlands of Palestine and the coastal area, as far as about 35 miles (60 km) inland, receive any appreciable and dependable amounts of rainfall. South of Gaza and Beer-sheba rainfall is negligible, but evidence of ancient settlements in the Negeb, the area south of Beer-sheba, suggest that it was either wetter in biblical times or extremely efficiently irrigated. Tree felling during historical times has also increased the aridity and erosion, just as it has in Greece.

In the Bible the country is described as '... a land of wheat and barley, of vines, of figs, of pomegranates, a land of olives, of oil, of honey, ... a land where the stones are of iron, where the hills may be quarried for copper ... your flocks and herds increase' (Deut 8:8-13). The farming Canaanites tended the fertile areas by day, returning at night to fortified centres which could withstand long sieges. Thus, when the Hebrews began their occupation in the thirteenth century BC, Canaan formed a patchwork of city-states combined in various alliances. The nomadic Hebrews soon adopted the Canaanite way of life. This placed considerable strain on their religious traditions, as they adapted them to agricultural needs.

Nomadic shepherds continued to graze sheep and goats through the marginal areas, as part of their long routes from Egypt to Mesopotamia. The area was also able to support a larger population than might be expected because of the great international trading routes which passed through it. The country exported grain, oil, wine and honey, and was famous for the healing properties of the 'balm of Gilead' (Gen 37:25 and Jer 8:22). Luxuries and wood were imported into Egypt.

Trading increased during the biblical period. The Philistines hindered Hebrew participation in this trade by occupying the southern coastal area until the Hebrew King David gained control in about 1000 BC.

LEFT The Near and Middle East evoke images of citrus fruits, olives and dates, or of more exotic produce sent to the world's markets. It would be more true to think of cereals, which have always been the staple of the population in the agricultural areas – even the nomadic herdsmen supplement their milk diet with grains. Barley, growing here in strips on a hillside in Palestine, originated in the Middle East and was the most important crop until modern times. In ancient Mesopotamia, measures of barley were a standard currency for taxation and exchange.

The Old Trading Roads

Donkey and camel caravans trudged along the main routes of the ancient world, which stretched through Palestine's narrow strip of fertile land, carrying olive oil, grains, building materials and cloths, as well as such exotic items as frankincense and ivory, between the main centres of civilization.

The major trade routes in the Near and Middle East were arguably the most important routes in the ancient world. At a time when shipbuilding and sailing techniques made it impracticable to use the sea for serious travel, Palestine's narrow strip of fertile land between the sea and the desert formed a bridge between the main centres of civilization in Egypt, Asia Minor and Mesopotamia.

For most of this early biblical period, the donkey was the normal means of transporting goods. Roads capable of taking wheeled vehicles did not exist, but donkeys could manage any convenient track provided they were fed and watered. Hence the importance of routes through comparatively fertile country. By the thirteenth century BC, camels began to be used so goods could be taken across desert areas. But trade flows naturally through more populated areas so Palestine remained a vital link in the great international routes.

For most of the second millenium BC Egypt controlled Palestine which was inhabited by Canaanites in scattered fortified agricultural centres such as Megiddo. Control of the area was easy to maintain for, at that time, no rival power was capable of sustaining an attack on Egypt itself. The Canaanite cities were frequently at war with each other, and each looked to Egypt for support.

Egypt could supply gold, linen and, in times of famine, grain, in exchange for slaves, wood and luxuries. Even African goods which were exported to Egypt from the south found their way by trade up through Palestine to the north and across eastwards into Mesopotamia, by way of Damascus and Hamath.

The main coastal route was known in later times as 'The Way of the Sea' (Isa 9:1) because it followed the Palestinian coastline from Egypt, skirting Gaza to avoid soft ground, through Aphek as far as the ridge of Mount

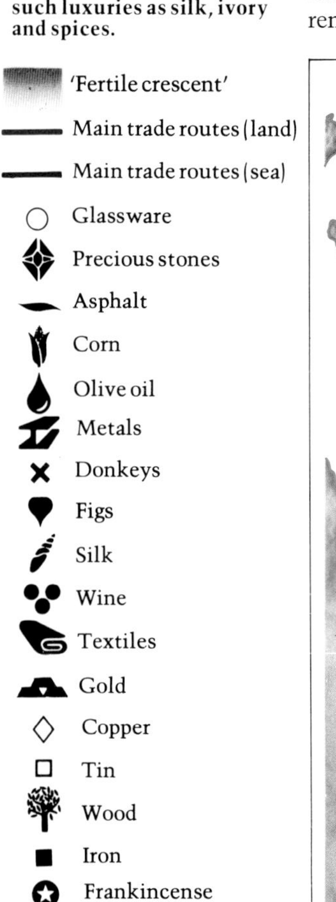

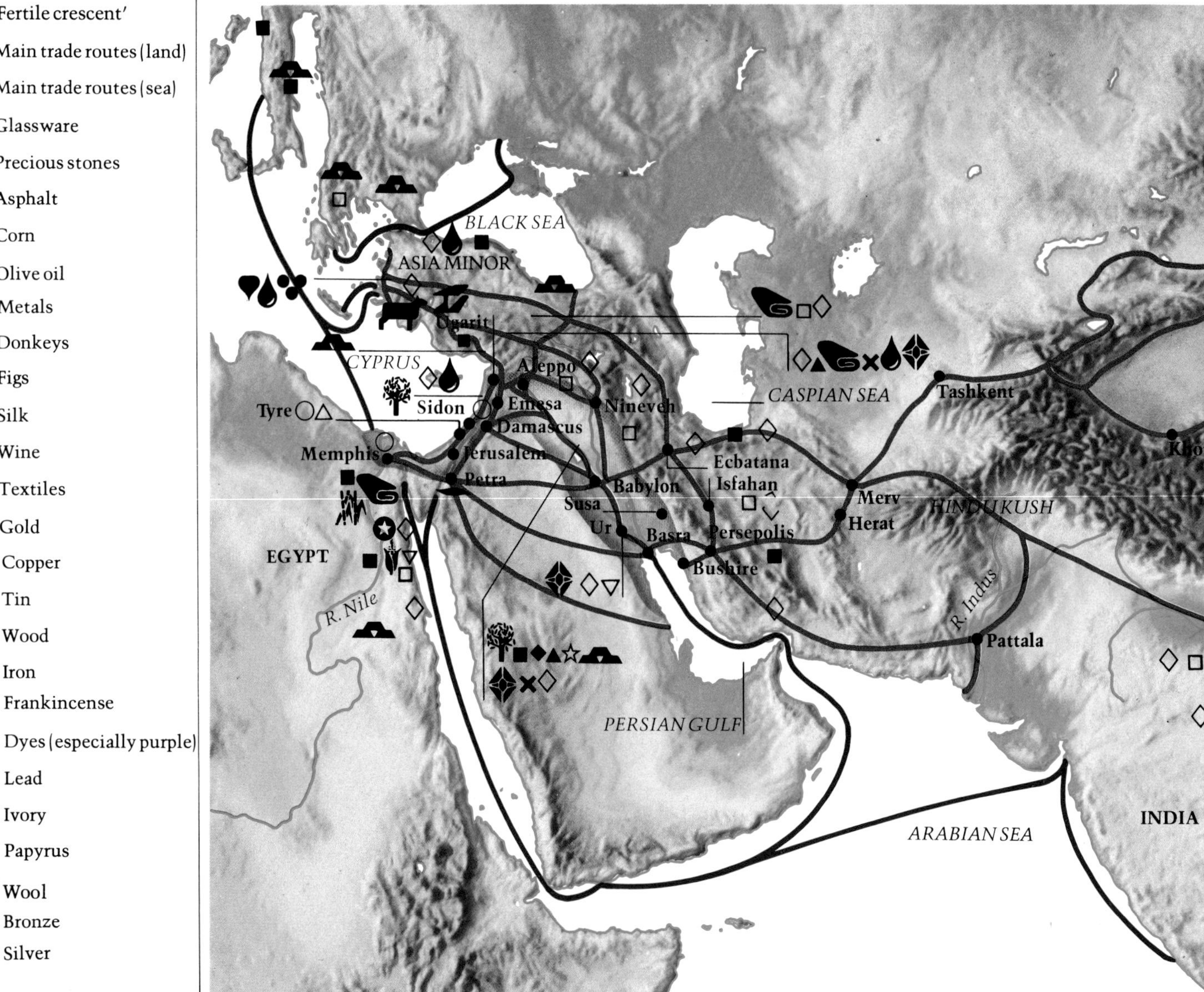

TRADE ROUTES **Ancient roads were mainly tracks for pack animals, but they stretched the length and breadth of the known world as far as India, China and into Central Africa, for such luxuries as silk, ivory and spices.**

Carmel, which it crossed to enter the Valley of Jezreel at Megiddo. There it branched. One route hugged the coast northwards by way of Acco, Tyre, Byblos, some 19 miles (30 km) north of modern Beirut and Ugarit. The eastward branch passed west of the Sea of Chinnereth (Sea of Galilee) to Hazor, and south of the small Lake Huleh to Damascus on its way across to Mesopotamia.

From Damascus, the only other main route through Palestine passed south down the highlands to the east of the Jordan Valley, diverting only to cross the short, deep canyons which drop steeply to the River Jordan and the Salt Sea (Dead Sea). It led through semi-desert areas to the open sea, and an important branch crossed to Egypt.

Although such routes were important, settlements were self-sufficient, at least at subsistence levels. The travels of nomadic shepherds, such as the Hebrews, were controlled by grazing needs of the flocks rather than by roads.

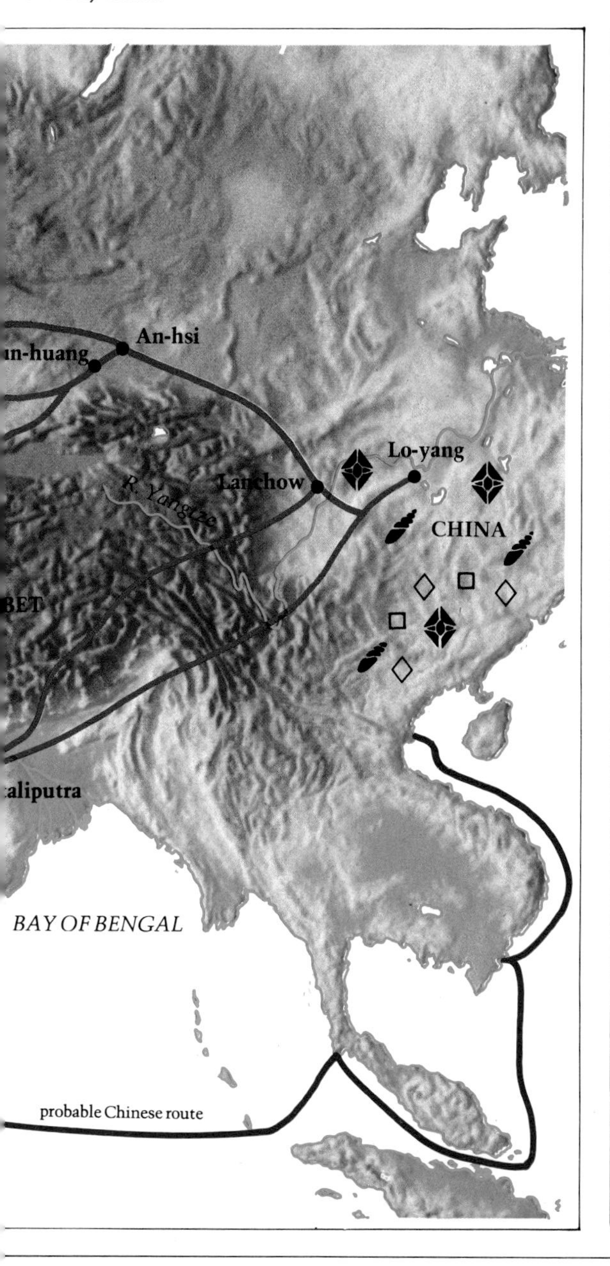

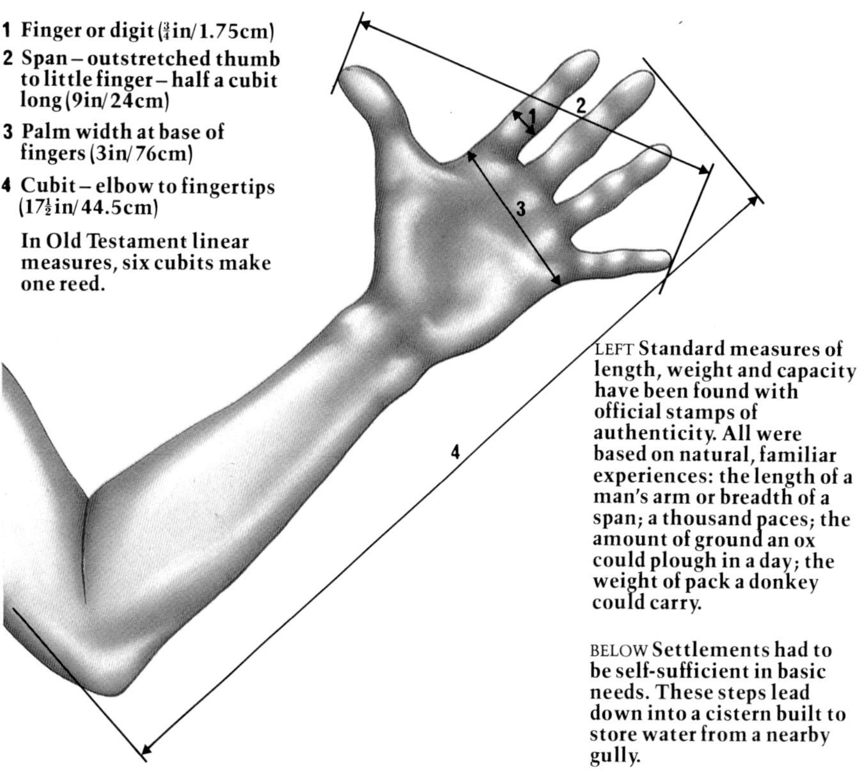

1 Finger or digit (¾in/1.75cm)

2 Span – outstretched thumb to little finger – half a cubit long (9in/24cm)

3 Palm width at base of fingers (3in/76cm)

4 Cubit – elbow to fingertips (17½in/44.5cm)

In Old Testament linear measures, six cubits make one reed.

LEFT Standard measures of length, weight and capacity have been found with official stamps of authenticity. All were based on natural, familiar experiences: the length of a man's arm or breadth of a span; a thousand paces; the amount of ground an ox could plough in a day; the weight of pack a donkey could carry.

BELOW Settlements had to be self-sufficient in basic needs. These steps lead down into a cistern built to store water from a nearby gully.

Ancient Cultures and Religions

During the second millenium BC local power struggles in Mesopotamia prevented any effective challenge to Egyptian control of Canaan, which was inhabited by peoples who worshipped fertility deities. The Egyptians themselves idolized the sun and believed in an afterlife.

The main inhabitants of the 'fertile crescent' during the first half of the second millenium BC ranged from the Sumerians of the lower part of Mesopotamia to the Egyptians of the Nile Valley. The Canaanites straddled the narrow land bridge of Palestine at the eastern end of the Mediterranean. The two great river valleys of the Nile and the Mesopotamian area watered by the Tigris and Euphrates had been drained and irrigated for nearly two millenia already, and had been the seat of great kingdoms for more than 1,000 years. In each case, the river system provided the fertility necessary to support a stable population. This gave the inhabitants good reason to create and maintain the irrigation and drainage works needed to realize the full potential of each river.

Since those times, the Persian Gulf has silted up to a distance of about 125 miles (200 km) where the Tigris and Euphrates now flow into it. However, during the height of the Sumerian civilization in the third millenium BC the two rivers entered it separately, and the Sumerians occupied the area on the Euphrates between Babylon and the sea. At first they were a group of city-states, each built round a temple dedicated to the local deity. Ur, near the mouth of the Euphrates, was under the patronage of the moon god and goddess, Nanna and Ningal, worshipped at a towering temple called a ziggurat.

The Sumerian civilization was already in decline at the beginning of the second millenium BC, when Abraham left it for Haran and eventually Canaan. But its enlightened legal traditions may be seen in the fragments of law found at Isin, north of Ur. They date from Abraham's time when the Sumerian and Akkadian areas had been united. The law gave women and slaves much lower status than freemen but it is perhaps more remarkable in view of later practice that they were accorded any rights at all. Other written records show well developed agricultural techniques of irrigation, ploughing, sowing, harvesting and threshing, all under the protection of the gods.

BELOW **Massive ruins in the Near and Middle East bear testimony to the energy of ancient peoples, their imaginative use of local materials, and their vivid expressions of religious belief. This reconstruction of a Mesopotamian ziggurat is typical of the temples built in honour of the astrological gods worshipped in the region.**

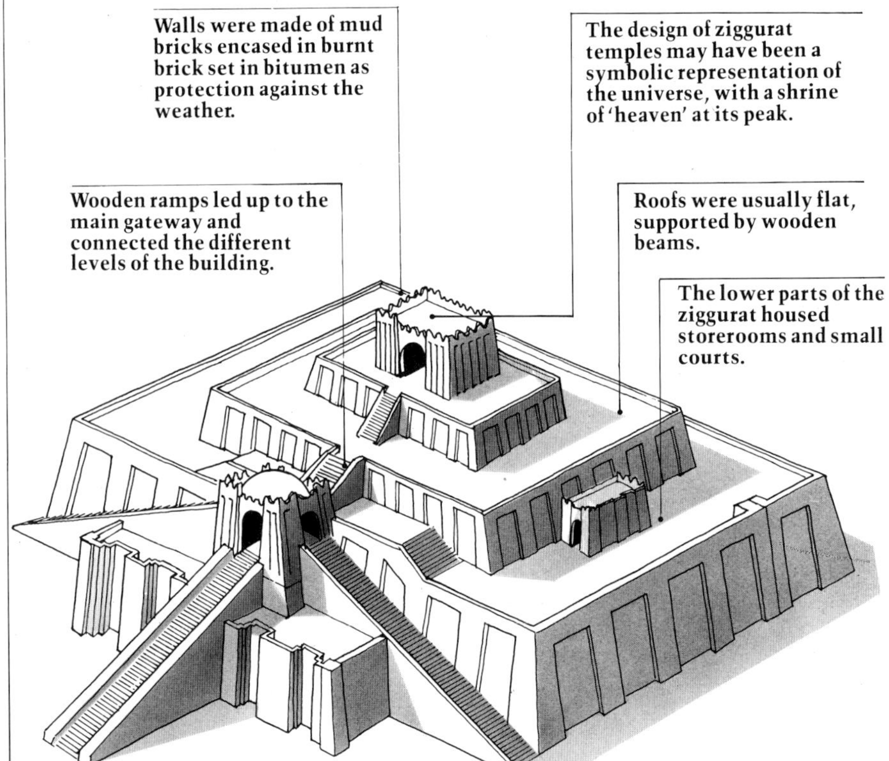

Walls were made of mud bricks encased in burnt brick set in bitumen as protection against the weather.
The design of ziggurat temples may have been a symbolic representation of the universe, with a shrine of 'heaven' at its peak.
Wooden ramps led up to the main gateway and connected the different levels of the building.
Roofs were usually flat, supported by wooden beams.
The lower parts of the ziggurat housed storerooms and small courts.

The power pattern of Mesopotamia was transformed around 1724 BC when Hammurabi became king of Babylon, which had until then been a typical city-state on the River Euphrates. Within 40 years, he conquered every other city or group of peoples in Mesopotamia, from the Persian Gulf to the Mediterranean, and gave the area a unity which remained effective long after this, the Old Babylonian Empire, had itself been conquered. Excavations of the site of one of the conquered cities, Mari, revealed archives which provide extensive information about Hammurabi and his times. Also the law code of Hammurabi was discovered at Susa and showed nearly 300 laws.

This legal material showed that case law, based on precedent, was the normal form of law in the ancient Middle East. These findings have made it possible to compare and contrast Hebrew law with the legal systems which influenced its development. Other important influences were the Babylonian creation myths, and the great Babylonian *Epic of Gilgamesh* which has similarities to material used in the opening chapters of Genesis.

Around 1595 BC, the Old Babylonian Empire fell to the Kassites after an abortive attempt by the Hittites to defeat Babylon. The Kassites have left little trace of their influence on biblical peoples. They were, however, a crucial part of the balance of power in the Mesopotamian area which prevented any one group making an effective challenge to Egyptian control of Canaan. Other contenders at this time were the Assyrians, similarly checked by the Kassites, and the Hittites. The Assyrians occupied the eastern area of central Mesopotamia, on the River Tigris, and the Hittites posed a more serious threat from Asia Minor.

The Hittites are sometimes mentioned in the Old Testament as being among the inhabitants of Canaan, but there is no question of the Hittite kingdom controlling the area. For 200 years, from *c*1500 BC, they resisted Egyptian attempts to extend their control northwards and across into Asia Minor. Finally, they defeated Rameses II at Kadesh *c*1285 BC and made a treaty which brought peace but limited Egyptian control of Canaan to the area south of Damascus. Such a treaty would account for the presence of Hittites living in Canaan and gives some indication of the variety of peoples generally referred to as 'Canaanites'.

As would be expected of a restricted area with major international routes crossing it, Canaan contained a mixture of peoples before the Hebrews dominated the southern part of it. This created problems for the Egyptians, who themselves had a domestic upheaval in the sixteenth century BC, when they expelled their Asiatic Hyksos rulers and created a New Kingdom. The new Egyptian rulers faced rebellions from the many settlements of Canaan whose people probably had blood ties with the Hyksos. Some of the Egyptian records give meticulous details of the Canaanite settlements conquered in the subsequent wars. More than a hundred cities are listed in the campaigns which ended with a decisive Egyptian victory near Megiddo – 924 chariots are listed amongst the loot when the city fell after a siege lasting seven months.

Megiddo is typical of many Canaanite fortified settlements, including Jerusalem, with its heavy walls defending the top of a rocky hill or ridge, and an elaborate water system with a staired shaft and tunnel to give safe access to the city's spring. The gate was often constructed so that an enemy had to expose his unshielded right-hand side when approaching it.

The Canaanites worshipped a multitude of gods and goddesses but the dominant characteristic was fertility, expressed through sexual intercourse between the gods and imitated in worship to ensure the fertility of the crops on which the Canaanites depended. Human sacrifice also occurred, to avert disaster or to ensure the fertility of the fields. The main festivals were associated with the various phases of the harvest and the area contained a number of religious centres with temples or sacred places, in addition to the sacred places of each city. Of interest for Hebrew religion are the Ugaritic myths. Their form is similar to the Hebrew commemoration of major religious events and they contain divine names and titles which are echoed in the Old Testament. After the Hebrew occupation of Canaan, Hebrew religion nearly succumbed to the religion of the Canaanites.

The most famous remains in ancient Egypt are the pyramids, monuments of the pharoahs. There are 48 which have survived to modern times, mostly in the region extending about 60 miles (100 km) south of modern Cairo. The majority of them belong to the very earliest period of known Egyptian history, the third millenium BC, and even the most recent were built at the beginning of the second millenium up to the 13th Dynasty in the eighteenth century BC.

By the time Abraham visited Egypt (Gen 12), temple complexes had replaced pyramids as royal tombs, but the oldest of the pyramids, the Step Pyramid at Saqqara near Memphis, had been standing for nearly 1,000 years.

Like the slim, pointed obelisks also found in Egypt, the pyramids are an architectural expression of fundamental Egyptian religious beliefs. They express belief in human survival after death and provide information about the guidance and support needed by the dead on their journey to heaven. They are also architectural expressions of the religious importance of the sun for ancient Egypt. The tip of the pyramid caught the first rays of the rising sun and conducted its power to the mummified body, similarly the tall obelisks conducted the sun's powers to the earth on which they were standing.

Sun worship was an important part of early Egyptian history. It formed a common religion uniting different political groups and by the middle of the third millenium BC, the names of Egyptian kings began to contain the name of the sun god, 'Re'. Rameses, a favourite name of the Egyptian kings, means 'Re has begotten him'.

Everywhere in Egyptian life, and death, religion played a central role. The king was the representative of the gods and mediated between them and the people of Egypt. Most of the gods had associations with social needs or social groups, such as crafts or women, and gods were also connected with particular localities. Solar worship associated the rising of the sun with creation and renewal, while the journey of the sun god through the underworld at night expressed the awareness of decay and regeneration fundamental to an agricultural economy. During the 18th Dynasty of Egyptian kings, about a century before the Hebrew escape in the thirteenth century BC, King Akhnaton attempted to suppress all religions other than the worship of the sun. He closed all temples to deities other than the sun and built a new capital at el-Amarna, between Thebes and Memphis. The reform did not survive the death of Akhnaton and the new capital was abandoned three years later at the beginning of the reign of Tut'ankhamun.

This failure points to the influence of the priesthood which served the many temples. As religion permeated every aspect of life, the priests became the administrators and intellectuals of Egypt whose powers increased enormously during the period of the New Kingdom of the 18th and 19th Dynasties. The contest between Moses and the Egyptian priests, depicted in Exodus, threatened the whole basis of Egyptian society.

BELOW **Wherever the international routes crossed inhabited areas, great fortresses arose to guard the settlements. These hilltop ruins look across the rich Valley of Jezreel towards Galilee, where the main coastal route between Egypt and the north branched for Asia Minor and Mesopotamia.**

BELOW The sun was Egypt's principal god, so the temples were carefully oriented to ensure that the rays of the rising sun shone through to the innermost sanctuary.

BELOW **The ancient Canaanite city of Megiddo had a temple area, where the city's fertility gods were worshipped. The design of such temples influenced the Hebrew Temple in Jerusalem, but the Hebrews repudiated the excesses of the Canaanite religion.**

BOTTOM **The Egyptian pyramids were temples as well as royal tombs. These are some of the earliest at Saqqara near modern Cairo. The rays of the rising sun first reached the apex of a pyramid, and the Egyptians believed that its divine power was transmitted to the mummified king buried deep within the stonework.**

- Until 1000 BC Canaanite settlements, Egypt controls coast
- 2030-1640 BC Middle Kingdom
- *c*1850 BC Abraham
- *c*1724-1595 BC Old Babylonian Empire
- *c*1720 BC Code of Hammurabi
- 1640-1530 BC Hyksos kings, Hebrews in Egypt
- *c*1595 BC Kassites overthrow Babylon
- 1550-1070 BC New Kingdom
- 1290-1224 BC Reign of Rameses II
- 1250 BC The exodus

Egypt: Unified and Prosperous

The dynasties unified Egypt under a king. He had religious authority as representative of the gods, backed up by a powerful bureaucracy and a highly efficient army. The annual fluctuations of the Nile was another unifying factor, providing food when the rest of the Near East experienced famine.

Apart from the creation narratives, the events described in the Books of Genesis and Exodus belong to about the 11th to 19th Dynasties of Egyptian kings, between the twentieth and twelfth centuries BC. Pharaoh is the Hebrew form of the Egyptian Per-'o, which referred to the royal palaces and estates. It became a royal title in the 18th Dynasty during the sixteenth century BC. These dynasties span about 900 years and cover the Middle Kingdom and the New Kingdom, separated by the Hyksos period when Lower Egypt and the delta were governed by foreign, Asiatic kings who invaded the country around 1640 BC and ruled during the 15th and 16th Dynasties.

The River Nile was the only geographical feature to give unity to the country and even this caused difficulties. The contrast between the delta area, some 90 miles (150 km) long where the river splits into many channels at its mouth, and the 600 miles (1000 km) of narrow river from the First Cataract near Syene (Aswan) to the delta, made it difficult to maintain a single central government. Power tended to shift between Lower Egypt, with its capital at Memphis, and Upper Egypt, ruled from Thebes.

The successful dynasties solved the problem of unifying the country by creating a powerful bureaucracy under the control of a king as the representative of the gods and the sole authority in the country. This authority was threatened somewhat by the priesthood particularly when a king attempted to make radical changes in the traditional religion, but priests normally served the gods as representatives of the kings. Kings are themselves shown as gods, as was the case with Rameses II who ruled Egypt at the time of the Hebrew escape, and the kings made offerings to themselves as gods.

The country was divided into 42 administrative divisions called nomes, 22 in Upper Egypt and 20 in Lower Egypt. Upper Egypt extended north from the First Cataract of the Nile, to just south of Memphis, virtually where the delta begins. Lower Egypt took in Memphis and the Nile Delta. Originally the nomes may have been separate little kingdoms but during dynastic Egypt they were administered by royal officials or a local aristocracy, responsible in each case to the king.

Apart from his religious authority, the king's power rested on the army, which had become a highly efficient and mobile force by the time of Rameses II, armed with bows, spears, swords and axes, and organized in groups of about 250 foot soldiers supported by light chariots. After the Hyksos period, weapons were made out of iron rather than bronze which had been used before.

There was no central code of law, such as was found in the Mesopotamian countries, but each nome had its court, and courts were presided over by higher officials of the central government. No doubt decisions were influenced by precedent, but there was no need for a legal code in a country ruled by a divine dictator.

There is virtually no rainfall in the Nile Valley, and the river draws its waters from the Ethiopian highlands and the tropical rain forests of central Africa. During the final 750 miles (1200 km) of its flow through Egypt to the Mediterranean, below the First Cataract, the river only falls about 1500 feet (500 metres) and has a huge amount of silt. The summer monsoons strike Ethiopia and flood the Blue Nile, augmenting the steady flow of the White Nile, so that the subsequent annual flooding in Egypt itself spreads the silt on which the country's agriculture depends. The art of geometry originated in Egypt to reestablish land boundaries after the annual flooding. This pattern of flooding and silting gave Egypt food when people in the rest of the Near East were starving because of famine.

Successful agriculture depended first on controlling the flooded areas where the river silt had broken through the flood channels in the river banks to the lower land beyond, and then on distributing water to the planted areas after the crops had been sown in October and November when the river level fell again. A lake just to the west of the Nile, at the junction of Upper and Lower Egypt, created an oasis called the Faiyum, where irrigation techniques using the lake water created an agricultural area of about 170 sq miles (450 sq km). The whole of the country's agriculture probably utilized about 13,000 sq miles (34,000 sq km) of land.

The staple crops were grain for bread, barley for beer (the main drink), chickpeas, lentils, onions, garlic, lettuce, animal fodder, dates and oil-producing plants. Vines were grown in the delta, but the wine was a luxury product. Models and paintings show grain being sown by hand, reaped with short sickles, threshed by animals driven over ears of grain, and winnowed. Other important crops were flax and papyrus, used for textiles and paper. Ploughs were drawn by oxen. Cattle were kept for both meat and milk; sheep, goats and pigs were also herded. Hunting, fishing and fowling occurred wherever there was opportunity, using hooks, spears, nets and bows and arrows. In the absence of wood, boats were constructed from bundles of papyrus reed lashed together with raised bows and sterns, and could be large enough for ocean voyages.

There was no coinage until the fourth century BC, but gold was a valued export quite apart from its use for jewellery and ornamentation. Weights and measures were standardized and were mainly needed for taxation purposes. Trade, including international trade, was conducted by barter, as is shown by a story from the end of this period describing the negotiations for wooden beams needed for a temple at Karnak. Among the items offered in exchange were ox hides, rolls of papyrus, bags of lentils, lengths of linen cloth and measures of fish – presumably dried.

Much evidence about life in ancient Egypt has come from the pyramids and other burial grounds. The Egyptians furnished their tombs lavishly with tools, furniture, weapons, food and models of the many things the dead would need during their journey through the underworld to judgement, and in the afterlife. Paintings and reliefs on the walls provide further information on the whole range of Egyptian society about which records had been kept from as early as 3000 BC.

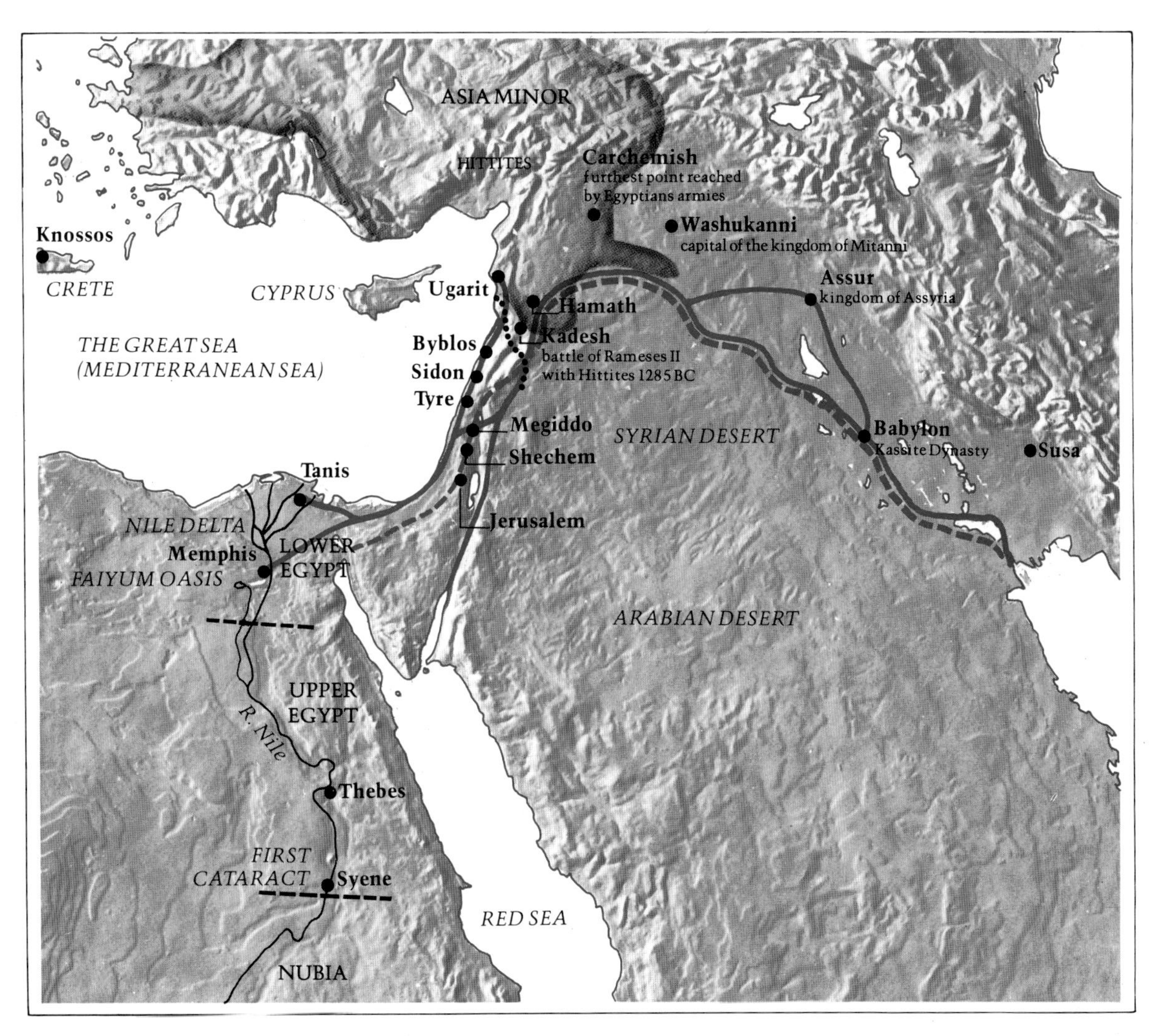

THE EXTENT OF EGYPTIAN CONTROL Egypt was exposed to attack from the north-east, where the main routes to Mesopotamia and Asia Minor entered the country. The extended lines of communication within Egypt, along the length of the River Nile, made it difficult to maintain internal unity. When Egypt had strong kings, the Egyptian army could be deployed right through Palestine and Syria, to prevent enemies from approaching the frontier. Strong kingdoms in Asia Minor and in the north of Mesopotamia, such as Mittani and the Hittite kingdom, stopped Egypt from penetrating any further than the border city of Carchemish. For a brief period in the eighteenth and seventeenth centuries, Lower Egypt was conquered by Semitic peoples, the Hyksos, who imposed their rule, and allowed the Hebrews to settle.

LEFT The pyramids were already over 1,000 years old when the Hebrews settled on the borders of Egypt during the second millenium BC. They symbolized the Egyptian belief both in the immortality and the divinity of their kings. Most of the pyramids were built in Lower Egypt, not far from the region where the Hebrews were allowed to live.

The pyramids have become the main symbol of ancient Egypt, but these royal tombs belong only to the earliest period of the country's history in the third and second millenia BC. The three pyramids of Giza all date from the 4th Dynasty in the middle of the third millenium BC and include 'The Great Pyramid of Cheops', the largest ever built. Lesser pyramids for royal relatives surrounded the main ones in which the kings were buried. The Great Sphinx (BELOW) stands near the two larger pyramids on a lower level, but it is not known what its function was or what it originally represented. The Giza area contains many tombs (RIGHT) cut into the rock ledges to face the rising sun. Modern repairs to ancient ruins at Giza (FAR RIGHT) typify the care lavished on the preservation of ancient monuments in Egypt.

The World in 1200 BC

Towards the end of the second millenium BC, migrants flooded into Mesopotamia and northern India, and then continued westwards, upsetting the existing power balance. Further afield, in the Indus Valley and China, advanced cultures with well organized social structures had developed.

BELOW This reconstruction of an eastern Mediterranean warship from the later part of the second millenium BC gives a vivid impression of the swift power of the 'Sea Peoples', who fell on Asia Minor, Palestine and Egypt. They were repulsed by the Egyptians, but established a foothold in Palestine as the Philistines, and destroyed the prevailing powers in Asia Minor.

The great civilizations of the ancient world seemed so secure that they appeared to be vulnerable only to neighbours of equal power. Periodic confrontations between the powers of Egypt, Asia Minor and Mesopotamia lend weight to this view. However, a greater threat emerged from the wide grasslands of eastern Europe and central Asia towards the end of the second millenium BC and changed the shape of the political map from Europe to India.

The newcomers were migrants, rather than invaders, who flooded into the Near East and northern India through the mountain passes, and continued westwards into central Europe. They are usually referred to as Indo-Europeans, because of common features in the languages they are thought to have influenced. Another name for these people is the Aryans. There is evidence for similar migratory waves in earlier periods and all of them may have been the result of population growths, or of pressure from other northern Asian groups.

The Hittites of Asia Minor, whose main confrontations had been with the Egyptians in Canaan and with the Kassites of northern Mesopotamia, fell either to the migrants themselves, or to the peoples they displaced as they penetrated into the Balkans. The city of Mycenae had dominated Greece while Knossos dominated Crete and the neighbouring islands. Both these centres were overrun by migrants from the north around 1200 BC and Greece entered a dark age which was to last for four centuries. An important aspect of the period was that iron ceased to be a rare metal and displaced bronze, an alloy of copper and tin, for making tools and weapons.

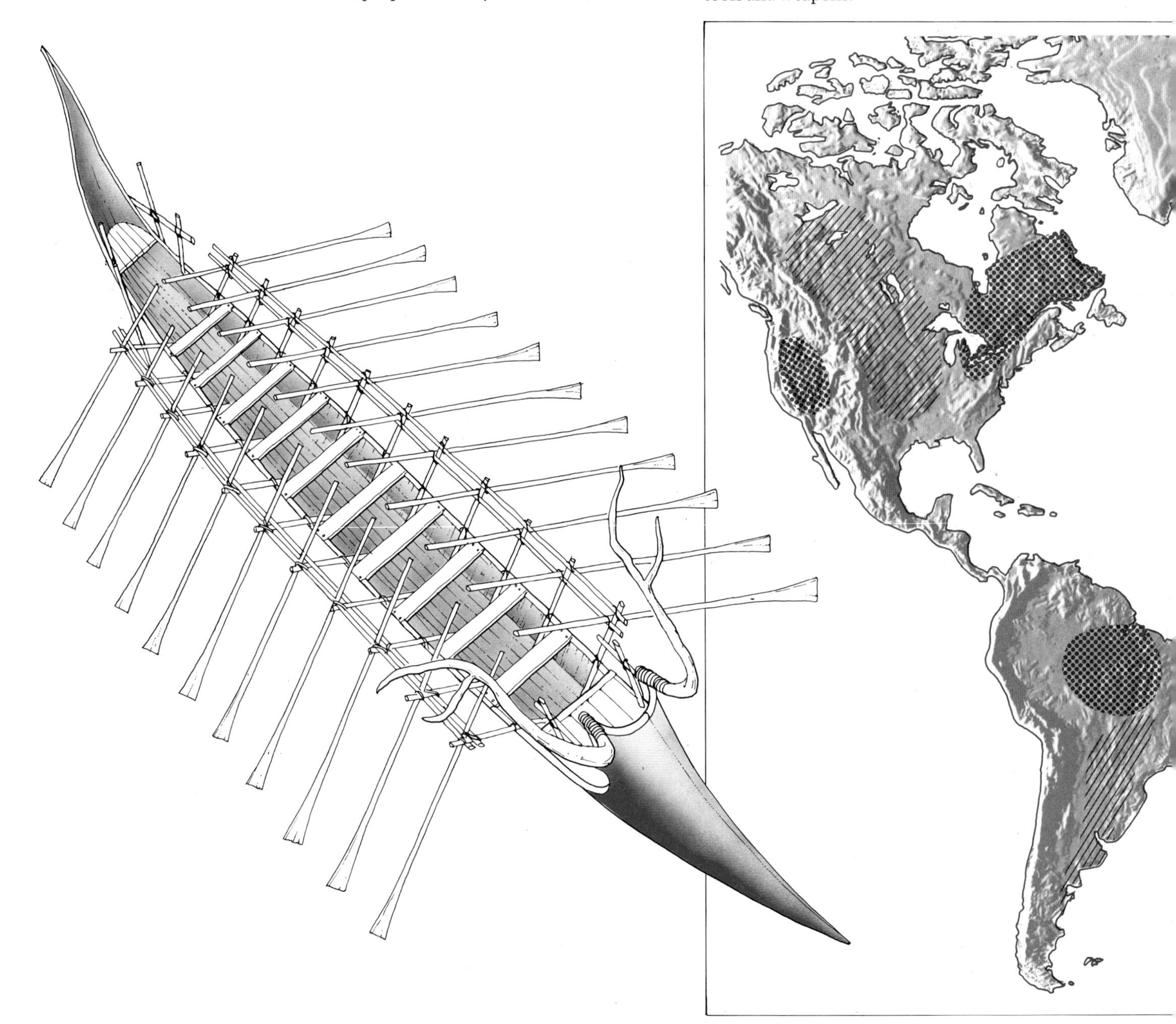

In India, during this period, the Indo-Europeans penetrated into the north, ending the first Indian civilization in the Indus Valley and establishing new cultural and religious patterns. Those new patterns are now thought of as characteristically Indian, particularly the language, Sanskrit, and the Veda literature, the first great collections of Indian religious writing.

The first royal dynasty in China of which there is evidence was the Shang Dynasty which ruled from about the eighteenth to the twelfth century BC. Its centre of power lay in the central parts of the Yellow River Valley in northern China. Other states existed at the time, but the Shang have left written records on divination bones from which a list of all the Shang kings can be constructed, as well as information about the organization of the state and military campaigns. Shang burial sites show that they had developed chariots with spoked wheels by 1300 BC. The culture is also characterized by beautiful bronze bowls of elaborate design cast in ceramic moulds and carved jade of similarly advanced design and technique. These finds point to a well organized society ruled by kings, with a developed social structure and organization of labour. Certainly the Shang seem to have had a complex agricultural civilization of peasants and city-dwelling craftspeople, with a priestly class, nobles, and a king, who was also high priest. A feature still to be found in Chinese society today – the patriarchial family system – was developed by this time.

Trading routes already existed between India and the Near and Middle East, and throughout the Mediterranean and for tin, possibly as far as Britain.

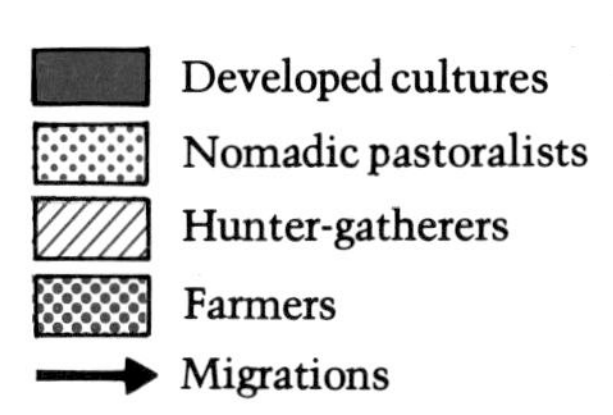

A TIME OF CHANGE For the biblical world, the most significant new influences were the migrant peoples who invaded the east Mediterranean area and Mesopotamia. In China the Shang Dynasty was nearing the end of its power, while the massive River Indus was spurning its own brand of culture.

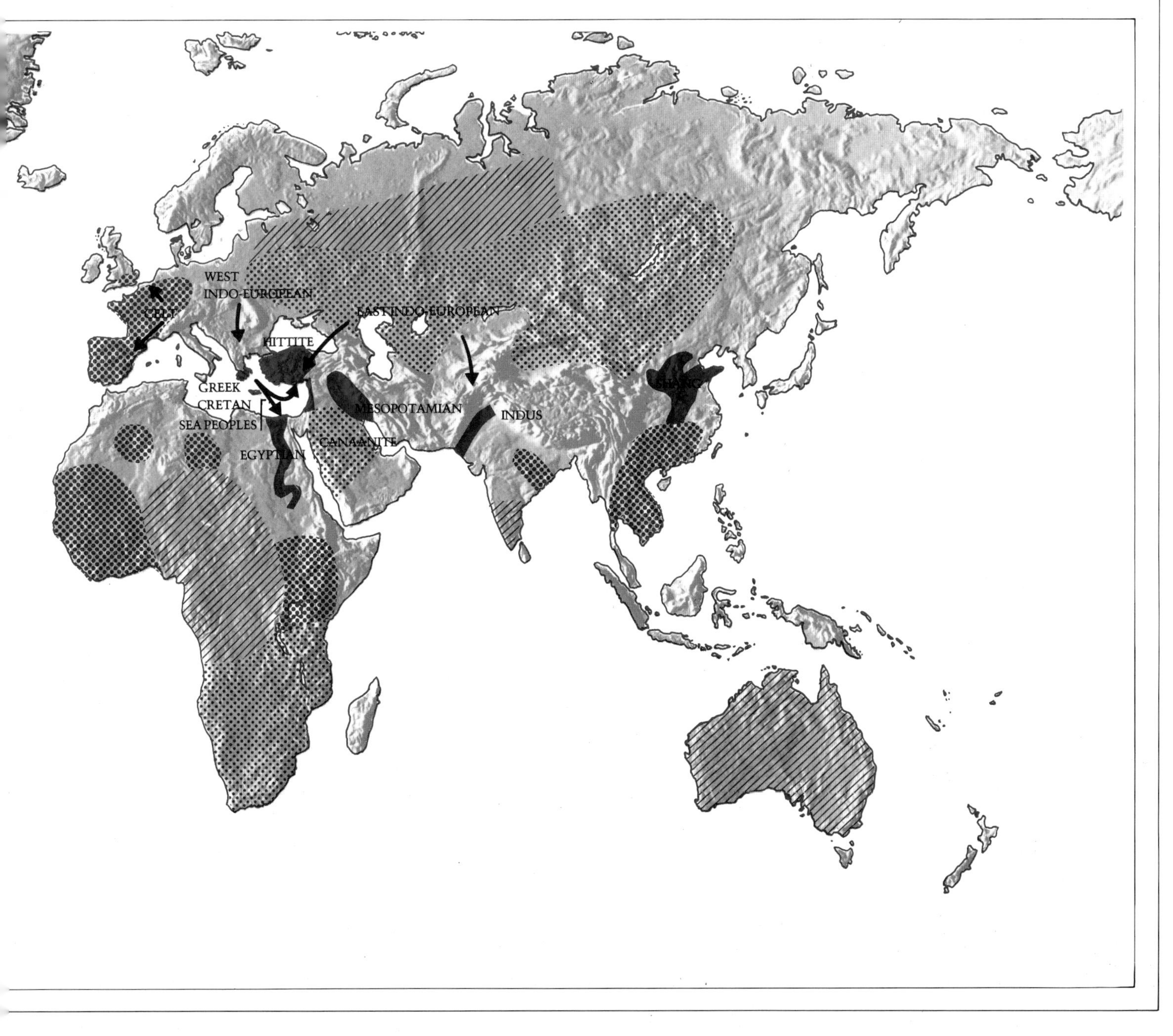

Creation Traditions

The accounts of creation in Genesis were seen as a preface to the exodus from Egypt, the main historical event in Hebrew tradition. They present one God with absolute power, and an ordered, coherent world administered by his representatives – the human race – who are responsible for their own actions, good or evil.

RIGHT The creation stories in the opening chapters of the Book of Genesis were shaped by the needs of the nomadic Hebrew herdsmen who preserved them in their oral traditions. The material contains features found in many Middle Eastern creation myths, but the Hebrew shepherds changed them to express their clear belief in the Hebrew God, Yahweh.

The opening chapters of the Book of Genesis stand apart from the rest of the Bible in both their content and purpose. Most of the material in the Bible was written at times close to the events described and there is at least a clear historical tradition behind the information. This is far less evident in Genesis 1-11. These chapters do not seem to describe events and people. Rather than recording history, they are explaining it. They present a view of the world which formed the basis for the beliefs, worship and way of life of, first, the Hebrews and, then, the Christians.

The material in these chapters was finally edited late in the Old Testament period, probably around 500 BC, after the exile in Babylon. It was seen as an introduction to the main event in all Hebrew tradition, the exodus, the great escape from Egypt in the thirteenth century BC, and was thus only written in its final form after some seven centuries of reflection on the significance of that event. The final editors used materials inherited from previous generations of Hebrews and from other parts of the Near and Middle East, but they shaped it into a general introduction for the rest of the Book of Genesis and the four books which follow – Exodus, Leviticus, Numbers and Deuteronomy. These five books contain the history of the Hebrew people from Abraham to the moment when they are poised to enter Canaan (Palestine) after escaping from Egypt under Moses.

There are two accounts of the creation. The first (Gen 1: 1-2:4a) is the final editors' preface which presents an ordered and coherent world with mankind as its administrator. The whole universe and everything in it is part of one perfect and benevolent plan which God, as sole source of all existence and of salvation, entrusts to mankind. The second account of creation (Gen 2: 4b-2:25) is more primitive and personal. It explains sexual desire and sets the scene for the emergence of discord and evil in a perfect world where there is only one God.

Both accounts provide insights into the world both as the Hebrews experienced it and as they hoped it might be. The escape from Egypt, and the covenant which followed it at Mount Sinai, showed that the good and benevolent God on whom the whole universe depended was prepared to save them from the evil mankind produced, and to restore the original perfection of the creation.

The subsequent chapters (Gen 3-11) which deal with Noah and the flood, the tower of Babel and the family trees, serve to show how the saviour God can be both just and merciful. Mankind is incapable of correcting the disorder it has introduced into creation, but the purpose of the lengthy family trees is to trace the thread of God's original intention through the generation from Adam to Abraham. Noah is a key figure in this. Not only was he chosen to preserve the creation after the flood, but he also received the first covenant from God (Gen 9). The covenant is the means by which God enters into or confirms his special relationship with mankind. As Noah is seen as the ancestor of everyone, this first covenant, which expresses the promise of universal salvation, benefits all peoples. Genesis 12 opens with the call of Abraham and the first of the covenants specifically with the Hebrew people. These opening chapters of Genesis thus express the considered

LEFT **Each head of a family represented both his own children and the people from whom he was descended. His identity epitomized the whole nation, which could trace its descent back through Abraham and Noah to Adam himself. In this way generation after generation was linked to the creation events and the promises of God implicit in them. At first the Hebrews could only see this process in their own nation, but as their religious perceptions developed they saw that the promises of God and his creative power extended to all peoples. The covenant with Noah was a covenant with everyone on earth.**

conclusions which the Hebrews reached about God and their fundamental relationship with him.

The earliest accounts of the Hebrews depict them as nomadic shepherds, grazing sheep along the sparse grasslands of the 'fertile crescent' between the Persian Gulf and the borders of Egypt, where the agricultural land meets the desert. They were not competing for land with any of the farming peoples, but their contacts with them meant that Hebrew writings had to explain how these other nations fitted into God's plan of creation. This is provided in Genesis 10.

The whole of this chapter consists of a genealogical table, or extended family tree, of Noah's descendants, which continues after the history of the tower of Babel in Genesis 11. In these chapters, the final editors of this material used older, oral traditions to demonstrate the link between the creation and Abraham, and also provided a 'map' of the world, as Hebrews saw it. The Hebrews believed they were all descended from one person – a common ancestor who provided a blood bond linking all the people and creating a tribal and national unity. They applied this same thinking to all other peoples, as these chapters of Genesis show.

To the Hebrews, all mankind was descended from Noah and his sons, the survivors of the flood. All people therefore shared in the promises made by God to Noah (Gen 9: 1-17). In this account, the three sons of Noah separated, creating the three main groups of 'nations', divided according to their direction from Palestine. The eastward peoples, including the Hebrews themselves, were 'sons of Shem'. The southern peoples of the Nile Valley and Libya, including the Canaanites of Palestine were 'sons of Ham'. The peoples to the north and west were 'sons of Japheth'.

This apparently simple division was complicated by the connection the Hebrews saw between Ethiopia, south of Egypt, and the peoples of the eastern Arabian desert and Babylonia, both of whom they considered to be 'sons of Ham'. In addition, the Hebrews believed that most of the Mediterranean people descended from Japheth. This included the people of southern Spain (Tarshish) whom they knew of through the Phoenician traders who sailed from Tyre to Sidon.

The 'sons of Shem' were commonly called the Semites. They included all the peoples with whom the Hebrews felt they had a close relationship, including the Assyrians of northern Mesopotamia and the tribes of the Arabian desert. Before they settled in Palestine, the main nomadic grazing areas for the Hebrews extended into Mesopotamia.

The creation accounts in Genesis 1-11 contain so many features in common with creation traditions in Mesopotamia and Canaan that it is impossible to ignore the connections. But the Hebrews modified the elements they borrowed from the creation myths of their neighbours, to make them serve the Hebrew beliefs about God. In the other traditions there are many gods in a continuous conflict which determines human nature and history without any possibility of human responsibility. The Hebrews, on the other hand, present creation in terms of a thoroughly moral God whose absolute power is mediated through his representatives, mankind, to whom he gives responsibility for the rest of the creation.

Gen 1-11.

God said, 'Let the earth produce every kind of living creature: cattle, reptiles, and every kind of wild beast'. And so it was. God made every kind of wild beast, every kind of cattle, and every kind of land reptile. God saw that it was good.
God said, 'Let us make man in our own image, in the likeness of ourselves, and let them be masters of the fish of the sea, the birds of heaven, the cattle, all the wild beasts and all the reptiles that crawl upon the earth'.
God created man in the image of himself,
in the image of God he created him,
male and female he created them. (Gen 1: 24-27)

Hebrew Roots

God gave a series of covenants to a nomad named Abraham, his son Isaac and grandson Jacob (Israel), which established Hebrew rights to the territory they later occupied. Meanwhile, under the protection of Joseph, one of Jacob's sons who held high office there, the Hebrews migrated to Egypt.

Abraham entered Canaan as leader of a family group of nomadic Amorite shepherds, moving sheep along their traditional grazing route between Mesopotamia and Egypt. However, the people descended from him, those who shaped the traditions as they talked of the past around camp fires, thought of him as the father of their nation.

By the time those traditions were recorded in writing, the Hebrew descendants of Abraham had experienced the escape from Egypt under Moses and had occupied Canaan. The land was by then the symbol of the covenant God had made with them as his chosen people, and this belief is reflected in the way the stories about Abraham are presented. Abraham's movements from Ur of the Chaldeans (Gen 11:31) where the River Euphrates once joined the Persian Gulf, to Haran near the headwaters of the Euphrates, and then southwards into Canaan, were all part of the saving acts of God which reached their climax with the covenant at Mount Sinai (Exod 19-24).

The stories are organized around a series of covenants made by God with Abraham, his son Isaac and his grandson Jacob (Gen 12-28). Jacob's name was changed to Israel (Gen 32:29) to give the name 'Israelite' to the Hebrew tribes which traced their descent from Israel's 12 sons.

The early covenants establish the Hebrews' rights to possession of the land, and define its boundaries roughly 'from the wadi of Egypt to the Great River, the River Euphrates, the Kenites, the Kenizzites, the Kadmonites, the Hittites, the Perizzites, the Rephaim, the Amorites, the Canaanites, the Girgashites, and the Jebusites' (Gen 15: 18-21). The list names the territory the Hebrews later occupied and the peoples they controlled when the Hebrew kingdom was most powerful under David and Solomon in the tenth century BC. It covered approximately the area from the Egyptian border to Syria and from the coast to the eastern parts of the Jordan rift valley.

These narrative traditions also associate the Hebrews with sanctuaries, originally Canaanite, which became important centres of the Hebrew religion, particularly Shechem, Bethel, and Hebron where Abraham, Isaac and Jacob were buried. Although later Hebrew legislation forbade any association with the Canaanite religion and its sanctuaries, it would appear that the Hebrews had adopted the traditional sanctuaries of the country when they finally occupied it. Even Jerusalem is mentioned, under the name of Salem (Ps 76:2 and Gen 14:18), when its king, 'a priest of God Most High' brought Abraham bread and wine and blessed him 'by God Most High, creator of heaven and earth'. Jerusalem did not become a Hebrew city until it was captured by King David in 1000 BC and made the capital of his kingdom.

The Canaanites were farmers, who worked the land surrounding their fortified cities, each of which had a secure water supply and storage pits for grain. There was no competition from the Canaanites for the sparse pastures used by the Hebrew nomadic shepherds. Throughout the biblical period, Egyptian grain was available at a price in times of famine, made sure by the dependable waters of the River Nile.

The times and events described by the Book of Genesis in connection with Abraham, Isaac and Jacob are related to the 12th and 13th Dynasties in Egypt. They cover the period from the twentieth century BC to about 1640. Then Lower Egypt was taken over by foreign rulers from the north-east. The invaders have been given the general name Hyksos (15th and 16th Dynasties), and appear to have taken advantage of growing numbers of non-Egyptians settling in the Delta region of Lower Egypt.

Until the Hyksos, Egypt had controlled Canaan, but this, together with Lower Egypt, was now taken over and ruled from the two Hyksos capitals – Tanis, known as Zoan in the Bible, and Avaris, at the eastern extreme of the Nile Delta. The native Egyptian rulers retained control of Upper Egypt, which they ruled from Thebes.

This situation helps to explain the final 15 chapters of the Book of Genesis, which describe the Hebrew migration to Egypt. The main figure is Joseph, one of the sons of Jacob (Israel), who was sold into slavery by his brothers and sold again in Egypt to a court official. His wisdom in interpreting dreams brought him promotion by the Egyptian king to a position of high responsibility, and he married the daughter of the priest of On (Heliopolis), the centre of worship of Re, the sun god, at the southern end of the Nile Delta near what is now the city of Cairo.

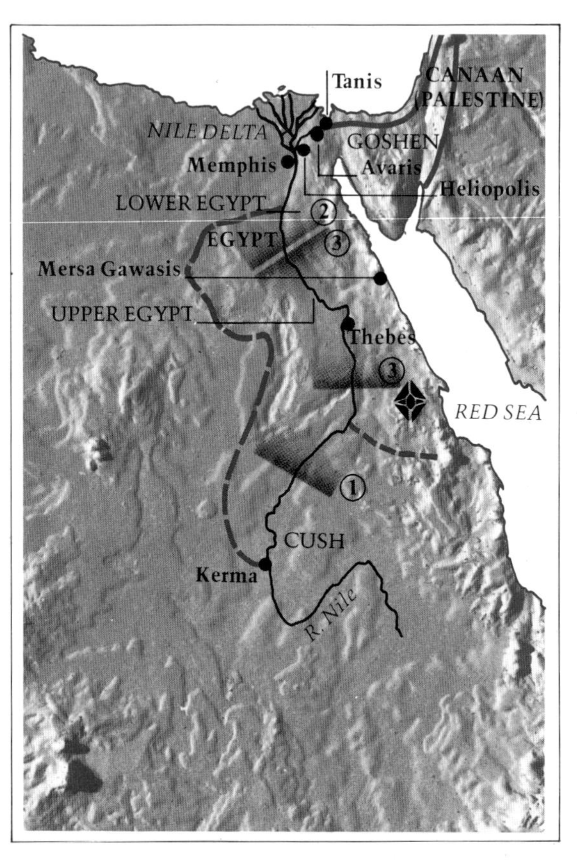

(1) Possible frontier during 12th-13th Dynasty
(2) Possible frontier during 15th Dynasty
(3) Possible frontiers during 17th Dynasty
Desert communication 15th Dynasty
Route to gold mines
 Amethyst quarries
Main trade routes

DESERT RICHES **The Hebrew nomads who came to Egypt under Joseph's protection lived in Goshen, to the east of the Nile Delta, far from Upper Egypt where the gold mines and amethyst quarries were to be found. These riches were the impetus for Egyptian domination of the area. Inevitably, with such expansion, communication routes were established.**

In addition to Re, the city was also a centre for the worship of the creator god, Atum, and exercised considerable influence over Egyptian religion and politics. Among the Egyptian titles of the On high priest were 'Greatest of the Seers' and 'King's Son of his Body'. Joseph was also a seer and held in high regard by the king, so he would have been accepted readily at On, and the Hebrews welcomed into Egypt. In addition, he is important as the ancestor of the most powerful Hebrew tribes to settle in Palestine after escaping from Egypt. It is now generally felt that the Hyksos period is the background for the Joseph stories. They become much more credible through the conjunction of Egyptian rulers – with whom the Hebrews would feel they had blood ties because the Hyskos were Semitic.

The Hebrews settled in Goshen, a place not mentioned in Egyptian records but which may have been a Canaanite name for the region to the east of the Nile Delta. Egyptian records do show permissions for nomadic groups to enter Egypt, and it fits both the nomadic shepherd origins of the Hebrews and the territorial claims of the Egyptian gods that such a group as the Hebrews should settle just beyond the borders of Egyptian territory.

During the 17th Dynasty of Thebes, in the seventeenth and sixteenth centuries BC, the native Egyptian rulers began their attempts to regain control over all Egypt. But it was not until the 18th Dynasty, in the sixteenth century BC, that they succeeded in defeating the Hyksos rulers. This began in the period of the New Kingdom, from the sixteenth to the eleventh centuries BC. This was probably the period when the 'new king who knew nothing of Joseph' (Exod 1:8) gained power in Egypt.

Gen 12-50.

'You shall no longer be called Abram; your name shall be Abraham, for I make you father of a multitude of nations. I will make you most fruitful. I will make you into nations, and your issue shall be kings. I will establish my Covenant between myself and you, and your descendants ... I will give to you and to your descendants after you the land you are living in, the whole land of Canaan, to own in perpetuity, and I will be your God.'
(Gen 17: 5-8)

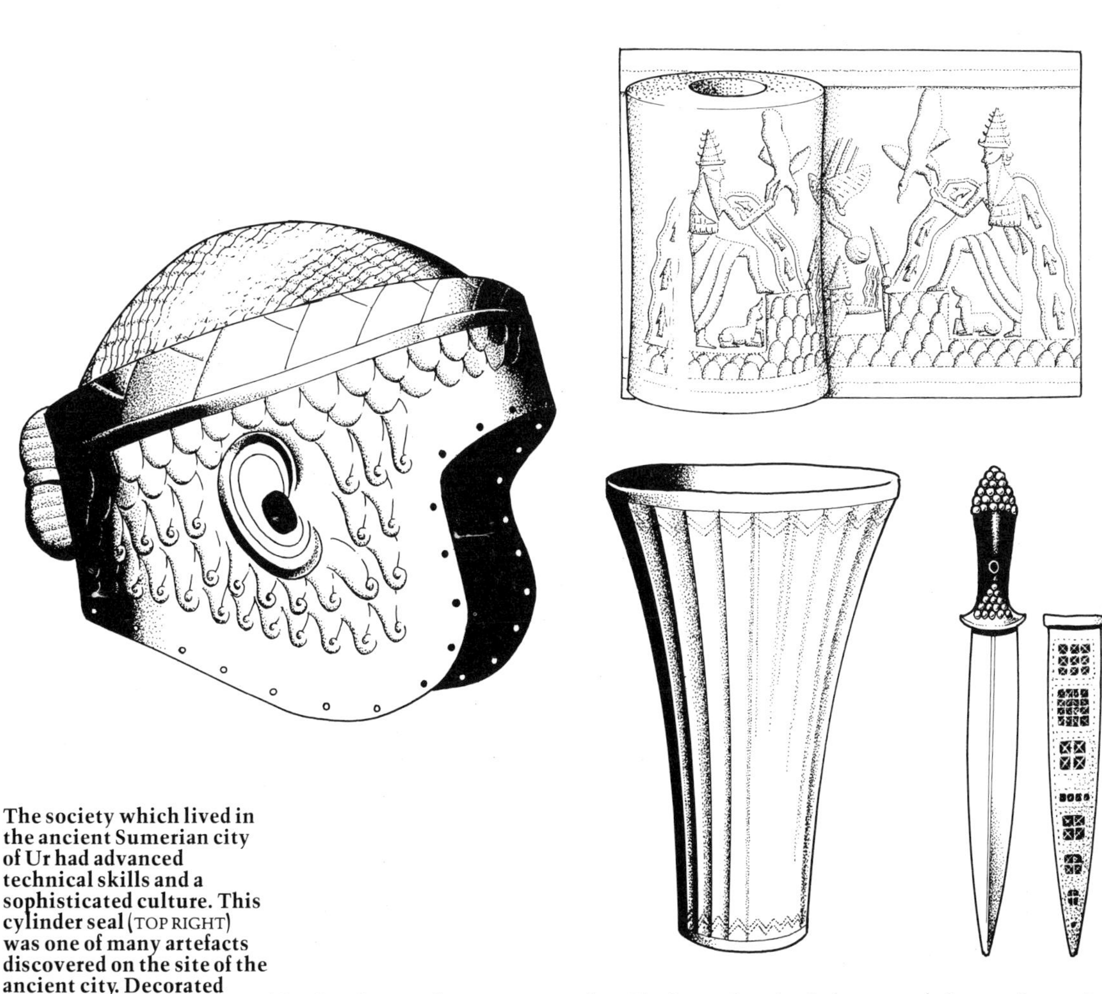

The society which lived in the ancient Sumerian city of Ur had advanced technical skills and a sophisticated culture. This cylinder seal (TOP RIGHT) was one of many artefacts discovered on the site of the ancient city. Decorated seals were used to authenticate documents. The seal was rolled over soft clay in which wedge-shaped writing (cuneiform) had been impressed, so that it left behind the owner's recognized symbols. Then the clay tablet was baked hard. Other artefacts discovered on the site include the ceremonial helmet (ABOVE) which was found in a royal tomb. The helmet was originally lined with quilting which was attached by lacing through holes visible around its edge. The Sumerians buried their royalty in style, ensuring that their dead kings and queens were dressed in the finest clothes and with everything they might need on their journey to the next world. The excavations at Ur have revealed many decorative objects. The fluted gold beaker (LEFT) was found in a queen's tomb. Also discovered was the gold dagger and its sheath (RIGHT). All these artefacts verify the extent of the citizens' wealth and skills.

- Until 1000 BC Canaanite settlements; Egypt controls coast
- 2030-1640 BC Middle Kingdom, 11th-14th Dynasties, capitals: Memphis and Thebes
- c1800-1600 BC Abraham, Isaac and Jacob
- c1724-1595 BC Old Babylonian Empire
- c1720 BC Code of Hammurabi
- 1640-1530 BC 2nd Intermediate Period; 15th-16th Dynasties, Hyksos kings, capital: Avaris; 17th Dynasty, capital: Thebes
- 1640-1530 BC Hebrew groups settle in Egypt
- c1595-1360 BC Kassites overthrow Babylon; Mitanni, Hurrians, Assyrians, Kassites and Hittites in Mesopotamian area
- 1550-1070 BC New Kingdom, 18th-20th Dynasties, capital: Thebes; Hyksos rulers expelled; Egypt united; wars with Mitanni
- 1550-1070 BC Canaanites under Egyptian control
- c1360 BC Hebrew groups settle in Canaan
- 1290-1224 BC Reign of Rameses II, capital: Pi-Rameses
- 1250 BC Hebrew escape from Egypt (the exodus)
- 1220-1200 BC Hebrew domination of Canaan begins under Joshua
- 1200-900 BC Philistines occupy the Palestinian coast
- c1200-1025 BC The Judges

BELOW **The refugee camps of the Near and Middle East are a harsh reminder of the sudden changes which have always marked the political realities of the area. At the time described in the early chapters of the Book of Exodus, the Hebrews found themselves in a similarly hopeless situation on the borders of Egypt. The old security of the days of Joseph had ended forever.**

+ Main sanctuaries associated with the Hebrews of Gen 12-50

— Main trade routes

① The Way of the Sea

② The King's Highway

HEBREW SANCTUARIES **The places where the patriarchs – Abraham, Isaac and Jacob – received covenants from God have been designated sacred from ancient times.**

LEFT **The Judean Desert seems an inhospitable area, but its sparse pasturage supported hardy sheep.**

Deliverance from Egypt

Increasingly, the Hebrews were regarded as aliens by the Egyptians. Around the 13th century BC they escaped to Canaan during the Passover. They were led by Moses who had been given a sacred covenant naming the Hebrews as God's 'chosen people'. Thereafter all Hebrew law was an expression of the people's gratitude.

Exod 1-24; 32-34, Num 10-14; 20-25.

Yahweh looked down on the army of the Egyptians from the pillar of fire and of cloud, and threw the army into confusion. He so clogged their chariot wheels that they could scarcely make headway. 'Let us flee from the Israelites,' the Egyptians cried 'Yahweh is fighting for them against the Egyptians!' 'Stretch out your hand over the sea,' Yahweh said to Moses 'that the waters may flow back on the Egyptians and their chariots and their horsemen.' Moses stretched out his hand over the sea and, as day broke, the sea returned to its bed. The fleeing Egyptians marched right into it, and Yahweh overthrew the Egyptians in the very middle of the sea. The returning waters overwhelmed the chariots and the horsemen of Pharaoh's whole army, which had followed the Israelites into the sea; not a single one of them was left.
(Exod 14: 24-28)

In about 1285 BC, an Egyptian army led by King Rameses II (1290-1224 BC) ran into a trap at Kadesh in northern Palestine, just north of what is now Lebanon. The front section of the army, with Rameses, was cut off by Hittite chariots who attacked the second section leaving the king and his section isolated. Only desperate fighting saved the situation.

Kadesh appears as a victory in Egyptian records, but the treaty which eventually followed left the Egyptian frontier in Palestine further south than it had ever been. Earlier in Rameses II's reign, the Egyptian capital had been moved to a site near the old Hyksos capital at Avaris, in the north-eastern part of the delta, as part of a vast, extensive building programme. Thus, the Nile Delta was once more the most important part of Egypt, and was vital to Egyptian security with mounting pressure from Libya to the west, and the uneasy peace with the Hittites.

These developments in Egyptian history have clear links with events described in the Bible. As a result, it is assumed that it was during the reign of Rameses II that the Hebrews escaped from Egypt, as described in the Book of Exodus. When the Asiatic Hyksos rulers of Egypt were overthrown around 1550 BC, the descendants of the Hebrew nomadic shepherds who had settled near the delta found themselves under increasing suspicion as aliens. They would certainly have been chosen as one of many groups forced into labour gangs to build Rameses' new capital and frontier fortifications. This is described in Exodus 1:11: 'Accordingly they put slave-drivers over the Israelites to wear them down under heavy loads. In this way, they built the store-cities of Pithom and Rameses for Pharaoh.'

The Hebrew leader, Moses, is presented as the adopted child of an Egyptian princess. He therefore had access to the royal court. But of equal importance are his contacts with the Midianites of the Sinai desert, who gave him shelter, and a wife, when he first had to flee Egypt. The Midianites, who were descendants of Abraham through his second wife, worshipped the same God as the Hebrews, and Moses returned to Egypt with the conviction that God had chosen him to lead his people to freedom.

The famous plagues described in Exodus 7-12 can all be seen as natural phenomena, but for both the Hebrews and the Egyptians they were contests between the Hebrew God and the Egyptian gods – of whom the king, Rameses II, was one. The broad background to the account in the Book of Exodus is entirely consistent with the situation in Egypt at the time. Religion was territorial and neither the Egyptians nor the Hebrews would want a Hebrew religious festival to be held on Egyptian soil, so the Hebrews asked permission to go into the desert for it. This was the request which the Egyptian king at first refused and then granted after the series of plagues.

The Hebrew escape or exodus from Egypt is described in the Book of Exodus 12-15. These chapters, and the subsequent ones which deal with the covenant at Mount Sinai, must be the most heavily edited passages in the Old Testament, for the events they describe are as central to the Hebrew religion as the crucifixion and resurrection of Jesus are to Christianity. The account of the exodus and covenant reached its present form in the Book of Exodus about seven centuries after the events occurred. But the final editors were able to refer to very old written sources and firm traditions kept alive through their regular use in Hebrew worship.

The description of the escape starts with the Passover regulations in Exodus 12. This celebration was, and still is, the key to Hebrew worship and the festival to which the other major feasts are linked. It was originally a protection rite for nomadic shepherds as they moved along the routes in search of pasture. The blood of a sacrificed lamb, symbolizing, and containing, the life-giving power of God, gave them protection against any evil forces, and the meal then sealed the links between God and his people. The escape from Egypt gave this rite new meaning, as a commemoration of the Hebrew God's victory over the Egyptian gods and his covenant with his chosen people. All subsequent acts of deliverance throughout Hebrew history were then seen as consequences of this exodus and God's deliverance and were celebrated therefore as extensions of the Passover. When the Hebrews became farmers, after the occupation of Canaan, the Canaanite harvest festivals were celebrated as manifestations of the same power of God which had brought the people safely out of Egypt.

The actual crossing out of Egypt pursued by Egyptian soldiers, depicted in Exodus 14, occurred at what the Hebrews called *yam-suph*. When this was translated into Greek, about 1,000 years later, a phrase meaning 'Red Sea' was used, implying that the Hebrews crossed the Gulf of Suez. However, the Hebrew should more properly be translated 'Sea of Reeds', which also agrees with the place names given in the early part of the journey (Exod 13:17 – 14:2). The 'road to the land of the Philistines' (Palestine) left the north-east edge of the Nile Delta, where the Egyptian capital was then located, and followed the coast into Canaan. Succoth, where the Israelites first camped on their journey, was probably west of Lake Timsah (and today's Suez Canal), while Migdol was a border fortress near the coast at Tell el-Heir. Pi-hahiroth (Exod 14:9) faced Baal-zephon, where there was a temple for sailors on a narrow peninsula.

This route takes the Hebrew escape well north of the Gulf of Suez, into the marshy area near the Mediterranean coast, and fits both the Hebrew 'Sea of Reeds' and the account of Egyptian chariot wheels being clogged which comes from one of the earlier strands of the traditions woven together in Exodus 14. The crossing therefore probably occurred north of Lake Timsah. After this the Hebrews turned south, both to avoid Egyptian officials on the main routes into Palestine and to reach the wilderness areas grazed by the nomadic shepherd tribes, one of which was the Midianites to whom Moses had fled before returning to Egypt as his people's leader. The exodus took place in about 1250 BC, in the middle of the long reign of Rameses II.

Despite a wealth of information in the Books of Exodus, Leviticus, Numbers and Deuteronomy, there can be no absolute certainty about the route the escaping Hebrews took from Egypt to the mountain of the covenant and Canaan, nor how long the whole journey took. There are also some different views about the actual location of the mountain.

Some of the contradictory information becomes much clearer if it is accepted that the biblical accounts of the journey combine traditions about several waves of Hebrew penetration into Canaan, with at least two distinct journeys. One of these was opposed by kingdoms in the plains of Moab to the east of the Dead Sea, while an earlier journey was able to pass unhindered. In addition, there would have been Hebrews living in southern Canaan who had not gone to Egypt at the time of the entry of Joseph and his brothers.

Egyptian records lend support to such a view, for it appears that there were no organized kingdoms east of the Dead Sea in the 14th century BC, but, by the 13th century BC, kingdoms had emerged in Edom and Moab which would account for opposition to a Hebrew group during the latter part of the reign of Rameses II. In any event, there were fortified Canaanite cities across the south of Canaan which could prevent Hebrew groups of any size from penetrating past the region of Kadesh-barnea. Such groups would then have to cross eastwards to take the traditional nomadic route, the King's Highway. There need be far less uncertainty about the location of the mountain itself. It is referred to variously as Mount Sinai, Mount Horeb and Mount Paran, and all three names point to the granite mountains in the southern Sinai peninsula.

The most important incident of the whole tradition need not be doubted and would account for the mingling of all the traditions into one. That incident is the covenant at the sacred mountain, from which the Hebrews derived their national identity and their sense of religious unity. All Hebrews would have the strongest motives for associating their ancestors with the covenant tradition and for seeing the covenant as their entitlement to the land of Palestine.

The events at Mount Sinai are cast in a form similar to treaties between so-called saviour-kings and their subjects, whose relationships were based on a great victory or deed which placed the subjects under an obligation to their king. The relationship between them was then specified by laws accepted by the people, backed by the power of the gods and by sanctions. The Hebrew covenant was thus based on the escape from Egypt, the supreme manifestation of God's power and of his choice of the Hebrew people. Hebrew law then became the expression of the people's gratitude, and their obligations to God and to each other as God's chosen ones. All Hebrew law, whether it already existed or developed subsequently, was an expression of the covenant, and so was incorporated into the covenant narrative.

The Ten Commandments (Exod 20: 1-17 and Deut 5: 1-21) are in a class of their own. As direct, absolute commands, rather than laws presented in the form of cases and precedents, the Ten Commandments have no known parallels in the ancient Near East and could well go back to Moses himself.

LEFT **The sacred Ark of the Covenant of the Hebrew people was a portable shrine appropriate for nomads. The biblical descriptions make it difficult to reconstruct the Hebrew shrine, but the portable chest found in the tomb of the Egyptian King Tut'ankhamun would have been similar.**

BOTTOM **The shepherd origins of the Hebrew people remained an ideal, but they quickly accepted the farming methods of the Canaanites.**

BELOW **This palm tree decorates a wall of a synagogue in Capernaum, a town on the northern shore of the Sea of Galilee where Jesus once stayed.**

Exodus route

Main trade routes

THE GREAT ESCAPE **Most probably, the Hebrews crossed the marshy region to the east of the Nile Delta – Moses's parting of the waters would have occurred here – before journeying to the sacred mountain. The experience there, in the Sinai Peninsula, became the foundation of the nation's religion and identity.**

- *c*1595-1360 BC Mitanni in north, Hurrians under Aryan rulers; Assyria controls central Mesopotamia; Kassites overthrow Babylon
- 1550-1070 BC New Kingdom, 18th-20th Dynasties, capital: Thebes; Hyksos rulers expelled; Egypt united
- 1550-1070 BC Canaanites under Egyptian control
- 1360 BC Akhnaton tries to impose monotheism; capital: Tell el-Amarna
- *c*1360 BC Hebrew groups settle in Canaan
- 1290-1224 BC Reign of Rameses II, capital: Pi-Rameses
- 1285 BC Battle of Kadesh, narrow Egyptian victory over Hittites
- 1250 BC Hebrew escape from Egypt (the exodus)
- 1220-1200 BC Hebrew domination of Canaan begins under Joshua
- 1200-900 BC Philistines occupy Palestinian coast
- *c*1200-1025 BC The Judges
- 1194-1184 BC Trojan War
- 1194-1163 BC Reign of Rameses III
- 1175 BC Victory over the 'Sea Peoples'

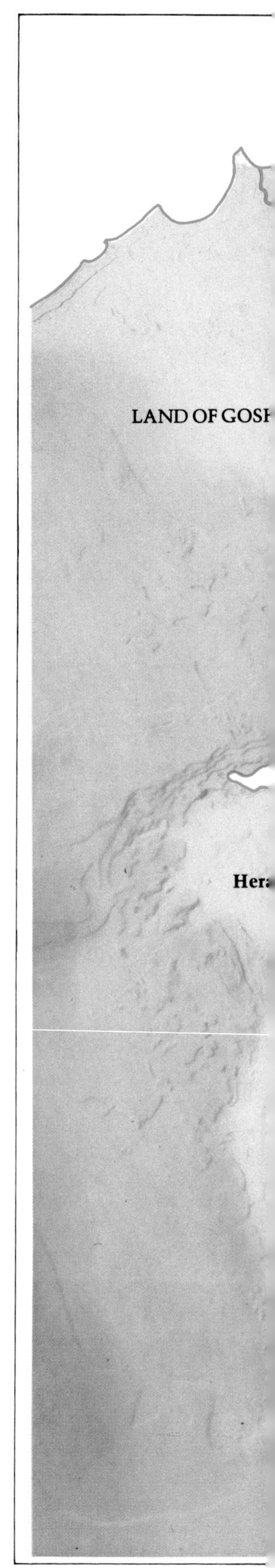

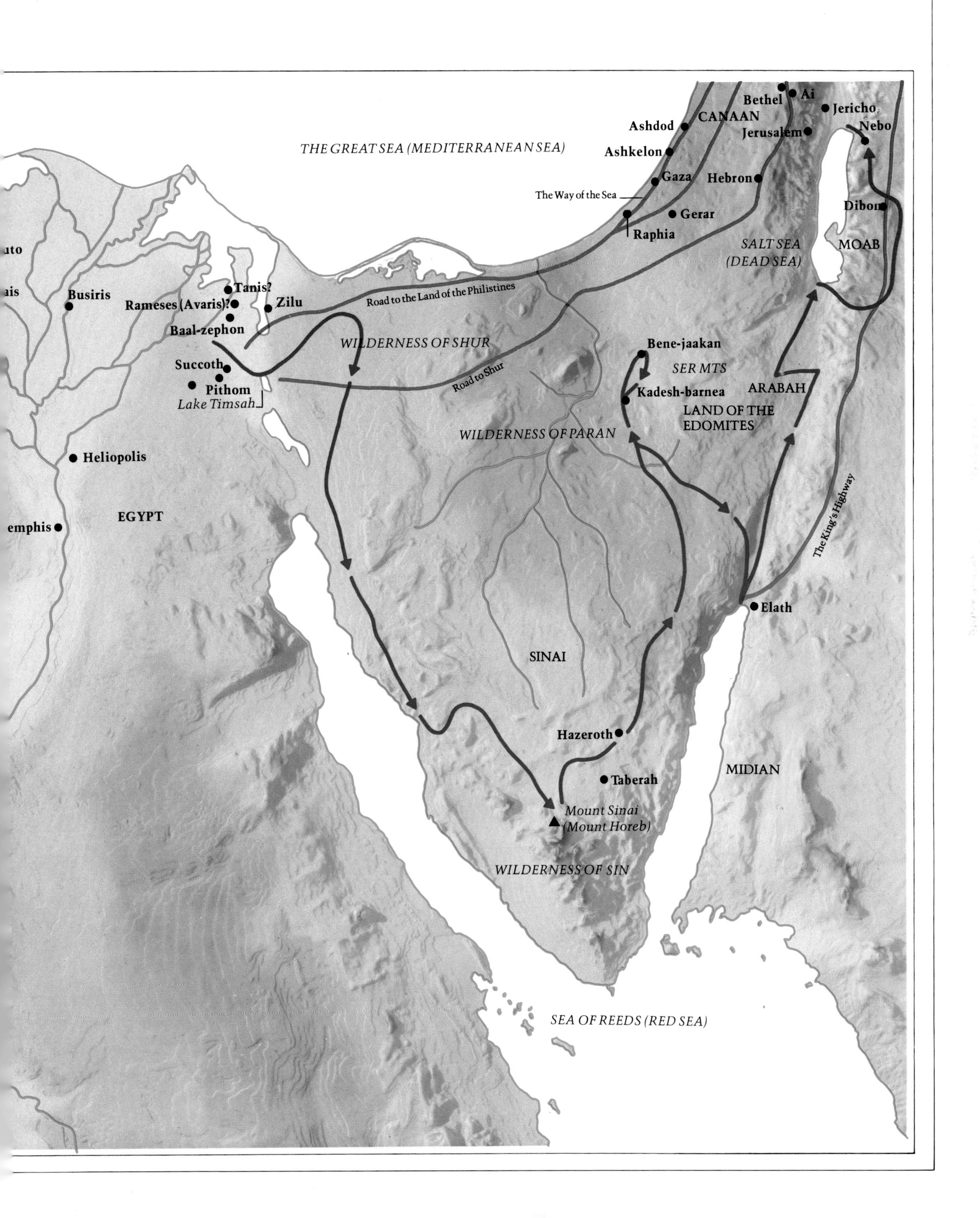

THE GREAT SEA (MEDITERRANEAN SEA)
Bethel
Ai
Jericho
CANAAN
Ashdod
Jerusalem
Nebo
Ashkelon
Gaza
Hebron
The Way of the Sea
Gerar
Raphia
Dibon
SALT SEA (DEAD SEA)
MOAB
Busiris
Tanis?
Rameses (Avaris)?
Zilu
Road to the Land of the Philistines
Baal-zephon
WILDERNESS OF SHUR
Bene-jaakan
Succoth
SER MTS
Pithom
Road to Shur
Kadesh-barnea
ARABAH
Lake Timsah
LAND OF THE EDOMITES
WILDERNESS OF PARAN
Heliopolis
EGYPT
emphis
The King's Highway
Elath
SINAI
Hazeroth
MIDIAN
Taberah
Mount Sinai (Mount Horeb)
WILDERNESS OF SIN
SEA OF REEDS (RED SEA)

2 · *THE BIRTH*

OF PALESTINE

The people shouted, the trumpets sounded. When they heard the sound of the trumpet, the people raised a mighty war cry and the wall collapsed then and there.
(Josh 6:20)

A Long Period of Turmoil

The exodus took place about the time the Near and Middle East was entering a long period of turmoil. The powers which had previously occupied Canaan collapsed or were wracked by civil wars. It was local peoples or migrants, such as the Philistines and Hebrews, who struggled for control of the Canaanite area.

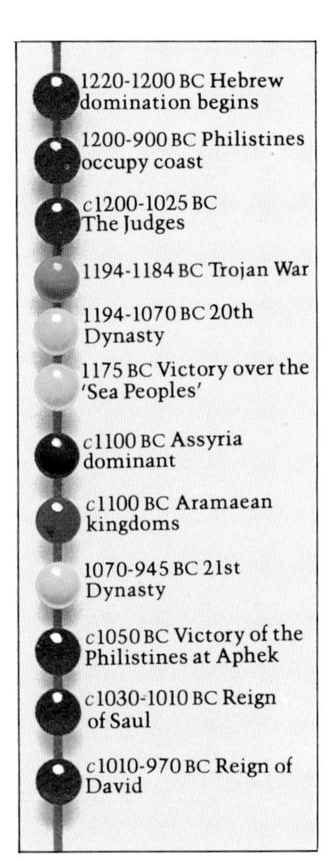

1220-1200 BC Hebrew domination begins
1200-900 BC Philistines occupy coast
c1200-1025 BC The Judges
1194-1184 BC Trojan War
1194-1070 BC 20th Dynasty
1175 BC Victory over the 'Sea Peoples'
c1100 BC Assyria dominant
c1100 BC Aramaean kingdoms
1070-945 BC 21st Dynasty
c1050 BC Victory of the Philistines at Aphek
c1030-1010 BC Reign of Saul
c1010-970 BC Reign of David

BELOW **The Egyptian temples were treasuries and store houses, as well as centres for worship. Reliefs from Old Kingdom tombs, such as these at Saqqara, just south of modern Cairo, record and depict the offerings brought to the temple, and to the tombs for use by the dead.**

The most probable date for the Hebrew escape from Egypt, the Exodus, is the latter part of the reign of King Rameses II of Egypt (1290-1224 BC), which would mean that the Hebrews penetrated into Canaan from the east at the end of the thirteenth, or beginning of the twelfth, century BC. Canaan was soon to become known as 'Land of the Philistines', and, eventually, Palestine. This time marks the beginning of nearly three centuries of weakness and turmoil for the great powers which normally considered Canaan an essential part of their defences and trading interests. It was not a period of peace for the area, far from it, but the protagonists were local to Canaan, or migrants such as the Hebrews.

The geography of the area forced the international routes from Egypt to Mesopotamia and Asia Minor through the narrow land of Canaan, between the desert and the sea. Throughout its recorded history, Canaan was at the mercy of the dominant powers of the Near and Middle East. It was nearly always occupied by one or other of them or was a battleground between them. During most of the second millenium BC, Canaan had been under the control of Egypt. The Canaanite city-states, always at war among themselves, had seen Egypt as a source of support against each other. But from the beginning of the fifteenth century BC, the powers of Asia Minor and upper Mesopotamia had resisted Egyptian pressure and forced the Egyptians back from Carchemish in the north. The battle of Kadesh (c1285 BC), between Egyptians and the Hittites of Asia Minor, left the northern limits of Egyptian control running from Damascus to the Phoenician coast. Egyptian controlled territory would probably have been pushed back to the Nile Delta itself if the Hittites had not themselves been overwhelmed by migrants known as the 'Sea Peoples' who had probably been driven out of the Balkans and Greece.

Egypt might have regained full control of Canaan but in turn had to fight off the 'Sea Peoples' who attacked the delta region of Lower Egypt during the reign of Rameses II's successor, Merneptah (1224-1214 BC). Egypt repulsed the migrants from the delta but could not prevent them gaining control of the coastal strip in southern Canaan, where they become known as the Philistines. They established themselves in five main cities: Gaza, Ashkelon, Ashdod, Gath and Ekron, where they were technically subject people of the Egyptians. Their presence points to Egyptian weakness. Egypt was entering a period of internal disorders and economic problems. The priests grew enormously powerful on wealth which they built up through the temples and kept secure from the state. Gradually Upper Egypt fell under the control of the priests of Thebes, while Lower Egypt was ruled by the kings from Tanis in the delta. Meanwhile, Libya increased its pressure on Egypt from the west and Nubia gained its independence. Egypt would not be fully united and powerful again for several centuries.

Assyria might have taken advantage of Egyptian weakness and the collapse of the Hittites, but it too moved into a period of civil war and rebellion. The Babylonians, near the Persian Gulf, briefly gained power over Assyria. Although the Babylonians were defeated, the Assyrians were still not in a position to take control of Canaan. The struggle for Canaan in this period took place between the Canaanites, Philistines, Hebrews and the Aramite tribes of the Syrian desert, until the Hebrew King David established overall control and made Jerusalem his capital around 1000 BC.

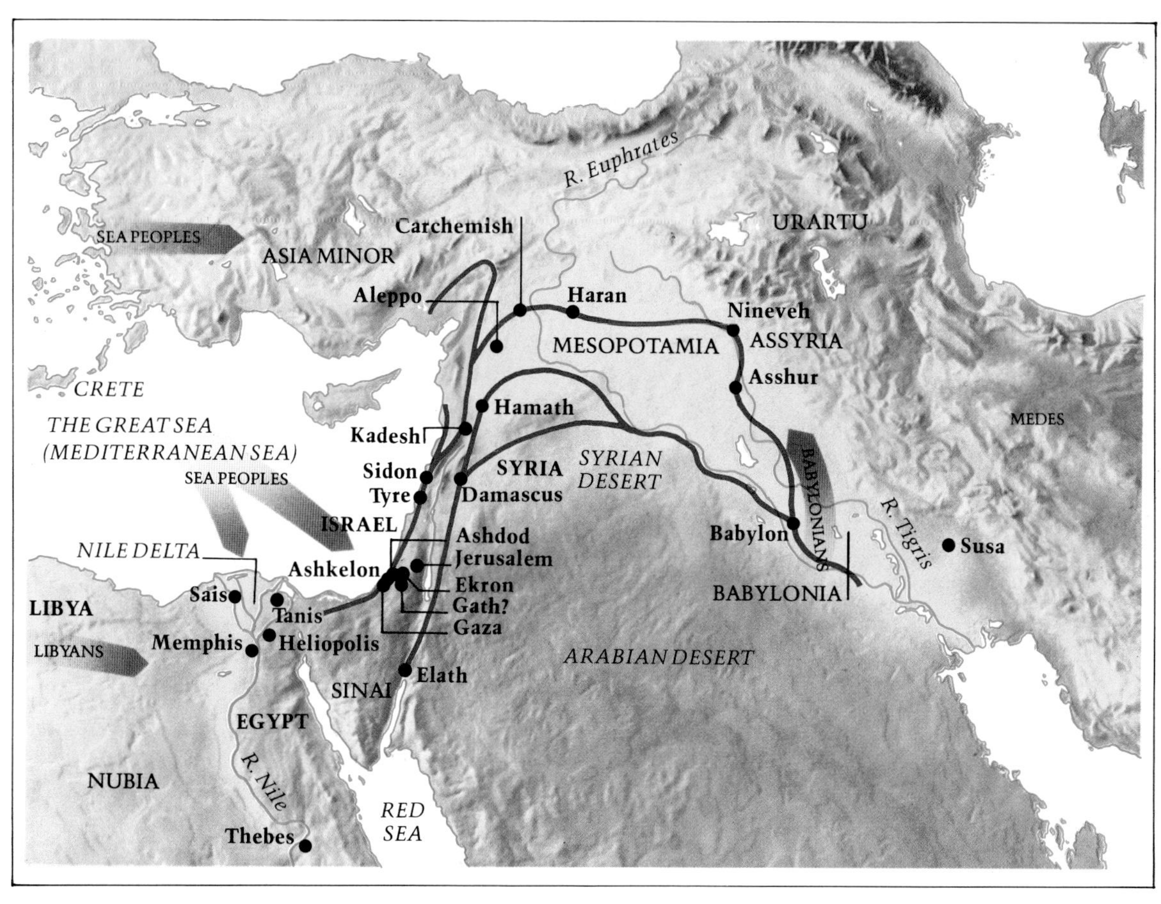

A NEW POWER VACUUM **Waves of migrants from the Mediterranean area and from Libya exerted tremendous pressure on the old powers – especially Egypt, which committed itself to defending its interests in Canaan. Meanwhile, in Mesopotamia, the Babylonians were beginning their long struggle with the Assyrians.**

Everyday Life in Canaan

For most people living in ancient Canaan, every detail of life revolved around basic survival, with no clear division between religion and the secular. Although the area was inhabited by peoples of many different origins, impressive ruins and archaeological finds do reveal an unmistakable cultural unity.

The impressive remains of Canaanite culture can still be seen in the Palestinian area in the ruins of great fortified towns and in artefacts displayed in museums. Egyptian lists of the places conquered during their various campaigns in Canaan show how heavily populated the area was. King Tuthmosis III (*c*1479-1425 BC), for example, carried out at least 16 campaigns throughout Canaan and Syria as far as the River Euphrates, and described a war he fought against a league of more than 100 Canaanite cities. The list contains 119 names, beginning with the main Canaanite centres Kadesh and Megiddo.

Although peoples of many different origins lived in Canaan, there was a certain cultural unity extending from Ugarit, on the coast of Syria, to the Egyptian border and inland to the River Orontes and the Jordan Valley. This would have included the sea-trading Phoenicians. However, the key to the whole of Canaanite culture probably lies in the trade interests by sea and along the international land routes which passed through Canaan. The Canaanites were, however, predominantly farmers living in heavily fortified settlements from which they could work the fertile land within safe reach. Agriculture and defence were the two keys to their way of life and religion, but the rivalry between the many fortified towns meant they did not achieve political unity, and the shifting patterns of alliances and leagues are similar to those of Greece during the classical period about 1,000 years later. It is possible that the Hyksos rulers of Egypt, from the mid-seventeenth to mid-sixteenth century BC, were Canaanite in origin, and that this was a brief period of political unity and power in an area stretching from Lower Egypt to the borders of Asia Minor.

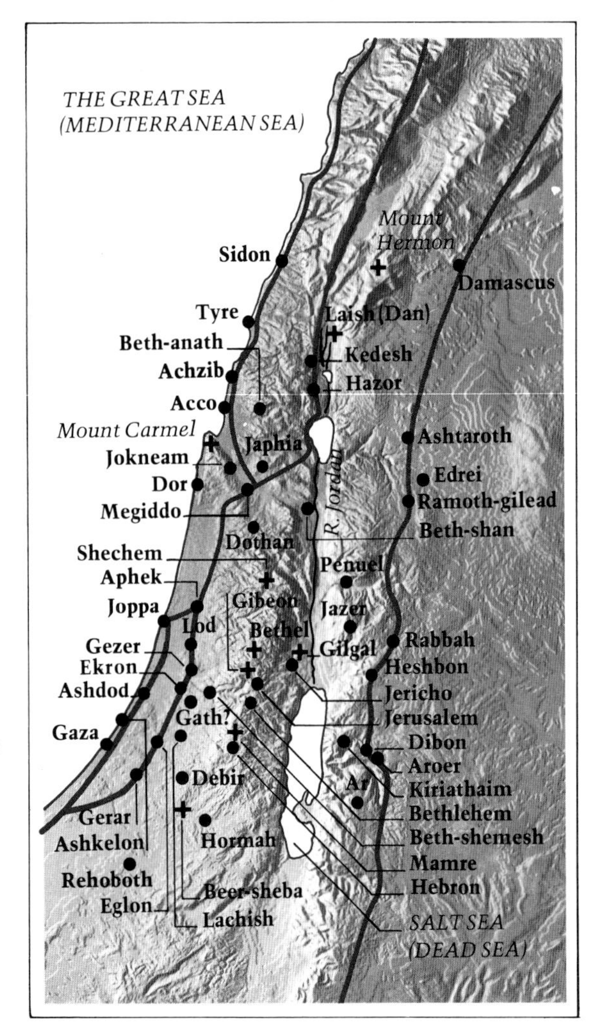

Main trade routes

+ Sanctuaries

AN INFLUENTIAL SOCIETY
The Canaanites occupied the area now called Palestine from the earliest times. They developed the methods of writing from pictorial systems which eventually spread throughout the Near and Middle East. They were farmers living in fortified cities; archaeological remains and artefacts which have been discovered reveal an advanced society. Some of the cities became important Hebrew sanctuaries after the exodus, and Jerusalem housed the Ark of the Covenant in a tent on a threshing floor. Their religion was mainly concerned with the fertility of their crops, which was linked to that of the gods themselves. The Canaanites were never sufficiently united to extend their rule beyond the narrow corridor of territory they held between the Mediterranean Sea and the Arabian Desert. In the end, both the Philistines and the Hebrews were able to overthrow them.

The Canaanite city of Megiddo was on a fortified hill, commanding the coastal road where it emerged into the Valley of Jezreel from a pass in the ridge of Mount Carmel, and branched into its northern and Mesopotamian routes. The city was repeatedly destroyed and rebuilt as each victor in turn took advantage of its strategic position. Excavations there have revealed some 20 layers of occupation. It was to receive its most impressive additions during the reign of the Hebrew King Solomon (*c*970-931 BC), but it was also powerful and wealthy during the thirteenth century BC. At that time it already possessed a great fortified palace to the east of the main gate, and a fortified temple. A hoard of carved ivory plaques, jewellery, gold vessels and precious beads point to the wealth in the city at this time. It was a feudal society, under the absolute authority of a king.

To Canaan must go the credit for developing methods and skills in writing which were to affect the whole Near East and, ultimately, the world. It would appear that Canaanite scribes developed the first alphabet which made it possible to pass from pictorial scripts, such as the Egyptian hieroglyphs, to the more flexible and economical single-letter scripts, based on vocal sounds and representing the smallest components of words, which form the basis of the modern Western alphabet. Although the symbols were originally pictograms, in which meaning is conveyed through stylized images, they gradually became independent of their origins and were limited in number.

Most of the Canaanite cities were dependent on agriculture and water supplies within their fortifications. Therefore, they were almost all situated near the coastal plain, with a few scattered across to the edges of the Jordan Valley. The destruction of the coastal city of Ugarit by the Philistines about 1200 BC makes it possible to put a final date to the hundreds of written texts discovered on the site. They were in the form of clay tablets, which included religious and mythological material. From these, and the excavations of Canaanite sanctuaries, it is possible to reconstruct something of the beliefs and practices of Canaanite religion without having to depend too closely on the hostile and critical descriptions contained in the Bible.

The Canaanites worshipped a complex pantheon of gods and goddesses of whom the chief god was named El, the father of the gods. The goddess most associated with El is Asherah, and the god most frequently denounced in the Old Testament, Baal, was the son of El and Asherah. Prominent, too, was Baal's sister Anat.

Baal was at war with other gods, particularly Mot, the god of death, Yamm, the god of the seas, and Nahar, the river god. But the various myths indicate that it is dangerous to be too precise about the identities and characters of the various gods, for a variety of religious myths are often combined.

The Old Testament shows that some of the language and symbolism of the Canaanite religion was also used by the Hebrews, particularly the name of the chief god, El, and some of the aspects of the Canaanite creation myths. El is called 'El the Bull' in some of the Canaanite texts, while Baal has titles such as 'Rider of the Clouds', with control over the storms and rain which water the soil for the crops. In the creation myths, Baal fights the death god and the god of the chaotic waters, and at one stage is himself killed. His sister forces the death god, Mot, to give Baal life for half of the year, and the water god is banished to the sea. Wherever the Hebrews have drawn on such ideas, they have subordinated them to the unique saviour-God of the escape from Egypt and the covenant. However, the influence of the Canaanites can most be seen in the Hebrew sacrifices and festivals.

The Canaanites offered animals, crops and incense both as sacrifices in which all or some of the offering was burnt, and as communion sacrifices with an associated sacred meal. The main Canaanite festivals were celebrations of the various stages of the harvest. They appear in Hebrew religious celebrations as the three major harvest festivals, known in English translations of the Bible as the festivals of Unleavened Bread, Pentecost (or Weeks), and Tabernacles. Whatever their origins, the Hebrews associated these festivals with the God of the covenant, and so detached them from their Canaanite origins.

The function of Canaanite religion was, above all, to secure the fertility of the crops and livestock, and also to ensure success in war. Its characteristic forms of worship were sexual sacred rites, known as sacral prostitution in which the fertility of the male and female gods was directed to human needs by re-enacting the gods' own intercourse. A darker element imitated the death and rising again of Baal, with suggestions of the ritual killing of Canaanite kings. Canaanite fertility rites were condemned by the Hebrew religion with a vehemence which suggests that the sacred prostitution ritual may have been widespread after the Hebrews became farmers.

Excavations at the Phoenician colony of Carthage in North Africa confirmed the practice of sacrificing infant children to the god Molech. At a time of deep national corruption in the eighth and and seventh centuries BC, a shrine for this purpose was built outside the south wall of Jerusalem and bitterly condemned by the prophets (Jer 7:31).

PROVIDING THE ESSENTIALS

Everyday life for the great majority of people in the ancient world was almost totally concerned with survival. The essentials of life were food, which had to come from their crops and livestock, and protection, which came from being part of a social unit which could defend its members. For the nomadic pastoral peoples, such as the Hebrews during the earlier part of their history, their herds provided food and the extended family, clan or tribe, provided protection. For all others, security depended on being a member of a territorial group, as small as a fortified town or as large as a country. Their security was only as sure as their ability to defend that territory. To be conquered by invaders, whether by a great power or by a neighbouring town, meant slavery or death. Every detail of life, housing, family structures, religion, and even the selection of children for survival, evolved as a result of these basic concerns – food and security.

In the nomadic tribes the social structure reflected the natural authority and the basis of the family. Blood ties were all important. The family was polygamous (men had more than one wife), but the

LEFT **It is believed that the camel was not domesticated until the latter part of the second millenium BC, when it was used by the tribes of the Syrian and Arabian Desert. It enabled the tribesmen to attack the agricultural areas and retreat again to the safety of the desert. Even when the Palestine area was free from the great military powers of the Near and Middle East, it was always under threat of lesser raids from the desert regions to the east of it.**

Hazor is one of the oldest inhabited sites and centres of worship, a major Canaanite sanctuary until it was destroyed by the Hebrews. Its fortified mound was the centre of an extensive settlement.

INSETS **After the Hebrews had destroyed Canaanite Hazor, they rebuilt it as a major fortress guarding the route north to Asia Minor and Mesopotamia. The pillared building is ninth century** BC.

INSET **The remains of Hebrew buildings, erected on the ruins of Canaanite Hazor, show how deeply the Hebrews were influenced by the culture they tried to destroy.**

basic rights of members of the extended family were recognized and protected. Even slaves related to the family by blood had limited rights, other slaves had no rights. The flocks and herds were the common property of the group.

The social systems of agricultural settlements dependent on a particular territory were far more rigidly structured. A strict hierarchy of authority and subordination existed, with rule by an absolute monarch. Egypt does not even appear to have had codified laws, but Mesopotamia regulated its social structures with a written code from at least the beginning of the second millenium BC. Houses were built of mud brick with flat roofs which could be used for drying crops. They were normally just one room with a raised sleeping platform on which a mat would be spread. For defensive reasons, at least in Canaan, the houses were clustered in positions which could be fortified and surrounded by heavy defensive walls. The main gate was usually approached by a ramp, set at an angle so that attackers had to expose their right, unshielded, sides to the defendants. Access to water during siege, either by storage or fortified spring, was important, as were safe storage facilities for harvested crops. The olive tree was much valued as a source of oil from the pressed fruits, for use in lamps, cooking, cosmetics and in medicine. It was such a universal symbol of health, prosperity and security that the Hebrews eventually used it to show that authority had been conferred on a person, by anointing them with olive oil. From this practice comes the word 'messiah', literally meaning 'the anointed one'.

In monarchical systems, law was administered by the king or his delegates. For the patriarchal nomads the father or grandfather judged cases in the presence of the whole family or tribal group. This practice continued after the Hebrews developed a monarchy, in the form of town elders sitting in judgement in the open area just inside the town gate. Just as there was no clear boundary between religion and the secular, so the law dealt with religious and secular offences in the same 'court'. Education was within the family group and related to the family's trade, unless the child was destined for one of the specialized administrative skills, such as scribe, priest or royal official, when specialist training would be given. Such professions were not usually distinct from each other, especially in the earlier period.

There were no extensive roads in any modern sense of the word, until the Romans developed their system of paved roads wide enough to take wheeled vehicles. The donkey was the usual means of transport, used as a pack animal, although the camel came into use for crossing desert areas towards the end of the second millenium BC. But it was a static world for most non-nomadic peoples who by modern standards had a very short life expectancy and harsh standards of living.

BELOW **The religion of the Canaanites was mainly concerned with the fertility of the land. The chief god, Baal, was associated with three goddesses, Anath, Asherah and Astarte, who were all deifications of the sexual aspects of fertility. Their worship was usually associated with sexual intercourse, and the images of the gods emphasized their sexuality. The Hebrews tried to stamp out the religion.**

TEMPLES AND RELIGION

Temples in the ancient Near East were not places in which large numbers of people worshipped, but rather, were buildings which provided a focus for worship. Only priests could enter them. They may have marked a place with sacred associations in the history or mythology of the people, or symbolized the presence of the gods within the city, or both, while their architecture expressed the peoples' beliefs visually.

The most dramatic of the Egyptian temples to have survived, at Abu Simbel in Upper Egypt, was built early in the reign of King Rameses II (1290-1224 BC), the Egyptian ruler at the time of the Hebrew escape. It expresses both the central importance of the sun in Egyptian worship, and the role of Rameses himself as a god. The temple facade, facing the River Nile, contains four seated statues of Rameses, each about 65 feet (20 metres) high. Between his legs stand statues of various relatives, suitably diminished to show their lesser importance. In the temple's innermost sanctuary, four statues of smaller size depict the three most important state gods of the time and the king himself, all seated in a row.

Central to Egyptian religion was the worship of the sun. The name of Re, the sun god, was incorporated into the official names of the Egyptian kings. The Abu Simbel temple was designed to demonstrate the sun god's support for the king. Twice each year, the first rays of the rising sun shone right through the full length of the complex interior of the temple. The rays entered through the narrow entrance, passed through the great hall, on through another vestibule, into a smaller hall, through a further vestibule and, finally, into the innermost sanctuary where it illuminated the four seated statues of the king and his fellow gods.

The temple at Hazor, north of the Lake of Gennesaret (Sea of Galilee), was most important to the Canaanites. Hazor was the largest Canaanite city and a major commercial centre on the main route between Egypt and Mesopotamia. From excavations, it appears that the city was destroyed early in the twelfth century BC and that, at the time of its destruction, its temple was constructed with a succession of rectangular rooms, reached by narrow doorways through the thick stone walls. The whole structure was about 90 feet (30 metres) long by 50 feet (15 metres) wide. Inside the first doorway was a spacious porch, then a further chamber through a doorway, and finally another doorway leading to the large, innermost room, which contained a niche in its far wall.

This room contained a square altar carved with the symbol of the storm-god, Baal, large and small basalt basins, several tables for wine offerings, and a seated statue. Between the porch and the middle chamber, the positions of two round bases for pillars show that they were not for roof supports but had a place in the temple worship.

The Hazor temple has particular significance because its general architecture is so similar to that of the Hebrew Temple in Jerusalem built by the Hebrew King Solomon in the tenth century BC. In the court outside the temple building at Hazor were several smaller altars, and a drainage channel to carry away the blood from the sacrificed animals. At the Hebrew Temple, as at Hazor, the animal sacrifices took place outside the building itself, while incense was sacrificed inside. Other Canaanite temples, particularly at Shechem and Megiddo, had features similar to the Hazor temple.

For the Hebrews, as for other people of the time, sacred places were used for the worship of their own national god even when they had associations with other gods. The Hebrews found no problems in using Canaanite sacred centres, but not for the worship of Canaanite gods.

BELOW **The temple at Luxor in Egypt was built on the site of an ancient sanctuary. The inner part of the temple was built by Amenophis III while the outer was constructed during the reign of Rameses II. The temple was dedicated to the god Amun.**

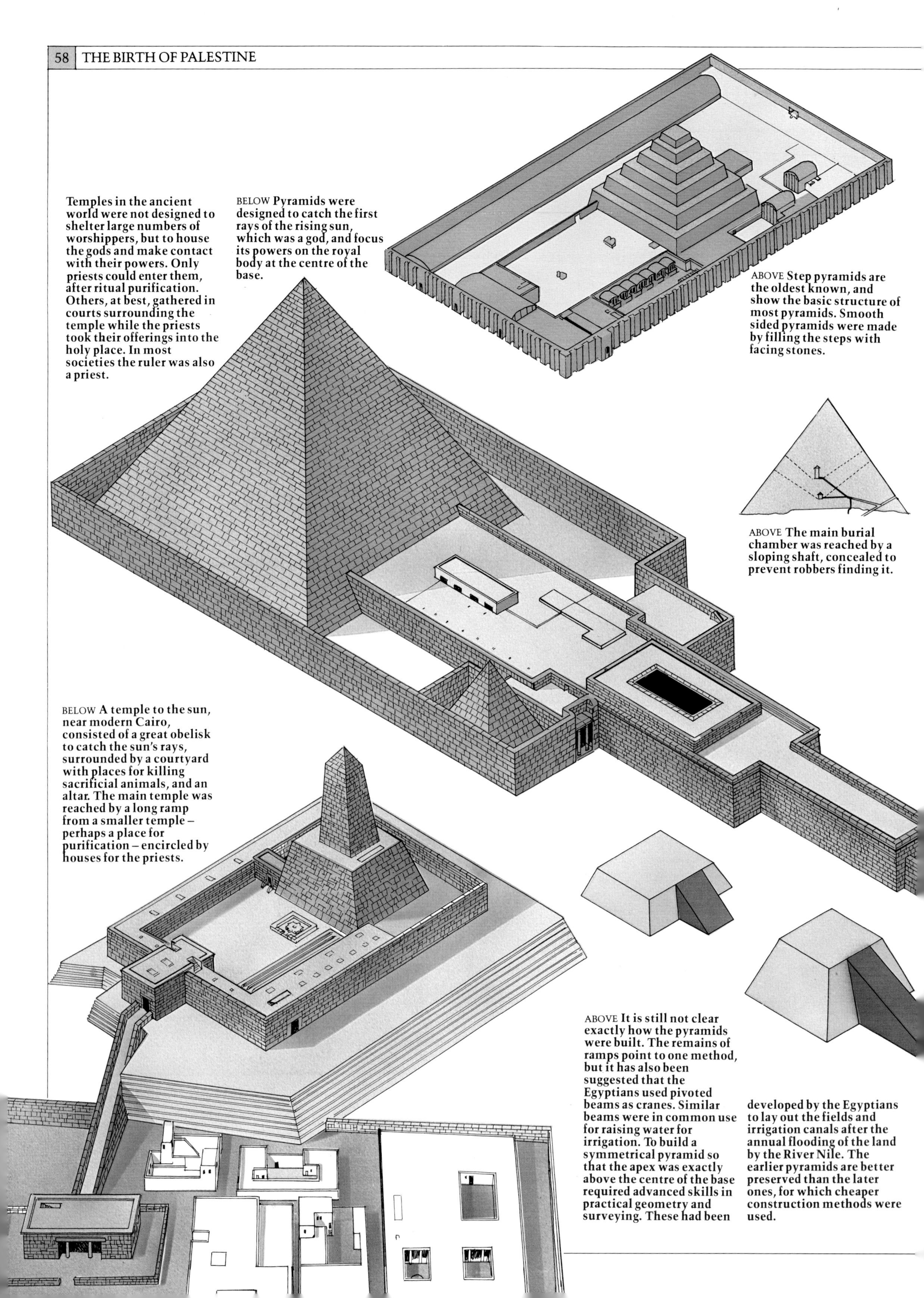

Temples in the ancient world were not designed to shelter large numbers of worshippers, but to house the gods and make contact with their powers. Only priests could enter them, after ritual purification. Others, at best, gathered in courts surrounding the temple while the priests took their offerings into the holy place. In most societies the ruler was also a priest.

BELOW **Pyramids were designed to catch the first rays of the rising sun, which was a god, and focus its powers on the royal body at the centre of the base.**

ABOVE **Step pyramids are the oldest known, and show the basic structure of most pyramids. Smooth sided pyramids were made by filling the steps with facing stones.**

ABOVE **The main burial chamber was reached by a sloping shaft, concealed to prevent robbers finding it.**

BELOW **A temple to the sun, near modern Cairo, consisted of a great obelisk to catch the sun's rays, surrounded by a courtyard with places for killing sacrificial animals, and an altar. The main temple was reached by a long ramp from a smaller temple – perhaps a place for purification – encircled by houses for the priests.**

ABOVE **It is still not clear exactly how the pyramids were built. The remains of ramps point to one method, but it has also been suggested that the Egyptians used pivoted beams as cranes. Similar beams were in common use for raising water for irrigation. To build a symmetrical pyramid so that the apex was exactly above the centre of the base required advanced skills in practical geometry and surveying. These had been developed by the Egyptians to lay out the fields and irrigation canals after the annual flooding of the land by the River Nile. The earlier pyramids are better preserved than the later ones, for which cheaper construction methods were used.**

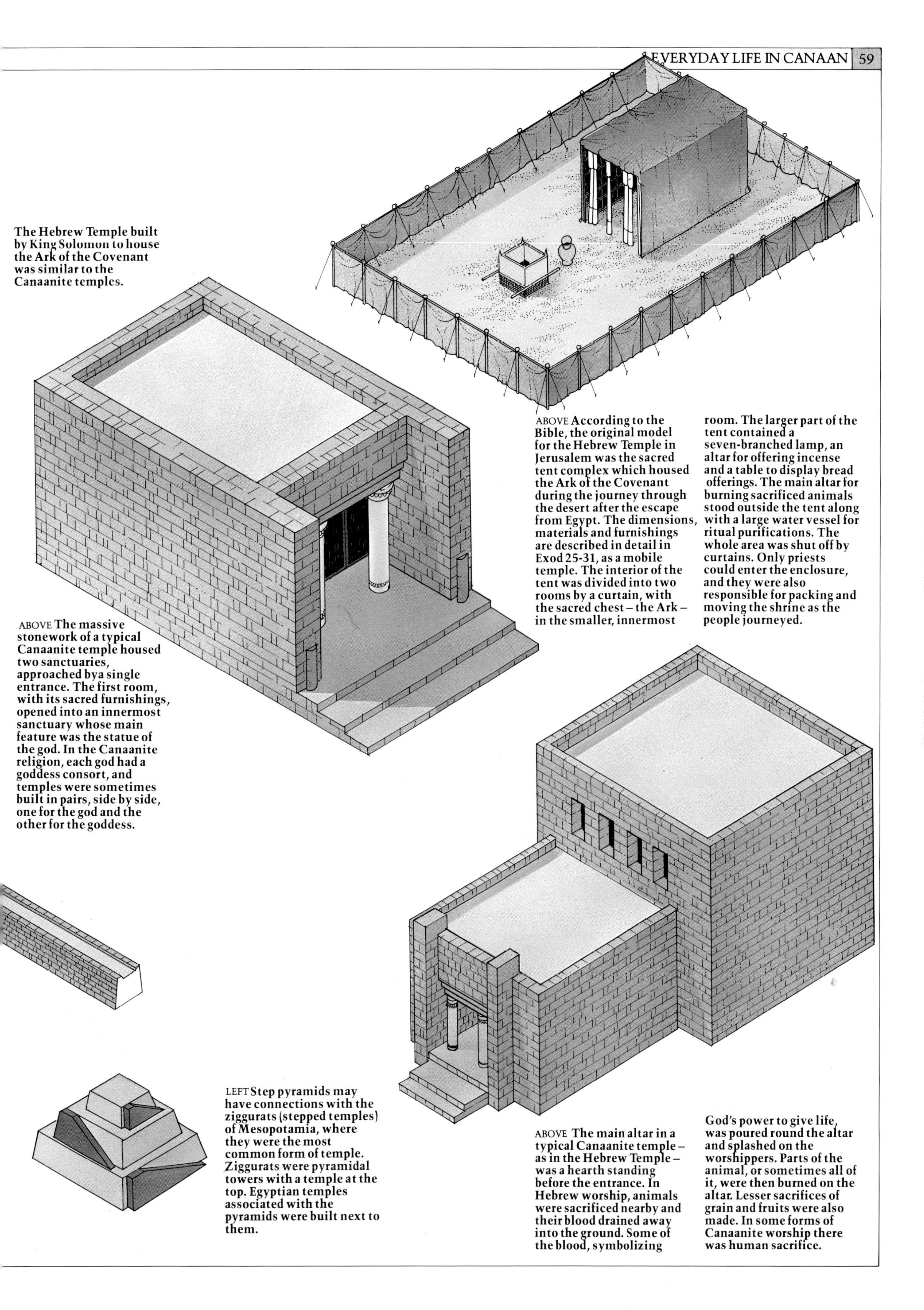

The Hebrew Temple built by King Solomon to house the Ark of the Covenant was similar to the Canaanite temples.

ABOVE According to the Bible, the original model for the Hebrew Temple in Jerusalem was the sacred tent complex which housed the Ark of the Covenant during the journey through the desert after the escape from Egypt. The dimensions, materials and furnishings are described in detail in Exod 25-31, as a mobile temple. The interior of the tent was divided into two rooms by a curtain, with the sacred chest – the Ark – in the smaller, innermost room. The larger part of the tent contained a seven-branched lamp, an altar for offering incense and a table to display bread offerings. The main altar for burning sacrificed animals stood outside the tent along with a large water vessel for ritual purifications. The whole area was shut off by curtains. Only priests could enter the enclosure, and they were also responsible for packing and moving the shrine as the people journeyed.

ABOVE The massive stonework of a typical Canaanite temple housed two sanctuaries, approached bya single entrance. The first room, with its sacred furnishings, opened into an innermost sanctuary whose main feature was the statue of the god. In the Canaanite religion, each god had a goddess consort, and temples were sometimes built in pairs, side by side, one for the god and the other for the goddess.

LEFT Step pyramids may have connections with the ziggurats (stepped temples) of Mesopotamia, where they were the most common form of temple. Ziggurats were pyramidal towers with a temple at the top. Egyptian temples associated with the pyramids were built next to them.

ABOVE The main altar in a typical Canaanite temple – as in the Hebrew Temple – was a hearth standing before the entrance. In Hebrew worship, animals were sacrificed nearby and their blood drained away into the ground. Some of the blood, symbolizing God's power to give life, was poured round the altar and splashed on the worshippers. Parts of the animal, or sometimes all of it, were then burned on the altar. Lesser sacrifices of grain and fruits were also made. In some forms of Canaanite worship there was human sacrifice.

The First Scripts

Both the Sumerians and the Egyptians seem to have developed similar writing methods around 3000 BC. The first scripts employed pictorial symbols to depict objects and also represent sounds. They were gradually refined into systems of phonic symbols and were used like an alphabet.

Writing, as a means of communication and of recording information, seems to have been developed independently at two places, about the same time: by the Sumerians, near the Persian Gulf, and by the Egyptians, both in about 3000 BC. Graphic methods of communication and expression may have been in use before then, but there is no evidence for the existence of a systematic set of symbols to express ideas and words in written form – in other words, writing.

In both places, the first scripts were pictograms, pictorial representations of objects in the natural world, stylized and given a fixed form. They probably continued to be used in this primary sense, but their value for communication lay in the sounds they represented. Originally the sound would be the name of the object which the sign depicted, and the sign could then be used for other words containing that sound. Ancient Egyptians used about 100 phonograms, signs expressing sounds, but 24 of them expressed only one sound and were used like an alphabet. All the signs expressed a combination of two consonants, except one which expressed three consonants to indicate a form of plural. As the system developed, signs were also attached to words to show the exact sense in which signs were being used in order to prevent ambiguity—by the time Egyptian writing had developed fully almost all words normally had them. The sequence of signs could be written in either direction from side to side, or vertically, and the direction of the writing was shown by the way the signs were pointing.

From the earliest times, the signs were written in flowing or cursive form, and this remained the common form. However, for more formal purposes, such as public records and inscriptions, monumental hieroglyphic script was used. 'Hieroglyphic' is the Greek word for Egyptian writing, and literally means 'sacred scratching'. This form of writing retained its pictorial form and required a large number of symbols. Later, the form of cursive writing developed in Lower Egypt became the form used throughout the country.

BELOW **Egyptian writing used pictures, usually called hieroglyphs. They became symbolic and only loosely associated with their pictorial origins, with the advantage that a limited number of symbols could be used to express a wide range of meanings.**

	OX	HOUSE
EGYPTIAN HIEROGLYPHICS *c*3000 BC		
CANAANITE *c*2000 BC		
PHOENICIAN *c*1000 BC		
HEBREW *c*700 BC		
OLD GREEK *c*650 BC		
ARAMAIC *c*350 BC		
FORMAL HEBREW *c*150 BC		
FORMAL GREEK *c*450 BC	A	B
ROMAN *c*550 BC	A	B

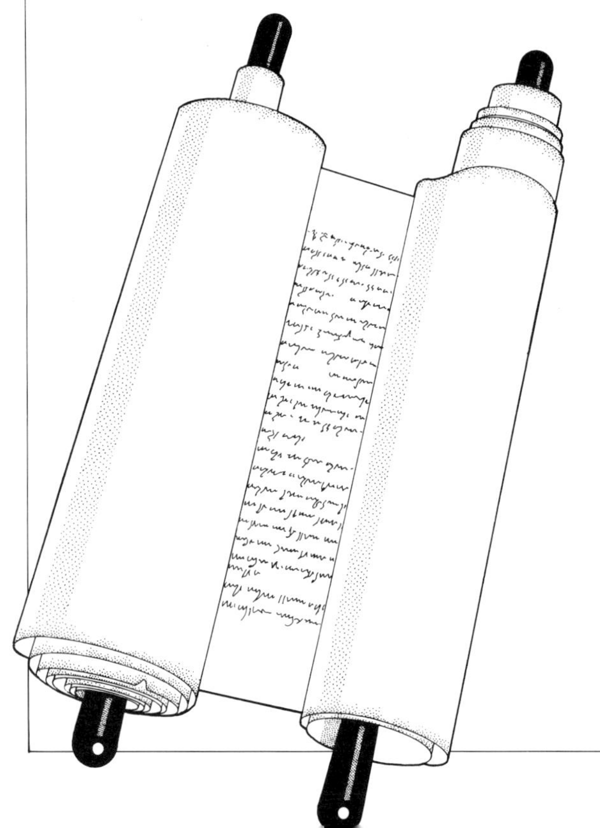

Any flat surface, from wax and pottery to beaten metal and stone, was used for writing, but the most distinctive writing material was made from the papyrus reed, which grows as thick as 3 in (7 cm) and up to about 15 feet (5 metres) high. The stem was split into strips which were laid at right-angles across each other. They were held together by soaking or pasting to form long sheets of various standard widths, ranging from about 5 in (12.5 cm) to 10 in (25cm). These sheets were pasted together to make scrolls about 30 feet (10 metres) long. The surface was smoothed using various hammering and polishing techniques.

In Mesopotamia, the normal writing material, clay, determined the form of script. As in Egypt, Sumerian writing developed from pictograms to phonograms, but far fewer signs were used to specify the precise meaning of a word. Ambiguity was thus possible, but, in practice, the context provided the meaning. This form of script was known as 'cuneiform'. The names comes from the Latin for wedge because of the wedge-shaped stylus used for writing by pressing into soft clay blocks which were then baked hard. The original pictures became highly stylized, but as in Egyptian hieroglyphic, a comparatively large number of symbols were needed to express the different combination of syllables and the sounds they made.

The first true alphabet seems to have been developed by the Canaanites during the second millenium BC. A very limited number of consonantal sounds were each represented by a fixed symbol. These basic symbols, of which there were 22, could be used with great flexibility. They made it possible to construct words from their sounds and even to write different languages. The Hebrews adopted these signs around the time of their escape from Egypt, and they also spread from Phoenicia through Greece into the rest of the ancient world in various forms. Egyptian continued to be written in hieroglyphic, but Greek became the common language of the ancient world following the conquests of Alexander in the fourth century BC.

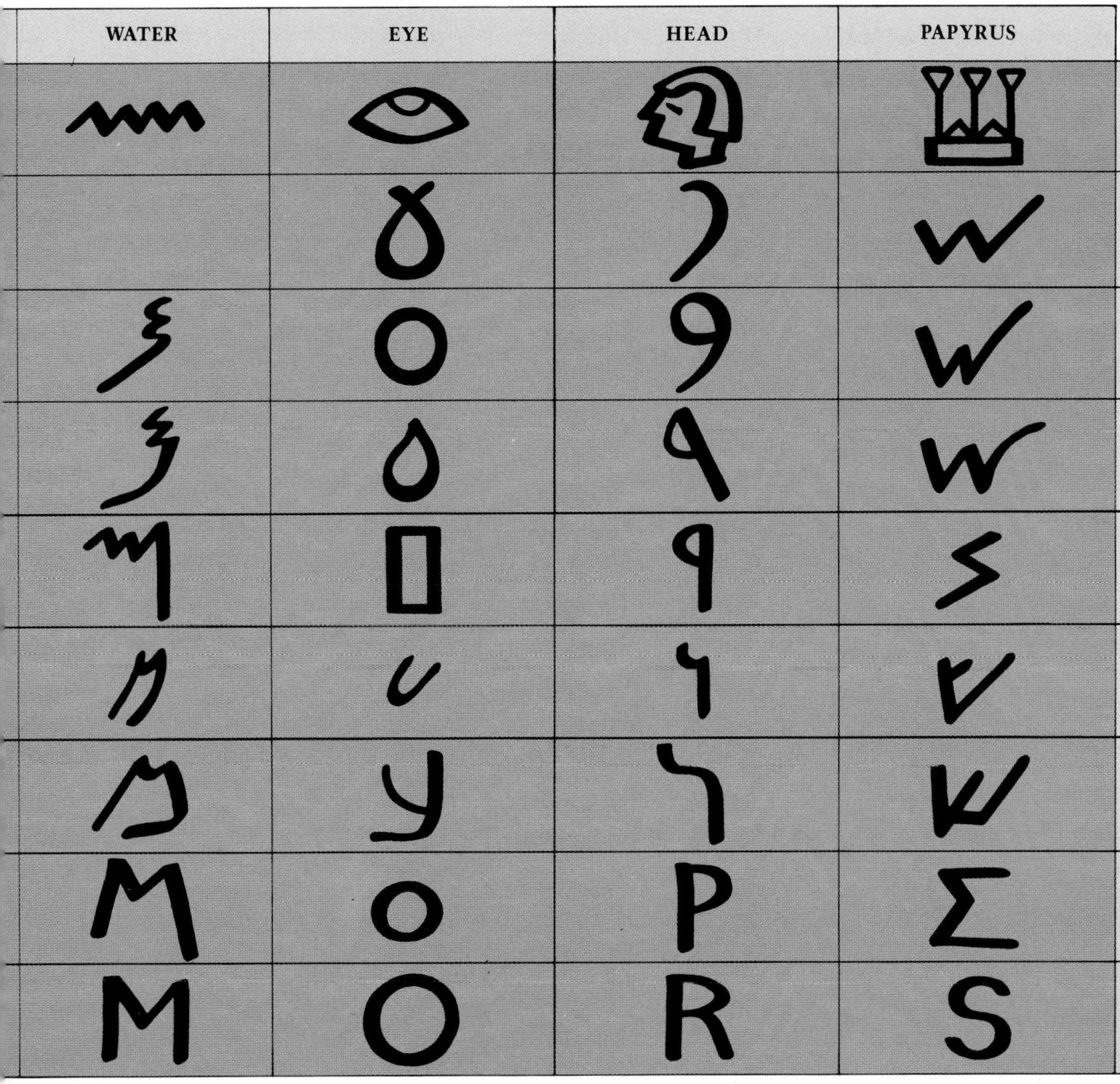

WATER	EYE	HEAD	PAPYRUS	
				Egyptian writing did not develop far from the use of pictorial symbols.
				Canaanite writing shows its pictorial origins, but in fact symbolizes basic sounds.
				The 22 basic symbols of the Canaanite system became the standard for the region.
				The Hebrews adopted the Canaanite alphabet in a modified form.
				The Canaanite origins can still be seen in archaic Greek script.
				Aramaic was the main language of the Persian Empire, and displaced Hebrew in Palestine.
				Classical Hebrew was written in a 'square' form of the common script of the region.
M	O	P	Σ	The Greek alphabet allocated vowel sounds to some of the letters, and added more symbols.
M	O	R	S	The Romans gained their alphabet from the Etruscans and Greek colonists.

Decline of The Egyptian Empire

Egypt's power began disintegrating in about 1200 BC. External threats stretched its defences to the limit. The country itself was breaking into two: the Tanis kings still controlled the delta area, but the Theban priests effectively ruled upper Egypt. By the 8th century BC, the Egyptian influence had waned.

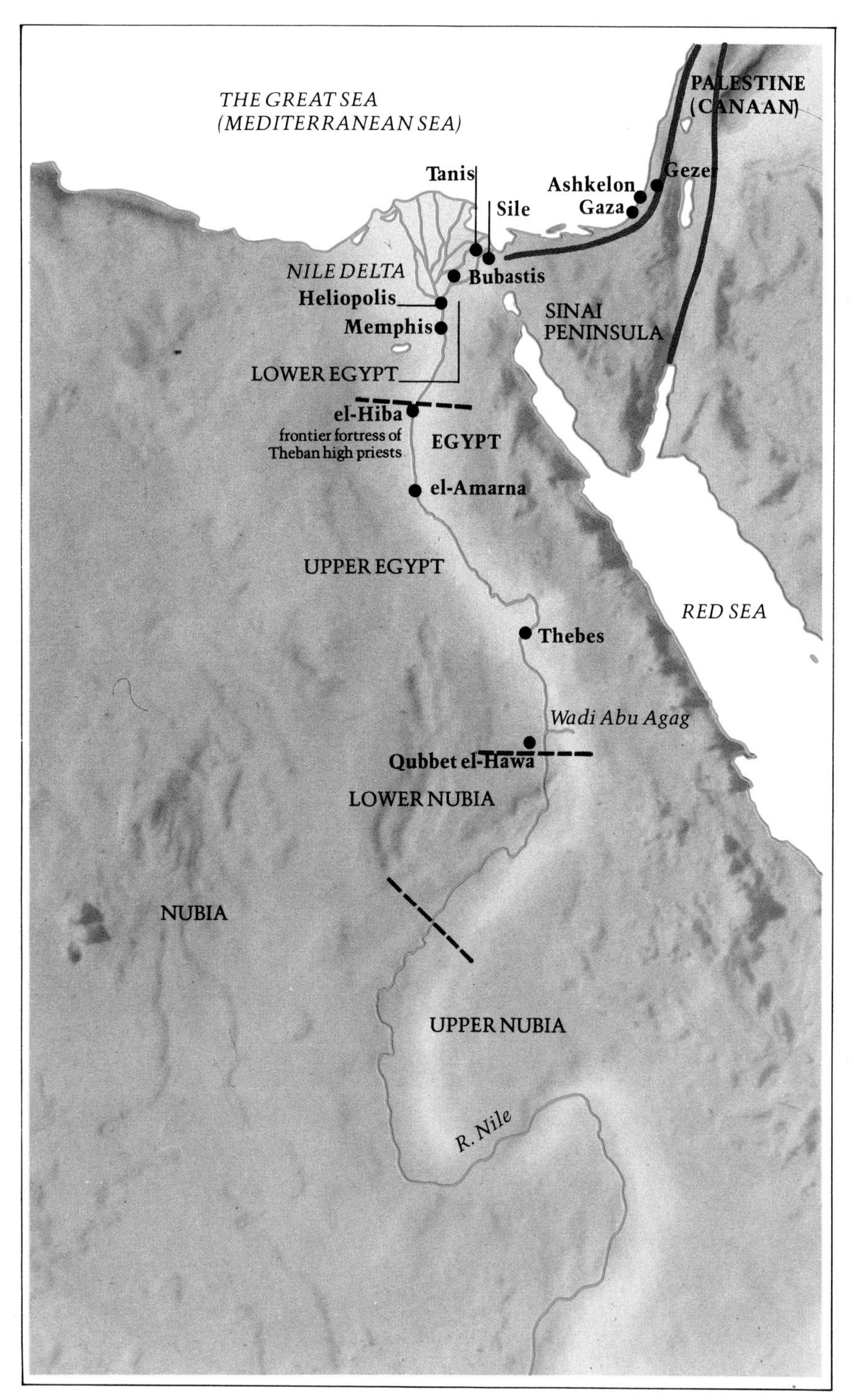

DIVIDED RULE **The Tanis kings of the 21st–23rd Dynasties were only nominally sovereigns of Upper Egypt–the area stretching south from the fortress of el-Hiba as far as Qubbet el-Hawa (close to present-day Aswan). Previously, during the 18th Dynasty, the capital had been in Thebes, but gradually it had moved north – first to el-Amarna, then to Tanis. Left alone, the Theban high priests soon established control of the area, although most still acknowledged the Tanis kings.**

At the time of the Hebrew escape from Egypt, the Egyptian kings still retained control over southern Canaan, but their hold was slipping. Egypt itself was breaking into its two 'natural' parts of Upper and Lower Egypt, and threats from the migrant 'Sea Peoples', coming in from the Balkans, and Libyan enemies to the west of Egypt were soon to stretch the defensive resources of the state to their limits. The Hebrews were able to penetrate into eastern Canaan, away from the coastal road, without interference from Egypt. Although Egypt successfully repulsed them during the reign of King Rameses III (1194-1163 BC) of the 20th Dynasty, the 'Sea Peoples' established themselves on the southern coast of Canaan shortly afterwards, and became known as the Philistines.

During the reigns of the seven kings of the 21st Dynasty (1070-945 BC) the country was ruled from Tanis, in the Nile Delta near the point where the coastal road leaves for the north and for Mesopotamia. Theoretically, their rule extended into Upper Egypt as well, but, in practice, the priests of Thebes ruled the area independently under the hereditary leadership of their high priest. The Tanis kings could only enforce their authority as far as el-Hiba, the frontier fortress of the

RIGHT **The enormous statues of the Egyptian kings symbolize their power and their status as gods. Despite their brief period of forced labour under the Egyptians and their dramatic exodus, it was here the Hebrews looked for protection from the powers of Assyria and Babylon. This limestone statue of Rameses II can be seen at Memphis today.**

Theban high priests, little more than 60 miles (100 km) up the River Nile from Memphis. Some of the 21st Dynasty may even have been Libyan, showing that the Libyans had gained control of Lower Egypt, just as the Hyksos had done 500 years earlier.

The first king of the 22nd Dynasty, which lasted from the tenth to the eight centuries BC, was Sheshonk I (945-924 BC). He was of Libyan descent, coming from a family which had been influential in Egypt during the preceding Dynasty. He was 'Shishak' of the Old Testament who invaded the southern Hebrew Kingdom of Judah and took the royal and Temple treasures from Jerusalem (1 Kgs 14:25f). For a while he managed to unite the two parts of Egypt again, by making his son high priest of Thebes when the hereditary line of high priests became extinct. But the unity was not to last, and Egypt disintegrated again by the middle of the ninth century BC into overlapping dynasties and areas ruled by cities with their own kings. At one stage there appear to have been no less than seven independent areas of rule in Lower Egypt and two in Upper Egypt, a situation which made it impossible for Egypt to exert any effective power. By then, the mid-eighth century BC, Assyrian influence was rolling across the Near East and would shortly extend its power into Egypt itself.

Something of the unstable Egyptian situation during the eleventh century BC, when the Hebrews were establishing themselves in Canaan and resisting domination by the Philistines, can be seen from Egyptian monuments of the period. At Karnak, in the great temple complex just south of the capital of Upper Egypt, Thebes, a long avenue of ram-headed sphinxes erected to protect the king bear the name of the high priest of Amun. At that time the high priests were becoming the effective rulers of Upper Egypt. Opposite Thebes itself, on the other side of the River Nile, the Valley of the Kings contains secret burial places where the bodies of the kings of the 17th to 20th Dynasties had been collected for reburial in the 21st Dynasty.

The uncertain times demanded massive fortifications of the temple areas, which were both treasuries and the shrines of the bodies of Egypt's divine kings. Collections of royal tombs from the 21st Dynasty have been found within the temple area at Tanis, the capital of Lower Egypt, enclosed by a brick-built enclosure measuring over 500 yards (430 metres) long by some 400 yards (370 metres) wide, and with walls 30 feet (10 metres) high and 45 feet (15 metres) thick.

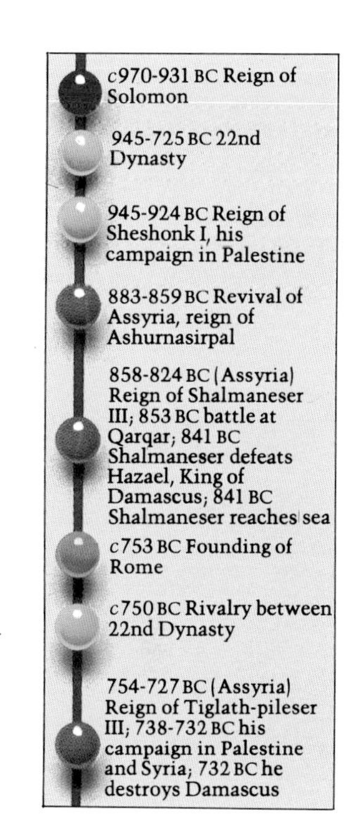

c970-931 BC Reign of Solomon
945-725 BC 22nd Dynasty
945-924 BC Reign of Sheshonk I, his campaign in Palestine
883-859 BC Revival of Assyria, reign of Ashurnasirpal
858-824 BC (Assyria) Reign of Shalmaneser III; 853 BC battle at Qarqar; 841 BC Shalmaneser defeats Hazael, King of Damascus; 841 BC Shalmaneser reaches sea
c753 BC Founding of Rome
c750 BC Rivalry between 22nd Dynasty
754-727 BC (Assyria) Reign of Tiglath-pileser III; 738-732 BC his campaign in Palestine and Syria; 732 BC he destroys Damascus

The World in 900 BC

Strong cultural and religious bases had developed in China, the Americas and in India by 900 BC. But it was a period of decline for the Egyptians and a dark age for the other Mediterranean states, although nearby the Assyrians and Babylonians were on the brink of power.

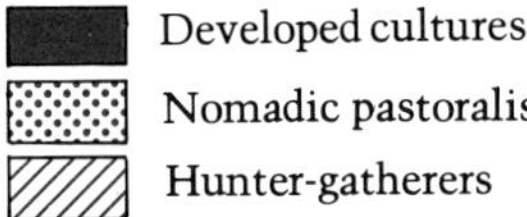

OLD AND NEW POWER PATTERNS **The Near and Middle East were still the main centres of civilization during the early part of this period, both in Egypt and in Mesopotamia. But a brilliant culture was developing in China, with advanced bronze casting techniques. The Aryan migrations were firmly established in north-western India, and had already set the pattern for the forthcoming developments in Indian religion and culture.**

The migrations of the end of the second millenium BC produced a dark age in the main parts of the Mediterranean from which the brilliance of Greek classical civilization would emerge around the fifth century BC. But further east, in India, the invaders from the north – variously referred to as Indo-Europeans or Aryans – had established themselves firmly in the Indus Valley and were beginning to extend their power still further eastwards.

These peoples, who were to set the pattern for classical Indian culture, were nomadic herdsmen who overran the fortified citadels of the Indus Valley cities with attacks supported by light, horse-drawn chariots. Like the Canaanite fortified settlements, the Indian cities were small independent states farming the land round their fortifications, and unable or unwilling to form a single defensive organization against the invading Indo-Europeans. For the incomers, wealth lay with their cattle, rather than land, and most of their fundamental needs were met from their herds. The origins of the characteristic Indian reverence for cattle as expressions of the divine life-force may lie in the part cattle played in the lives of these conquerors.

There are very few archaeological remains from the Indo-Europeans of India at this time, but there is a vast body of religious literature which laid the foundations of classical Indian religion. The priests recorded their people's religious beliefs and practices in great detail. As in other religious literature from the ancient world, including the Old Testament, the material had circulated among the people and been passed down the generations by word of mouth before it reached written form. By then it had been shaped in a poetic style appropriate for community recitation, which also helped to preserve the contents during their transmission. The earliest of these writings are the four Vedas, composed around the tenth and ninth centuries BC when the Indo-Europeans were consolidating their power. They consist of the Rig-Veda, the Sama-Veda, the Yajur-Veda and the Atharva-Veda. These would later be expanded by commentaries which became equally influential. The Vedas contain prayers, nature poems, instructions for ritual and other material representing a cross-section of the people's experience, together with more explicitly religious material such as directions for the priests, and formulas for rituals and magic. The rituals were the direct means of communication with the gods, particularly by sacrifice. In the early period there were no temples or images of the gods, and the rituals were carried out at an open altar as might be expected of a people with nomadic origins.

Further east, in China, around 1100 BC, the Chou peoples from the modern province of Shaanxi had conquered the Shang Dynasty to the east of them and established their capital further up the Huang Ho river valley. They were to rule northern China until about the eighth century BC, and established a second capital for their eastern provinces near Luoyang. There is evidence of large-scale population movements, reminiscent of the policies employed a little later in the Near East by the Assyrians. Poetry and an important collection of historical records from this period still exist. The Chou showed reverence for the Shang they had displaced and at first gave them a share in rule. Such respect may help to explain why the Chou were able to keep firm control of the north but had little direct control over southern China.

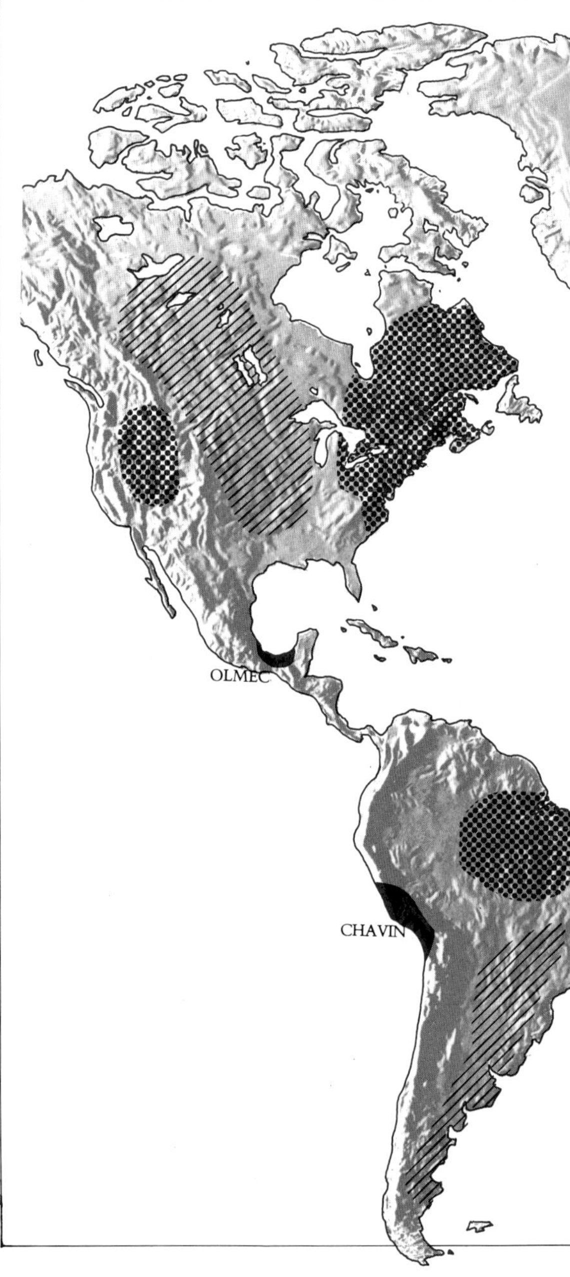

In the Americas, the Olmec culture of Mexico was spreading eastwards into what is now Guatemala, where it would provide the foundations for the Mayan civilization. In the western coastal areas of South America, the Chavin culture of Peru was worshipping jaguar-headed gods similar to those of the Mexican Olmecs. There was no central government, it seems, but their technical achievements are shown by the great stone temples they built for their gods.

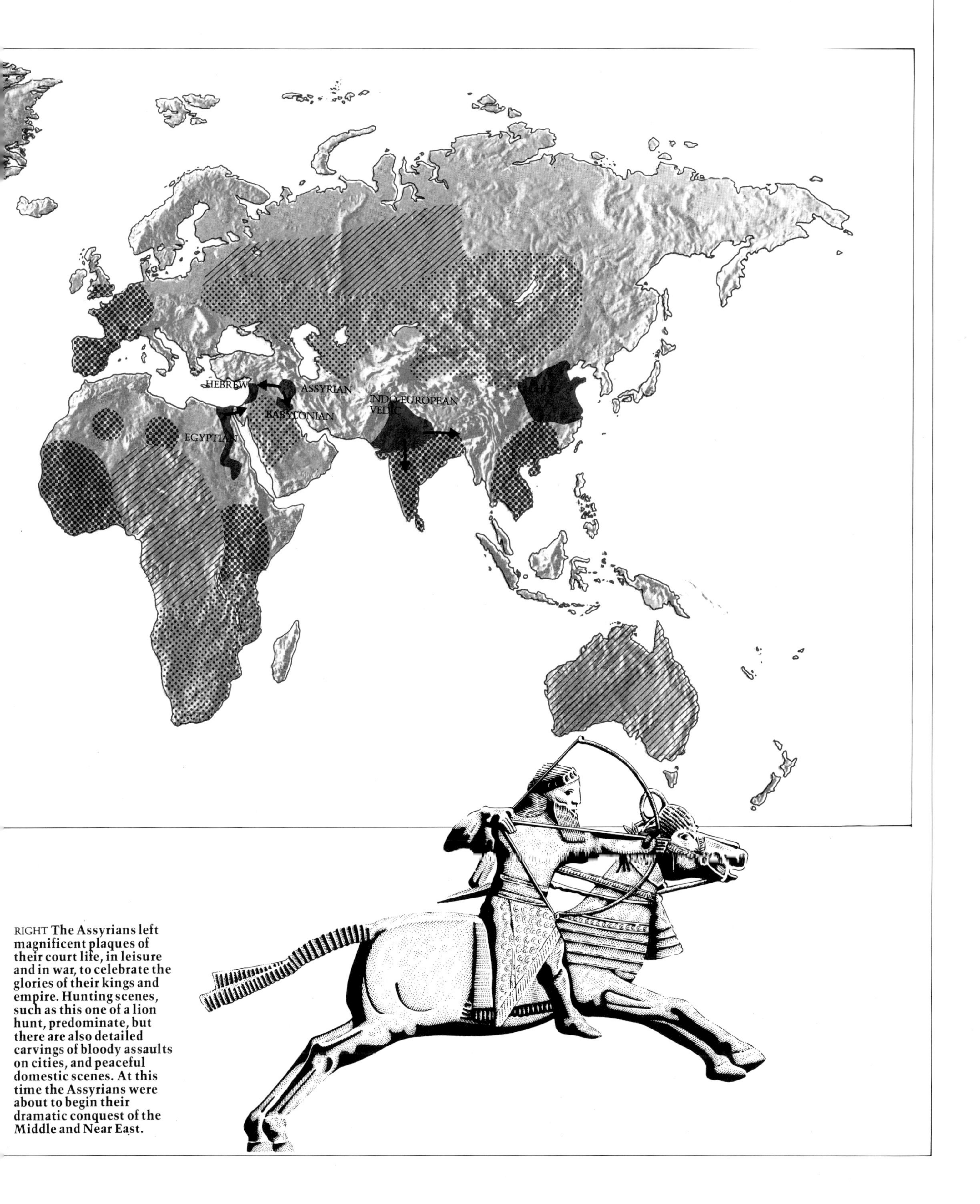

RIGHT **The Assyrians left magnificent plaques of their court life, in leisure and in war, to celebrate the glories of their kings and empire. Hunting scenes, such as this one of a lion hunt, predominate, but there are also detailed carvings of bloody assaults on cities, and peaceful domestic scenes. At this time the Assyrians were about to begin their dramatic conquest of the Middle and Near East.**

The Hebrews in Canaan

There was little central Hebrew organization – although various tribes fought many bitter wars against the Canaanites and other common enemies – until Saul was chosen as king about 1030 BC. By then, the Hebrews were challenging the rule of the Philistines, who had conquered much of Canaan and renamed it Palestine.

RIGHT **The Hebrews established a central sanctuary in the middle of Canaan for their mobile shrine, the Ark of the Covenant.**
INSET **Ashkelon was one of the five coastal cities from which the Philistines managed to dominate Palestine.**
INSET RIGHT **Gezer was one of the last of the Canaanite cities to fall into Hebrew hands.**

The combined evidence of Egyptian records (which, interestingly, do not mention the exodus of the Hebrew people) archaeological excavations, and the Old Testament, suggests that the Hebrew occupation of Canaan (Palestine) was long and complex. The biblical accounts are now believed to be closer to what probably happened than was at one time thought. In their current form, the Old Testament explanations of the conquest of Canaan were not finally edited until some seven centuries after the events they describe, and it is reasonable to suppose that the account is coloured by the needs of later Hebrews to establish their divine right to possession of the land. Moreover, later generations of Hebrews, particularly around the time of the exile in Babylon (598-539 BC), had to be taught that national security depended on strict obedience and loyalty to God, and this lesson is the main motif of the Old Testament's historical writings.

If the biblical version of the conquest of Canaan is correct, then the Canaanite fortified cities were more numerous in the west than near the Jordan Valley. There were also Hebrews living in Canaan, possibly in considerable numbers, before the arrival of the Hebrews from Egypt, and the Hebrews associated with Egypt entered Canaan in at least two waves, one during the fourteenth and the other towards the end of the thirteenth century BC.

The Book of Joshua contains extensive lists, both of the conquered Canaanite kings and of the ones the Hebrews were unable to defeat, and lists of the various territories eventually occupied by the Hebrew tribes. The most interesting list occurs in Joshua 12:7-24 where 31 kings are listed as being defeated by the Hebrews. The list is similar to Egyptian lists of cities defeated during their campaigns, which follow the order of the campaign rather than a geographical or alphabetical order. When considering the history of this period, it is vital to realize that it is the kings and their armies who are defeated, and that this does not necessarily mean that the cities themselves were always captured.

Taking exaggerations into account, the Book of Joshua summarizes the first stages of occupation in three phases. The first phase took Jericho in the Jordan Valley and then moved into the region of the Judean hills south of Jerusalem. This would have been an alliance of the king of Jerusalem (Jebus), and the kings of the cities of the Shephelah, the hilly area facing the coastal plain. Success of this type does not imply that the Hebrews were able to take Jerusalem itself.

The next part of the list mentions places in the central hill country, including Bethel, and the Sharon, the coastal area north of Joppa. This part of the list should perhaps include Tirzah, north of the sanctuary of Shechem, and all of this section may refer to places where there was isolated warfare, rather than a coherent campaign. Finally, there are the wars of the northern cities, including the great trading centre of Hazor, where archaeological evidence points to its destruction early in the twelfth century BC.

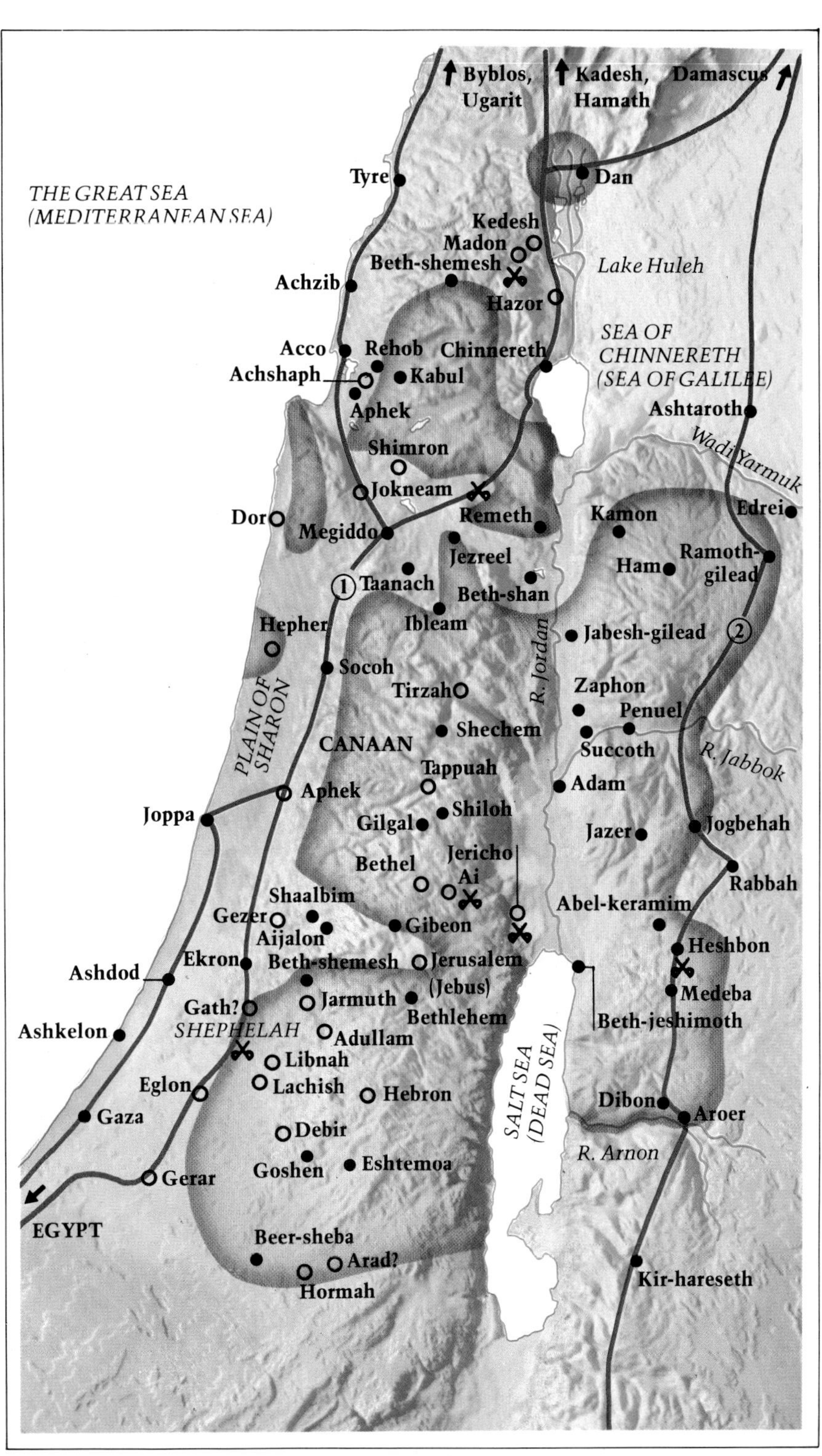

Sites of conflicts

Early Hebrew settlement regions

Conquered cities

Main trade routes

(1) The Way of the Sea

(2) The King's Highway

THE UNIFICATION PROCESS
The Hebrews who escaped from Egypt tended at first to occupy the marginal land which had not been brought under cultivation by the Canaanites, and only later did they capture the cities. Too disunited to be able to offer any coherent resistance themselves, the Canaanites normally would have appealed for help to Egypt: however, it was beset by internal problems.

The areas should be seen not so much as conquered territories, with the Hebrews immediately occupying and the Canaanites destroyed, but rather as areas where Canaanite resistance was neutralized by the defeat of Canaanite coalitions. Where a city was captured and destroyed, the successful event became a model for later descriptions, at a time when the Hebrews were in danger of losing their distinctive religious identity through adopting so many Canaanite religious beliefs and practices.

Joshua 24 describes a solemn renewal of the covenant at the sanctuary of Shechem. It has been suggested that this is the event which first united the various Hebrew groups, both those already in the land and those which had come from Egypt, so that they all identified themselves as the chosen people of the God who had delivered them from slavery.

The Hebrew settlement of Canaan took place during the late fourteenth, thirteenth and early twelfth centuries BC. It needs to be viewed over that long period – a century and a half – to take account of its diversity.

The Hebrews who entered Canaan were nomadic pastoral peoples, who could infiltrate into marginal land without causing too much anxiety to the farmers of the fortified cities. The two communities coexisted reasonably amicably for many years. Even at the time of David, the very end of the twelfth century BC, the city of Jerusalem, then known as Jebus, was still a Canaanite stronghold. So it appears that the Hebrews first controlled the land between the cities and only later occupied the cities themselves. Only in one case, that of the tribe of Dan, is there any indication that a Hebrew group had to move because of the opposition of the cities in the area (Judg 1:34). The Danites travelled to Laish, north of the Sea of Chinnereth (Galilee) where they marked the northern frontier of Hebrew territory.

The Book of Judges is organized around the deeds of 12 'judges' who at various times rallied groups of

BELOW **During the twelfth and eleventh centuries BC, migratory peoples arrived by sea from the Greek mainland and the islands of Aegean, and tried to occupy the Nile Delta. The Egyptians drove them off and they occupied the territory later known as Palestine.**

Hebrews to resist attack from Canaanites or from peoples beyond the borders of Canaan. These people were deliverers, with a special gift for leadership in times of danger, rather than part of the normal Hebrew authority structure, based on heads of families and clans. One of them, Deborah, was a woman. Their success during the various crises gave them an extraordinary authority as people who could restore God's rule – in private matters of dispute as well as in times of public danger.

Of the 12 judges, details are given of the campaigns fought by five of them, and six receive little more than a mention. At the time there was no great international power fighting to control Palestine. The Canaanite cities were weakened by rivalries between themselves, and the smaller ones could be captured in time by various groups of Hebrews. Only the Philistines posed a serious threat to final Hebrew domination.

The five campaigns of the judges throw light on relationships between the various Hebrew tribes during the thirteenth and twelfth centuries BC, as well as the foes they faced. Clearly, there was no central tribal organization, only a feeling of some kind of solidarity between the various Hebrew groups which could be appealed to in times of crisis. Only once is there any evidence of concerted action. The prophetess Deborah rallied six northern Hebrew tribes who lived along the western highlands to Mount Carmel and in the valley beyond, under the leadership of Barak of Naphtali, to fight a league of Canaanite cities. The victory song (Judg 5) rebukes four other northern Hebrew groups for failing to join the campaign and makes no mention of the tribes south of Jerusalem.

Other peoples singled out as enemies are the Edomites, Moabites and Ammonites. They were associated with the territories through which the King's Highway passed on its way northwards to the east of the Salt Sea (Dead Sea) and the Jordan Valley, and were bitter enemies of the Hebrews during the monarchy period. The last enemy identified is the Midianites, a nomadic tribe who had helped the Hebrews during the escape from Egypt (Exod 18). It seems the Hebrews were now settled and had begun to resent nomads.

Twice the Philistines are the enemy of the Hebrews. One of these occasions is a very brief mention early in the Book of Judges (3:31), where 300 are routed by Shamgah, but there are good textual reasons for placing this incident after the exploits of Samson, which only appear towards the end of the book. Other evidence also places the arrival of the Philistines in the middle of the twelfth century BC, a century after the Hebrew escape from Egypt, and a century and a half before the Hebrew King David finally defeated them.

The final sections of the Book of Judges and the First Book of Samuel describe the struggles of the Hebrews against the Philistine domination of at least the southern part of Canaan. The Philistine migrants had established themselves in the coastal area between the Shephelah and the sea, part of which is now the Gaza Strip. The five Philistine cities were Gaza, Ashkelon, Ashdod, Gath and Ekron. The last two could control the main route of the coastal road from Egypt to the north and to Mesopotamia. The other three were on the route to Joppa, the only sheltered harbour south of Acco, now part of Tel Aviv. The Philistines gave their name to this part of the Canaanite territory as 'Palestine', and it will be convenient to use this name from now on.

The Philistines were part of the 'Sea Peoples' who migrated into the eastern seaboard of the Mediterranean during the early part of the twelfth century BC. They overran the Hittites of Asia Minor, and were repulsed by the Egyptians as they attempted to take over the delta area of Lower Egypt where the River Nile runs into the Mediterranean. The Egyptians successfully resisted

Josh, Judg, 1 Sam 1-70.

Then Joshua came and wiped out the Anakim from the highlands, from Hebron, from Debir, from Anab, from all the highlands of Judah and all the highlands of Israel; he delivered them and their towns over to the ban. No more Anakim were left in Israelite territory except at Gaza, Gath and Ashdod. Joshua mastered the whole country, just as Yahweh had told Moses, and he gave it to Israel as an inheritance according to their division by tribes. And the country had rest from war. (Josh 11: 21-23)

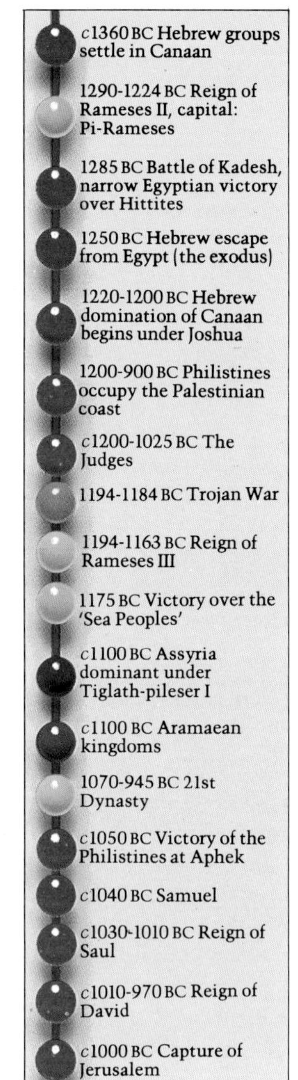

them during the reign of King Rameses III (*c*1194-1163 BC), and shortly afterwards the Philistines gained a foothold further up the coast and took over the five Canaanite cities which were to become their centres of strength. Under the Philistines, each city had its own king, but it was a closely-knit federation which appointed a single leader for warfare. They were technologically more advanced than the Canaanites or the Hebrews, for they introduced iron and kept control over its use. With iron weapons, chariots and good discipline, the Philistines soon extended their control into the Negeb, the central mountains and the Valley of Jezreel. Neither the Canaanites nor the Hebrews were able to withstand them, and they effectively ended Egyptian control of the area.

In the eleventh century BC, Samson, as 'judge' or charismatic leader, was a resistance fighter who organized guerilla tactics against the Philistines in the Shephelah, which contained a group of cities where the hills begin to rise out of the coastal plain. But if Samson ever intended to unite the Hebrew tribes, he failed to do so, and a central belt remained under Canaanite control, including Jerusalem. The Song of Deborah (Judg 5) demonstrates how difficult it was for the Hebrews to take concerted action.

Such unity as there was centred on the sanctuary of Shiloh, in the highlands north of Jerusalem, where the Ark of the Covenant – the portable shrine of the nomadic Hebrew religion – was tended by a priestly family. Samuel was dedicated to the shrine by his parents, in the ancient Near Eastern way of training priests, and would have been serving the shrine when the sacred Ark was taken into battle by the Hebrews against the Philistines at Aphek, around 1050 BC. The Hebrews were defeated, the Ark captured by the Philistines and Shiloh destroyed.

The First Book of Samuel has been compiled from two sources, which present differing views of Samuel. One of them, which is anti-monarchist, presents Samuel as king in all but name, ruling the country, humiliating the Philistines, and resenting popular demands for a king. The other source presents him as a local seer, who willingly sanctifies the people's choice of Saul as the first Hebrew king. The latter is the more likely, because a Hebrew desire for a central authority, able to organize the tribes against the Philistines, would have been logical. The old informal Hebrew federation of independent tribes could no more defend Hebrew territory than the old federations of Canaanite cities could prevent the Canaanites from being overwhelmed.

King Saul was unlucky. He had come to prominence as a gifted military leader, like the judges before him, but his reign ended in tragedy. He parted with Samuel, lost confidence, and allowed himself to be drawn into battle with the Philistines near Mount Gilboa in the Valley of Jezreel where the Philistines could deploy their chariots. It should have spelt the end of Hebrew independence, but in fact it gave David his opportunity, after his early years as a favourite of Saul and his years as an outlaw when King Saul turned against him.

INSET TOP **The coastal route through Palestine from Egypt passed through strongholds such as Gezer.**
INSET BOTTOM **Excavations at the site of ancient Jericho have revealed one of the city's defence towers.**

BELOW **Ancient megaliths, stand near the coastal plain in southern Palestine. The Hebrews fought a long guerrilla campaign against the Philistines in these parts, under Samson and other leaders.**

United under David and Solomon

Faced with a divisive political situation after Saul's death, David united rival Hebrew tribes, secured their loyalty by providing a neutral capital – Jerusalem – and subdued their various enemies. Solomon consolidated David's centralized administrative system and extended his influence through trade.

1 Sam 8-31, 2 Sam, 1 Kgs 1-11, Gen 1-11 (parts), Prov 10-31, Ps (parts).

David and his men marched on Jerusalem against the Jebusites living there. These said to David, 'You will not get in here. The blind and the lame will hold you off.' (That is to say: David will never get in here.) But David captured the fortress of Zion... David went to live in the fortress and called it the Citadel of David. David then built a wall round it, from the Millo going inwards. David grew greater and greater, and Yahweh, God of Sabaoth, was with him.
(2 Sam 5: 6-10)

The main sources of information about Kings David and Solomon were heavily edited by the historians of the southern Hebrew kingdom of Judah. Jerusalem was the capital of Judah, the city David had captured and made the first effective capital of the united Hebrew people. The sources are therefore suspect and may underrate Saul and the northern Hebrews in order to emphasize the glories of David and Solomon. But unattractive aspects, such as David's military murder of his officer, Uriah (2 Sam 11), are included to show that the accounts are not mere propaganda. However biased they may be, 1 and 2 Samuel present a convincing picture of David as an outstanding personality.

After he had been made king, Saul exercised loose control over the central highlands from Judah to the edge of Mount Carmel, the area east of the River Jordan, the Valley of Jezreel, and Galilee. The centres of his power lay in Benjamin country, just north of Jerusalem (which was still in Canaanite hands), and Bethlehem, just south of Jerusalem. The recognition by Samuel of the young David as future leader of the country (1 Sam 16) is consistent with the role of Samuel as a seer, but the account has been written with hindsight. David was born at Bethlehem, the most northerly town in Judah. He joined Saul's court as other young Hebrews from various tribal areas would have done, and became a successful officer and a favourite of Saul's. There must be doubts about David's killing of Goliath at an engagement with Philistine forces on the edge of the Shephelah between Socoh and Azekah (1 Sam 17), for, in a brief summary of David's clashes with Philistines, the killing of Goliath is attributed to one of his soldiers (2 Sam 21:19).

David's marriage to one of Saul's daughters is told within the context of Saul's mounting jealousy of David, whose popular reputation as a warrior had now surpassed Saul's own (1 Sam 18). This would have been dangerous at any time in the turbulent history of Hebrew kings, including David's own reign, and so the marriage should be seen as a way of securing David's loyalty to Saul. Shortly afterwards, Saul attempted to kill David because he was a threat to his authority. This is still a period when the leader's authority rested on his pre-eminence in battle, as it had for the judges, and Saul could not afford to have his own reputation surpassed by one of his court.

The subsequent actions of David, after his flight from King Saul, all show the political skill which he would eventually use to unite the various Hebrew groups and factions. He was helped by the members of the sacred city of Nob, near Jerusalem, where the priests of the central sanctuary had fled when Shiloh was captured and destroyed by the Philistines after the battle of Aphek. David welcomed the survivor, Ahimelek, when Saul had Nob's priests executed. During this period David lived as an outlaw in the Judean hills and in caves along the shores of the Salt Sea (Dead Sea). He gathered around him the men who would become the nucleus of his own court. Eventually, he and his group became mercenaries in the service of the Philistines, following a long Hebrew tradition of service as mercenary soldiers. Even during this time, his sense of political realities kept him from antagonizing any Hebrews whose support he would need if he were to unite the people. Saul died at the Battle of Gilboa (*c*1010) after the Philistines had defeated him. David and his men had been left behind because of their previous service under Saul. Thus, no Hebrew group could claim that David had fought against them.

King Saul's reign ended in disaster. He lost the support of Samuel and of the traditional Hebrew religion, and eventually was defeated by the Philistines he had successfully resisted during his reign. Despite his reputation as a failed king, Saul did, for most of his reign, force the Philistines to relinquish control over the whole of the central highlands from Judah to the Valley of Jezreel. Saul's reign should be seen as an essential interlude of monarchical experiment between the ineffectiveness of the judges and the successful monarchy founded by King David.

David heard the news of Saul's defeat and death while he was at Ziklag, deep in the southern part of Judah, and immediately set about securing his own succession and acceptance by all the Hebrew tribes. He faced a delicate political situation, and his first steps were to dissociate himself from any involvement with the death of King Saul at the hands of the Philistines. David composed a beautiful lament for Saul and his son Jonathan (2 Sam 1:19-27). It is in the strong tradition of David as poet and musician who wrote at least some of the psalms. The lament demonstrated to Saul's supporters that David mourned his death. David also executed the messenger who said that he had killed King Saul, at Saul's own request, when it was obvious that the Battle of Gilboa was lost. In fact, Saul took his own life (1 Sam 31:4; 2 Sam 1:5-16). As he was about to become king himself, David had every reason to enforce respect for the person of the king.

It is clear that the Hebrew tribes constituted two distinct groups at this time – a southern group consisting mainly of Judah and Simeon, to which David belonged, and the northern tribes of the central highlands, Galilee and the Jordan area. The land between them, which included Jerusalem, may not yet have been under Hebrew control, and in any case the northern tribes had not looked for help from the southern ones during the period of the judges. It is even probable that the southern Hebrews had not been amongst the Hebrews who escaped from Egypt.

The southern Hebrews anointed David king at the ancient southern sanctuary of Hebron, and at first there was open war between the southern and northern Hebrew tribes. Saul had been succeeded by his son Ishbaal, but he offended his senior army commander, Abner, who then negotiated with David to transfer his loyalties and those of the northern tribes. Fortunately for David, Abner was murdered by David's own senior army officer, Joab. David could dissociate himself from the murder and give Abner a solemn funeral to show his disapproval of the deed. King Ishbaal was now the only

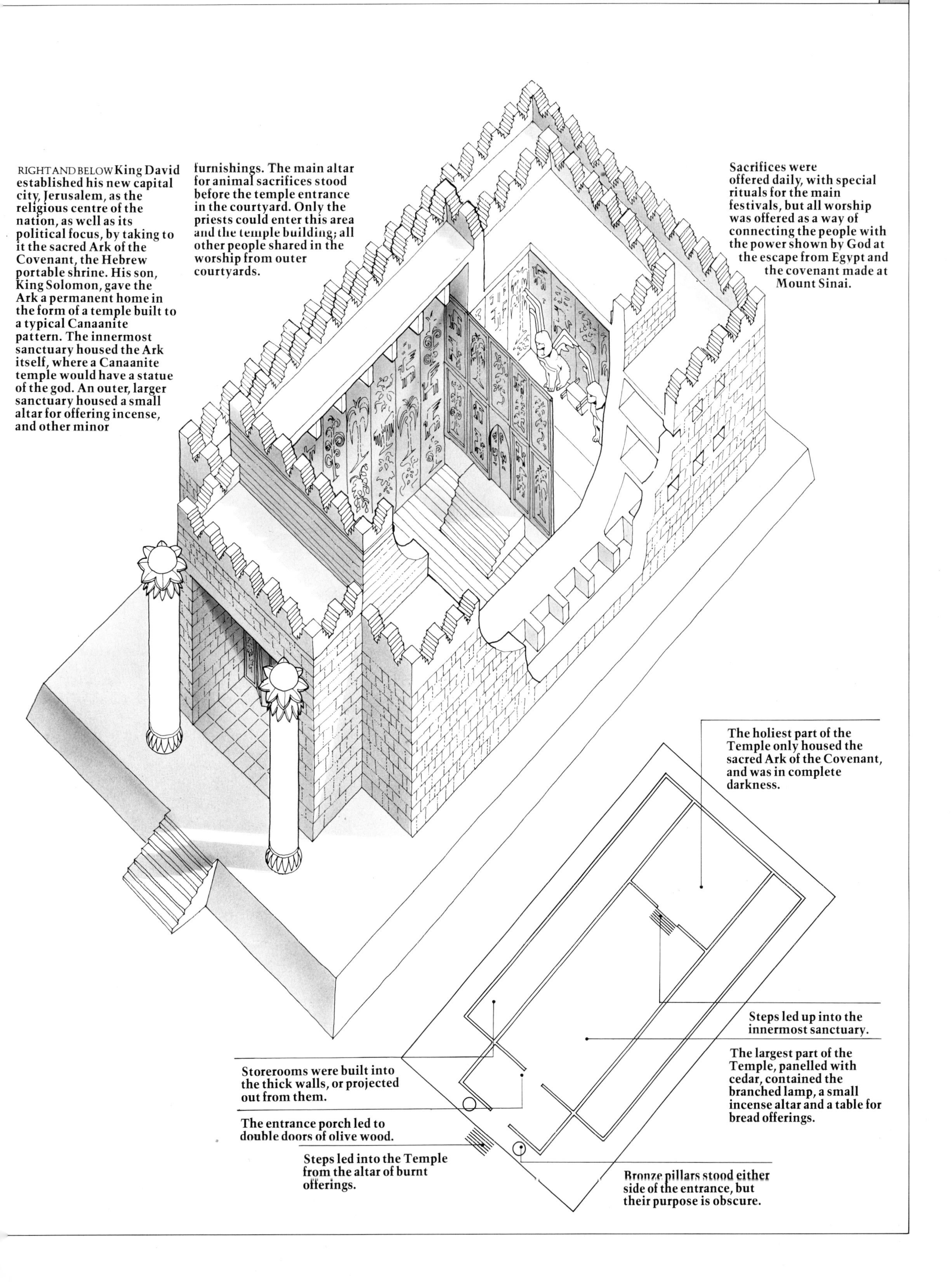

The holiest part of the Temple only housed the sacred Ark of the Covenant, and was in complete darkness.
Steps led up into the innermost sanctuary.
The largest part of the Temple, panelled with cedar, contained the branched lamp, a small incense altar and a table for bread offerings.
Storerooms were built into the thick walls, or projected out from them.
The entrance porch led to double doors of olive wood.
Steps led into the Temple from the altar of burnt offerings.
Bronze pillars stood either side of the entrance, but their purpose is obscure.

RIGHT AND BELOW King David established his new capital city, Jerusalem, as the religious centre of the nation, as well as its political focus, by taking to it the sacred Ark of the Covenant, the Hebrew portable shrine. His son, King Solomon, gave the Ark a permanent home in the form of a temple built to a typical Canaanite pattern. The innermost sanctuary housed the Ark itself, where a Canaanite temple would have a statue of the god. An outer, larger sanctuary housed a small altar for offering incense, and other minor furnishings. The main altar for animal sacrifices stood before the temple entrance in the courtyard. Only the priests could enter this area and the temple building; all other people shared in the worship from outer courtyards.

Sacrifices were offered daily, with special rituals for the main festivals, but all worship was offered as a way of connecting the people with the power shown by God at the escape from Egypt and the covenant made at Mount Sinai.

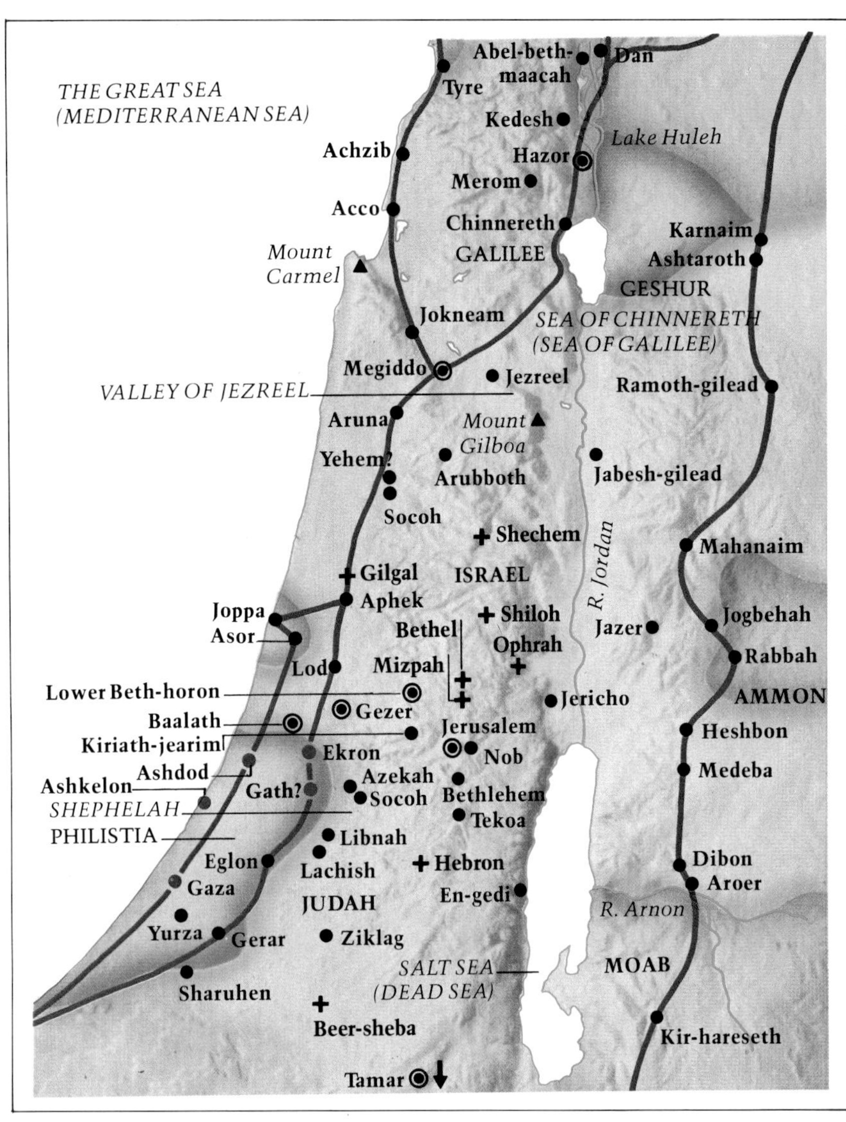

● Philistine cities
✚ Sanctuaries during the early monarchy
◉ Cities strengthened by King Solomon
The Land of Israel
Conquered region under Israel's rule
Region under vassal treaty
Main trade routes

THE KINGDOM **The whole coast, from below Joppa up to Mount Carmel, was controlled by David. Around the 12 Hebrew territories there was a ring of vassal states, which were usually administered in David's name by a governor. Later strategically-placed cities were strengthened by Solomon.**

remaining obstacle, and he was assassinated by two of his own officers who were then foolish enough to take Ishbaal's head to David. Once more David could demonstrate his disapproval of murdering kings by having the assassins executed. David's way was clear, and his reign over the united Hebrew tribes dates from his acceptance as king by the northern group of Hebrews, whose leaders went to Hebron to anoint him, as the southern group had already done.

David secured his hold over the united Hebrew people by providing them with a capital which had no political or religious associations for any of the Hebrew tribes – Jerusalem. The small Canaanite city was on a narrow ridge which fell away each side at a steep angle and flattened out at the northern end to form a gentle hill. The Gihon spring at the foot of the eastern slopes of the ridge provided a dependable water supply and was protected by the city's defensive walls and a water shaft. When David's soldiers captured it, Jerusalem, situated between the two main Hebrew groups, had never been in Hebrew hands before. Both groups could accept it without loss of face, and David sealed its new significance for his people by fetching the sacred Ark of the Covenant, the Hebrew portable shrine, from the borders of Philistine territory and installing it in its tent at the northern end of the city.

Once he had secured the loyalty of all the Hebrew tribes, David turned to their various enemies – the remaining Canaanite cities, the Philistines, the small kingdoms east of the Jordan Valley and the nomadic groups who attempted to settle in what was now Hebrew territory. Although the Philistines retained their foothold in the southern coastal area with its five cities, David took control of the cities of the Shephelah immediately inland, and of the coastal plain north of the Philistines. The Philistines were only able to survive as subservient to the Hebrews. King David's successor, Solomon, inherited the areas transversed by the coastal road as Hebrew territory, and David also imposed his rule over the areas through which the eastern route passed, the King's Highway. He thus controlled both of the great international routes through Palestine, as well as the land area from Damascus to the Egyptian frontier, and from the Great Sea (the Mediterranean) to the Syrian desert.

King David's political success was confirmed and secured by a major act of religious symbolism. David planned to build a temple to house the Ark of the Covenant (2 Sam 7) and his successor, Solomon, was to do so. The prophet Nathan had told David that a dream had revealed that David and his descendants were to be the 'house' of God's covenant with the Hebrew people. The Hebrew monarchy itself was to be the sign of the covenant and its guardian, so the Davidic succession became a form of divine right which should have provided the people with a secure and just administration. This idea of kingly responsibility was very important. For instance, when David had one of his officers murdered, so that he could take the officer's wife without scandal, Nathan rebuked him. This would have been normal behaviour, perhaps, for a Canaanite king who owned his subjects in the name of the god Baal, but a Hebrew king must administer Hebrew covenant law and be bound by it himself. The king was to be the guardian of the covenant. David's reign (c1070 BC) included a major rebellion, (c980 BC) led by one of his sons, Absalom. However, David regained control, and was able to nominate his son Solomon as his successor just before his death.

The triumph of Solomon in the succession struggle marked the eclipse of the older, conservative religious traditions, and the ascendancy of the new way of life introduced by the conquest of Canaan. The Hebrews had become a predominantly settled, agricultural people, rather than nomadic shepherds. The priest of David's court, Abiathar, who had survived the slaughter of the old Hebrew priest-guardians of the Ark of the Covenant by King Saul, backed the losing side and was banished by Solomon to Anathoth. A priest who first appeared after the capture of Jerusalem, Zadok, became the most prominent religious figure in Solomon's court.

BELOW In David's time Jerusalem lay to the south of the present 'old city', along the steep and narrow ridge of Ophel. Later it spread to the north and west after King Solomon built the Temple.

INSET Traditionally, this is supposed to be the entrance to David's citadel although its authenticity is extremely doubtful. Despite this, it is a popular tourist attraction in modern Jerusalem.

BELOW **King Solomon began the extensions to Jerusalem, which transformed it from a small Canaanite city into a larger capital. The water supply enabled the city to withstand a siege, and was reached from within the main fortifications.**

It is reasonable to assume that Zadok was the priest of Jerusalem in its Canaanite days, before its capture by King David, and that his prominence under King Solomon marks a distinct movement towards Canaanite expressions of religion.

If religious symbolism does not alter with the changing needs of the people, it fossilizes and becomes irrelevant. From the time of Solomon onwards, a tension can be detected within the Hebrews. Some of them remained loyal to the old Hebrew religion of the nomadic shepherds, while others expressed the essentials of the covenant religion in ways which reflected the Hebrew's needs in their new economic, social and political situation. The Hebrew Temple in Jerusalem, built by King Solomon, became the visible sign that the nomadic religion of the Hebrew escape from Egypt was being expressed in new forms.

The new Temple built by King Solomon in Jerusalem was more than a permanent home for the Ark of the Covenant, the mobile Hebrew shrine of the covenant God had made with his chosen people after their escape from Egypt. The Temple asserted that the Hebrew people had taken over the Canaanite way of life, with its fortified settlements, its agricultural economy, and its monarchical form of government. Not only was the Temple the shrine of the Ark, it was also the royal chapel administered by priests appointed by the king. At about this time a separate class of priests emerged to serve the Temple.

The plan of Solomon's Temple is similar to that of other temples in Canaanite areas, particularly the temple destroyed by the Hebrews at Hazor. The Temple itself was a comparatively small building, at most some 120-150 feet (35-40 metres) long by 45-60 feet (15-20 metres) wide, as it was not designed to accommodate worshippers. It stood in the great court which also contained the royal palace, and had its own inner court to which there was direct access from the palace. The Temple was entered by a porch between two ceremonial pillars, the significance of which has been lost. It then opened out into the Hekal or main hall. This communicated with the Debir, the innermost shrine, which was raised higher than the rest of the building and housed the Ark of the Covenant.

The main hall of the Temple contained an altar for burning incense, the table for the 'bread of the presence' – which originally may have been a food-offering to God – and 10 lampstands. The main focus for worship was the bronze altar of whole burnt offerings, a great raised hearth about 30 feet (10 metres) square and 15 feet (5 metres) high which stood before the Temple porch and on which the main sacrifices were offered. Near it was a bronze water basin some 15 feet (5 metres) in diameter and 8 feet (2.5 metres) high, with 10 wheeled basins for carrying water. As in Canaanite temples, there would have been channels to drain away the blood of the sacrificed animals.

Solomon employed Phoenician architects and workmen for the Temple, sent by King Hiram of Tyre, who also supplied the cedarwood with which it was panelled. It is no longer possible to say precisely where the Temple was situated in relation to modern Jerusalem, for it was destroyed by the Babylonians in 587 BC, and its successor, the Temple King Herod the Great built, was destroyed by the Romans in AD 70. It probably stood where the spectacular Moslem Dome of the Rock today protects a rocky outcrop with sacred associations.

The Temple and the royal palace were only a small part of the vast programme of building undertaken by Solomon for which he used forced labour, a normal practice of the times. A number of Palestinian cities have remains of massive fortifications constructed in Solomon's time. These included recessed stone gateways designed to provide several lines of defence, and walls of great thickness with hollow chambers built between the inner and outer surfaces, which have been found at Megiddo, Hazor and Gezer. The great shaft and tunnel at Megiddo, which gives access to the water supply, are now thought to date from the period immediately following Solomon.

Solomon consolidated the centralized administrative system begun by King David, from which come the first reliable Hebrew written records. Moreover, he took advantage of Palestine's central position in order to develop extensive trading connections both by land and by sea, with caravan routes into the Arabian desert and a merchant fleet in the Red Sea. He also developed the Hebrew copper industry from ore deposits in the Jordan Valley and the area south of the Salt Sea (Dead Sea). King Solomon's administrative ability is the foundation of his reputation for 'wisdom', which created a golden age for the Hebrew people. His achievements required large-scale organization of labour, and his success owes much to his understanding of divisive tendencies in Hebrew society, with its traditions of tribal loyalties. Solomon managed to maintain national unity, but it collapsed at his death in about 931 BC.

Land routes

Sea routes

TRADING LINKS **During King Solomon's reign, the Hebrews began to develop their trading potential. They were centrally situated and because they occupied Palestine, controlled the main trading routes and a large section of the Mediterranean coast. With their enemies defeated, they could afford a merchant fleet for the Red Sea and beyond.**

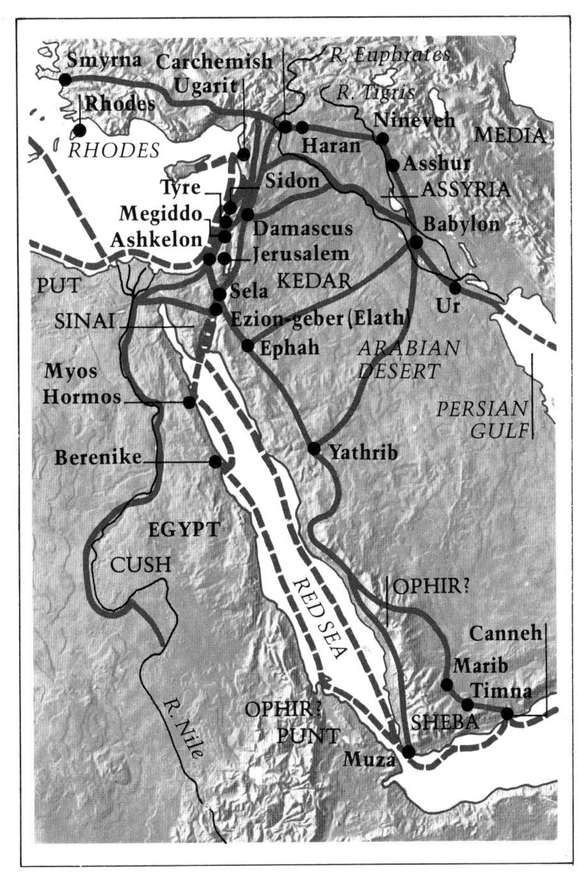

- c1050 BC Victory of the Philistines at Aphek
- c1040 BC Samuel
- c1030-1010 BC Reign of Saul
- c1010-970 BC Reign of David
- c1000 BC Capture of Jerusalem
- c970-931 BC Reign of Solomon
- 945-725 BC 22nd Dynasty, capital: Bubastis
- 945-924 BC Reign of Sheshonk I, his campaign against Palestine
- 931-910 BC (Israel) Reign of Jeroboam I
- 931-913 BC (Judah) Reign of Rehoboam

BELOW **King David's victories over the Philistines, and King Solomon's great fortresses, gave the Hebrews security. The nation looked back to these times as a golden age. This vineyard is on the edge of the coastal plain which the Hebrews seized from the Philistines.**

BELOW **Under King Solomon, the city of Jerusalem expanded to the north and west. Today, the area where Solomon built the first Hebrew Temple is covered by the great platform, built nearly 1,000 years later, as foundation for the Temple started by Herod the Great.**

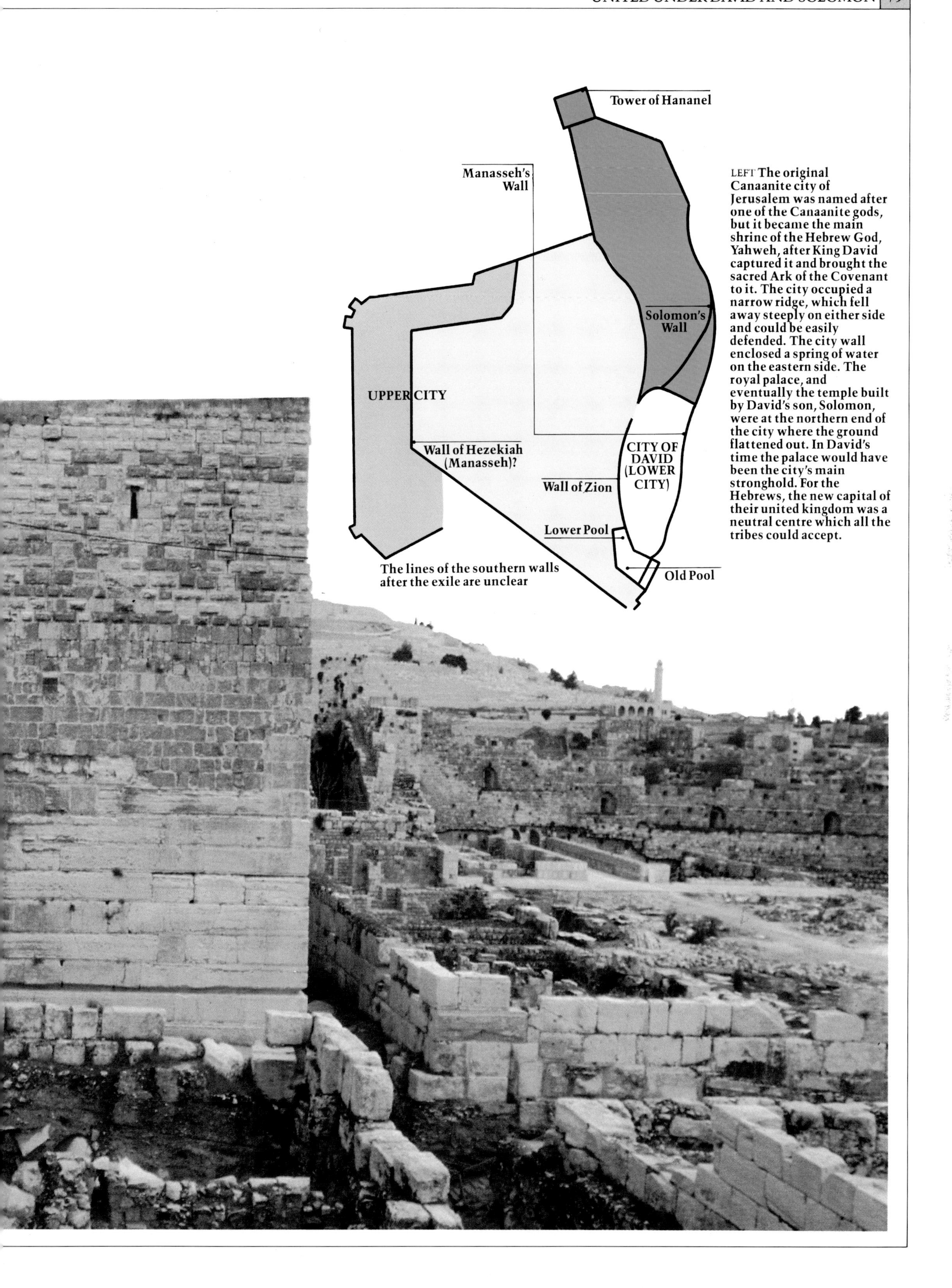

LEFT The original Canaanite city of Jerusalem was named after one of the Canaanite gods, but it became the main shrine of the Hebrew God, Yahweh, after King David captured it and brought the sacred Ark of the Covenant to it. The city occupied a narrow ridge, which fell away steeply on either side and could be easily defended. The city wall enclosed a spring of water on the eastern side. The royal palace, and eventually the temple built by David's son, Solomon, were at the northern end of the city where the ground flattened out. In David's time the palace would have been the city's main stronghold. For the Hebrews, the new capital of their united kingdom was a neutral centre which all the tribes could accept.

The Hebrew Collapse

Shortly after Solomon's death, differences between the northern tribes – who were angry at being economically exploited and uneasy about religious changes – and the southerners culminated in the kingdom's collapse. The Old Testament was written during the centuries of civil strife, invasion and exile which followed.

1 Kgs 12-22.

Jeroboam thought to himself, 'As things are, the kingdom will revert to the House of David. If this people continues to go up to the Temple of Yahweh in Jerusalem to offer sacrifices, the people's heart will turn back again to their lord, Rehoboam king of Judah, and they will put me to death.' So the king thought this over and then made two golden calves; he said to the people, 'You have been going up to Jerusalem long enough. Here are your gods, Israel; these brought you up out of the land of Egypt!' He set up one in Bethel and the people went in procession all the way to Dan in front of the other.
(1 Kgs 12: 26-30)

Kings David and Solomon proved to be the only kings to reign over a union of the various Hebrew tribal groups – traditionally 12 in number – settled in Palestine. At the death of Solomon in about 931 BC, the united kingdom split into two factions, consisting of the northern and southern groups of tribes, along the old demarcation line through the centre of Palestine. The split led to two separate Hebrew kingdoms. The southern one, Judah, with Jerusalem as its capital, was ruled by descendants of David until it was destroyed by the Babylonians in 587 BC. The northern group formed the kingdom of Israel, ruled by a series of dynasties with, eventually, Samaria as its capital. It survived until 721 BC when it was destroyed by the Assyrians.

The precarious unity of the Hebrew peoples had lasted little more than 70 years, from the choice of David as king by the two main groups of Hebrews, to the death of Solomon. Unity was only maintained by the outstanding abilities of these two kings. Shortly after the death of Solomon, Egypt reasserted her control over Palestine, but the Egyptians did not cause the split. The main causes were economic and religious, which amplified all the tensions which already existed between the two Hebrew groups.

The economic problems can be understood from the scale of King Solomon's building activities and the splendour of his court. Archaeology has confirmed the building programme, while, even allowing for exaggeration in the biblical accounts, it can be assumed that his court was resplendent. Both the taxation and the forced labour required for this building were sources of anger, and there is biblical evidence that at least part of the taxation fell more heavily on the northern group of Hebrews. A list of Solomon's administrators, given in the First Book of Kings (4:7-19), shows that the territory north of Jerusalem, from the coast to the eastern side of the Jordan Valley and the Salt Sea (Dead Sea), was divided into 12 districts. Eight of the districts consisted of Hebrew tribal areas, while the four districts along the western coast, from the Philistine border to Mount Carmel, consisted of former Canaanite cities occupied by the Hebrews late in the settlement period. Between them, these twelve northern districts were made responsible for the expenses of Solomon's court, each district covering the cost of one month of the year. There is no mention of the southern Hebrew areas, occupied by David's tribe of Judah and by Simeon. Undoubtedly the northern Hebrews were far more prosperous and numerous than the southern ones, but this evidence of inequality of taxation provides at least one good reason for their subsequent split.

To economic differences must be added differences in religious traditions. When David made his capital, Jerusalem, the religious centre for the Hebrew people, and Solomon built the Temple for the Ark of the Covenant, they made it possible for the old Hebrew religion to serve the new needs of the Hebrew people as they changed from nomadic shepherds to settled farmers. But many Hebrews remained loyal to the old nomadic symbolism of the Hebrew religion, associated with such ancient sanctuaries as Bethel, Shiloh and Shechem. The new Temple at Jerusalem could easily be seen as a departure from tradition, especially as the traditional priestly organization of the old tribal confederation had been eclipsed by the new line of priests associated with the Temple. The rebellion of the northern group, late in the tenth century BC, was led, eventually, by one of Solomon's own senior officials, Jeroboam, who was in charge of the forced labour levies drawn from the northern Hebrew areas.

The biblical accounts of the Hebrew monarchy were edited into their present form after the destruction of the northern Hebrew kingdom, Israel, by the Assyrians in 721 BC. So this occurred at a time when only the southern kingdom, Judah, remained. It is therefore reasonable to beware of a certain bias in favour of the southern kingdom and so of the Davidic dynasty, reigning from Jerusalem, and the religion of the Temple. This is borne out by the historical books themselves, which select incidents to be included for their religious significance and their effects on the survival of the kingdom of Judah. The reader is told that the rest of the information, that which applies to the northern kingdom, Israel, is available in other records, since lost (2 Kgs 8:23 and 2 Kgs 10:34).

The leader of the split between the two Hebrew

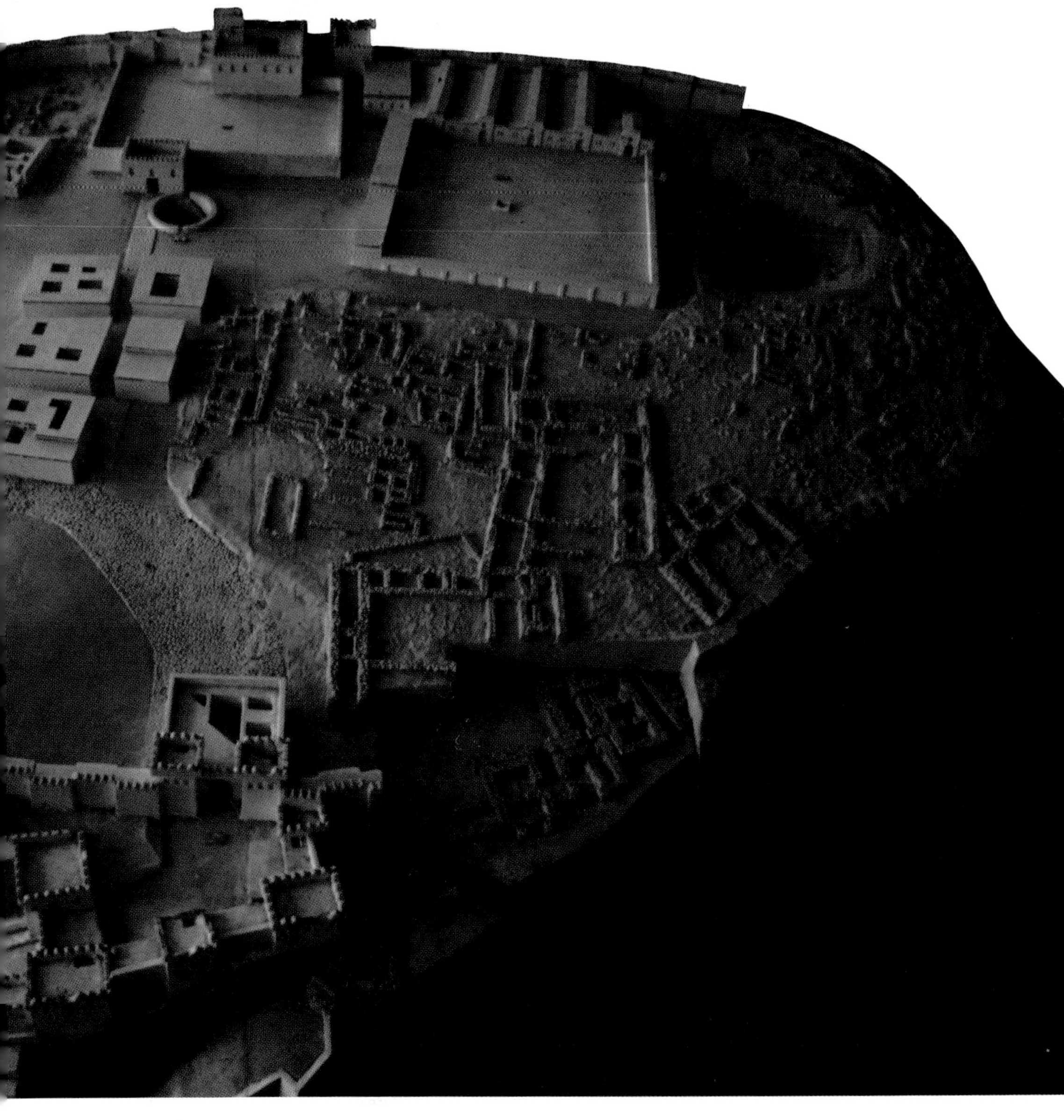

LEFT **Excavations at Megiddo have exposed the great walls and gateway built by King Solomon to strengthen Palestine after the Hebrews captured it. Solomon's numerous building projects depended on heavy taxation and forced labour, which were particularly resented by the Hebrews of the northern parts of the kingdom. This resentment was one of the main causes of the split in the Hebrew kingdom at King Solomon's death.**

groups, Jeroboam, was an important official in King Solomon's administration. He had rebelled during Solomon's lifetime and fled to Egypt. When Solomon's successor, Rehoboam, refused concessions to a delegation of northern Hebrews and threatened to increase their burden, they made Jeroboam king of the northern tribes and fortified Shechem and Penuel. King Rehoboam of Judah assembled an army to put down the rebellion, but prophetic advice dissuaded him from attacking the northerners. It is possible that the prophets, as distinct from the royal priests, sympathized with the northern desire to curb the power of the Jerusalem kings and the Temple priests. In any case, the northern group was by far the stronger of the two, and in the many years of civil warfare between the two Hebrew kingdoms, the northern kingdom became dominant.

The split was sealed by the northern emphasis on the importance of two sanctuaries, Bethel, near the southern frontier with the kingdom of Judah, and Dan, in the far north of the kingdom of Israel. The one at Bethel, in particular, would provide a centre for northern Hebrews inclined to look to Jerusalem. Each of them contained a religious image in the form of a golden bull, a traditional symbol for the Hebrew God, Yahweh, but one which could easily be seen as a representation of the Canaanite god, Baal. The traditional Canaanite fertility religion was to be the main danger for the Hebrew people, both northerners and southerners, for the rest of the period of the monarchy. It is only natural, therefore, that the biblical histories roundly condemn these two sanctuaries of the northern Hebrew kingdom.

However, the internal struggles between the two Hebrew kingdoms was not the only factor to lead to their losing control of Palestine. A few years after King Solomon died in about 931 BC, the Egyptian King Sheshonk I, the first king of the 22nd Dynasty, reestablished Egyptian control of Palestine by a military campaign which took him as far as the Phoenician cities and revived Egypt's trading relationships with Byblos, north of Damascus. Egypt thus once more had command of the coastal road to the north and to Mesopotamia. In the course of the campaign, Sheshonk took Jerusalem and stripped the royal palace and the Temple of its treasures. Egyptian supremacy in the region was comparatively short lived, for the 22nd Dynasty collapsed in civil war late in the eighth century BC. By then the Hebrew kingdoms were too weakened by their mutual enmity to take advantage of Egyptian weakness. Moreover, the Assyrians had begun their great expansion, and would soon be the dominant power of both the Near and Middle East.

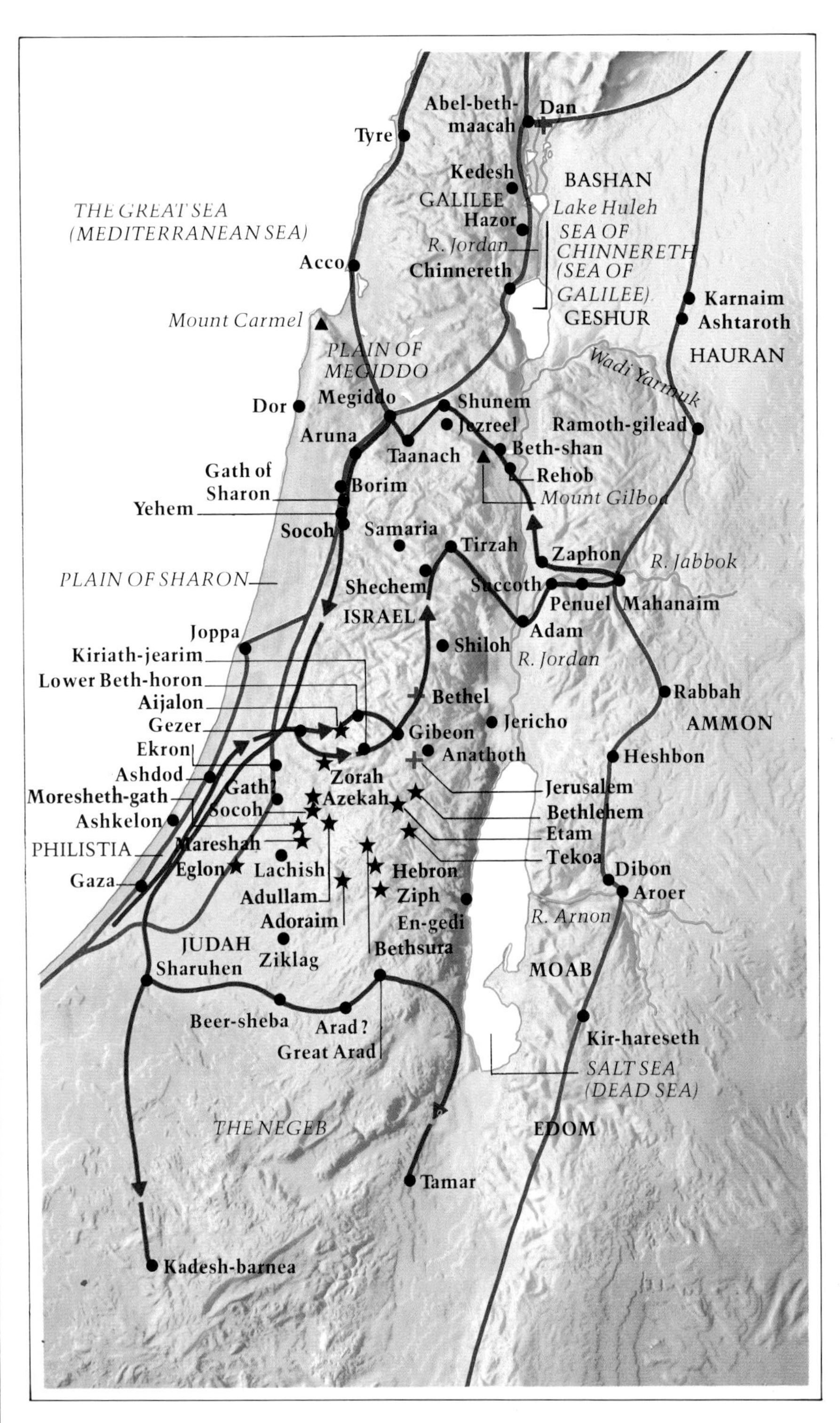

- Egyptian campaign of Sheshonk I, c 928 BC
- ★ Fortresses of King Rehoboam of Judah
- + Royal sanctuaries
- Main trade routes

DISSOLUTION OF THE KINGDOM **Not long after Solomon's death, Sheshonk I's Egyptian army surged through Palestine, taking Jerusalem and gaining control of the trading routes. Meanwhile, Solomon's successor, Rehoboam, had a power base in the south, and he quickly alienated the northern tribes. During the two centuries of its existence, the northern kingdom was by far the stronger and more prosperous. Eventually, in 721 BC, it was crushed by the Assyrians who destroyed its capital.**

A NATION'S RELIGIOUS WRITINGS

The national memory of the early days of the Hebrew people included the lives of the founding patriarchs and of Moses, and the accounts of the exodus from Egypt which were passed down by word of mouth. Popular religious experiences influenced tradition, for the stories were selected and shaped by the people's own needs and by their own beliefs about God which changed over the years.

At the exodus from Egypt c1250 BC, and when the people were united into one kingdom by King David c1070 BC, the tribal traditions merged into one organic whole. At much the same time, the need for court records gave a stimulus to the recording in writing of the nation's ancient historical traditions. An early collection of Hebrew law, recorded in The Book of the Covenant (Exod 20:22-23:19) influenced the later development of law in Deuteronomy.

During this same period, in the two centuries following the death of Solomon in c931 BC, the first books of prophetic teaching and preaching were written. As the nation grew in prosperity, it appears to have moved away from the religious and social morality of the Mosaic covenant and showed that it was incapable of appreciating the issues involved in the Assyrian invasion in the eighth century BC. Under the leadership of its successive kings, with the notable exception of Hezekiah and Josiah, the nation ignored the warnings of the prophets and slid ever deeper into religious compromise and complacency.

The 48 years of exile from 587-539 BC were a great period of vitality. Historians presented the national traditions in ways which brought out the principles of the covenant and the effects of God's presence among his people. Above all, the priests in exile collected and edited the traditions about the patriarchs, the exodus from Egypt, the covenant and the nation's laws, and set them all within a framework of the creation of the universe, to produce the first five books of the Old Testament. The work of rebuilding Jerusalem and restoring the covenant community proved more difficult than the returning exiles anticipated. All the writings testify to the disillusionment which the people experienced.

In the remaining five and a half centuries of the Old Testament period, the great empires of Persia, Greece and Rome dominated the area and made their contributions to Hebrew culture. For a brief period the Hebrews even managed to shake off foreign rule. During these centuries, the collection of the Psalms reached its final form and contributed to the worship in the new Temple in Jerusalem. Scribes also made collections of proverbs and folk-sayings. Under the stimulus of Greek thought, the ancient questions of life, death and of man's place in God's world were explored again in the Wisdom writings and in cryptic expressions of hope and encouragement in times of persecution. The total result was a collection of writings, the Old Testament, which contained the accumulated religious experience of a whole nation, covering 2,000 years of its history.

BELOW **The fortified water system at Megiddo, with its great shaft and long tunnel, was constructed during the early years of the northern Hebrew kingdom, after the death of King Solomon, so that the city could reach its water supply in safety when it was under attack.**

c1000 BC Capture of Jerusalem
c970-931 BC Reign of Solomon
945-725 BC 22nd Dynasty
945-924 BC Reign of Sheshonk I, his campaign in Palestine
931-910 BC (Israel) Reign of Jeroboam I
931-913 BC (Judah) Reign of Rehoboam
913-911 BC (Judah) Reign of Abijah
911-870 BC (Judah) Reign of Asa
910-909 BC (Israel) Reign of Nadab
909-886 BC (Israel) Reign of Baasha
886-885 BC (Israel) Reign of Elah
885 BC (Israel) Reign of Zimri (7 days)
885-874 BC (Israel) Reign of Omri
883-859 BC Revival of Assyria, reign of Ashurnasirpal
9th and first half of 8th century BC Egypt weak
874-853 BC (Israel) Reign of Ahab; Elijah
858-824 BC (Assyria) Reign of Shalmaneser III; 853 BC battle at Qarqar; 841 BC Shalmaneser defeats Hazael, King of Damascus
852-841 BC (Israel) Reign Jehoram; Elisha
841-814 BC (Israel) Reign of Jehu
783-745 BC Assyria weak
c753 BC Founding of Rome
750 BC (Israel) Amos and Hosea
c750 BC Rivalry between 22nd Dynasty and 23rd Dynasty
754-727 BC (Assyria) Reign of Tiglath-pileser III; 732 BC he destroys Damascus
732-724 BC (Israel) Reign of Hoshea
726-722 BC (Assyria) Reign of Shalmaneser V
721-705 BC (Assyria) Reign of Sargon II; 721 BC he captures Samaria

3 · *THE FALL O*

THE KINGDOM

My friend had a vineyard
on a fertile hillside.
He dug the soil, cleared it of stones,
and planted choice vines in it.
In the middle he built a tower,
he dug a press there too.
He expected it to yield grapes, but sour grapes
were all that it gave.
(Isa 5:2)

Faith and Nationalism

The next 400 years saw the Near and Middle East in turmoil. The Hebrews were exiled, their kingdoms destroyed. Only the southern people retained their identity, aided by the prophets who used the experience of national disaster to explain their religious inheritance, and eventually returned to Palestine.

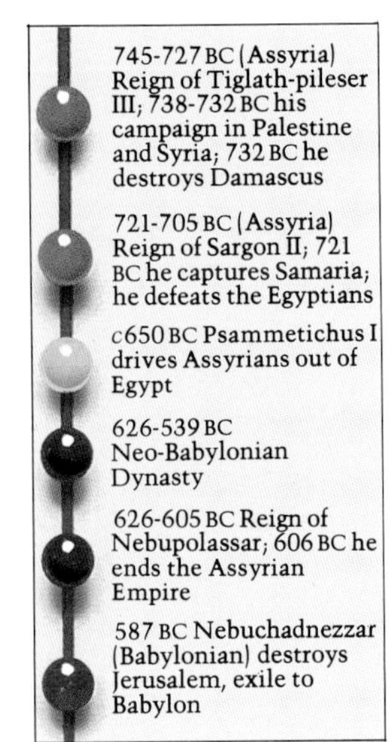

745-727 BC (Assyria) Reign of Tiglath-pileser III; 738-732 BC his campaign in Palestine and Syria; 732 BC he destroys Damascus
721-705 BC (Assyria) Reign of Sargon II; 721 BC he captures Samaria; he defeats the Egyptians
c650 BC Psammetichus I drives Assyrians out of Egypt
626-539 BC Neo-Babylonian Dynasty
626-605 BC Reign of Nebupolassar; 606 BC he ends the Assyrian Empire
587 BC Nebuchadnezzar (Babylonian) destroys Jerusalem, exile to Babylon

From the end of the tenth century BC, when the united Hebrew kingdom of David and Solomon split up, to the end of the sixth century BC, when the exiled Hebrews returned to rebuild their ruined country, the Near and Middle East were a turmoil of shifting power patterns, as Egypt was finally eclipsed, and three great Mesopotamian powers in succession took control of the area. As the main international routes passed through the narrow land of Palestine, between the Syrian Desert and the Great Sea (Mediterranean Sea), the Hebrews were caught in the age-old dilemma of small nations trying to survive when the great international powers fought each other.

During these centuries each of the Hebrew kingdoms was destroyed. When the northern kingdom of Israel was overthrown in 721 BC by the Assyrians, its people were deported never to return. But although the southern kingdom of Judah was destroyed in 587 BC by the Babylonians and its people deported, they managed to retain their national identity and return to start again in Palestine after nearly 50 years of exile. Much of the Old Testament was shaped during this period, for the Hebrews' records of events in their two kingdoms formed the basis for the historical books. It was at this time that the Hebrew historians edited the nation's traditions of the times of the patriarchs, the great escape from Egypt and the settlement of Palestine. The experience of national disaster provided a framework for understanding the pattern of the nation's relationship with the God who had made them the people of his covenant.

A succession of outstandingly influential and independent religious teachers, the Hebrew prophets, helped to form the national understanding of its religious inheritance and point to the relevance of its religious beliefs in the turmoil of historical events. The first of these were Elijah and Elisha. They lived in the ninth century BC and their actions are recounted in the Books of Kings. However, the prophetic movement continued with men whose teaching was recorded either by themselves or by their followers. They included Amos, Isaiah, Jeremiah, and Ezekiel. More would teach and write immediately after the return from exile, but the most influential were active as the Hebrew monarchy declined into corruption and was eventually extinguished between the eighth and sixth centuries BC.

Other major influences in Hebrew religious understanding were less conspicuous than the prophets but nevertheless provided the people with their main religious resources. These were the traditions of worship which eventually focused on the Temple in Jerusalem, the evolving insights of Hebrew law, the popular expressions of religion which had been passed down in the songs, and the expressions of folk wisdom in proverbs and poems, found in such books as Psalms, Proverbs and Ecclesiasticus.

There was no distinction between the secular and the sacred aspects of everyday life. Hebrew religious insights developed in response to the actions first of the Assyrians, as they expanded their empire from its base in Mesopotamia to the rest of the Middle and Near East during the eighth century BC, then of the Babylonians, as they destroyed the Assyrian empire at the end of the seventh century BC and briefly ruled for 70 years. Finally the Persians overthrew the Babylonians in the latter half of the sixth century BC. Additionally, for a brief period of four years, from 609 BC to 605 BC, Egypt tried to take control, but the Babylonians were too strong for them. Each power in turn left its deep imprint on the Hebrew people and influenced the ways in which the Hebrews expressed their religion.

BELOW AND RIGHT **The faith and resilience of ordinary people kept the nation alive as successive great powers conquered their land.**

The Laws in Context

The whole body of Hebrew law is placed within the context of the covenant given to Moses. And even when changing social and political conditions necessitate amending the laws of the society, they must always be controlled by the principles of the covenant, in which personal values are determined by God.

The Old Testament places the whole body of Hebrew law within the context of the escape from Egypt, the exodus, and the account of the covenant given to the people by God during the journey from Egypt to Palestine. Every detail of the law is formulated as the direct command of God to the Hebrew people, revealed to Moses. It covers religious, criminal and civil law. However, the contents suggest that the collection of laws in the Books of Exodus, Leviticus, Numbers and Deuteronomy represents developments in Hebrew law over the course of several centuries, from before the escape from Egypt in the thirteenth century BC to the later period of the Hebrew monarchy in the seventh century BC.

As the political institutions of the Hebrew state changed to meet new situations, so too the laws of the society changed, but they were always to be controlled by the principles of the covenant, in which personal values were determined by God. The covenant was meant to create 'a kingdom of priests, a consecrated nation' (Exod 19:6), and the nation's laws set out the pattern of relationships between the members of such a group. Placing them all within the covenant narratives made this point in a concrete way.

Two main forms of law are contained in the collection. The first took the form of direct, absolute commandments, referred to in Hebrew as *debarim* (literally 'words') of God. These include the Ten Commandments (Exod 20:1-17 and Deut 5:6-22). The second was law cast in the form of precedents or cases, usually referred to as *mishpatim* (Exod 21:1). This type of case law is the normal form for other ancient legal codes of the Near and Middle East, and it clearly consists of the precedents built up in the courts, whether at local level or in the courts of the central national authority. However, the Hebrew laws of absolute divine command seem to be unique, and it has been suggested that they reflect the fundamental principles of Moses himself.

Different collections of law can be distinguished among the laws as they now appear, two of which are 'codes' of law covering the whole range of Hebrew life. The first, the Book of the Covenant (Exod 20:22-23:19), is placed within the description of the divine revelation at Mount Sinai, immediately after the Ten Commandments, and is probably the oldest collection of Hebrew case law, dating from at least the early years of the monarchy. The second consists of the major part of the Book of Deuteronomy (Deut 12-26), and is thought by many to be a revision of the earlier Book of the Covenant made at a time when the Hebrew monarchy had become so corrupt that it could no longer be trusted to administer the principles of the covenant. This Deuteronomic Code was the stimulus for the reform carried out by King Josiah in 622 BC (2 Kgs 22-23) during the final years of the monarchy. Two other collections are the Holiness Code (Lev 17-26), which applies the principles of 'holiness' – being in a fit state to participate in religious rites – to a wide range of religious, civil and criminal offences, and the Priestly Code which legislated for the priesthood and all that was needed for the official sacrificial expression of the Hebrew religion which was centred on the Temple.

During the monarchy, the law was administered by the kings themselves, royal officials, and the elders of local Hebrew communities who continued the traditions of justice handed down from the period before the monarchy. Increasingly, the official priesthood became responsible for all law, secular and religious, until at times, after the Babylonian exile, all state authority was in the hands of the priests of the Temple at Jerusalem.

Exod 20:1-17, 20:22-23:19, 25-31:18, 34:10-26, Lev 1-7, 11-16, 17-27, Num 5-6, 8-10:10, 15, 18-19, 28-30, Deut 5:1-22, 12-26.

'See, today I set before you life and prosperity, death and disaster. If you obey the commandments of Yahweh your God that I enjoin on you today, if you love Yahweh your God and follow his ways, if you keep his commandments, his laws, his customs, you will live and increase, and Yahweh your God will bless you. . . . But if your heart strays, if you refuse to listen, if you let yourself be drawn into worshipping other gods and serving them, I tell you today, you will most certainly perish. . . . I call heaven and earth to witness against you today: I set before you life or death, blessing or curse. Choose life, then, so that you and your descendants may live, in the love of Yahweh your God, obeying his voice, clinging to him.' (Deut 30:15-19)

BELOW **Despite the failure of the Hebrew kings, it was during their times that the Hebrews developed such a strong sense of identity, expressed by the 'Star of David', and symbols of prosperity.**

Dangers from the East

After several centuries of ruthlessly dominating Mesopotamia, Assyria forged through Syria and Palestine in the 8th century BC, going on to conquer the entire 'fertile crescent' from the Persian Gulf to Lower Egypt. But it was overthrown by the rebellious Babylonians who, in turn, were defeated by the Persians.

From the time of the Hebrew escape from Egypt in the mid-thirteenth century BC to the collapse of the united Hebrew kingdom of Kings David and Solomon in the mid-tenth century BC, the centre of power in Mesopotamia lay far to the south, well away from Palestine. This, together with Egyptian weakness during the same period, created a power vacuum which gave the Hebrews the opportunity to conquer Palestine and dominate the neighbouring small countries. For a brief time after the death of Solomon in *c*931 BC, the Egyptians regained control of the area, but civil war in Egypt ended their expansionist ambitions again, and opened the way for the Assyrians.

Assyria lay around the upper reaches of the River Tigris, now mainly northern Iraq. Its name is a Greek form of Asshur, the oldest Assyrian city and its original capital, but the Assyrian kings administered their empire from various cities on the River Tigris, with Nineveh, north of Asshur, eventually becoming the capital of the Assyrian Empire when it was at its most powerful. The Assyrians were always under threat from the peoples of the eastern mountains which separate Mesopotamia from the Caspian Sea. But a succession of Assyrian kings, from the tenth century BC, broke the power of the mountain kingdoms and of the Babylonians to the south and made them vassal kingdoms whose kings ruled only by permission of the greater power. The Assyrians then set about expanding west towards the Great Sea (Mediterranean Sea). King Ashurnasirpal II (883-859 BC) took tribute from the Phoenician ports of Tyre and Sidon, and from Arvad further north on the Syrian coast. He did not take Damascus, the capital of Syria, and seems to have been more concerned to bring the Phoenician trading ports under his control.

The next Assyrian king, Shalmaneser III (858-824 BC), found himself facing a coalition of 11 kings from Syria, Lebanon and Palestine, who withstood him in battle at Qarqar on the River Orontes about 854 BC. The Assyrian Chronicle, recorded on clay tablets, some of which still exist, lists Kings Ahab of the Hebrew kingdom of Israel, Hadadezer of Damascus and Irhuleni of Hamath among the rulers who opposed Shalmaneser, and naturally records it as a great Assyrian victory in which the River Orontes was dammed by the numerous enemy dead and the Assyrians captured chariots, horses and armour. There is no mention of the battle in the Old Testament (which goes into great detail about Ahab's reign), for the Hebrew author of the First Book of Kings was mainly concerned with the religious struggle against the Canaanite religion, and with Hebrew relationships with Syria. In view of later Assyrian advances into Palestine and Egypt, the Battle of Qarqar must have prevented further Assyrian expansion at that time.

However, the Palestinian kingdoms were beginning to feel the effects of Assyria. Assyrian records state that King Jehu of Israel (841-814 BC) paid tribute of silver and gold, and vessels made from gold, to Shalmaneser III, while a later Assyrian king, Adadnirari III (810-783 BC), boasted that he subjugated Phoenicia, Israel, Edom and the Philistine territory. This probably means that Assyrian patrols penetrated down the coastal road and the major leading route, the King's Highway, but did not stay to occupy the area, for there is no mention in the Old Testament of Assyrian presence during this period. The situation soon changed, however. After a brief period of Assyrian weakness in the eighth century BC, King Tiglath-pileser III (745-727 BC) restored Assyrian power and began to drive the frontiers of the empire into Syria and Palestine.

Tiglath-pileser III gave the Assyrian expansion the new impetus which was to enable it even to incorporate Egypt into the Assyrian Empire. The Assyrians were the first power to make an empire of the 'fertile crescent' from the Persian Gulf to Lower Egypt, with the international routes through Palestine as its main arteries. The new Assyrian king restored the territories temporarily lost through the pressures of the mountain peoples to the east of the Assyrian homeland, made himself king of the puppet kingdom of Babylonia at the south-eastern end of Mesopotamia, and secured his western frontiers by capturing Damascus, the capital of Syria, usually called Aram in the Old Testament. He was now poised to thrust south along the coastal route towards Egypt.

In the eighth century BC, the small kingdoms of Palestine and Syria had apparently expected again to withstand the Assyrians by a coalition, as they had done at the Battle of Qarqar a century earlier, but this time their efforts were to fail disastrously. The Book of Isaiah records the attempts of Syria and the northern Hebrew kingdom of Israel to form a coalition of Palestinian states. They were resisted by the southern Hebrew kingdom, Judah, whose King Ahaz preferred to sit out a siege of Jerusalem by his two small northern neighbours rather than allow himself to be drawn into war against Assyria (Isa 7). Tiglath-pileser easily overran the feeble coalition, made northern Palestine part of an Assyrian province, which also included most of the kingdom of Israel, and accepted tribute from the kingdom of Judah. Despite the fierce opposition of the prophet Isaiah, King Ahaz of Jerusalem turned his small Hebrew kingdom into an outpost of Assyrian power and brought Assyrian religious rites into the Temple to prove his loyalty.

The next Assyrian King, Shalmaneser V (726-722 BC), suppressed the rebellious Hebrews of the kingdom of Israel. His successor, Sargon II (721-705 BC), ensured that there would be no more opposition from them by deporting the Hebrew population from the capital, Samaria, and the surrounding districts, and bringing in settlers from other parts of the Assyrian Empire to replace them. This was to be the end of the northern Hebrew tribes as an identifiable entity. Sargon also destroyed the mountain kingdom of Urartu, east of Assyria, and thereby unwittingly removed the buffer state between Mesopotamia and the fierce nomadic tribesmen of the Caucasus area and beyond, who were to play a large part in the overthrow of Assyria a century later when Scythian hordes flooded into Mesopotamia from the north and east.

At Sargon's death, his successor, Sennacherib (704-681 BC), had to deal with revolts throughout the empire, and the Palestinian states looked to Egypt for help. There had already been a skirmish between Assyrians and Egyptians in Sargon's reign at Raphia on the Egyptian frontier, but now an Egyptian army marched north and was defeated in 701 BC at Eltekeh on the branch of the coastal road from Gaza to Joppa. The King of Judah, Hezekiah (715-687 BC), had attempted to throw off Assyrian rule and reform his country's religion, but he too submitted and paid tribute despite the Assyrian failure to capture Jerusalem (2 Kgs 18-20). Sennacherib also dealt with the Babylonians by destroying Babylon. During his reign the Assyrian capital was moved to Nineveh.

Assyria finally defeated the Egyptians under Esarhaddon (680-669 BC), captured Memphis, the capital in Lower Egypt, and forced the Egyptian King Taharka of the 25th Dynasty (*c*715-663 BC) to flee to Upper Egypt. The Assyrians never managed to maintain effective control of their Egyptian possessions, for by now their empire was too extended to keep subdued. Incursions of Scythians through the eastern mountain passes about 625 BC were the signal for rebellion by the Babylonians again, this time supported by the Medes to the east of southern Mesopotamia in what is now western Iran. Assyria fought bitterly for several years, but finally succumbed to the Babylonians around 612 BC.

The Assyrians struck terror into the hearts of the people of the Near and Middle East to a degree beyond any power before them, and arguably anyone since. The Assyrian military machine was utterly ruthless with any area where it experienced resistance, as is shown by the Assyrian records and the great victory plaques on which they carved a pictorial description of their campaigns. The plaques show Assyrian troops besieging fortified cities, such as the Palestinian city of Lachish, which fell to Sennacherib in 701 BC and was made Assyrian army headquarters for the campaign. Ramps have been built against the city walls, captives are being led away, prisoners are impaled on stakes outside the walls and the heads of prisoners taken earlier are fired over the walls from catapults. It confirms the bitter poems of triumph written by the Hebrew prophet Nahum to celebrate and vividly describe the fall of the Assryian capital, Nineveh, when 'the bloody city, stuffed with loot' received the kind of treatment it had meted out to so many others: '... the chariots storm through the streets, they hurtle across the squares, they look like blazing flames, ... the crack of whip, the rumble of wheels, galloping horse, jolting chariot, charging cavalry, flash of swords, gleam of spears, a mass of wounded, hosts of dead, countless dead, they stumble over the dead' (Nah 2-3).

The Assyrian army was conscripted by means of a census taken in provincial districts, and organized in multiples of 10s and 50s. Originally it was only called out in times of war or for the forced labour needed for state building works, but a standing army was maintained from the time of Tiglath-pileser III (745-727 BC) as Assyrian campaigns reached down into Palestine and the inevitable rebellions broke out whenever there was a change of king. Unlike the Egyptians, the Assyrians did not employ mercenaries, but made conquered territories contribute their quota of men for the army. The bulk of the army consisted of infantry, but in the ninth century BC the cavalry was organized as an independent division, and a pioneer corps was formed in the following century to provide military roads and the specialized skills needed for siege operations. Bridges of boats spanned rivers, and there are Assyrian relief carvings of soldiers swimming rivers with the aid of inflated animal skins. The soldiers were armed with conical helmets, round shields, spears, bows and swords, and tackled fortified positions behind the protection of large, light structures of plaited reeds.

The extent and thoroughness of Assyrian records, written on clay tablets and carved in stone, point to a well developed administrative system. By the time of the Palestinian campaigns there were army commanders for the eastern and western provinces of the empire, and a commander of the royal bodyguard. Governors were assigned to the provinces created as the army advanced, to organize taxation, tribute and the levies for the army and for forced labour. There is evidence that countries which cooperated with the Assyrians, as the southern Hebrew kingdom of Judah did, were unmolested provided there was no suspicion of disloyalty.

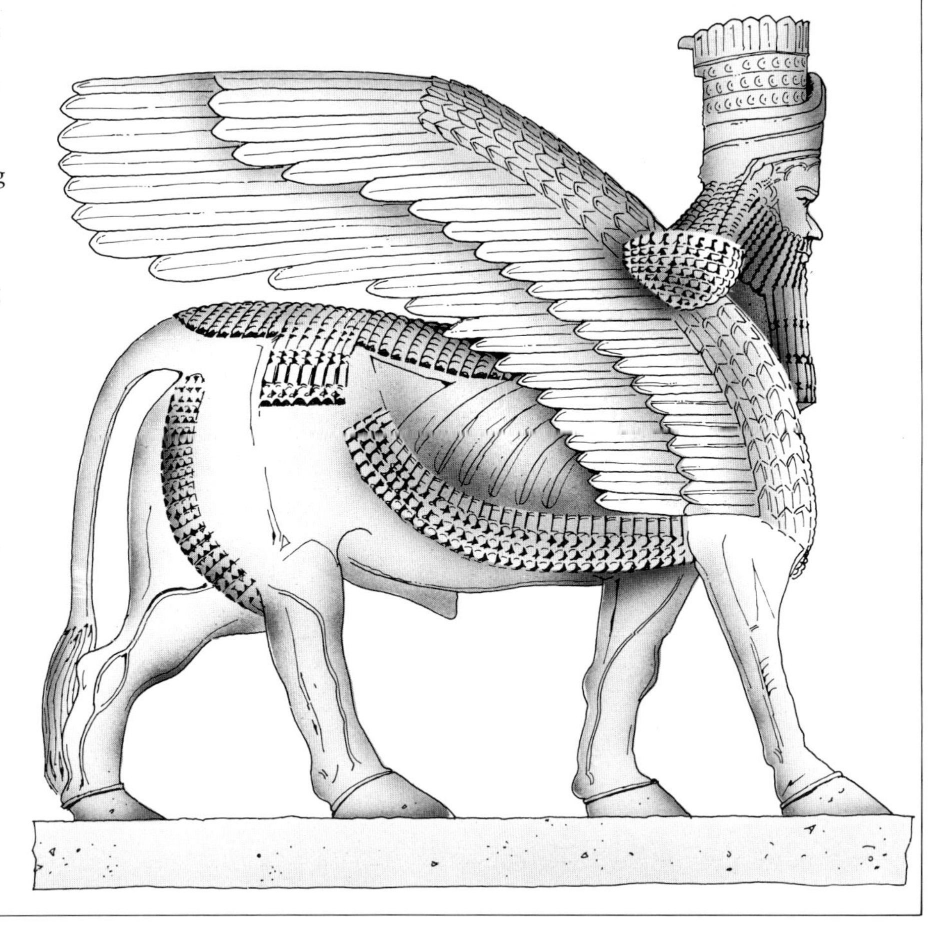

BELOW **The great winged bulls which guarded the gateways of the Assyrian royal palaces are powerful symbols of Assyrian might and ruthlessness.**

BELOW **The northern Hebrews established a new capital at Samaria, after their break with Jerusalem. They soon became so strong that they thought they could stop the Assyrian advance into Palestine. The Assyrians crushed them in 721** BC.

BELOW **The coastal plain through Palestine was of great strategic importance, as it was the only route between Egypt and the rest of the Near and Middle East. Every great power in the ancient world fought for control of Hebrew territory.**

745-727 BC (Assyria) Reign of Tiglath-pileser III; 738-732 BC his campaign in Palestine and Syria; 732 BC he destroys Damascus

721-705 BC (Assyria) Reign of Sargon II; 721 BC he captures Samaria; he defeats the Egyptians at Raphia

601 BC Babylonians defeated in Egypt

c650 BC Psammetichus I drives Assyrians out of Egypt

626-539 BC Neo-Babylonian Dynasty

626-605 BC Reign of Nebupolassar; 606 BC he ends the Assyrian Empire

587 BC Nebuchadnezzar (Babylonian) destroys Jerusalem, exile to Babylon

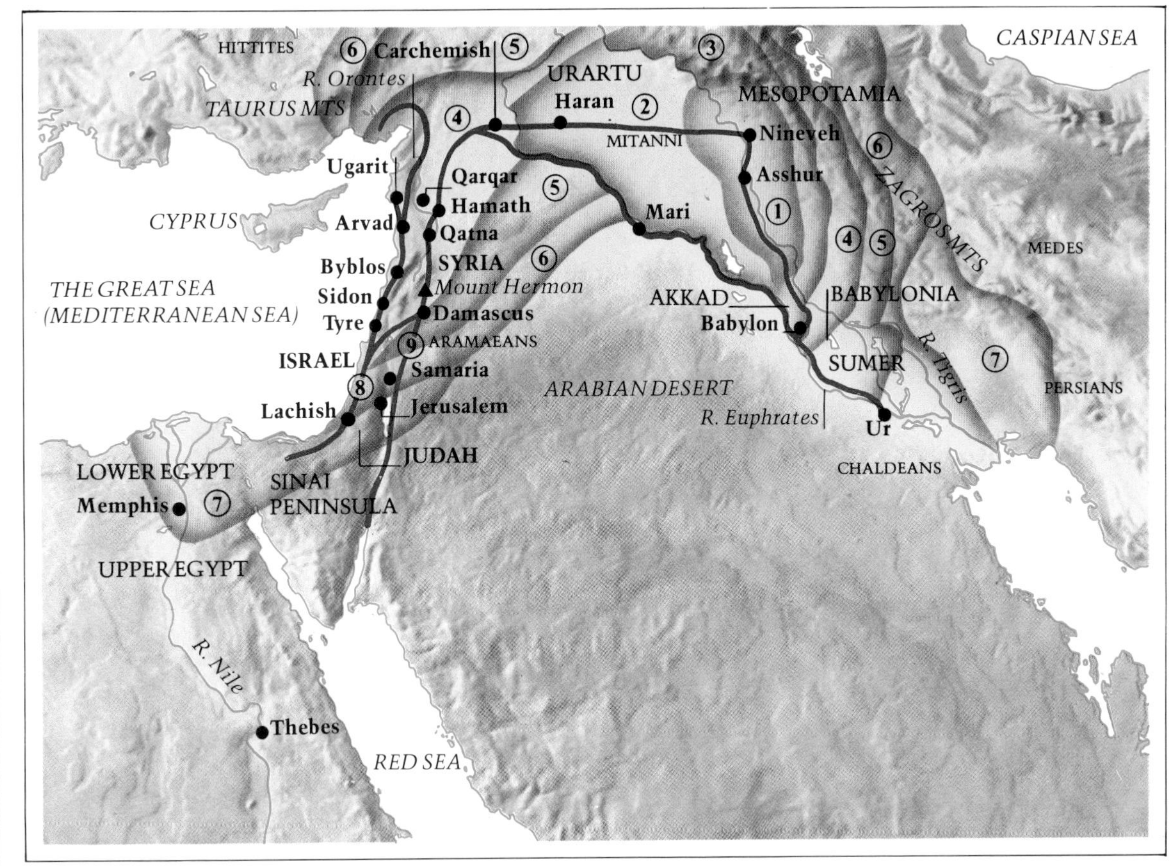

1. Nucleus of Assyrian Empire
2. Expansion in 14th century BC
3. Expansion in 13th century BC
4. Expansion in 9th century BC
5. Expansion during reign of Tiglath-pileser III (745-727 BC)
6. Expansion during reigns of Sargon II (721-705 BC) and Sennacherib (704-681 BC)
7. Expansion during reigns of Esarhaddon (680-669 BC) and Ashurbanipal (668-630 BC)
8. The Way of the Sea
9. The King's Highway

— Main trade routes

ASSYRIAN EXPANSIONISM **Over 700 years, the empire grew into a vast domain, gradually stretching deep into Asia Minor and curving through the 'fertile crescent' as far as Egypt.**

BELOW **The city of Lachish was the scene of one of the most dramatic sieges by the Assyrians in 701 BC. It was a key fortress in southern Palestine guarding the approaches to Egypt.**

Assyrian religion followed the traditional religious beliefs and practices of the rest of Mesopotamia, of which the most dramatic remains are the great temple-towers or ziggurats which have been found from the upper waters of the River Euphrates to the Persian Gulf. Sometimes they had a straight staircase leading to the sanctuary at the top, and sometimes a spiral ramp winding round the outside. The Assyrians had a complex pantheon of 600 planetary and stellar deities, and 300 gods of the land of the dead, with complex liturgies and a creation myth which included a tradition of a universal flood. Divination, particularly from the livers of sacrificed animals, was a prominent feature, as were magical formulae to guard against the many demons thought to threaten everyday life. The national god Asshur was a god of war, symbolized by an archer within a winged disc.

The region of Babylonia lay near the south-eastern end of Mesopotamia, and took its name from the principal city, Babylon, on the River Euphrates. The Babylonians figure prominently in the Old Testament, and 'Babylon' became an instantly recognizable symbol of any great oppressive power for both Jews and Christians. However, their actual period of domination after they had defeated the Assyrians only lasted some 80 years. They were overthrown by the Persians in 539 BC.

The Old Babylonian Empire had collapsed under pressure from the Kassites in the middle of the second millenium BC, ending a period of power and splendour, of which the law code of Hammurabi from the eighteenth century BC is ample evidence. The

Babylonians were rebellious subjects of the Assyrians for five centuries, repeatedly brought to heel and at one time ruled directly by Assyrian kings. As with most of the nations of the Near and Middle East, they were a mixture of peoples, and, during the main part of the Assyrian ascendancy, the dominant Babylonian group were Aramaean nomads from the Syrian Desert who invaded Babylonia during the early part of the first millenium BC and merged with the Chaldeans of southern Babylonia. One of these Aramaen Chaldean chiefs seized power in 721 BC and opposed Sargon II of Assyria. That attempt at Babylonian independence failed, but another Aramaean descendant, Nabopolassar, successfully rebelled in 626 BC and began the war which was to end some 20 years later with the Babylonians in control of the Assyrian Empire.

The destruction of Assyria was assisted by incursions of wild, disorganized mounted tribesmen through the eastern mountains, who fanned out through Mesopotamia and the Near East as far as the Egyptian frontier. These hordes were part of the Scythian migration which has left its mark on Hebrew and Christian writings as the armies of Gog and Magog (Ezek 38-39; Rev 20:8). Their tombs have yielded delightful gold, silver and bronze figures of wild animals and mounted horsemen. They settled nowhere, but their threat, combined with the Babylonian rebellion, forced the Assyrians to withdraw their troops from Palestine. This gave the Hebrews one of their brief periods of freedom from foreign control which lasted from 625 BC to 609 BC, before first the Egyptians and then the Babylonians once more took over Palestine.

The Babylonians under King Nabopolassar destroyed the Assyrian capital Nineveh in 612 BC. Then his successor, Nebuchadnezzar (605-562 BC) defeated the Egyptian King Necho II (609-594 BC) of the 26th Dynasty far up the River Euphrates at Carchemish, now known as Cerabulus, on the borders of modern day Syria and Turkey. At first the Babylonians did little to interfere with the only remaining Hebrew kingdom, Judah, and allowed King Jehoiakim (609-598 BC) to continue to rule the country from its capital, Jerusalem. However, the Hebrews intrigued to get the Egyptians to free them from Babylonian rule, but this failed and in 598 BC the Babylonians captured Jerusalem after a siege which had lasted for three months.

The king and his leading officials were deported to Babylon, where they were allowed to live in some comfort at Babylonian state expense, and another descendant of King David, Zedekiah (597-587 BC) was placed on the throne of Judah. The intrigues with Egypt continued, and in 589 BC the Babylonians again attacked Jerusalem. This time they besieged it for more than two years. There was a brief respite when an Egyptian army tried to relieve the city but the Babylonians finally destroyed it. The king and people were deported to Babylonia, where the Hebrew monarchy ended. The territory was lost to Hebrew control for the 48 years of the exile, until the Babylonians in their turn were overthrown by the Persians in 539 BC.

Babylonian religion, like that of the Assyrians, was the common religion of Mesopotamia. It included temple-towers, a vast pantheon of gods, divination and belief in a multitude of demons.

BELOW **The Assyrians left vivid records of their kings' activities, both in peace and war, on great plaques. The war murals depict the details of military techniques and ruthlessness, but the domestic scenes show how the kings were waited upon by servants.**

The Egyptian Renaissance

Strong and independent once again, Egypt drove the Assyrians out of the country about 650 BC, led by a king of the 26th Dynasty, which, ironically, had been installed by the occupiers. The dynasty pursued a sophisticated foreign policy and lasted until defeated by the Persians well over a century later.

- Frontiers
- Cultivated areas
- Main trade route
- Main internal routes
- 22nd Dynasty (Tanis)
- 23rd Dynasty (Leontopolis)
- Princes of the 22nd-23rd Dynasties
- Independent chiefs
- Realm of the West (Sais)
- Disputed areas
- Heracleopolitan territory
- Hermopolitan territory
- Theban territory

Egyptian politics during the first four centuries of the first millenium BC were a chaos of competing and simultaneous rulers reflecting the decline of this great power. The only exception was the comparatively stable reign of Sheshonk I (945-924 BC), who reimposed Egyptian rule over Palestine and returned to Egypt with the gold furnishings of the Temple in Jerusalem and of the royal palace. Thus, for the most part, Egypt was in no state to control events in the Near East.

The first major cause of dissension was the office of high priest at Thebes. This was one of the wealthiest and most influential positions in Egypt, carrying military power as well as the authority of the official state religion. During the 22nd Dynasty, the kings tried to reduce the power of the Theban priests in Upper Egypt, who ruled with little regard for the royal authority based on Lower Egypt. But Thebes proved to be too strong to control, and the 23rd Dynasty (*c*828-712 BC) brought in a period when there were numerous kings in various parts of Egypt, recognized in different major centres such as Thebes, Hermopolis, Heracleopolis, Leontopolis and Tanis. In 770 BC, King Kashta from Nubia, south of Syene (Aswan), added Upper Egypt as far north as Thebes to his dominions and became the first king of the 25th Dynasty. There had been a brief 24th Dynasty, consisting of two kings who ruled from Sais in the western part of the Nile Delta, near what is now Alexandria, for 12 years from about 724 BC.

It was to this former great power that the Hebrew kings looked for protection from the Assyrians, who destroyed the northern Hebrew kingdom of Israel in 721 BC. For a brief period the Nubian rulers of Egypt managed to impose a form of central control over the whole country. This stability at home enabled them to help Judah against the Assyrians in 701 BC. In 674 BC an Assyrian attack was repulsed at the Egyptian frontier itself. In 671 BC the Assyrians won through, occupying all Lower Egypt for two years. They were then forced out of Memphis, recaptured it in 667 BC with the aid of Egyptian rulers of the eastern delta region, were forced out yet again, and finally, about 660 BC, plundered the whole country from the delta to the Nubian borders in the south.

The 26th Dynasty was founded in 663 BC by the rulers from the eastern delta who had supported the Assyrians in their attacks on the rest of Egypt, and were then given the throne of all Egypt. The second king of this dynasty, Psammetichus I (663-609 BC), eliminated the many local rulers and imposed unity on the whole

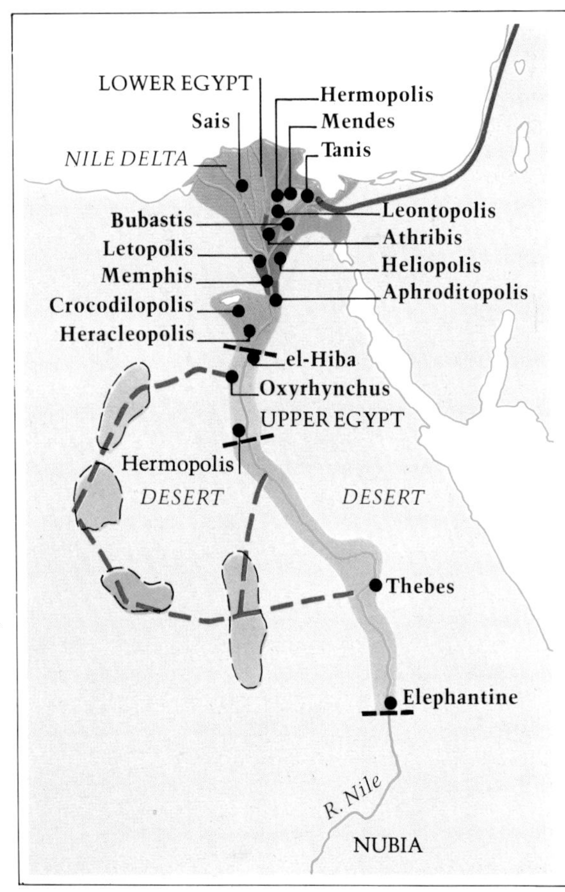

EGYPTIAN INSTABILITY **The chaos caused by civil war between the 22nd and 23rd Dynasties was complicated by minor disputes.**

RIGHT **Healthy oxen in ancient Egypt indicated a period of prosperity. The country produced a wide range of crops.**

country with the aid of mercenary troops. Psammetichus pursued a sophisticated foreign policy, based on maintaining a balance of power in the Near and Middle East which would prevent any one people from becoming strong enough to threaten Egypt again. Around 650 BC, he succeeded in driving the Assyrians out of Egypt and then supported the Babylonians against Assyria until the Babylonians began to overwhelm the Assyrians. He then supported the Assyrians from about 620 BC, and his successor, Necho II (609-594 BC), took an army to the aid of the Assyrians in their final desperate struggles against the Babylonians after the fall of the Assyrian capital, Nineveh. Necho was himself defeated by the Babylonians at Carchemish in 605 BC. However, on his march north he had defeated and killed the independent Hebrew King Josiah of Judah when the Judeans foolishly withstood the Egyptian march north at Megiddo, ending one of their rare periods of independence from foreign rule.

In 601 BC the Babylonians tried to take Egypt, but Necho repulsed them at the frontier, and Judah became the furthest outpost of the Babylonian Empire. The 26th Dynasty survived until 525 BC, ruling an independent Egypt until the Persians captured it with little effort after their brilliant defeat of the Babylonians.

RIGHT **Egyptian civilization supported a wide range of professions under the patronage of the kings. Surviving monuments, such as this statue of a chief physician, show what status and wealth such men could gain. He is holding a representation of the temple of Neith, a goddess in the Egyptian pantheon.**

The World in 600 BC

There were now pockets of Greek colonies in the Mediterranean and the East, and Phoenicia was building up extensive trading links. But it was Persia which soon would challenge Egypt and Babylonia. In India a crucial religious realignment was taking place, while petty internal wars were irritating China's rulers.

By 600 BC other parts of the eastern Mediterranean were beginning to affect the peoples of the Near and Middle East. The need for iron was forcing Egypt to trade far from its frontiers. The Egyptian King Necho II (609-594 BC) established trading fleets in both the Red Sea and the Great Sea (Mediterranean Sea), and tried to link the two with a canal which the Persians completed a century later. The Greeks figure for the first time in Egyptian affairs – as mercenaries.

The history of Greece during the eighth and seventh centuries BC is obscure, but by the end of the seventh century in the many small Greek states the old monarchical governments had been replaced by rule by the land-owning classes. Details differ for the various independent states, but this period saw Greek expansion throughout the Mediterranean world. Unlike other expansions, the Greek colonists did not represent a Greek conquest of the areas where they settled. Each colony was independent of its mother city, although linked to it by bonds of tradition and loyalty. The epic poems, the *Iliad* and *Odyssey* by Homer, probably give a picture of Greek culture during this period, although they recount events from earlier times – iron replaces bronze, new formations, tactics and armour are developed for warfare, the cities are administered by magistrates, and elaborate temples built for the gods. From the first recorded Olympic Games in 776 BC, such regular festivals gave a form of unity to the scattered Greek communities, which was reinforced in the middle of the sixth century BC when the annual Panathenea festival featured dramatic readings of Homer. About 600 BC the beginnings of Greek philosophy can be seen in the works of Thales (*c*625-(*c*625-585 BC), Anaximander (*c*610-546 BC) and Anaximenes (*c*585-524 BC), who all came from the Greek colony of Miletus in Asia Minor.

The traditional date for the founding of Rome on the Palatine hill is 753 BC. Again according to tradition, it was ruled by seven kings until the last one was driven out and the republican form of government established about 509 BC. The Phoenician colony of Carthage dominated the central Mediterranean and provided the Phoenicians with a central base for their many trading posts in Sicily, Sardinia, Corsica and the western Mediterranean coast of Africa. Massilia (now Marseilles) was founded by Greeks about 600 BC. By

BELOW **The Greeks never gained lasting political control over their neighbours, but Greek art, drama, poetry, architecture, philosophy and political theory had enormous influence.**

Developed cultures
Nomadic pastoralists
Hunter-gatherers
Farmers
Nomadic pressures and farmer expansion
Trade

NURTURING THE GREAT CULTURES **Persia was about to eclipse the might of Babylonia, which had overthrown the Assyrians. But the Mediterranean region was flourishing too – Phoenician ships were dominating trade, Greece was nearing the height of its political maturity and its colonies were beginning to spread the Greek ideal. In Italy, Rome was slowly consolidating its position. Trade routes to India and the Far East linked the ancient world's civilizations and ended their isolation.**

539 BC the Persians had conquered the Babylonian Empire and had wiped out any remaining Assyrian strongholds.

In the India of 600 BC the northern area, conquered by Indo-European immigrants, had settled down into 16 or more independent states, which were eventually to be absorbed into one kingdom. The religious writings of the Vedas were followed by others which expanded their traditions and commented on them. In these later writings – the Brahmanas, Aranyakas and the Upanishads – Indian religion, including the caste system, was formulated more systematically. This religion, Hinduism, is not a polytheism worshipping many gods, but a pantheism, in which the ultimate reality is Brahman and the world (including individuals) is merely the expression of Brahman's self-limitation.

Two Indian religious leaders were born about this time, Vardhamana, the founder of Jainism, and Siddhartha Gautama, who became the Buddha, the 'Enlightened One', and founder of Buddhism. Each began from traditional elements in Indian religion, but developed them so distinctively that they became religions separate from Hinduism.

In China, the Chou rulers had been forced by nomadic pressures to move their capital eastwards to Luoyang in 771 BC, and until 481 BC events are carefully recorded in official chronicles. The period is marked by small-scale wars between more than a 100 petty states within the empire of the Eastern Chou. Iron casting developed for weapons and agricultural implements. Bronzes show a stylistic development from flat interlace decoration to full three-dimensional detail.

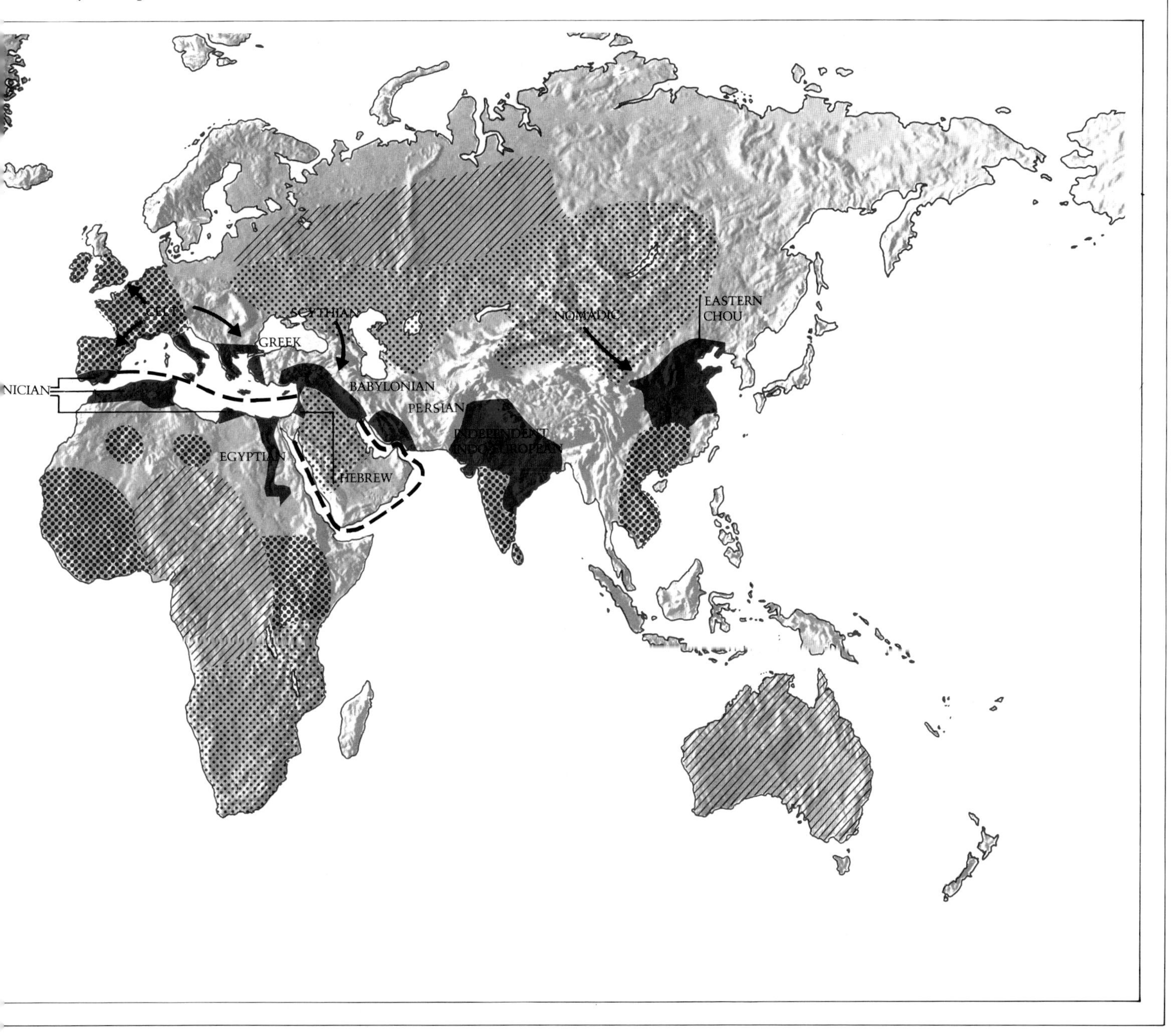

Assyrian Domination

For two centuries, a constant state of civil war existed between Israel and Judah, and each had continual skirmishes with neighbours. But the Assyrians who attacked in the 8th century BC were quite a different kind of foe. They destroyed the northern kingdom and Judah survived only as a small puppet state.

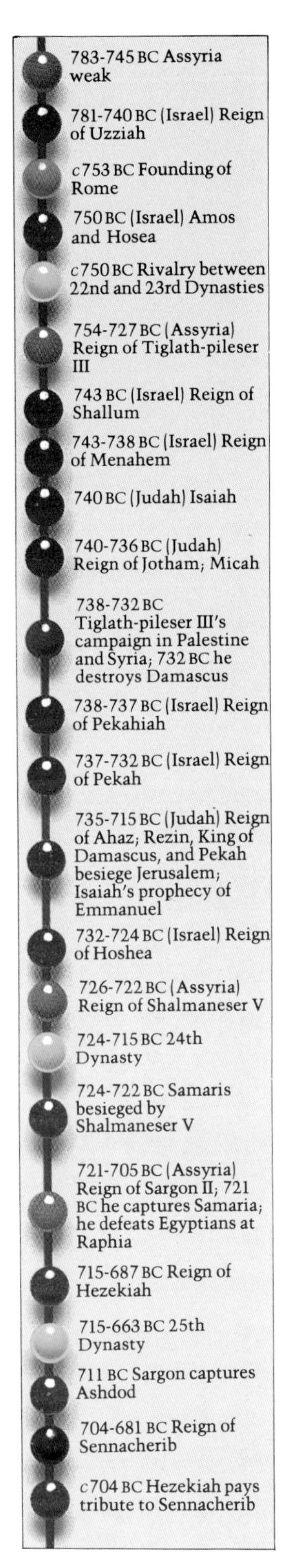

783-745 BC Assyria weak
781-740 BC (Israel) Reign of Uzziah
c753 BC Founding of Rome
750 BC (Israel) Amos and Hosea
c750 BC Rivalry between 22nd and 23rd Dynasties
754-727 BC (Assyria) Reign of Tiglath-pileser III
743 BC (Israel) Reign of Shallum
743-738 BC (Israel) Reign of Menahem
740 BC (Judah) Isaiah
740-736 BC (Judah) Reign of Jotham; Micah
738-732 BC Tiglath-pileser III's campaign in Palestine and Syria; 732 BC he destroys Damascus
738-737 BC (Israel) Reign of Pekahiah
737-732 BC (Israel) Reign of Pekah
735-715 BC (Judah) Reign of Ahaz; Rezin, King of Damascus, and Pekah besiege Jerusalem; Isaiah's prophecy of Emmanuel
732-724 BC (Israel) Reign of Hoshea
726-722 BC (Assyria) Reign of Shalmaneser V
724-715 BC 24th Dynasty
724-722 BC Samaris besieged by Shalmaneser V
721-705 BC (Assyria) Reign of Sargon II; 721 BC he captures Samaria; he defeats Egyptians at Raphia
715-687 BC Reign of Hezekiah
715-663 BC 25th Dynasty
711 BC Sargon captures Ashdod
704-681 BC Reign of Sennacherib
c704 BC Hezekiah pays tribute to Sennacherib

For about two centuries after the death of King Solomon in *c*931 BC and the division of the united Hebrew kingdom into two independent ones, the greatest dangers to the Hebrew people came from within their own kingdoms. These dangers were both political and religious.

The two Hebrew kingdoms were in a constant state of civil war. The northern kingdom of Israel, around its capital of Samaria, grew in prosperity by controlling the main trade routes, while the southern kingdom of Judah was safe from its northern brethren, as its capital, Jerusalem, was almost impregnable if resolutely defended. However, its territory comprised the less prosperous parts of Palestine. Egypt exercised general control of the area, but mainly left the Hebrews to their own devices.

The traditional Hebrew religion, having adapted to the new, agricultural way of life, was maintained at the ancient sanctuaries which were already religious centres when the Hebrews occupied Palestine. The chief of these were Beer-sheba, Hebron, Bethel, Shiloh, Shechem, Mount Carmel, and Mount Hermon. In addition, there were Jerusalem, with its Temple built by King Solomon to house the sacred Hebrew Ark of the Covenant, and Dan, which was probably an extremely ancient religious centre. It was made a Hebrew sanctuary by King Jeroboam I when he broke with his southern Hebrew brethren to found the kingdom of Israel in 931 BC. However, the source of later problems was that the Hebrews tended to accept the native Canaanite religion of Baal with its worship of the fertility gods and goddesses, and sacred prostitution at the 'high places'. In Canaanite religion, no moral censure or stigma was attached to sacred prostitution – sexual intercourse with priestesses or temple servants was viewed as a form of communion with the divine. The Baal religion, with its emphasis on fertility, was an essential part of agricultural life for many Hebrews. When kings married native Baal-worshippers, it was even recognized as an official religion, alongside the Hebrew covenant religion of Yahweh.

Despite the hostility between the two Hebrew kingdoms, the region grew in prosperity as it profited from the trade passing through their territory. But with the prosperity, and the acceptance of Canaanite social stratification, came stark inequality and injustice. The very shape of the towns changed as the wealthy enlarged their houses at the expense of the poor, and people sold their land and eventually went into slavery to their Hebrew neighbours to meet their debts.

In this situation a new group of religious teachers, the prophets, emerged. They were independent of the royal courts and the royal sanctuaries, including the Temple in Jerusalem, and – crucially – were prepared to denounce the kings and their religious officials whenever they showed signs of betraying the traditional Hebrew religion.

The prophets Elijah and Elisha stood out against the kings of the northern kingdom, Israel, during the reigns of King Ahab and his descendents (about 870-740 BC).

BELOW When the northern group of Hebrews broke away from Jerusalem's rule, they soon became more powerful than their southern brethren. The ruins of the ancient gate of their capital, Samaria, once led into a city greater than Jerusalem.

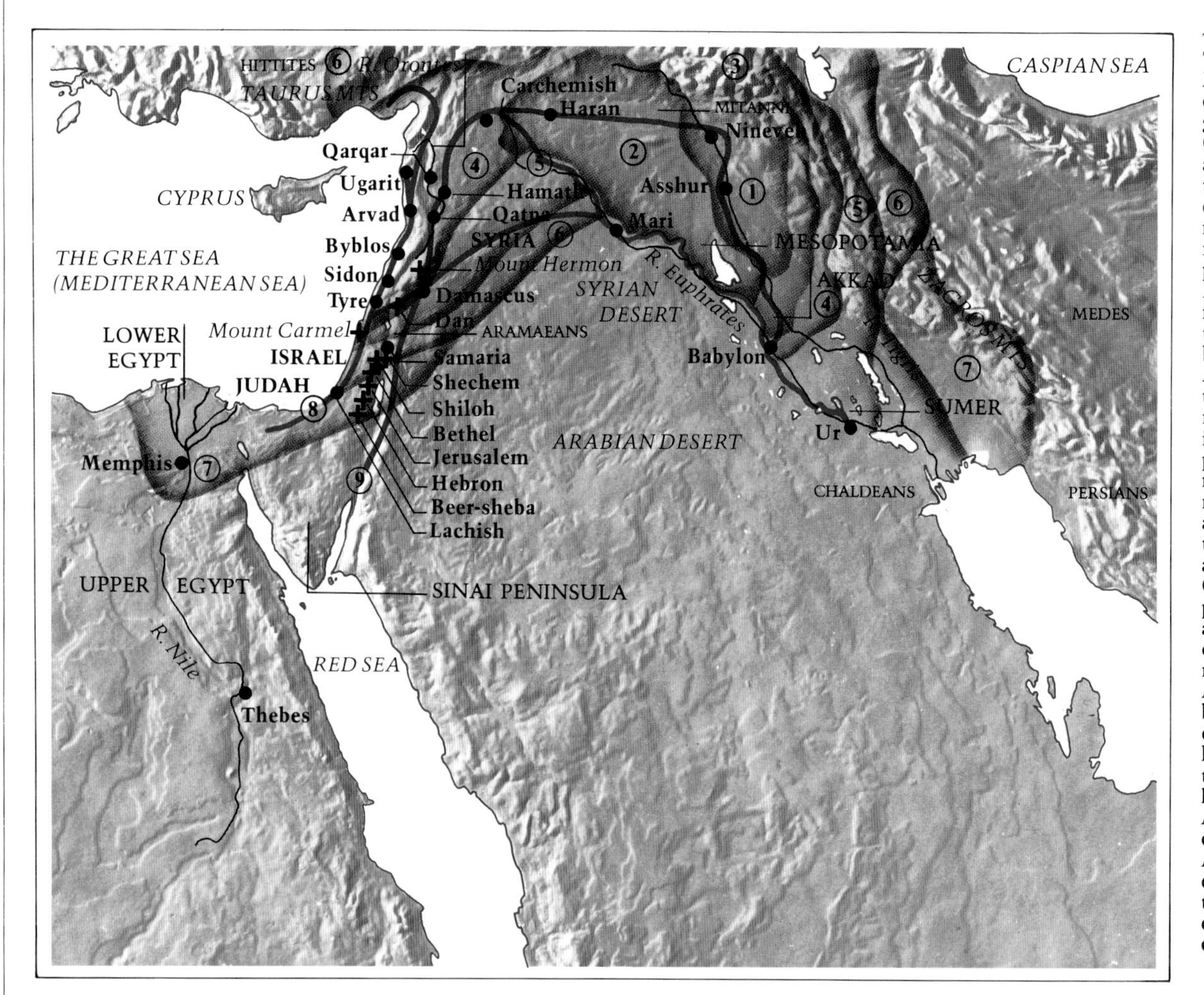

THE ASSYRIAN EXPANSION
The balance of power in Mesopotamia moved as one or other of the main cities gained control of the area. Overall control was always a precarious possession, for the region was at the mercy of the fierce tribes of the northern and eastern mountains, and subject peoples within Mesopotamia readily rebelled to sieze power themselves. There had been a period when the Assyrians were supreme at the end of the second millenium BC, but tribal invasions weakened their power. They recovered to regain control of their neighbours in the eleventh and tenth centuries BC, and then expanded to the west as far as the coast of the Great Sea, where they were poised to move on Palestine and Egypt. The small states of Syria and Palestine managed to check the Assyrians for a brief period, but their ruthless advance could not be stopped for long. Tiglath-pileser III thrust into Palestine, and his successors took the Assyrian advance on to capture Lower Egypt. Assyrian control of the empire was maintained through a ruthless policy of destruction and exile of all opponents.

(1) Nucleus of Assyrian Empire
(2) Expansion in 14th century BC
(3) Expansion in 13th century BC
(4) Expansion in 9th century BC
(5) Expansion during reign of Tiglath-pileser III (745-727 BC)
(6) Expansion during reigns of Sargon II (721-705 BC) and Sennacherib (704-681 BC)
(7) Expansion during reigns of Esarhaddon (680-669 BC) and Ashurbanipal (668-630 BC)
— Main trade routes
(8) The Way of the Sea
(9) The King's Highway
+ Sanctuaries

The kings expropriated their subjects' land, gave official recognition to the Baal religion, and gained or maintained their thrones by ruthless murder and terrorism. Finally Jehu ended this bloody dynasty. Having been anointed king by Elisha, Jehu made the elders of Samaria pile the severed heads of the descendants of Ahab and his queen, Jezebel, on either side of the city's main gate as proof of their loyalty

The first of the prophets who left books of their teachings was Amos, a shepherd from the southern kingdom who in the eighth century BC denounced the northern kings and their people at the royal sanctuary of Bethel. A little later Hosea, a native of the northern kingdom, continued Amos's work and taught that the Hebrew God, Yahweh, and not the Canaanite fertility gods, was the real source of his people's prosperity. Perhaps even more importantly, Hosea introduced the concept of God's faithfulness and tender love towards his people and thus opened the way to a new understanding of the covenant.

The prophets warned that God would punish his own people if they were disobedient in any way. Frequently, God had exacted this punishment on the northern Hebrew kingdom through attacks by its neighbours. But Israel was not the only disobedient nation, and in the opening two chapters of Amos the prophet tactfully reviews Israel's enemies before coming to the crimes of Israel itself. Amos lists Damascus, Gaza, Tyre, Edom, Ammon, Moab and even Judah as other peoples who have angered God. The worst punishment of all came in the latter half of the eighth century BC. Then Assyria began its drive south into Palestine to secure its frontiers with Egypt.

The Assyrian advance had been checked temporarily in 853 BC at Qarqar by an alliance of 12 kings, including the king of Israel. Although the Assyrians boasted of victory, they made no permanent advance until the accession of King Tiglath-pileser III (745-727 BC) brought in a new era of Assyrian expansion. By 738 BC Tiglath-pileser had exacted tribute from the states of Syria and northern Palestine as far as the coast, as punishment for an attempt to stop his advance. Israel was included in this, and her king, Menahem (743-738 BC), raised the 1,000 talents of silver by taxing all the landowners in the kingdom.

When Menahem of Israel died in 738 BC, his son Pekahiah only survived for two years before being assassinated by one of his own officers, Pekah, who took the throne and reigned for five years, from 737 BC to 732 BC. Menahem's fierce taxation to satisfy Assyria had aroused deep bitterness, and Pekah of Israel joined King Rezin of Damascus to oppose the Assyrians again.

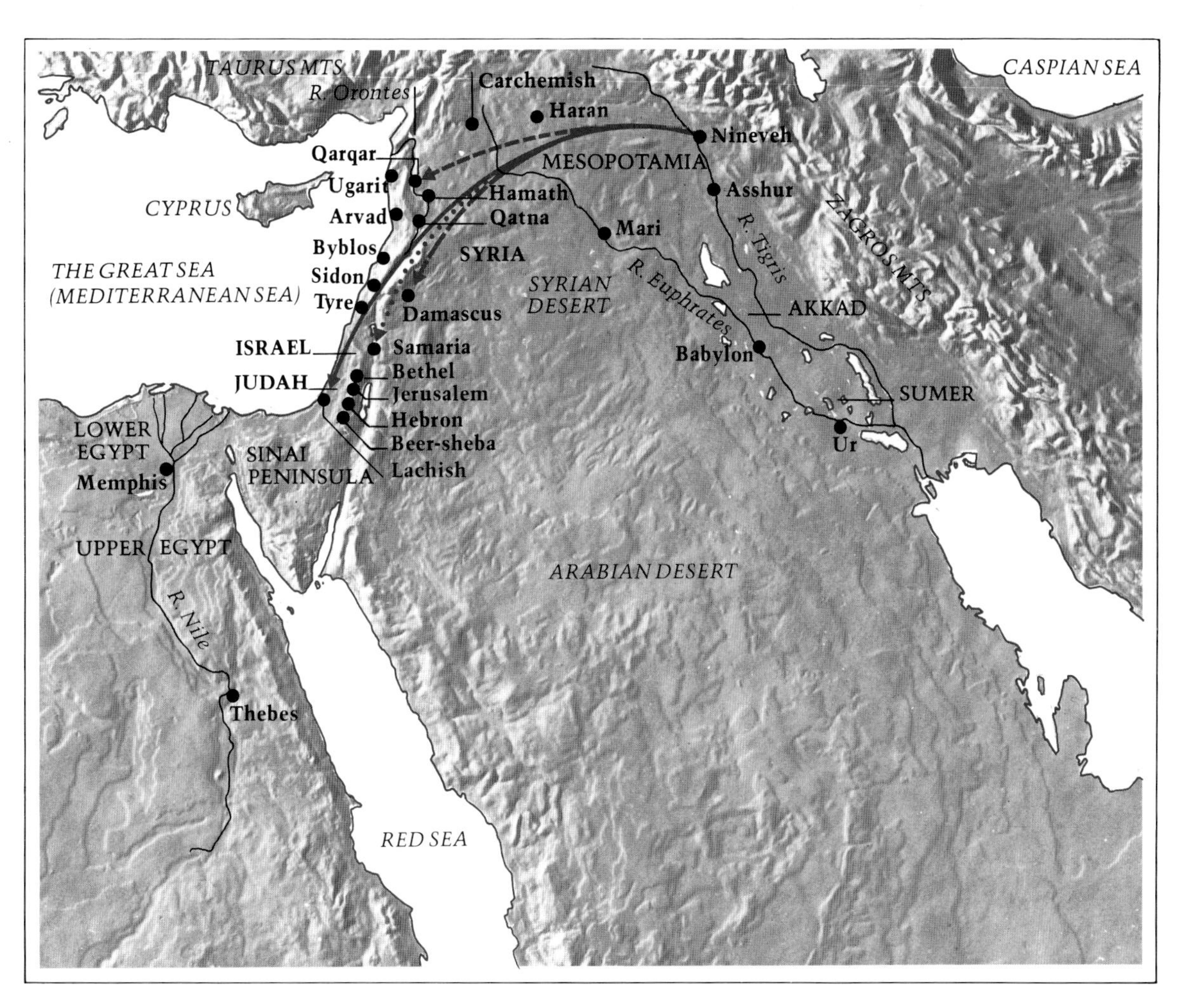

ASSYRIA AND PALESTINE
When the Assyrians had secured control of the whole of Mesopotamia, they thrust westwards along the international routes to Asia Minor and Egypt. They aimed to occupy the Syrian and Palestinian area, but an alliance of the area states, including Israel and Judah, slowed down the Assyrian advance in 853 BC. In the next century, the Assyrians pushed to the Egyptian border, and their campaigns exposed the deep enmity between the two Hebrew kingdoms, Israel and Judah. Syria and the Hebrew kingdom of Israel were destroyed in the campaigns of 732 and 721 BC. People from the Babylonian area were settled on the land. The other Hebrew kingdom, Judah, became an ally of the Assyrians. Despite protests from the prophet Isaiah, Judah rebelled, and even survived an Assyrian siege of Jerusalem in 701 BC, but the Assyrians kept control until about 625 BC.

They needed the support of the southern Hebrew kingdom of Judah to strengthen their armies, but King Ahaz of Judah (735-715 BC) would have none of it, so Rezin and Pekah attacked Jerusalem to force Ahaz from his throne and replace him with a king who would cooperate with them against the Assyrians.

These are the circumstances which bring the prophet Isaiah into public affairs for the first time. King Ahaz of Judah could see that the Assyrians were too powerful to be stopped, so he decided to become a puppet king of the Assyrians. To prove his loyalty to his new masters, he decided to impose the Assyrian religion on the Hebrews of Judah alongside the traditional Yahweh religion. Isaiah urged Ahaz to do nothing – neither join the alliance between Rezin and Pekah nor go out of his way to befriend the Assyrians. When Ahaz refused his advice, Isaiah gave him the famous 'Immanuel' warning, and went on to give the first explicit 'messianic' teaching, expressing the hope that God would give his people a faithful and just king (Isa 7-12).

The Assyrian king Tiglath-pileser moved south in 734 BC, down the coastal road through Philistia to the Egyptian border. In the following two years, 733-732 BC, he marched south again to take Damascus, Galilee as far as Megiddo, and most of the Jordan Valley. The people's leaders were deported and the territory made into three provinces of the Assyrian Empire. The kingdom of Israel was reduced to the mountain area around Samaria, and King Pekah was murdered by his successor, Hoshea (732-724 BC), who submitted to Assyria and paid tribute.

When Tiglath-pileser died in 727 BC, King Hoshea of Israel rebelled and tried to obtain Egyptian help, but the new Assyrian king, Shalmaneser V (726-722 BC) attacked Samaria, the capital of Israel. He did not live to complete the siege, but his successor, Sargon II (721-705 BC) captured the city and deported at least the leading people of the kingdom. In time they were replaced by people from other parts of the Assyrian Empire, who brought with them their own religious traditions. Judah survived as a puppet kingdom of the Assyrians, but the northern Hebrew kingdom, Israel, was finished.

After the fall of the kingdom of Israel, Samaria was made an Assyrian province, but King Sargon II of Assyria had to return to Syria and Palestine at least three more times to quell rebellions supported by Egypt. At one stage he even compelled the Egyptians to pay him tribute. His death in 705 BC was the signal for widespread rebellions. Hezekiah, King of Judah (715-687 BC), who succeeded Ahaz, the king who had first submitted to the Assyrians, also rebelled. Hezekiah

2 Kgs 1-14, Amos, Hos, 2 Kgs 15-20, Isa 1-12; 14-23; 29-32; 36-39, Mic 1-3.

'Come now, let us talk this over,
says Yahweh.
Though your sins are like scarlet,
they shall be as white as snow;
though they are red as crimson,
they shall be like wool.
'If you are willing to obey, you shall eat the good things of the earth.
But if you persist in rebellion,
the sword shall you eat instead.'
The mouth of Yahweh has spoken. (Isa 1: 18-20)

Tiglath-pileser III's route in 734 BC

Tiglath-pileser III's route in 733 BC

Tiglath-pileser III's route in 732 BC

Assyrian provinces

Shalmaneser V and Sargon II expansion and provinces

Sennacherib's route in 701 BC

Egyptian army defeated, 701 BC

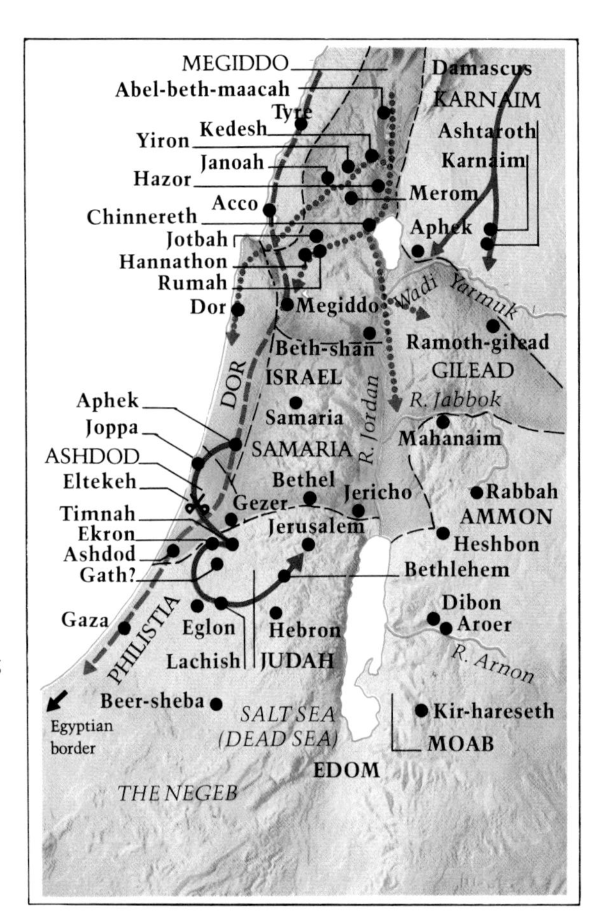

THE BATTLES FOR JUDAH

Under Tiglath-pileser III, the Assyrians made regular military excursions into the Hebrew kingdoms. In 734 BC, they drove down the coast into Egypt, and then conducted a major campaign against the Syrians in 732 BC, capturing Damascus. The campaign into Palestine in 701 BC was directed against Judah, which had survived by total submission when the Assyrians destroyed Samaria in 721 BC. Although supported by the Egyptians, Hezekiah was forced to pay tribute to the Assyrians.

attempted to sweep away the Assyrian religious practices introduced by Ahaz, and it seems that he was at least partly successful, for the Second Book of Kings records that 'No king of Judah after him could be compared with him, nor any of those before him' (2 Kgs 18;4-5).

Hezekiah realized that the Assyrians would not allow him to become independent, for he strengthened the fortifications of Jerusalem and constructed the famous tunnel which still carries water within the ancient limits of Jerusalem, through the solid rock from the Gihon spring to the Pool of Siloam. The taxation system was reorganized, and a census taken to prepare for expanding the army. The kingdom's borders were extended to include the old Philistine area, which commanded the coastal road as it approached Egypt, for Hezekiah could count on Egyptian intervention and would want to ensure that the Assyrians did not cut off the Egyptian route before an army could even reach Palestine. The Hebrews celebrated a solemn Passover of renewal of the covenant and rededication of the nation to God.

Sargon II of Assyria was succeeded by his son Sennacherib (704-681 BC). He began his reign by swiftly crushing a rebellion in Babylon, and then moved to remedy the situation in Palestine at the other extreme of the Assyrian Empire. In theory there were several routes available to him, but the only practicable one for an army was the road through Hamath and Qarqar, near the head of the River Orontes in Syria. On his way, Sennacherib received tribute as expressions of loyalty from Arvad, Byblos, Sidon and Ashdod on the coastal route, and from Ammon, Moab and Edom on the King's Highway east of the Jordan Valley and the Salt Sea (Dead Sea). The effect was to isolate the Hebrews of Judah. Next the Assyrians took the port of Joppa and the fortified towns which lay inland. The army moved on south along the two parallel branches of the coastal road, to secure Philistia, and then swept inland to capture Lachish, the strongest city of the Shephelah. Relief carvings discovered at the Assyrian capital, Nineveh, show the assault on Lachish in great detail, and after its capture Sennacherib made it his headquarters for the conquest of the rest of southern Palestine.

Jerusalem was besieged, and during the siege an Egyptian army managed to penetrate as far as Eltekeh, just south of Joppa, before it was defeated. But the Assyrians did not capture Jerusalem. The exact reasons for this are obscure. However, King Hezekiah paid a heavy tribute to Sennacherib, which may have satisfied the Assyrian king. Sickness swept through the Assyrian army (2 Kgs 19:35) and the Babylonians were again in rebellion. Sennacherib returned to Nineveh, and Judah gave no more trouble. When King Hezekiah of Judah died in 687 BC his son, Manasseh (687-642 BC), cooperated fully with the Assyrians.

The prophet Isaiah played a large part in advising Hezekiah during the rebellion (2 Kgs 18-20; Isa 36-39), and stiffened the king's resistance.

LEFT AND INSET **Archaeological exploration in Jerusalem arouses strong opposition because of the sacred associations every part of the ancient city has for Jews, Christians and Muslims. Nevertheless the State of Israel and many foreign sources finance extensive work carried out under strict supervision. Since the State of Israel gained control of the whole of Jerusalem, much work has been done to the old city and around the Temple area. Of particular interest are the discoveries about the extension and fortification of the city during the period of the Hebrew kingdom. King Hezekiah transformed the water supply and greatly strengthened the city's defences in anticipation of the Assyrian campaign against his kingdom. Much of his work can still be seen, despite subsequent destructions of the city.**

FAR LEFT **Although much later in date, fortifications in Jerusalem still give an idea of how strong the city could be made in ancient time. Whenever it was vigorously defended, Jerusalem was able to withstand long sieges by great military powers.**

The Great Hebrew Reform

During Josiah's reign as king of Judah, the Assyrians withdrew in order to fight the Babylonians at home. Josiah quickly destroyed all traces of the Baal cult and the Assyrian religion, and began to restore Hebrew rule over the whole of Palestine, meanwhile reaffirming the covenant basis of the laws.

2 Kgs 21-23, Zeph, Jer 1-12, Deut, Nah.

The king then had all the elders of Judah and of Jerusalem summoned to him, and the king went up to the Temple of Yahweh with all the men of Judah and all the inhabitants of Jerusalem, priests, prophets and all the people, of high or low degree. In their hearing he read out everything that was said in the book of the covenant found in the Temple of Yahweh. The king stood beside the pillar, and in the presence of Yahweh he made a covenant to follow Yahweh and keep his commandments and decrees and laws with all his heart and soul, in order to enforce the terms of the covenant as written in that book. All the people gave their allegiance to the covenant. (2 Kgs 23: 1-3)

BELOW LEFT AND RIGHT The great reform of Hebrew religion in 622 BC was based on a law book found in the Temple. King Josiah purged the nation of its corrupt worship and renewed its covenant with God – by force if any opposed him. He laid the foundations for Judaism as a religion of law. The books of the law became the most sacred symbols of the Hebrew religion in the synagogues after the exile in Babylon.

King Sennacherib of Assyria (704-681 BC) stabilized the situation in the far western provinces of the empire by his campaign in Palestine at the end of the eighth century BC, and his successors Esarhaddon (680-669 BC) and Ashurbanipal (668-630 BC) were able to extend Assyrian control into Egypt. Lower Egypt was captured from King Tirhakah of the 25th Dynasty about 671 BC, and, some three years later, the Assyrians were able to advance up the River Nile beyond Thebes, which they sacked about 663 BC. Their attacks put an end to the 25th Dynasty, and the following one was founded by Delta kings who at first supported the Assyrians. King Manasseh of Judah (687-642 BC) is mentioned in an Assyrian list of those who paid tribute to Esarhaddon, together with the kings of Arvad, Byblos, Tyre, Ashdod, Ashkelon, Gaza, Samaria, Beth-Ammon, Moab and Edom. The list helps show the limits of the Hebrew kingdom of Judah, which was allowed to continue as a puppet kingdom of the Assyrians. The Assyrian attacks on Egypt effectively stopped any hopes the Palestinian states might still have had of help from that quarter.

The long reign of King Manasseh over Judah was a period of complete subjection to the rule and culture of Assyria. The Second Book of Kings paints a bleak picture of religious conditions during his reign. The Canaanite religion was restored with its 'high places', altars to Baal, sacred prostitution, and images of the Canaanite gods set up in the Temple in Jerusalem. Assyrian astrological religion was prominently encouraged with its worship of 'the whole array of heaven' and prophecies. He practised human sacrifice in the terrible Molech rites of child sacrifice, first definitely mentioned in connection with his grandfather, King Ahaz (2 Kgs 21: 2-9).

The major parts of the Book of Deuteronomy probably drew in northern traditions secretly collected together during Manasseh's reign, to provide a programme of reform if the opportunity arose. It is basically a codification of a wide range of Hebrew laws from the previous six centuries, presented as if they had all been delivered by Moses as the Hebrew people were poised to invade Canaan after the escape from Egypt. By this means, the editors were able to show how the Mosaic religion of the covenant with Yahweh, the saviour God of the Hebrew people, could be applied to the contemporary task of bringing the nation back to God again. The attempts of Hezekiah, King Manasseh's father, had shown that no reform was possible while Assyria was in control of Palestine, so the programme of reform had to be kept hidden.

Manasseh died peacefully, his son Amon succeeded to the throne of Judah but only reigned for two years (642-640 BC) before he was assassinated, to be succeeded in his turn by his son Josiah (640-609 BC) aged only eight. It was during his reign that the opportunity for reform occurred.

At the death of King Ashurbanipal, about 630 BC, the Assyrian Empire began to disintegrate. Egypt had already broken away under the leadership of King Psammeticus of the 26th Dynasty. The province of Babylon successfully rebelled under the leadership of Nebupolassar (626-605 BC), the first king of the Neo-Babylonian Empire. Hordes of Scythians, the nomadic horsemen from the steppes of western Asia, swept into Mesopotamia from the mountains behind the Assyrian homeland. The Assyrians withdrew their troops from Palestine to meet the crisis in Mesopotamia. They never returned.

The reform of Judah began as soon as the Assyrians withdrew, though it is not entirely clear how the various phases of it proceeded under King Josiah. He was barely 18 years old when Ashurbanipal of Assyria died,

but it would appear that he quickly began to restore Hebrew rule over the whole of Palestine, and in the end he managed to extend his control to cover the two Assyrian provinces to the north of Judah – Samaria and Megiddo. This included Upper and Lower Galilee, and the territory east of the Jordan Valley from Lake Chinnereth (the Sea of Galilee) in the north to the Salt Sea (the Dead Sea) in the south.

Josiah's religious reforms reached their climax in 622 BC and were connected with restoration work on the Temple in Jerusalem. The prophet Jeremiah had been active for about three years by then, and at first saw the incursions of the Scythian hordes as punishment from God for Hebrew unfaithfulness. In fact, the Scythians do not appear to have troubled Judah, although they reached the Egyptian borders (Jer 1:13-16).

During repairs to the Temple, the Book of the Law was found. Undoubtedly it was the codification of Hebrew law which now forms the major part of the Book of Deuteronomy which makes explicit the covenant basis of Hebrew law. Undoubtedly, many of the laws in Deuteronomy were enacted long after Moses' time, to meet new needs and changes in the Hebrew way of life. The book presents old and new laws as direct commands made by God to Moses, when the people were waiting to enter Canaan after the escape from Egypt. Whenever it was written, probably during Manasseh's reign (687-642 BC), it made an ideal vehicle for reform, for it translated the general religious principles of the covenant into practical details covering the whole range of religious and secular life.

The religious reform was enforced throughout the territory controlled by King Josiah. The Second Book of Kings states that all traces of the Baal cult and the Assyrian religion were removed from the Temple in Jerusalem, and the buildings which housed the sacred prostitutes and the women who wove the vestments for the images of the gods were destroyed. The 'high places' were desecrated throughout the country, and wherever the royal reformers met opposition they killed the priests of the foreign cults. In particular, the shrine of Molech was destroyed which had been the place where children were sacrificed outside the southern walls of Jerusalem (2 Kgs 22-23).

Jeremiah accompanied the reformers in their purging of his native town of Anathoth, where his father was the priest of Yahweh, and was surprised when he too met with opposition (Jer 11:18-23). For Josiah not only destroyed the shrines of foreign religions throughout his territory, but also forbade sacrifices to the Hebrew God, Yahweh, anywhere except at the royal Temple in Jerusalem. The purpose was to control all expressions of religion to ensure that it reflected the principles of the covenant. However, it gave great powers to the Jerusalem priesthood and aroused bitter resentment in the rest of the country. From 622 BC on, the Temple was to be the only place where the main rites of the Hebrew religion could officially be performed. This is still the case, and explains why sacrifices are no longer a feature of the Jewish religion despite the extensive laws in the Old Testament commanding them to be offered. The Temple in Jerusalem no longer exists, and sacrifices may be offered in no other place.

Egypt made efforts to support Assyria during its final years, trying to maintain a balance of power in the Near and Middle East as Babylon rose to supremacy. An Egyptian army reached Mesopotamia in 616 BC, and King Necho II of Egypt took an army up the coastal road through Palestine in 609 BC to the aid of the Assyrians. Josiah attempted to stop the Egyptians at Megiddo, but he was defeated and killed.

704-681 BC Reign of Sennacherib; c704 BC he receives tribute from Hezekiah; 701 BC he defeats Egyptians at Eltekeh and captures Lachish

687-642 BC Reign of Manasseh

685-664 BC Reign of Tirhakah

680-669 BC Reign of Esarhaddon

663-609 BC Reign of Psammetichus I; c650 BC he drives the Assyrians out of Egypt

642-640 BC Reign of Amon

640-609 BC Reign of Josiah

c 630 BC Zephaniah

627 BC Call of Jeremiah

626-605 BC Reign of Nebupolassar

622 BC Religious reform

c612 BC Nahum

612 BC Nebupolassar and Cyaxares, king of Medes, take and destroy Nineveh

609-594 BC Reign of Necho II

609 BC Nebupolassar repulses the army of Necho II; 606 BC he ends the Assyrian Empire

BELOW Although Jerusalem owes so much to David and Solomon, its unique position as the sole centre of the Jewish religion was not secured until the reform of King Josiah, 300 years after Solomon's death. The Temple built by Solomon stood on the site of the present Muslim shrine, the Dome of the Rock, a beautiful structure which takes its name from its magnificent golden dome. In order to prevent corrupt practices entering the Hebrew religion, King Josiah made the Temple the only place in the world where Jews could legally offer the sacrifices essential for the full expression of Hebrew religion. The Temple was soon to be destroyed by the Babylonians, but after its restoration it was a centre of pilgrimage for Jews from every part.

INSET This young boy is at his bar mitzvah ceremony at the Wailing Wall in Jerusalem. At the age of 13, Jewish boys are initiated into the religious community and perform their first act as an adult – reading part of the Bible in Hebrew.

BELOW **The biblical writings associated with King Josiah's reforms connect the prosperity of the land with the people's faithfulness to the covenant and obedience to the divine laws.**

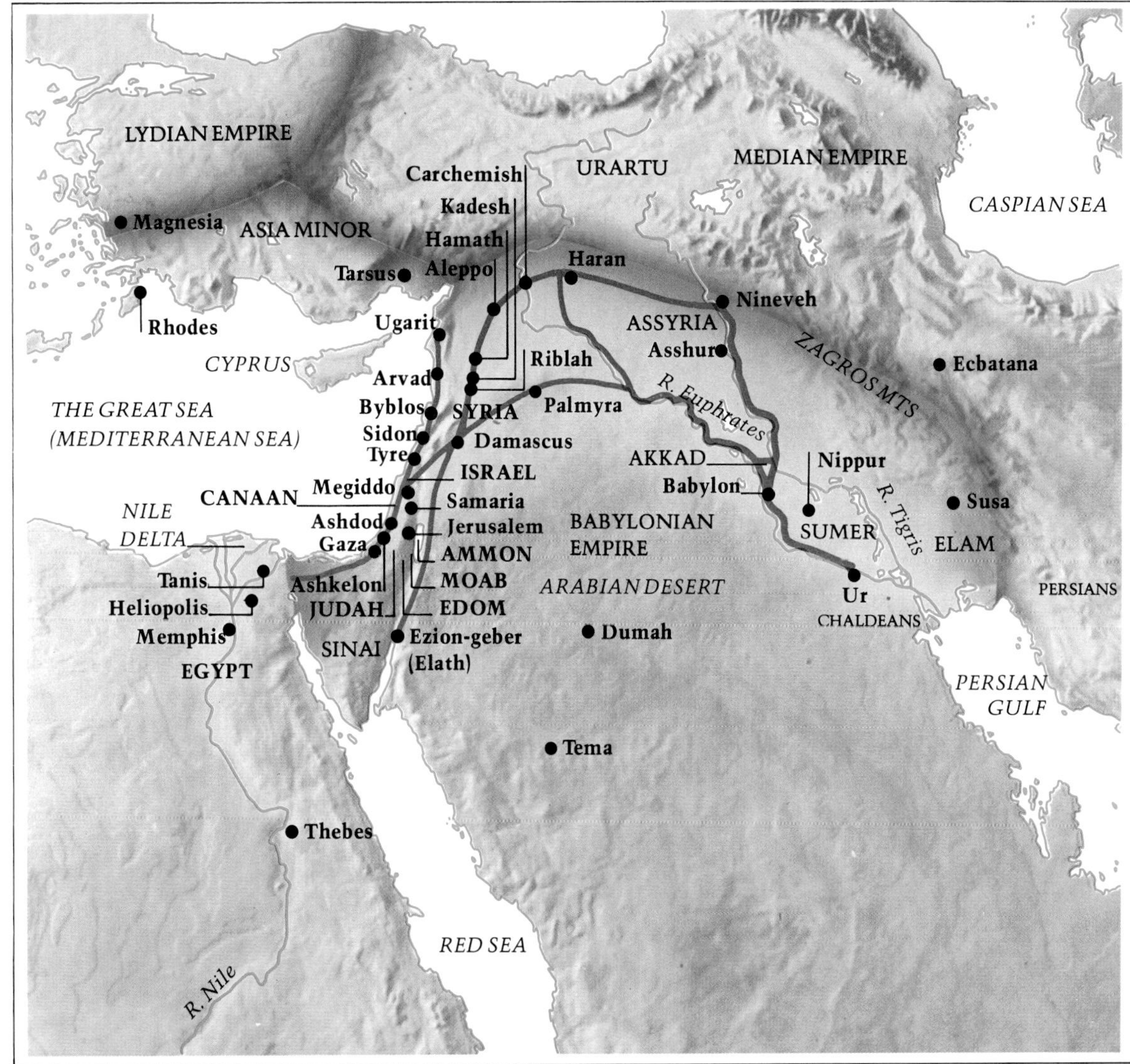

JOSIAH'S REFORM **When the Assyrian troops withdrew from Judah, during Josiah's reign, the Scythians attacked. But by 622 BC Josiah felt the time was ripe to repair the Temple in Jerusalem and free all former Hebrew territories from deviant religious practices. The wars to control the Near and Middle East raged for almost another 20 years. The Babylonians emerged as the victors after capturing the Assyrian capital, Nineveh, in 612 BC.**

Jerusalem Destroyed

The Egyptians defeated and killed Josiah, but were then forced out of Palestine by the Babylonians who exiled many Judean leaders When the Jerusalem Hebrews finally rebelled, their city and other fortified towns were destroyed and the people fled. It was to be nearly half a century before they returned.

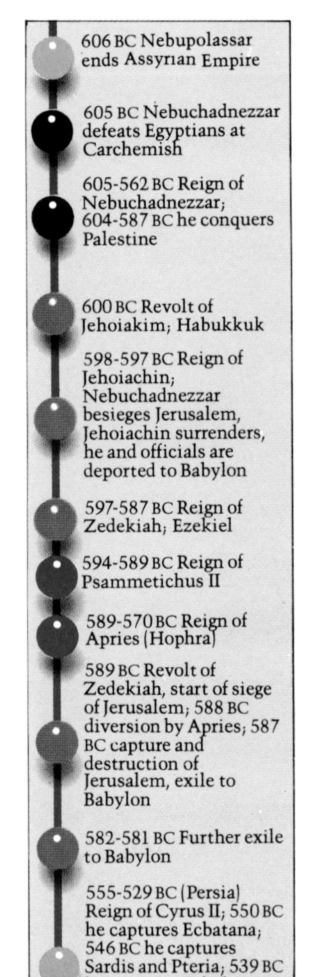

606 BC Nebupolassar ends Assyrian Empire
605 BC Nebuchadnezzar defeats Egyptians at Carchemish
605-562 BC Reign of Nebuchadnezzar; 604-587 BC he conquers Palestine
600 BC Revolt of Jehoiakim; Habukkuk
598-597 BC Reign of Jehoiachin; Nebuchadnezzar besieges Jerusalem, Jehoiachin surrenders, he and officials are deported to Babylon
597-587 BC Reign of Zedekiah; Ezekiel
594-589 BC Reign of Psammetichus II
589-570 BC Reign of Apries (Hophra)
589 BC Revolt of Zedekiah, start of siege of Jerusalem; 588 BC diversion by Apries; 587 BC capture and destruction of Jerusalem, exile to Babylon
582-581 BC Further exile to Babylon
555-529 BC (Persia) Reign of Cyrus II; 550 BC he captures Ecbatana; 546 BC he captures Sardis and Pteria; 539 BC he captures Babylon

King Josiah's death in 609 BC at the hands of the Egyptians was the beginning of the end for Judah and its capital, Jerusalem. Although the external appearance of Josiah's religious reforms was maintained for a while, their spirit died, and the prophet Jeremiah denounced king and people in the Temple courts (Jer 7). Josiah was succeeded by his son Jehoahaz (609 BC), who submitted to the Egyptians, but King Necho II of Egypt decided to install another son of Josiah, Jehoiakim (609-598 BC) and took the unfortunate Jehoahaz to Egypt.

Egyptian control of Palestine was only to last four years, for Necho had already been defeated by the Babylonians both at Carchemish and at Haran when he passed back through Palestine with his army in 609 BC. The capital of Assyria had fallen to the Babylonians in 612 BC, and the last Assyrian army was finally defeated and destroyed at Carchemish by Nebuchadnezzar in 605 BC. Later that year, Nebuchadnezzar (605-562 BC) succeeded Nebupolassar as King of Babylon, and began the Babylonian drive southwards through Palestine towards Egypt. King Jehoiakim of Judah submitted to him in 604 BC and paid tribute until 601 BC, when Nebuchadnezzar tried to invade Egypt and was repulsed with heavy losses.

Nebuchadnezzar returned to Babylon to recoup, and Jehoiakim saw this as the end of Babylonian control of Palestine, so he stopped paying the tribute and rebelled. The prophet Habakkuk probably belongs to this period, for he envisaged the Babylonians as God's agents who would return like the scorching winds from the eastern desert; '... if it comes slowly, wait, for come it will, without fail' (Hab 2:3). Come they did, but it was not until the end of 598 BC that Nebuchadnezzar began the siege of Jerusalem. King Jehoiakim died before the siege began and was succeeded by his son Jehoiachin (598-597 BC), who surrendered after three months of the Babylonian siege.

The Babylonians were remarkably lenient to the Hebrew leaders after the surrender of Jerusalem, possibly because they had been spared taking the city by assault. Jehoiachin – occasionally referred to as Jeconiah in the Old Testament – was deported to Babylon. With him went many of the royal family and the leading people of Jerusalem, all of whom were maintained at Babylonian expense in a comfortable captivity. The prophet Jeremiah's continual denunciations had brought him into conflict with the Hebrew leaders, and this was to continue under the next king, Zedekiah (597-587 BC), another of Josiah's sons. In one sense, this marked the beginning of the Babylonian exile, which was to have such deep effects on the Hebrews and their understanding of their religion. But it did not seem so at the time. The Jerusalem Hebrews expected the return of their leaders at any time, despite the repeated warnings of Jeremiah. The prophet Ezekiel went – or was taken – to Babylonia during this period, and tried to convince the exiles that they were there to stay. Indeed, Ezekiel's visions suggest that God had deserted Jerusalem and the Temple, and was now with the Hebrews in Babylonia (Ezek 1-2; 10-11). It cannot have been a comfortable position for King Zedekiah in Jerusalem, if some of his subjects were expecting the return of the 'rightful' king and his court from Babylon.

Both Jeremiah and Ezekiel refer to the expectations of a speedy return to Jerusalem by the exiles who had been taken to Babylon by Nebuchadnezzar in 598 BC (Jer 27; Ezek 13), and both are at great pains to disillusion them. Events soon proved them right. The peoples to the

south-east of Judah began to encroach on Judean territory, arousing doubts about Zedekiah's ability to defend his kingdom. Prophets among the Hebrews in exile in Babylon encouraged their hopes of returning home, particularly as Zedekiah was proving to be a weak king. Nebuchadnezzar executed some of these prophets for treason, and there were indications that Hebrews drafted into the Babylonian army were stirring up mutiny.

Zedekiah thought there might be a possibility of throwing off the Babylonian control of Palestine, so towards the end of 594 BC he called a meeting in Jerusalem of ambassadors from Edom, Moab, Ammon, Tyre and Sidon (Jer 27:3) to try to form a coalition to eject the Babylonians. The plans came to nothing, but Zedekiah tried again in 589 BC, possibly with the support of the new Egyptian king of the 26th Dynasty, Apries (589-570 BC). Only Tyre and Ammon supported Judah this time, and Edom eventually helped the Babylonians.

By the end of 589 BC, a Babylonian army had arrived in Judah and picked off its fortified towns one by one, until only Lachish and Azekah remained, apart from Jerusalem. Among the charred remains of the city gate of Lachish, archaeologists have found a message from one of the outposts reporting that the signal fires of Azekah could no longer be seen. Lachish itself fell shortly afterwards. In the middle of 588 BC the siege of Jerusalem was lifted temporarily when an Egyptian army moved into Palestine, but it was driven back by the Babylonians and the siege resumed. Jerusalem fell the following year, in the summer of 587 BC, to a Babylonian assault, just as Zedekiah was about to surrender the city.

King Zedekiah fled with some of his troops, but was captured near Jericho and taken to the Babylonian army base at Riblah in Syria, where Nebuchadnezzar executed Zedekiah's two sons and then had Zedekiah himself blinded and taken in chains to Babylon. Jerusalem was razed to the ground, its leading citizens executed and many others taken into exile in Babylonia. Jerusalem was to lie in ruins until the Persians defeated the Babylonians in 539 BC, 48 years later, and encouraged the Hebrew exiles to return and rebuild. The kingdom of Judah was ruined, its cities destroyed and only the poorest of its people left in the area. The Babylonians appointed a Hebrew, Gedaliah, to be governor of the territory, which he administered from Mizpah, between Jerusalem and Bethel, where he was joined by some of the Hebrews who had tried to oppose the rebellion against Babylon, including Jeremiah. Not long afterwards other Hebrews, who had fled from the Babylonians to Ammon, returned to Mizpah and murdered Gedaliah, together with the small garrison of Babylonian troops attached to him, and some of the Hebrews. They then fled back to Ammon. Fearing that Nebuchadnezzar would hold them responsible, the survivors of the massacre fled to Egypt, taking Jeremiah with them.

The Hebrew kingdoms had failed to solve the eternal dilemma of small nations caught between the struggles of great international powers as they fought one another for supremacy. Palestine had the misfortune to lie across the only viable international land routes from Egypt, and the Hebrews could never forget that four centuries before, in the days of Kings David and Solomon, they had been undisputed masters of Palestine from Damascus to the Egyptian frontier.

2 Kgs 23-25, Jer 12-39, Hab, Ezek 1-24.

In the fifth month, on the seventh day of the month — it was in the nineteenth year of Nebuchadnezzar king of Babylon — Nebuzaradan, commander of the guard, an officer of the king of Babylon, entered Jerusalem. He burned down the Temple of Yahweh, the royal palace and all the houses in Jerusalem. The Chaldaean troops who accompanied the commander of the guard demolished the walls surrounding Jerusalem. Nebuzaradan, commander of the guard, deported the remainder of the population left behind in the city, the deserters who had gone over to the king of Babylon, and the rest of the common people. (2 Kgs 25: 8-11)

BELOW **Southern Palestine was left a ruined country after the destruction of Jerusalem in 587 BC and the deportation of all its survivors. The poor who were left behind wandered the land with their meagre flocks, scraping a living wherever they could.**

BELOW Successive invaders of Palestine destroyed the cities they captured. When Jerusalem was levelled by the Babylonians in 587 BC, the citizens were fortunate to be exiled as a group to Babylonia. They kept their sense of national identity and their descendants were allowed to return and rebuild the city 48 years later, when the Persians defeated the Babylonians. INSET Although these fortifications in the background seem to be ancient, they are at least 1,500 years later than the walls in the foreground.

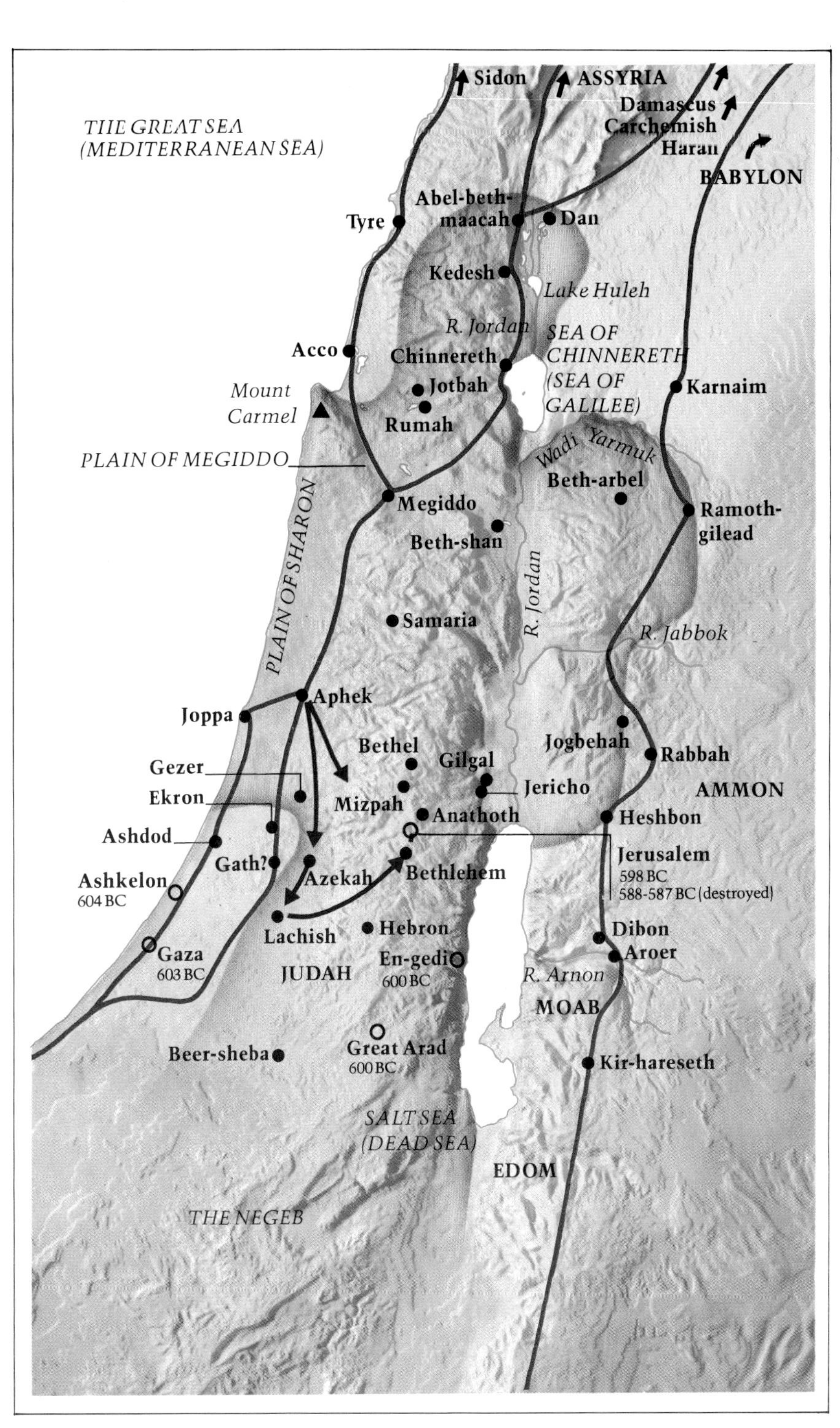

Kingdom of Josiah of Jerusalem (640-609 BC)

Babylonian conquest of Palestine by Nebuchadnezzar (605-562 BC)

Final campaign against Jerusalem (588-587 BC)

Main trade routes

THE BABYLONIANS IN JUDAH

After vanquishing the Assyrians in Mesopotamia, the Babylonians turned their attention west to the 'fertile crescent'. This was at a time when Josiah was giving new life to the old Hebrew laws of the covenant. But the invaders were a stronger and more unified force; under Nebuchadnezzar they captured important towns, including Jerusalem which was taken in 598 BC and finally destroyed 10 years later.

Exile in Babylon

During the exile in Babylon, the Hebrew priests organized their records and traditions within a narrative framework, underlining God's significance. Such a view of history, which included outstanding passages of hope, reassured the exiles that God's power was at work throughout all events and in all laws.

During the final days of Jerusalem, both Jeremiah in Jerusalem and Ezekiel in Babylonia wrote outstanding passages of hope, which promised a new covenant in which God would transform his people and make it possible for them to respond to his promises. The Babylonian exile did in fact stimulate new and impressive movements in Hebrew thought.

There is very little to show how the Hebrews were organized during their exile in Babylonia. Only one thing is certain, that they managed to retain their identity, and were not merely absorbed into the general culture of Babylon, as it would seem had happened to the exiles of the northern Hebrew kingdom, Israel, when the Assyrians deported them in 721 BC. The Babylonian Empire was short lived, barely surviving the death of Nebuchadnezzar in 562 BC. The Babylonians had mounted more campaigns into the Palestine area aimed at Tyre, Ammon and Moab. More Hebrews were deported to Babylon in 582 BC, while Egypt was invaded by Nebuchadnezzar in 568 BC, but not incorporated into the Babylonian empire. Three kings ruled Babylon within seven years after 562 BC, until Nabonidus (556-539 BC) seized power. He attempted to make the moon god the main deity in the Babylonian religion, and so antagonized the priests of Marduk, the god of the city of Babylon, that he eventually moved from Babylon to Tema, an oasis far to the south-west of Babylon in the Arabian Desert. His son Belshazzar was left in charge of affairs in Babylon, while Nabonidus developed caravan routes across the Arabian Desert. By this time, the middle of the sixth century BC, Cyrus of Persia had begun his swift rise to power east of Babylonia, and it was to him that the Babylonian Empire would fall.

For the Hebrews, the exile in Babylonia from 587 BC to 539 BC deprived them of most of the main symbols of their religion. Since 622 BC the Temple in Jerusalem had been the only place where the sacrifices could officially be offered, and the Temple had been destroyed. The Hebrew kings of David's line may have managed to exercise some kind of authority over the Hebrews in Babylonia, but if they did so it was not for long. King Jehoiachin was imprisoned by Nebuchadnezzar and

Extent of Babylonian Empire

Main trade routes

(1) Probable site of exile

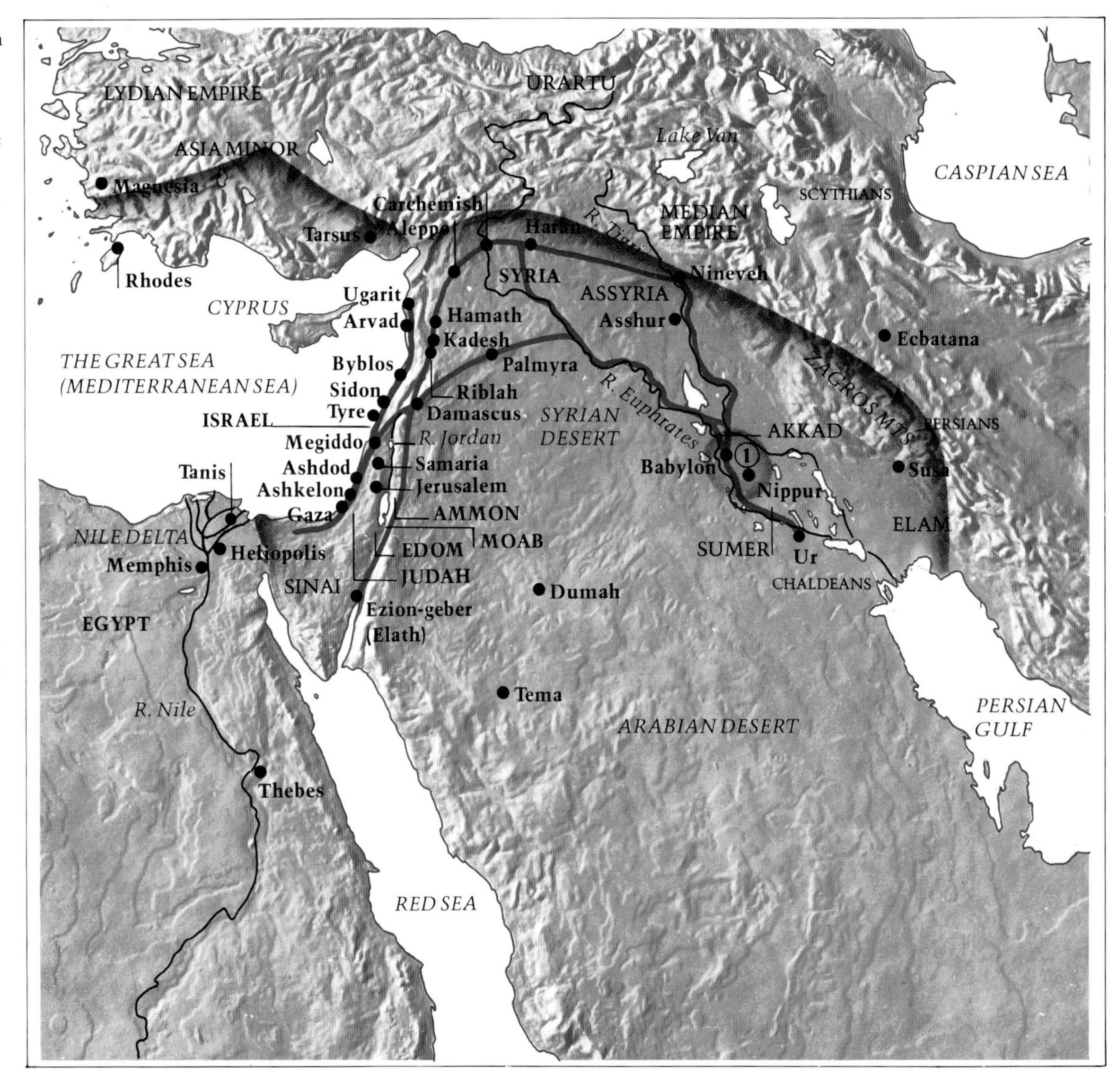

THE BABYLONIAN EXILE **The destruction of Jerusalem by the Babylonians in 587 BC came at the end of more than two years of siege, and was the second time in little more than a decade that the Babylonians had been forced to subdue the city. Its people were deported to Babylonia, where they remained until the Persians overthrew the Babylonians nearly 50 years later. These years constitute the historical exile, during which the Hebrews explored the significance of the disaster for their religious beliefs. They came to see it as a period of purification, and an opportunity to reform the nation when eventually they were allowed to return to Jerusalem.**

was not released until Nebuchadnezzar's death nearly 20 years after the destruction of Jerusalem; King Zedekiah had been taken to Babylon blinded and in chains after seeing his sons executed. The Davidic kings, as visible evidence of God's covenant (2 Sam 7:10-16), end with the Babylonian exile and the destruction of David's capital, Jerusalem. When the Hebrews returned to rebuild the city, it was to create a community ruled by the priests of the restored Temple. But Palestine itself was the most powerful symbol of all, mentioned again and again in the covenant statements of the Old Testament from Genesis onwards. The exiles bitterly resented that they were separated from their land, and reacted angrily to the news that others were occupying its ruins (Ezek 33:23-29).

As the remaining Hebrew kingdom was being destroyed, prophets were already teaching that the people would be brought back to Palestine by God, when their punishment was over (Jer 30-31). In Babylonia, after the destruction of Jerusalem, Ezekiel provided a detailed picture of the ideal Jerusalem which would emerge from the exile (Ezek 40-48), and the anonymous author of the final chapters of the Book of Isaiah (Isa 40-66) expressed powerful hopes of return as the news of the Persian king, Cyrus, began to reach the Hebrew exiles.

Although the Hebrew exiles in Babylonia were deprived of the visible symbols of their religion during the main years of exile (587-539 BC), they did take with them other symbols equally powerful – their historical traditions, their laws, and their memories of the sacred rituals of the Temple in Jerusalem, kept fresh by the Temple priests who had gone into exile and who became the leaders of the Hebrew community.

During the exile, the Hebrews were able to reflect on the nation's history, and organize their records and traditions to show the religious patterns in it all. As in all historical writings, there had to be selection from the large amount of material available, and then arrangement of the selection to bring out the lessons which could be learned from it. The philosophy of history presented in most of the historical books of the Old Testament was influenced by the authors of the Book of Deuteronomy. The key principle was obedience. If the people were faithful to the covenant and to the laws which applied it to everyday life, they would prosper in the land God had given to them, and be wisely ruled by King David's descendants. If they were disobedient, they would be punished to purify and reform them. Above all, they must maintain the purity of the Temple worship in the place which God 'himself will choose from among all your tribes, to set his name there and give it a home' (Deut 12:5) – that is, Jerusalem. The historians selected and arranged their material to demonstrate this, and at the same time reminded the reader that other information could be obtained from historical books which are now lost. Surrounded by all the magnificence of the Babylonian civilization and of its religion, such a view of history reassured the Hebrews in exile that their own God was not to be judged by their failure. They had brought their punishment on themselves, and their exile showed how powerful their God really was, as he used even history itself for his purposes.

This theme was developed further by another group among the exiles, the 'priestly school', so called because of their interest in the Hebrew priesthood and the regulations governing sacrificial worship. The priestly school is thought to have been responsible for the two Books of Chronicles, which present a parallel version of the period recorded in the Books of Samuel and Kings. However, their main influence can be seen in the material about the escape from Egypt (the exodus), and the journey through the wilderness when the covenant was made. The priestly school assembled a wide range of traditional material. This consisted of stories about the creation, the first human beings, the flood and the Tower of Babel; the history of the patriarchs, Abraham and his immediate descendants; the Hebrews in Egypt, their escape, the covenant and the journey; and collections of Hebrew law, including Deuteronomic law and the priestly laws about the facilities needed for worship and the way worship was to be performed. All the material was then arranged within a narrative framework to demonstrate how God's creative power was at work throughout the events and in all the laws. The opening of the Book of Genesis (1:1-2:4a) is the priestly introduction to the work, which is then arranged in five books – Genesis, Exodus, Leviticus, Numbers and Deuteronomy. This shows the ideal world which God still intends to restore, with mankind as the administrators of his plan.

This does not mean that the opening five books of the Old Testament – or even the historical books which follow – reached their final form during the Babylonian exile. However, they were given their main shape at this time in order to provide the Hebrews with confidence in the future and with fundamental religious principles for a fresh beginning when the exile ended.

PROPHETS OF THE EXILE
During the years leading up to the destruction of Jerusalem in 587 BC, and in the years of exile which followed, three outstanding teachers tried to transform the religious thinking of the Hebrew people.

JEREMIAH **(c645-580 BC) started his ministry in Jerusalem 40 years before it was destroyed and lived right through the attempted reforms and the disintegration of the nation. As the exile began he taught that there would be a 'new covenant' which would change the hearts of the people (Jer 31-32).**

EZEKIEL **(c625-550 BC) was a priest, probably of the Hebrew Temple in Jerusalem, who was taken to exile in Babylonia. He warned his fellow Hebrews that there would be no early return to Jerusalem. He gave vivid descriptions of God's presence amongst his exiled people, and also taught that there would be a new covenant. His book ends with plans for a new Jerusalem.**

THE 'SECOND ISAIAH' **is an anonymous prophet whose teaching occupy the last 26 chapters of Isaiah as the Persians were sending the Hebrews home again. This prophet taught that the people's suffering would be rewarded.**

2 Kgs 25, Jer 40-52, Lam, Mic 4-7, Isa 13-14; 32-35; 40-55, Ezek 40-48, Gen 1-11 (parts), Lev 17-26, Exod 25-31; 34-40, Lev 1-16; 27, Num 1-10; 15-19; 25-36.

But do not be afraid, my servant Jacob. . .
look, I will rescue you from distant countries
and your descendants from the country where they are captive.
Jacob will have quiet again and live at ease, with no one to trouble him.
Do not be afraid, my servant Jacob. . .
I will make an end of all the nations
where I have scattered you;
I will not make an end of you,
only discipline you in moderation,
so as not to let you go entirely unpunished.
(Jer 46: 27-28)

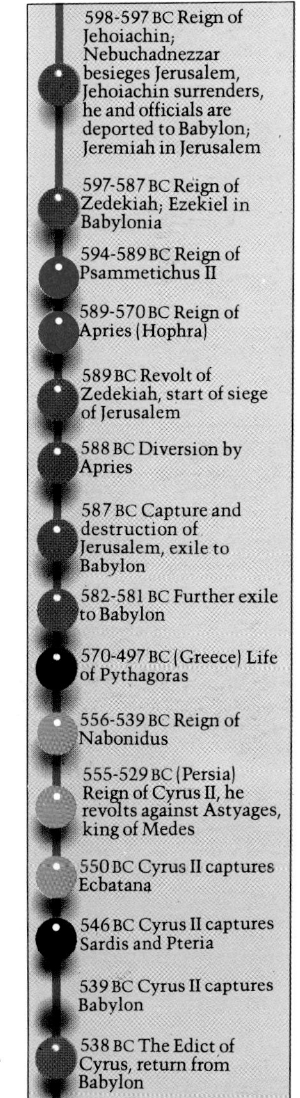

598-597 BC Reign of Jehoiachin; Nebuchadnezzar besieges Jerusalem, Jehoiachin surrenders, he and officials are deported to Babylon; Jeremiah in Jerusalem
597-587 BC Reign of Zedekiah; Ezekiel in Babylonia
594-589 BC Reign of Psammetichus II
589-570 BC Reign of Apries (Hophra)
589 BC Revolt of Zedekiah, start of siege of Jerusalem
588 BC Diversion by Apries
587 BC Capture and destruction of Jerusalem, exile to Babylon
582-581 BC Further exile to Babylon
570-497 BC (Greece) Life of Pythagoras
556-539 BC Reign of Nabonidus
555-529 BC (Persia) Reign of Cyrus II, he revolts against Astyages, king of Medes
550 BC Cyrus II captures Ecbatana
546 BC Cyrus II captures Sardis and Pteria
539 BC Cyrus II captures Babylon
538 BC The Edict of Cyrus, return from Babylon

The ancient city of Babylon lay a little to the south of modern Baghdad, on the River Euphrates, where its rulers could control all southern Mesopotamia. By the time of the Hebrew exile the great city straddled the river, and was defended by a double wall pierced by eight gates. Two bridges connected the old city with the new extensions. Great avenues crossed the city and divided it into sections, and there was also a network of canals. Built of hard baked mud bricks, the excavations have revealed its impressive architecture and imaginative use of relief sculptures built into the walls. It was the centre of a great empire in the second millenium BC, but fell into decline and became an Assyrian province. The Babylonians rebelled in 626 BC and overthrew the Assyrian Empire in 612 BC.

ABOVE The Ishtar Gate was the main entrance into Babylon, and was covered with blue enamelled brick reliefs of bulls and dragons. The great avenue inside the gate stretched across the city, paved with pink marble and limestone slabs. A frieze of lions ran along the walls of the adjacent buildings. The huge statue of Marduk, the chief god of Babylon, was carried in procession along the avenue and through the Ishtar Gate in the New Year festival.

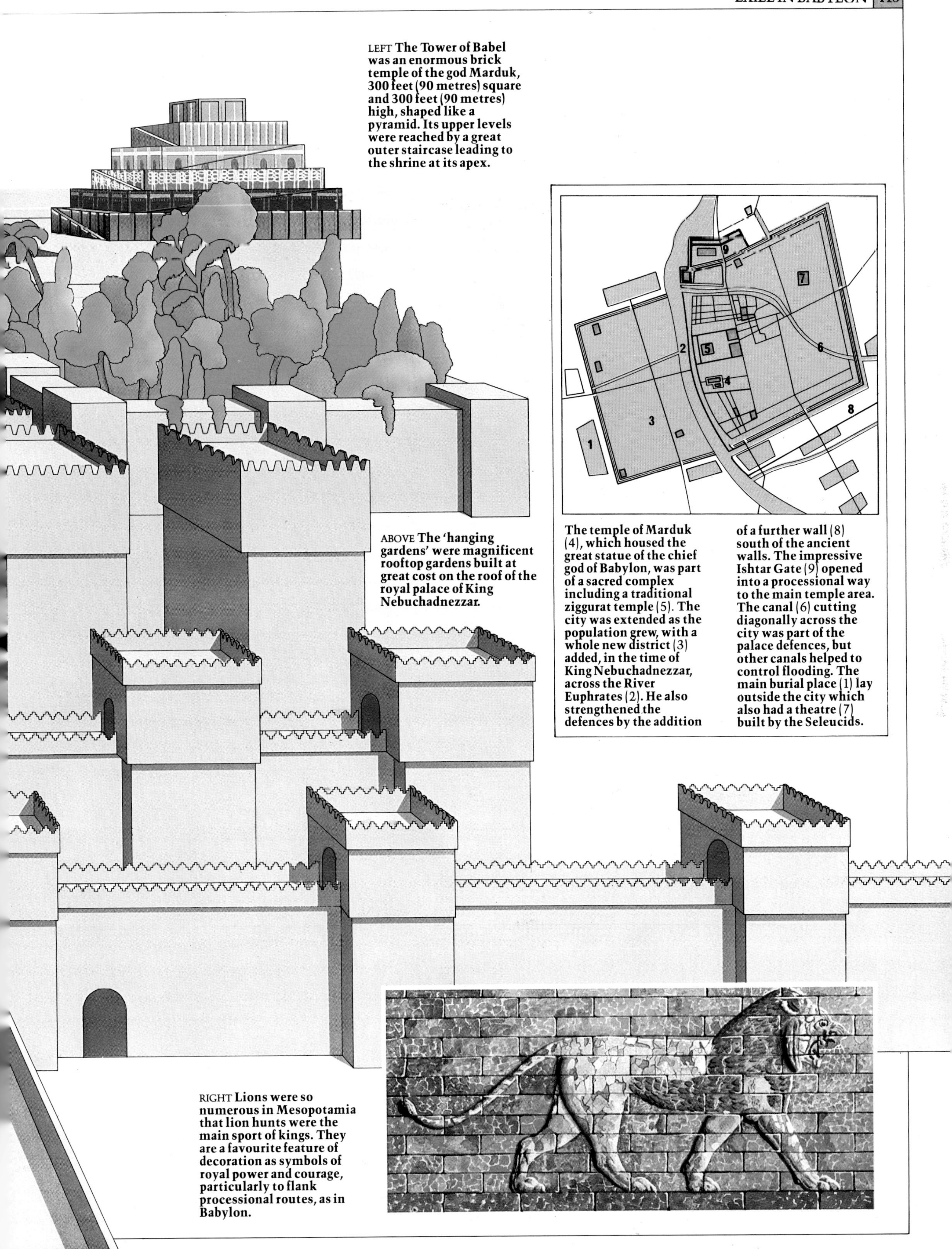

LEFT **The Tower of Babel was an enormous brick temple of the god Marduk, 300 feet (90 metres) square and 300 feet (90 metres) high, shaped like a pyramid. Its upper levels were reached by a great outer staircase leading to the shrine at its apex.**

ABOVE **The 'hanging gardens' were magnificent rooftop gardens built at great cost on the roof of the royal palace of King Nebuchadnezzar.**

The temple of Marduk (4), which housed the great statue of the chief god of Babylon, was part of a sacred complex including a traditional ziggurat temple (5). The city was extended as the population grew, with a whole new district (3) added, in the time of King Nebuchadnezzar, across the River Euphrates (2). He also strengthened the defences by the addition of a further wall (8) south of the ancient walls. The impressive Ishtar Gate (9) opened into a processional way to the main temple area. The canal (6) cutting diagonally across the city was part of the palace defences, but other canals helped to control flooding. The main burial place (1) lay outside the city which also had a theatre (7) built by the Seleucids.

RIGHT **Lions were so numerous in Mesopotamia that lion hunts were the main sport of kings. They are a favourite feature of decoration as symbols of royal power and courage, particularly to flank processional routes, as in Babylon.**

4 · REBUILDING TH

E HEBREW NATION

And Ezra read from the Law of God, translating and giving the sense, so that the people understood what was read.
(Neh 8:8)

New Beginnings under Persia

After a bloodless victory over the Babylonians in 539 BC, the Persian king, Cyrus, went on to build up a strong, tolerant empire, which extended as far south as Egypt. The Persians employed unusual military tactics, and remained the dominant power in the Near and Middle East for more than 200 years.

In 539 BC King Cyrus of Persia (555-529 BC) received the surrender of Babylon without having to fight. This was the climax of the campaign in which the Persian armies had swept across the eastern frontiers of the Babylonian empire from the Indian Ocean to the Black Sea, and then struck southwards into the heart of Mesopotamia. Tension between King Nabonidus of Babylon (556-539 BC) and the Babylonian priests of the chief god, Marduk, lay behind Cyrus's bloodless victory. Nabonidus had tried to replace the worship of Marduk with the worship of the moon god, Sin, and the Babylonian priests had moved against him.

It was wise of the priests of Babylon to welcome the Persian victor, for Persian rule proved to be remarkably sympathetic and tolerant. Subject races of the Persian empire had to give military and other kinds of service, but they were treated as equals by the Persian troops, and they reached high rank in both the army and the civil service. The exiled Hebrews in Babylonia were only one of many exiled national groups which received compassionate treatment at the hands of Cyrus. Such peoples were offered the opportunity of returning to their native lands together with the treasures looted from them by the Babylonians, and were provided with support from the Persian treasury to rebuild their cities and temples. There was certainly taxation and tribute exacted from all parts of the empire, but it was used to benefit the provinces. Although King Cyrus remained faithful to his own gods, it is not surprising that the Hebrews saw the hand of their own God in his victories (Isa 44-45).

The army was the key to Cyrus's rise to greatness. The tactics which brought this success depended on fighting at a distance and overwhelming the enemy with a hail of arrows while cavalry harassed the ranks. It was mobile warfare at a time when armies usually confronted each other in ranks, and the Persian bowmen fought with little personal protection so that they were free to move swiftly and fire repeatedly. Hand-to-hand fighting had to be avoided at all costs. When the Greeks did at last manage to make a Persian army stand and fight at close quarters at Marathon in 490 BC, the Persians were overwhelmed. The Athenians trapped the Persians against their ships in a narrow position, by giving them no chance to manoeuvre, and they were slaughtered in close fighting with the hoplites, the Greek infantry.

From his capital, Ecbatana, King Cyrus laid the foundations of an empire which was to last for more than 200 years, until it fell to Alexander the Great in 331 BC. Cyrus was succeeded by Cambyses II (529-522 BC) who extended Persian rule into Egypt. His

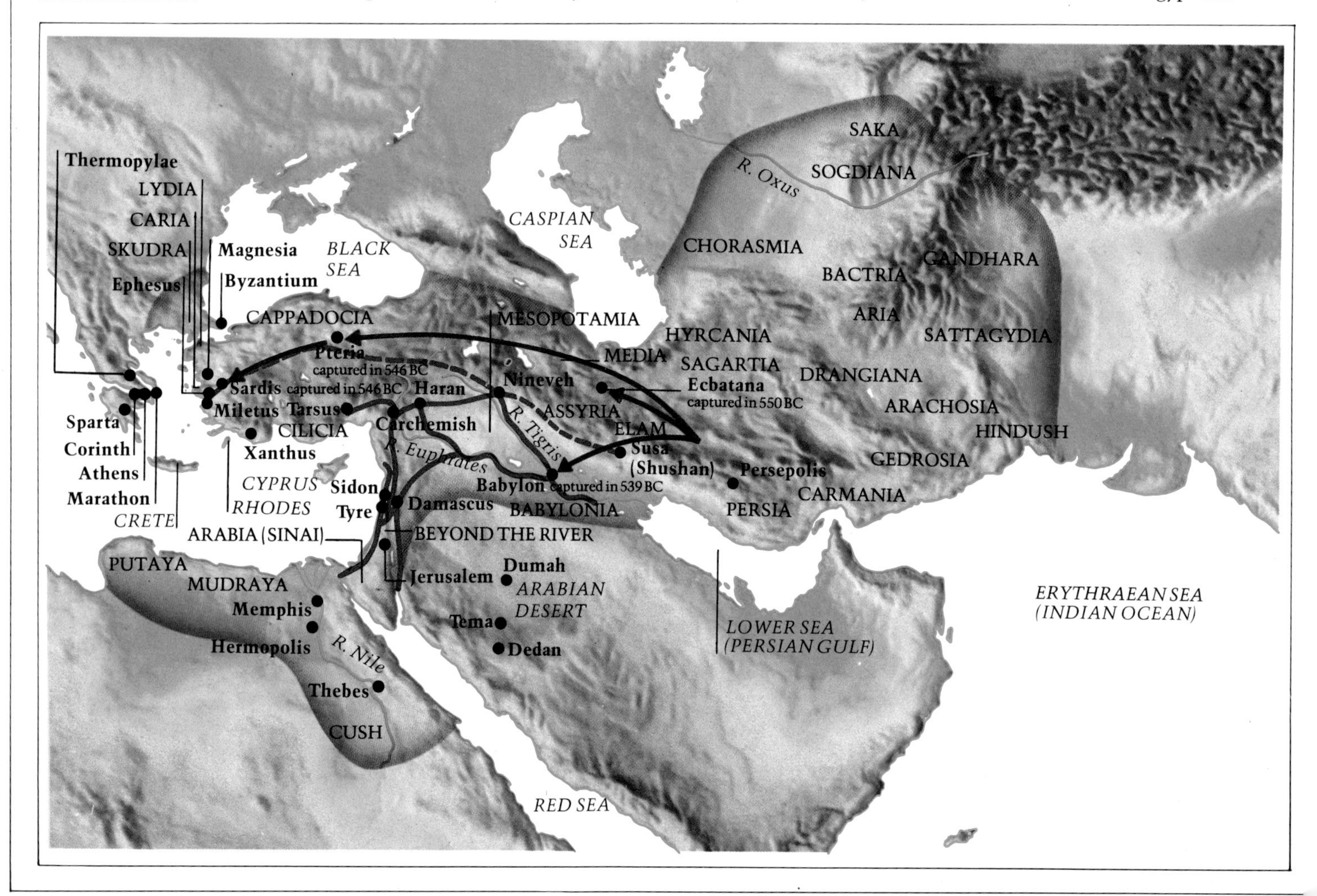

THE PERSIAN EMPIRE **The Persian expansion which eventually led to the overthrow of the Babylonian Empire began when Cyrus made Ecbatana his capital. The main Persian thrust took them up the eastern parts of Mesopotamia to conquer Asia Minor, and Babylon then fell when Cyrus took his army southwards again. Cambyses II, who succeeded to the Persian throne in 528 BC, extended the empire into Egypt, and the full organization of provinces was created by the next king, Darius I (521-486 BC). Persian rule was markedly more humane than in earlier empires, with the return of exiles and equal status for subject peoples in the army and administration.**

successor, Darius I (522-486 BC), moved the capital to Persepolis after a year of disorders following the succession. By then the empire stretched from the north-west of the Indus Valley to Asia Minor, and included all of Mesopotamia, Palestine and Egypt, where the Persian emperors constituted the 27th Dynasty. Control of Egypt was never easy, however, particularly after the Persian defeat by the Greeks at Marathon in 490 BC, and the Persians lost control of Egypt for 60 years during the 28th, 29th and 30th Dynasties (400-343 BC), only to regain it for a mere 10 years before Alexander took over.

The Persian Empire was organized in provinces controlled by satraps who were relatively independent of the central government, despite a system of separate military commands and a courier system unsurpassed in the ancient world until the Romans. Aramaic – a Semitic language – was adopted as the official language, and consequently became the common tongue of the Persian Empire.

The main religion of Persia at the height of its power was Zoroastrianism, which was a monotheism introduced by the prophet Zoroaster. Its god was Ahura Mazda, the creator and lawgiver. In this religion the world was viewed as a battle ground between equal forces of good and evil.

LEFT **The date palm has been a main source of food in the Near and Middle East for at least 4,000 years.**

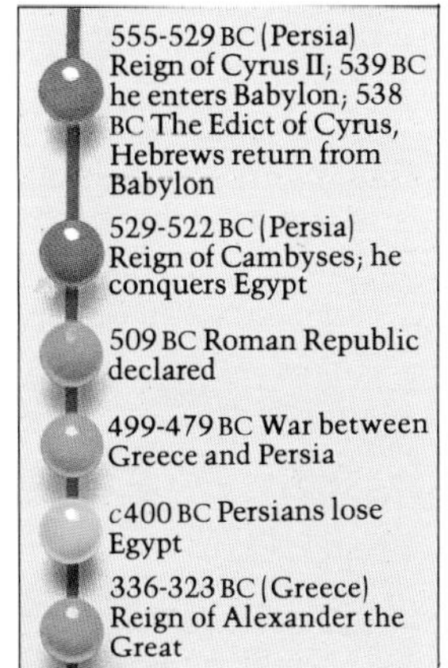

555-529 BC (Persia) Reign of Cyrus II; 539 BC he enters Babylon; 538 BC The Edict of Cyrus, Hebrews return from Babylon
529-522 BC (Persia) Reign of Cambyses; he conquers Egypt
509 BC Roman Republic declared
499-479 BC War between Greece and Persia
c400 BC Persians lose Egypt
336-323 BC (Greece) Reign of Alexander the Great

BELOW **Memphis, the capital of Lower Egypt, was near the western extreme of the Persian Empire. The problems of maintaining effective rule over such a vast area proved to be too great, and the empire fell easily to Alexander.**

Greek Civilization

The Greek city-states — loosely linked by shifting political alliances — had an extensive trading network and many colonies in the Mediterranean area. They created a culture which had a profound effect on the region and their influence was increased dramatically by the military successes of Alexander the Great.

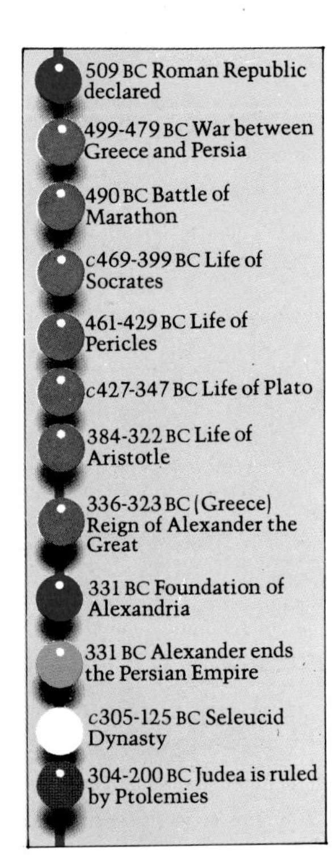

509 BC Roman Republic declared
499-479 BC War between Greece and Persia
490 BC Battle of Marathon
c469-399 BC Life of Socrates
461-429 BC Life of Pericles
c427-347 BC Life of Plato
384-322 BC Life of Aristotle
336-323 BC (Greece) Reign of Alexander the Great
331 BC Foundation of Alexandria
331 BC Alexander ends the Persian Empire
c305-125 BC Seleucid Dynasty
304-200 BC Judea is ruled by Ptolemies

Geography is often the key to understanding the history, and, to a large extent, the character of a people. As much of mainland Greece is made up of fertile valleys, separated from each other by steep mountainous ridges, settlements tended to develop independently as small agricultural states. In addition, the sea, never far from any part of the Greek peninsula, formed an important influence, drawing the peoples of Greece to the many islands of the Aegean, and to the coasts of the Black Sea, Asia Minor, southern Italy and northern Libya. By the sixth century BC, Greeks from the many small states had established colonies throughout the Mediterranean area, from what is now Rostov, where the River Don flows into the sea east of the Crimea, to Mainake (Malaga) in Spain. Colonies clustered thickly around the foot of Italy and Sicily, and in the Black Sea. The Aegean area – from mainland Greece and the islands to the western coast of Asia Minor – was the real heart of Greece. Location and ready access to the sea thus made the Greeks a trading nation, linking the great civilizations on their eastern borders with the rest of the Mediterranean world and the Black Sea area. Trade created the wealth of such cities as Athens, Corinth and Miletus.

City-states swiftly developed out of the small, self-sufficient communities. However, trading and the financing of ships and the cargoes they carried began to create internal tensions and bitter rivalries between the states. While this was to cause the ultimate downfall of Greece, the internal problems caused by large differences in wealth among the citizens in fact stimulated the development of Greek democracy. The extremes of social stratification and injustice, which could be maintained by force and by law in Egypt or Mesopotamia, were successfully resisted in Greece. The many colonies were relatively independent of their mother cities and learned the arts of self-government. There were many variations in the forms of government, and although democratic rule was fragile, it was successfully maintained in most of the city-states.

The Greek states survived their greatest external threat early in the fifth century BC when the Persians, who had already taken all Asia Minor and Thrace, tried to extend their empire to the Greek peninsula itself. At first, the Greek cities of Ionia in western Asia Minor welcomed the Persians for the increased trading opportunities they offered, but Persian support for wealthy factions, and control by the Persian provincial

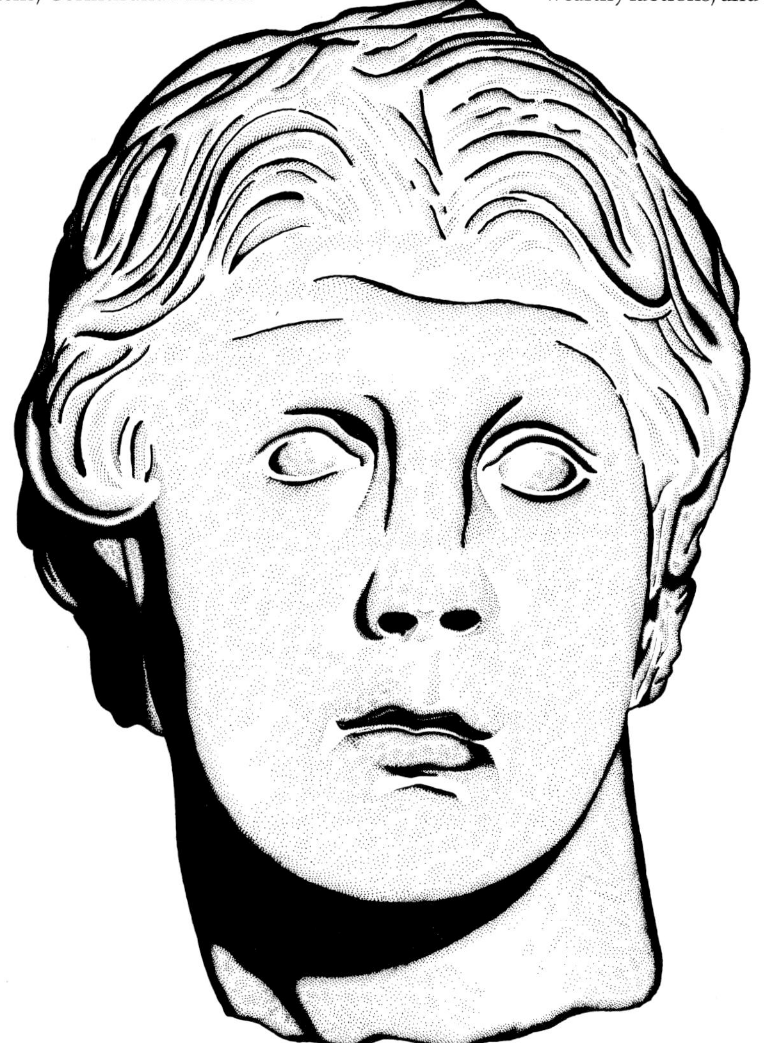

RIGHT **During his brief reign of 13 years, Alexander the Great conquered the Persian Empire from Egypt to India. He freed himself and his army from their Greek base when he crossed into Asia Minor in 337 BC to confront the Persians. He made the capital of his brief empire wherever his campaign headquarters happened to be at the time.**

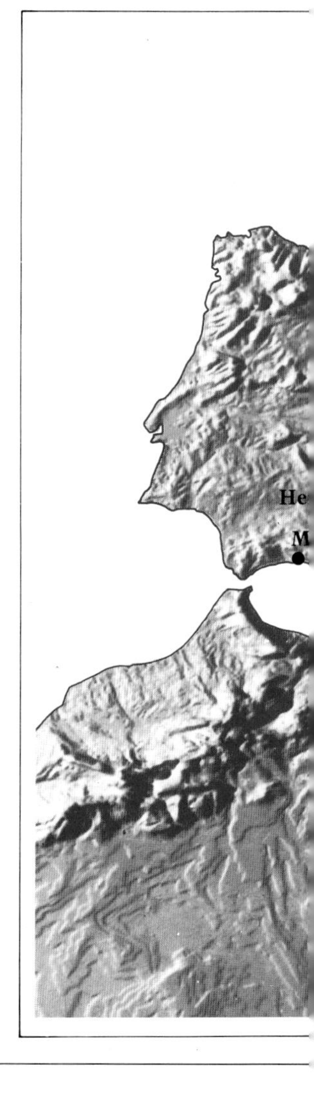

Coastal areas with numerous Greek colonies

Mother cities

Colonial cities

Area of the Ionian revolt (500-494 BC)

Routes taken by the Persians:

Fleet and army 492 BC

Fleet 490 BC

Fleet 480 BC

Army 480 BC

GREECE AND HER COLONIES (BELOW) **The heavily indented coast of mainland Greece, and the many islands by which it was surrounded, made the Greeks a nation of sailors and traders. The major mainland cities established colonies all through the Mediterranean and Black Sea regions, particularly in Asia Minor and southern Italy. Once established, the colonies became independent but retained ties with their mother cities by sacred festivals. After Alexander, there were colonies as far as the Indus.**

PERSIA AND GREECE IN THE 5TH CENTURY BC (RIGHT) **Wars between the Persians and the Greeks began when the Greek colonies on the coast of Asia Minor rebelled against their new Persian overlords. The Persians advanced against mainland Greece itself, and all but Athens and Sparta submitted. In 490 BC the Athenians defeated a second Persian campaign at Marathon. The Persians took Athens 10 years later, but the defeat of the Persian fleet at Salamis forced a withdrawal, with final defeat in 489 BC.**

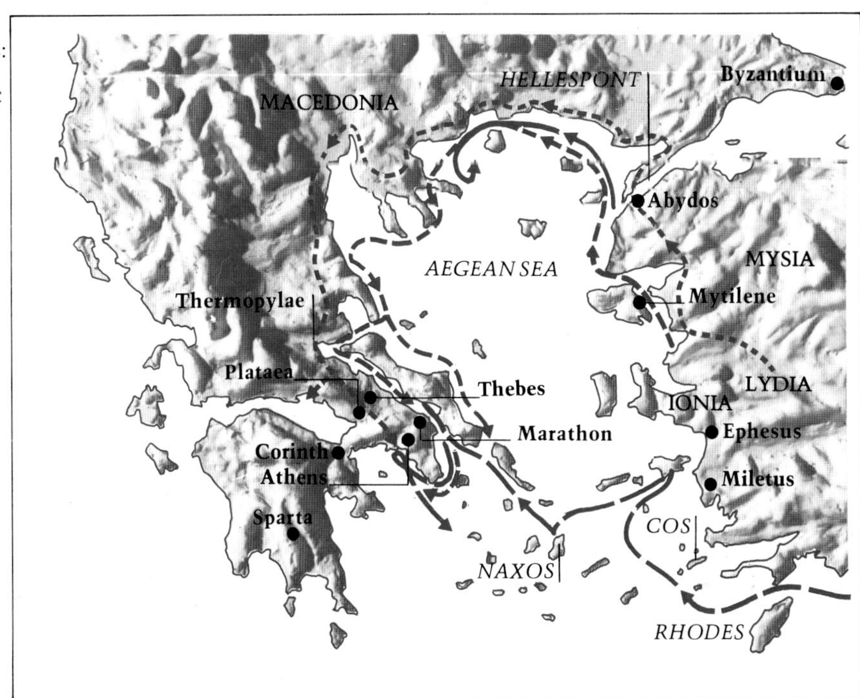

ABOVE AND RIGHT **The Near East contains much evidence of the influence the Greeks had on the area in the form of impressive ruins, such as this theatre a little to the south of the Sea of Galilee. They also gained a lasting reputation through their victories over the Persians, first when they repelled them after their invasion of mainland Greece, and later when Alexander the Great conquered the Persian Empire itself. The Greek states were rarely united, but their fierce independence was reflected in their political theories and the relentless pursuit of truth which characterized the great Greek philosophers. Men such as Socrates paid for their honesty with their lives, while others, such as Plato and Aristotle, tried to influence powerful rulers as advisers and tutors. They usually failed in this, but their writings became the main foundations of European thought both in ancient and modern times.**

governor, the satrap, caused growing tension which broke into rebellion in 499 BC. The Persians crushed the Ionian Greeks and destroyed the city of Miletus. Persia sent an army into Macedonia in 492 BC, but a storm wrecked the Persian supporting fleet. Two years later, in 490 BC, a Persian army ferried across the Aegean was defeated by the Athenians at Marathon. For a while the pressure eased, as the Persians coped with disorders following the death of the Persian king, Darius I, but his successor, Xerxes (486-465 BC), led a third army in 480 BC which bridged the Hellespont and advanced on Greece with the support of a great fleet. This time the Persians burned Athens and overran the whole of central Greece, even though the Spartans defended the narrow pass of Thermopylae to the last man. Only the crushing defeat of the Persian fleet at Salamis forced Xerxes to retreat, and in the following year, 479 BC, the united Greek armies defeated the Persians at Plataea.

The unity forced upon the Greek states by the Persian threat was short-lived. For a while Athens enjoyed pre-eminence, but by the end of the fifth century BC the city-states were locked in bitter civil war in which first Sparta and then Thebes became dominant. The Persians could have taken Greece at any time if the Persian provincial governors had not been causing disruption within the empire itself.

Despite the Persian wars and the bitter struggles between the Greek states, Greece created a culture which influenced the ancient world far more effectively than any military supremacy could have done, and which has had profound effects even on civilization

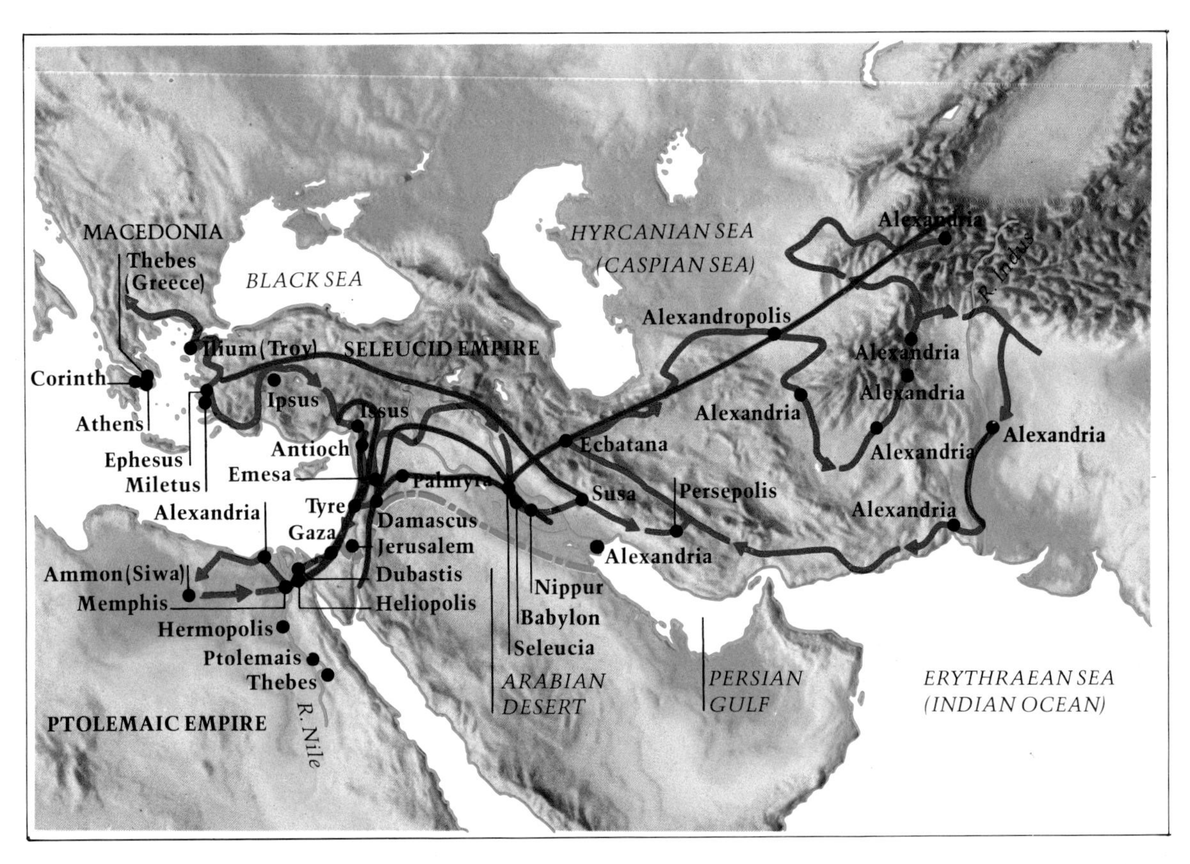

ALEXANDER'S EMPIRE In the 5th century BC, Greece was united under Alexander the Great in its fight against the Persian Empire. Once he had conquered Asia Minor, Alexander led his men into northern Syria where he defeated the Persian king Darius III at Issus. He then pressed south to Egypt where he founded the city of Alexandria. Wherever he went, Alexander built cities named after him and then used them as a base for his military operations. From Egypt, Alexander took his troops up into Mesopotamia, Babylon and Persia. He completely destroyed the Persian Empire and finally died in Babylon in 321 BC. After his death Ptolemy ruled in Egypt and Seleucus in Syria. The extent of their two empires is also shown on the map.

today. This culture had a unity which transcended the bitter rivalries between Greeks themselves, and was expressed supremely in architecture, sculpture, drama, historical writings, poetry and philosophy. A feeling for form and order pervading everything, was related to the world the Greeks encountered in their everyday lives and to the needs of their city-based society. Much of what they produced had an overtly religious theme, but underlying this was the celebration of the Greek way of life and of the 'polis' – the city-state which provided its citizens with their sense of identity. Their achievements became models for exploring and understanding the nature of the world, and for the organization of society. This influence was dramatically increased by the military achievements of Alexander the Great (336-323 BC). In the 13 years from 336 BC, when Alexander, aged 20, succeeded his father as king of Macedonia until his death aged 33, he conquered the whole of the Near and Middle East from Greece to the western parts of India.

Until Alexander, Greece had been a country of independent city-states, linked together politically by shifting combinations of leagues, and by a common language and culture. Macedonia, in the north, had been little different from the other states, but Alexander swiftly established its supremacy. He secured the northern frontiers of Macedonia, united the Greeks under his rule by destroying Thebes, and, in 334 BC, crossed the Hellespont with a Greek army to push back the western frontiers of the Persian Empire. The satraps of the western Persian provinces in Asia Minor failed to stop him, and he liberated the Greek cities of Ionia.

At this point Alexander and his 40,000 strong army became independent of Greek support, and pressed on through Asia Minor to confront and defeat the Persian King Darius III (336-330 BC) at Issus. The victory opened the way for Alexander to take Syria, Phoenicia, Palestine and Egypt. On his way down the coastal route, Alexander showed his determination and ruthlessness, when he captured the island of Tyre in 332 BC, then nearly a mile offshore, by building a causeway out to it and taking the city by assault. Since then Tyre has been a peninsula. In Egypt, he founded the port of Alexandria, and had his personal divinity confirmed by the oracle of Zeus at the Siwa oasis in the Sahara desert.

From Egypt, Alexander took his army back through Palestine and along the eastern branch of the coastal route through Damascus into Mesopotamia. By the winter of 331 BC he had again defeated the Persians, passed through Babylon and Susa, and destroyed the royal palaces at Persepolis. Much of the original Greek army had been allowed to return home before Babylon was reached, but Alexander continued north to Ecbatana with troops recruited in Persia, and fought his way eastwards to the upper reaches of the River Indus. Alexander returned to Babylon with his decimated and exhausted army, declaring that east and west had been united under his divine rule. He began to build a fleet to conquer the world, but died of a fever in Babylon. Although Alexander's empire did not survive his death, he had managed to impose a single rule on a larger part of the western world than anyone before him.

The Divided Empire

After Alexander's death in 323 BC, his generals divided up his empire and then fought amongst each other. In the process they destroyed the prosperity of the great trading ports of mainland Greece. The centre of wealth shifted to Alexandria, where both Hellenistic and Jewish culture thrived.

ABOVE **After Alexander the Great, the many cities he founded throughout the eastern Mediterranean area and as far as the borders of India, became centres of Greek culture. The theatre in particular, typified by the masks of tragedy and comedy, introduced Greek attitudes to life even to people who were illiterate. The many amphitheatre ruins show that most cities had regular drama festivals.**

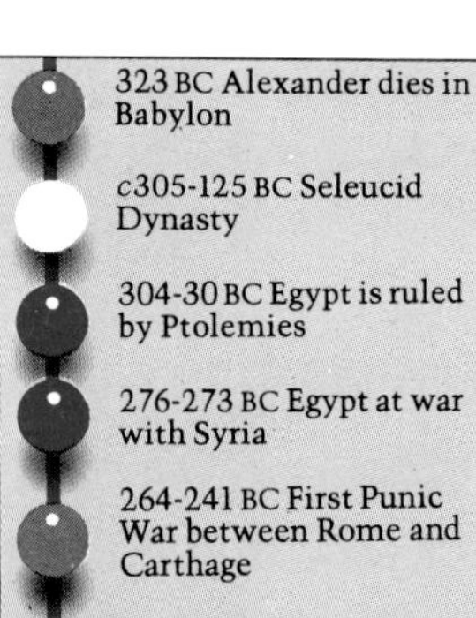

323 BC Alexander dies in Babylon
c305-125 BC Seleucid Dynasty
304-30 BC Egypt is ruled by Ptolemies
276-273 BC Egypt at war with Syria
264-241 BC First Punic War between Rome and Carthage
218-201 BC Second Punic War
217 BC Egyptian victory over Seleucids at Raphia
202-200 BC Seleucids reconquer Palestine
200-142 BC Judea ruled by Seleucids
166-160 BC Judas Maccabeus revolts; start of Maccabean Wars

Alexander the Great died at the age of 33 in Babylon, master of an empire spanning the Near and Middle East. After his death, his influence remained in the shape of the many cities he had founded on Greek lines, with Greek architecture and street plans which reflected a desire for clear, rational order. More than 20 of them were named Alexandria, and were scattered from the headwaters of the River Indus to the great new port at the western side of the Nile Delta in Egypt. Others were named after his companions. Many cities were replanned along Greek lines, and given new names, such as Ptolemais for the Palestinian port of Acco. However, the empire itself collapsed.

When Alexander died, his generals came into their own for the first time after years of being overshadowed by the towering personality and abilities of their leader. The far eastern parts of the empire in north-west India survived only briefly as independent kingdoms, although the Greek influence remained. At the other extreme, in Greece itself, the generals fought each other for control of Macedonia and of the cities of central and southern Greece. In the process they destroyed the prosperity of the great trading ports, including Athens. Migrating Gallic tribes plundered their way through Greece and on into Asia Minor. Then they created the kingdom of Galatia, which was later to become the nucleus of the Roman province of Galatia, which figures in the New Testament. By the time some sort of order was restored, after 50 years of chaos, some strong and wealthy ports had emerged including Rhodes, Ephesus and Smyrna.

Immediately after Alexander's rule, the major part of the empire was divided among Alexander's main generals – Antigonus ruled Asia Minor, Syria and Palestine; Seleucus ruled Mesopotamia, Persia and the eastern parts to the borders of India; and Ptolemy ruled Egypt and Libya. That division only lasted to the Battle of Ipsus in 301 BC, when Seleucus added Asia Minor and Syria to his possessions. Greek became the common tongue of the educated as the cities established schools, theatres, Greek temples and gymnasiums, while the Persian official language, Aramaic, continued to be used in the countryside – the situation still found in New Testament times. The Seleucids only managed to hold such a vast expanse of territory for some 50 years before the Parthians took control of eastern Mesopotamia – and eventually of most of the eastern parts of the Seleucid kingdom around the end of the third century BC. The Parthian Empire eventually prevented Roman expansion into the east.

Egypt remained under the control of the Ptolemies until the Romans conquered Egypt in 30 BC. Under Ptolemaic rule, Alexandria became the greatest trading port in the ancient world, and a major centre of learning with a great library, museum, and a community of scholars exempt from taxation and maintained at royal expense. The city became a multiracial society where foreign groups could live by their own customs and laws within the city's constitution. The Jewish community was particularly prominent.

Officially, Palestine had been allocated to the Seleucids after the Battle of Ipsus, but once again it was a vital frontier area between two great powers, and was in fact under Egyptian control until the end of the third century BC. This helps account for the growth and influence of the Jewish population of Egypt in settlements all over the country. By this time the 'dispersed' Jews far outnumbered Jews living in Palestine itself, and Hebrew had become a dead language for everyday purposes. To meet the needs of Jews who could no longer read Hebrew, the Jewish sacred books, the Old Testament, began to be translated into other languages, particularly Greek which so many Jews now used.

BELOW **Throughout the area conquered by Alexander later rulers rebuilt their main cities along Greek Lines. These ruins at Samaria, north of Jerusalem, show how completely the people were influenced by Greek architecture. In Jerusalem the priests themselves were leaders of the trend towards the Greek way of life.**

The Rise of Rome

Rome gradually became enormously powerful, and by 146 BC had destroyed its old adversary, Carthage. But its republican nature was doomed — upset by the corrupting combination of great wealth, military success and increasing colonial possessions — and was superseded by an emperor wielding absolute power.

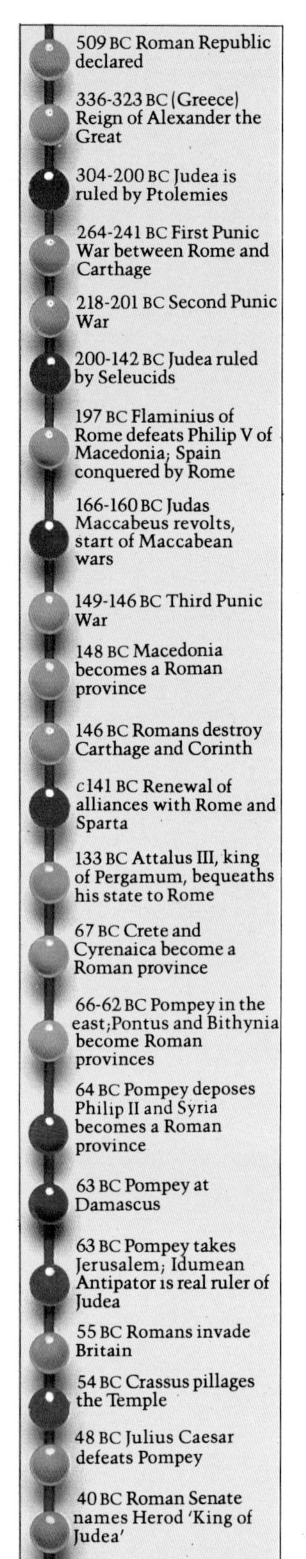

509 BC Roman Republic declared
336-323 BC (Greece) Reign of Alexander the Great
304-200 BC Judea is ruled by Ptolemies
264-241 BC First Punic War between Rome and Carthage
218-201 BC Second Punic War
200-142 BC Judea ruled by Seleucids
197 BC Flaminius of Rome defeats Philip V of Macedonia; Spain conquered by Rome
166-160 BC Judas Maccabeus revolts, start of Maccabean wars
149-146 BC Third Punic War
148 BC Macedonia becomes a Roman province
146 BC Romans destroy Carthage and Corinth
c141 BC Renewal of alliances with Rome and Sparta
133 BC Attalus III, king of Pergamum, bequeaths his state to Rome
67 BC Crete and Cyrenaica become a Roman province
66-62 BC Pompey in the east; Pontus and Bithynia become Roman provinces
64 BC Pompey deposes Philip II and Syria becomes a Roman province
63 BC Pompey at Damascus
63 BC Pompey takes Jerusalem; Idumean Antipator is real ruler of Judea
55 BC Romans invade Britain
54 BC Crassus pillages the Temple
48 BC Julius Caesar defeats Pompey
40 BC Roman Senate names Herod 'King of Judea'
30 BC Suicide of Antony and Cleopatra, Egypt becomes a Roman province

Tradition has ascribed the founding of Rome to Romulus in 753 BC, and dated the Roman republic from the expulsion of the last of the Etruscan kings in 509 BC. At this time it was still only a small city on the Palatine Hill, farming the surrounding countryside just as far as it could easily defend it, like so many other agricultural city-states of the ancient Mediterranean world. Its form of government changed radically during the 1000 years of its history, from the founding of the republic to the deposition of the last Roman western emperor in AD 476. However, the names and titles of the main social groups and the administrative structure from the early days remained in use throughout its history.

The ancient city was composed of a number of families or clans, whose heads, the 'patres', were members of the council, or senate, which advised the king. This group comprised the patricians. Other citizens constituted the plebeians, the common people, who in the early days of the republic were largely at the mercy of the patricians in the senate. Two magistrates, the consuls, who were appointed by the senate, ruled jointly for a year at a time. All citizens were members of two assemblies, originally one for civil and the other for military decisions. During the first two centuries of the republic, the city's politics were dominated by the struggle by the plebeians to gain protection from injustices and equality with the patricians, a battle largely won through compromise: by increasing the number of magistrates and by a complex system of legal controls over power.

To protect the city's existence and life, the Romans gradually extended their control over their neighbours, first by entering into league with them, then leading them, and finally conquering them until Rome had gained control of all central Italy. The secret of Roman success over her neighbours, and eventually the rest of the Mediterranean world, lay in her attitude towards military service. The army was manned by citizens conscripted in rotation, who accepted the very different kind of discipline needed for effective military service, and who were led in battle by the elected magistrates. Although it was a civilian 'militia', rather than a professional army, there were clear and consistent procedures for all military situations, from the pitching of a camp to the assault of a fortified stronghold. All the soldiers were trained in these procedures so that the conscripts during their period of duty, or the magistrates in office for that year, could take over without confusion. All that was needed to make such a force effective was mobility, and this was provided from 312 BC when the first of the great Roman roads, the Via Appia (Appian Way), was built. Such highways eventually linked almost every part of the Roman Empire.

Roman religion emphasized the sacredness of the family and the home by revering the spirits of the family's ancestors, and worshipping the household gods at the domestic altar in each home. The father was the family's priest, whose authority within the family – and as its representative in the city's

BELOW The great Hebrew fortress of Masada was typical of the strongholds which was unable to withstand a Roman army determined to capture it. the spread of Roman power throughout the Mediterranean region during the final centuries BC was largely unplanned. Rome subdued its neighbours to ensure its own safety, and then expanded beyond Italy to secure its shores. At first its armies were manned by its citizens, who were called to their military service in strict rotation, but it soon became necessary to have a standing army of Romans supplemented by auxiliary troops from other nations. Much of the later expansion of the empire came through the appeals for help from nations in the grip of civil war or under attack from powerful neighbours. Once they had restored peace, the Romans put their own administrators in charge, with native rulers assisting them.

INSET The Romans standardized their military methods and applied them throughout the empire. The layout of this Roman camp by the shores of the Dead Sea is the same as camps in Scotland. A marching legion could construct such a camp within hours, and have a secure base for its operations.

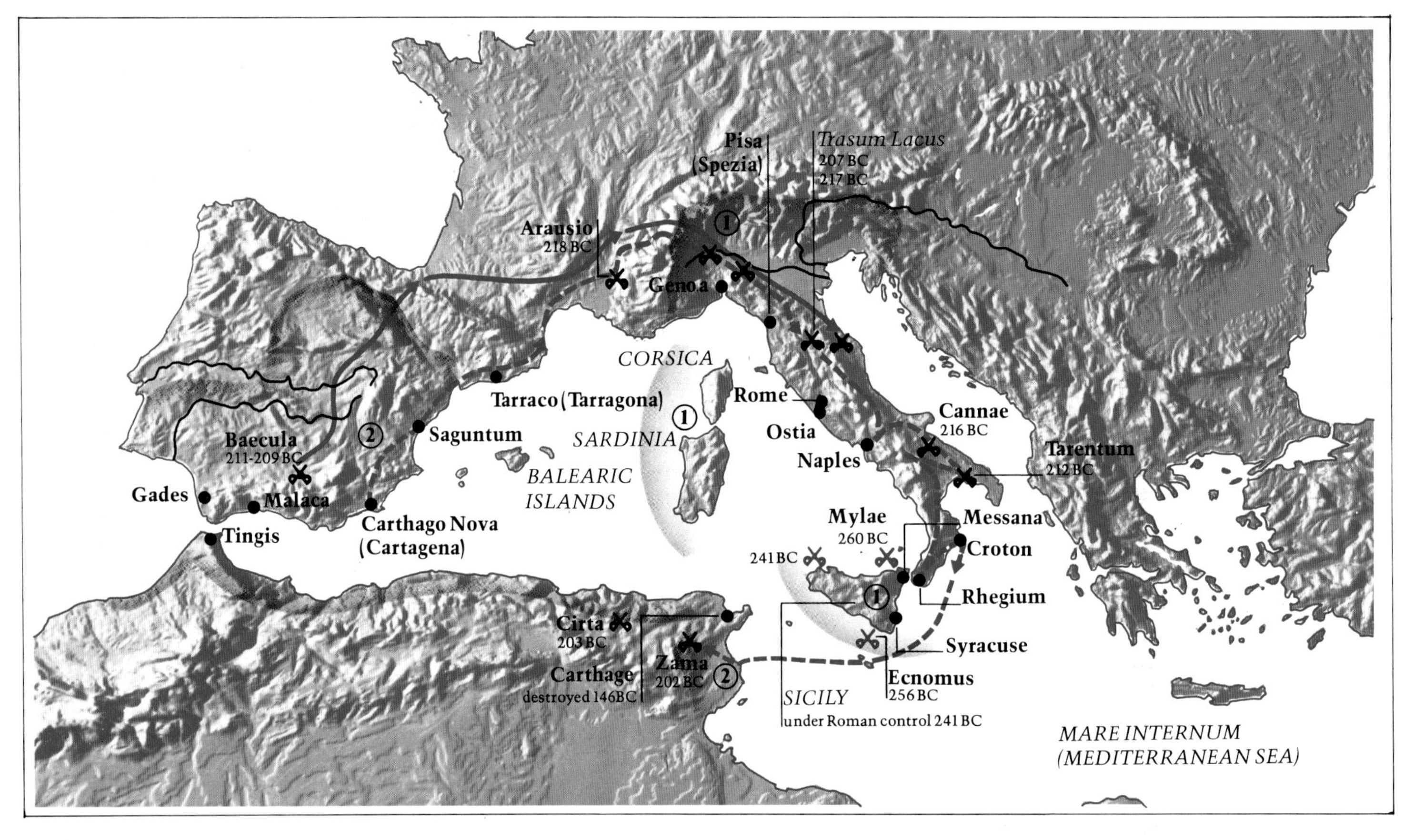

① Roman territory

② Carthaginian territory

First Punic War (264-241BC): Roman naval victories

Second Punic War (218-201BC): battle sites

Carthaginian land campaigns:

Hasdrubal (209-207BC)

Hannibal (219-202BC)

THE PUNIC WARS **The sack of Gaul in 390 BC made the Romans realize that they must control the whole of Italy. Carthage ruled the western Mediterranean and inevitably war broke out between the two powers. There were three Punic (Carthaginian) campaigns; the third one in 149-146 BC resulted in Carthage being razed to the ground. The Carthaginians were defeated after many battles and Rome took possession of all their territory.**

assemblies – was absolute. The same sense of the sacred was felt towards the natural world, and was expressed characteristically in the reading of omens to tell whether it was wise to proceed with any undertaking. The chief gods of the state were Jupiter, supreme deity and god of the heavens, and Mars, the god of war, who also controlled the time of growth and harvest – the season of the year when warfare was most practicable.

The first real conflict between Rome and powers beyond Italy came as Rome extended its control southwards until it began to impinge on the security of the many colonized Greek cities in the southern part of the Italian peninsula. Although independent of their mother cities, the Greek cities as a whole were deeply conscious of their common inheritance. Threatened by Rome, the Greek colony of Tarentum hired King Pyrrhus of Epirus (on the eastern side of the Greek mainland) who brought a professional army to the colony's aid and drove the Romans back in 280 BC and 279 BC. However, the Greeks incurred such heavy losses that Pyrrhus deserted his paymasters when he fought the Romans again in 275 BC, this time indecisively. Thus the Greek cities of Italy had no choice but to accept alliances with Rome.

At this time, the western Mediterranean was controlled by Carthage. Based around modern Tunis, Carthage was originally a Phoenician colony and held the key to the main sea routes through to Spain and beyond. As was to happen later in Palestine, the Romans came into conflict with Carthage through an appeal for help from a small group, the people of Messana in Sicily, who wanted to dislodge a Carthaginian garrison. The incident was the beginning of a long series of wars with Carthage lasting from 264 BC to 146 BC, with periods of truce and times when Rome thought it had forced Carthage into complete submission. Carthage was a strong sea power, and the early stages of the conflict forced the Romans to build a fleet and develop naval tactics. To overcome Carthaginian superiority in seamanship, the Romans fought by manning their ships with legionaries, grappling the enemy ships and fighting as if it were a land engagement. During the second of the wars, which began in 218 BC, the Carthaginian general Hannibal (247-c183 BC) attacked the Romans from the north, with the aid of the famous elephants which his army had led across the Alps. By the third conflict with Carthage in 146 BC, Rome had become a great power, and the conflict ended swiftly with the destruction of Carthage and the selling of its citizens into slavery.

During this part of the third and second centuries BC, Rome had almost been destroyed by defeats both in Italy and in Spain. However, by 205 BC Rome was master of Spain, and by 147 BC extended its rule into Greece and Macedonia, thus becoming sole ruler of the central and western Mediterranean and bringing enormous power and wealth to the city. A change in policy increased this power. Defeated areas were made into provinces of the Roman Empire ruled by an annually-appointed Roman magistrate, instead of being allowed to continue as states in alliance with their conquerors. With power and wealth came increased corruption in Rome, which proved to be beyond the powers of reforming magistrates, and a new situation developed at the end of the second century BC when the Roman army was turned into a professional body. This paved the way for victorious commanders to have a body of troops whose loyalties would be more to their generals than to anyone in Rome.

Rome gained a foothold in Asia Minor in 133 BC when the city was bequeathed the kingdom of Pergamum, which became the rich Roman province of Asia. But the first century BC saw Rome torn apart by civil wars as rival generals, including Julius Caesar, manoeuvred for power. The chaos was only brought to a close by giving power to a single person who would wield absolute authority. The person chosen was Octavius, who was proclaimed Augustus Caesar in 27 BC. His accession marked the end of Rome as a republic, even though he took office with the declared intention of restoring republican government and safeguarding it.

Rome gained control of Palestine with the capture of Jerusalem in 63 BC, at a request by the Jews to stop civil war between rival religious parties. Egypt was made a Roman province in 30 BC, thus ending the rule of the Ptolemies.

LEFT **The Roman road system extended throughout the empire and was standardized everywhere, so that troops and equipment could be moved swiftly wherever they were needed. Trade flourished with the efficient communications.**

ABOVE **The practical skills of Roman engineers can be found in the remains of their building works, seen throughout the empire. Aqueducts, with enclosed water channels, carried water from springs many miles away as towns outgrew their original sources of supply. The basic, simple arch was developed into barrel vaults, and domes of great strength formed from intersecting arches.**

Jews of the Diaspora

Jerusalem, which was rebuilt under the aegis of Persia, was regarded by the Diaspora — Jews who settled outside Palestine — as their religious centre and guardian of their traditions. They developed the synagogue as the distinctive Jewish meeting place and flourished in a number of trades and professions.

There is no definite date for the start of the dispersion of Jews in areas outside Palestine, also called the Diaspora. There are references to groups of people who are almost certainly Hebrews living outside Palestine from long before any of the great deportations began with the Assyrian destruction of the northern Hebrew kingdom of Israel in 721 BC. Hebrews were traders and mercenaries whose professions led to the establishment of Jewish settlements certainly in Egypt and in the trading centres of the Near and Middle East. Palestine, their 'homeland', lay across some of the most important international routes of the ancient world, and it would be surprising if Palestinian Hebrews had not utilized them. However, in normal usage, 'Diaspora' refers to Jews settled outside Palestine who regarded Jerusalem as the centre of their religion and the guardian of their traditions. After the Babylonian exile (587-539 BC), when the Temple of Jerusalem had been rebuilt and was the only officially recognized place for sacrifice, Jerusalem became more and more a centre for pilgrimage by the Jews living at a distance from it.

King Cyrus of Persia, the conqueror of Babylon, encouraged the exiled Jews to return to Palestine to rebuild Jerusalem and its Temple, but it is clear that a substantial number of Jews remained in what was then the Persian Empire. Jewish writings after the exile, such as the Books of Daniel, Tobit and Esther, as well as the histories, take for granted that there were Jews in important positions at the Persian royal court. The Diaspora expanded in number, thriving in a variety of trades and professions.

Many Jews had fled to Egypt at the Babylonian destruction of Jerusalem in 587 BC (2 Kgs 25:26), and there are records of a Jewish colony at Elephantine (near present day Aswan), where there were Jewish mercenary soldiers serving the Persians during the fifth century BC, with their own temple of Yahweh, the Hebrew God. Jewish mercenaries served as defensive forces for Egypt too in Cyrenaica, in present day Libya, and in the area east of the Nile Delta. When the empires, first of Alexander and then of Rome, opened administrative links between the Near East and the rest of the Mediterranean, the numbers of Jews living outside Palestine increased even more, and both Alexandria and Rome had substantial Jewish colonies.

The synagogue, which means 'assembly' in Greek, developed in the Diaspora as the distinctive Jewish meeting place for discussion and worship. This took the form of readings, prayers and reverence of the sacred books, but not of sacrifice. There would also have been such meeting houses in Palestine itself if the regulations restricting sacrifice to the Temple in Jerusalem were enforced.

As Hebrew became a dead language, both for Aramaic-speaking Jews and for the Greek-speaking Jews of the Mediterranean world, the sacred books were translated into other languages. The most important such translation is the Septuagint, the translation into Greek, which was almost certainly produced in Alexandria during the second century BC.

BELOW There are traces of Hebrew settlements outside Palestine from long before the Roman Empire, as Jews remained where they had been exiled, served as mercenaries or engaged in trade. Their meeting places became 'synagogues', where Jews could pray together, read the sacred scriptures and instruct their children. The full expression of Hebrew religion, by animal sacrifices, was only allowed in the Temple in Jerusalem.

INSET The symbol of the seven lamps joined to a single stem comes from the command that Moses was to make one for the original Hebrew shrine (Exod 26:31-40). It may have symbolized the seven days of creation.

The World in 300 BC

The Near and Middle East, soon to be dominated by Rome, had been transformed by its introduction to Hellenistic culture, while in India, the highly-organized Mauryan Empire expanded its control, spreading Buddhism as it went. It was a time of political chaos for China and stability for the American civilizations.

The 11 years which followed Alexander the Great's crossing of the Hellespont in 334 BC and defeat of the Persians on the River Granicus, until his death in 323 BC, transformed not only the Near and Middle East but also created Hellenism, the Greek way of life. Alexander's empire had stretched from the Sahara Desert west of Egypt to the Indus Valley in India, and from the Black Sea and Greece to the Persian Gulf and the Indian Ocean, but it split at his death into first three and then many kingdoms. Seleucus in Babylon gained control of the whole eastern part of the empire, eventually from Asia Minor to the Indus, but the Seleucids could not maintain the unity of so large an area. The Parthian tribesmen were gaining control of what is now northern Iran from their homelands east of the Caspian Sea, and eventually extended their empire throughout Mesopotamia to the borders of Syria. In 53 BC they destroyed a Roman army at Carrhae, and put an eastern limit to Roman expansion.

Further east, in India, Alexander's outposts soon crumbled. His invasion of India, which he thought was only a small peninsula, had extended his army beyond its powers. The army's departure left a power vacuum which was quickly filled by Chandragupta Maurya. About 322 BC, some two years after Alexander's retreat from India, Chandragupta began to expand from his Punjab base in the kingdom of Magadha to the rest of the Punjab and the whole Indus Valley. He defeated Seleucus Nicator in 305 BC and extended his power to take in what is now Afghanistan, so that he controlled all of northern India from his capital of Pataliputra (Patna) on the River Ganges. Within three generations, his dynasty ruled all India except the deep south and had created the Mauryan Empire. It had a highly organized,

BELOW **Alexandria became the greatest port in the ancient world after an old Egyptian port was enlarged by Alexander the Great. He joined the island of Pharos to the mainland to form two harbours, and extended the city to the west. His body was brought from Babylon to be buried there.**

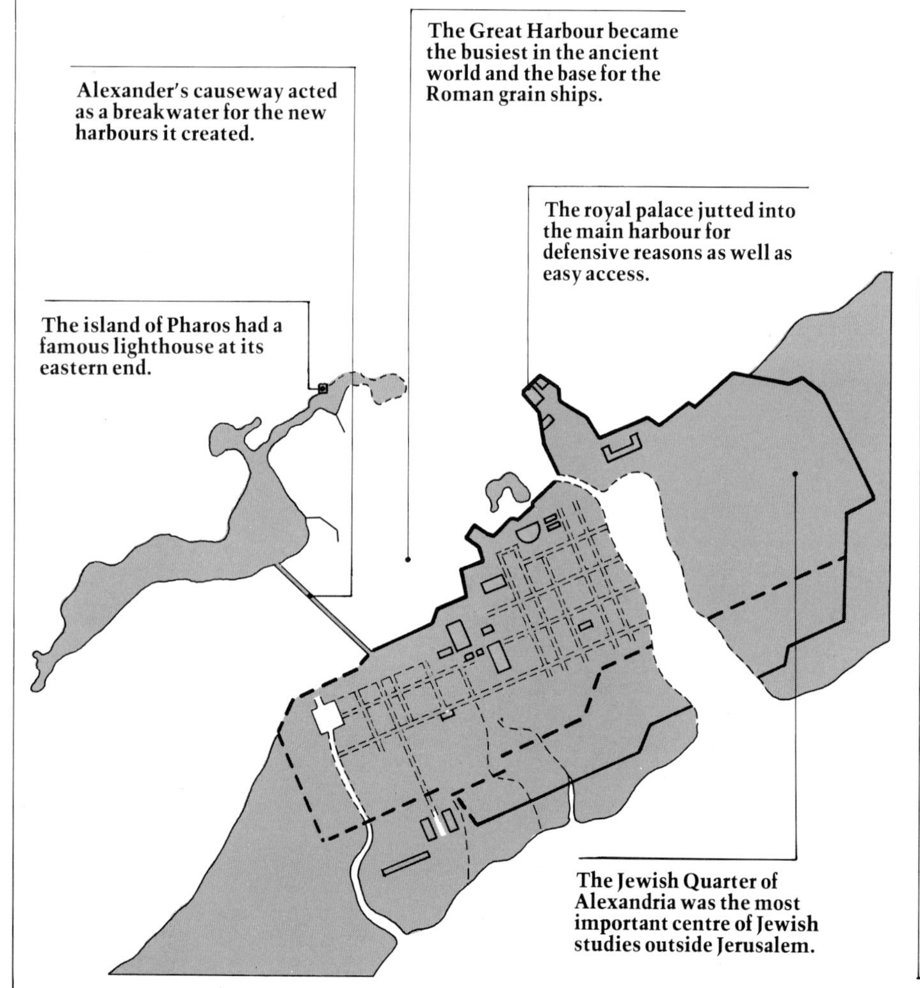

The Great Harbour became the busiest in the ancient world and the base for the Roman grain ships.

Alexander's causeway acted as a breakwater for the new harbours it created.

The royal palace jutted into the main harbour for defensive reasons as well as easy access.

The island of Pharos had a famous lighthouse at its eastern end.

The Jewish Quarter of Alexandria was the most important centre of Jewish studies outside Jerusalem.

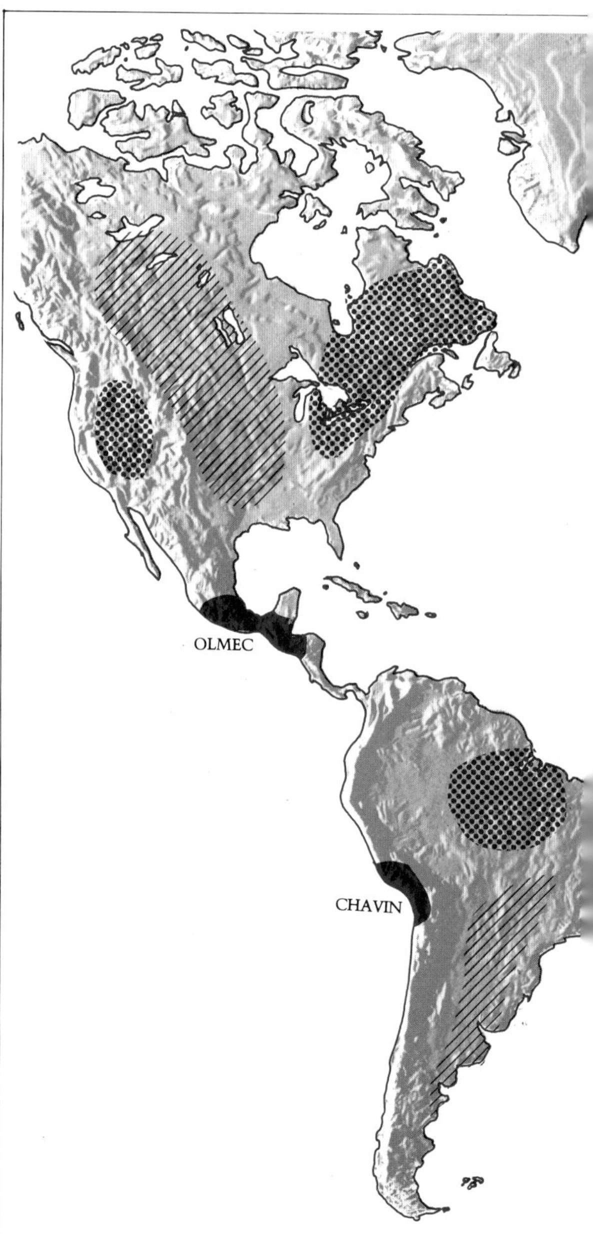

centralized bureaucracy, with separate departments for such concerns as agriculture, forestry, public works, and trade, each with its own provincial officials answerable to heads of department in the capital, and so to the emperor. The administrative hierarchy stretched down to the headman of each village. Chandragupta's grandson, Ashoka, was converted to Buddhism, and, under his rule, its beliefs and laws were codified. Buddhism spread throughout India, without displacing Hinduism, and became a missionary religion beyond.

Further east, China had entered a period of political chaos and vast armies. The situation stimulated the emergence of a series of great thinkers, comparable with the Greek philosophers of the same period, who tried to provide an approach to life which could form the basis for a stable and happy society. These philosophers included Confucius (c551-475 BC), Mencius (c372-289 BC) and Chuang Tzu (c369-286 BC).

In the Mediterranean area, the Greek city-states had only flowered for a brief period and repelled a Persian invasion in famous battles such as Marathon (490 BC) and Thermoplylae (480 BC), but then brought about their own decline in a series of bloody wars between the city states until Alexander imposed his rule. A legacy of outstanding literature, drama, philosophy, sculpture and architecture survives from this period.

By the end of the fourth century BC, Rome had gained control of central Italy and repulsed an invasion of Gauls, who in 390 BC briefly captured and sacked all Rome except the Capitol. In central America, Olmec missionaries were firmly established in the valley of Mexico where they built a pyramid temple. Further south, the unity of the Chavin religion had given way to several separate, local cults.

Developed cultures
Nomadic pastoralists
Hunter-gatherers
Farmers
Farmer expansion
Main trade routes
Silk route

BELOW The century before 300 BC was a time of dramatic change. Alexander swept away the Persian Empire and spread Greek thinking throughout its area. Rome broke out of Italy and Buddhism was becoming more popular in India.

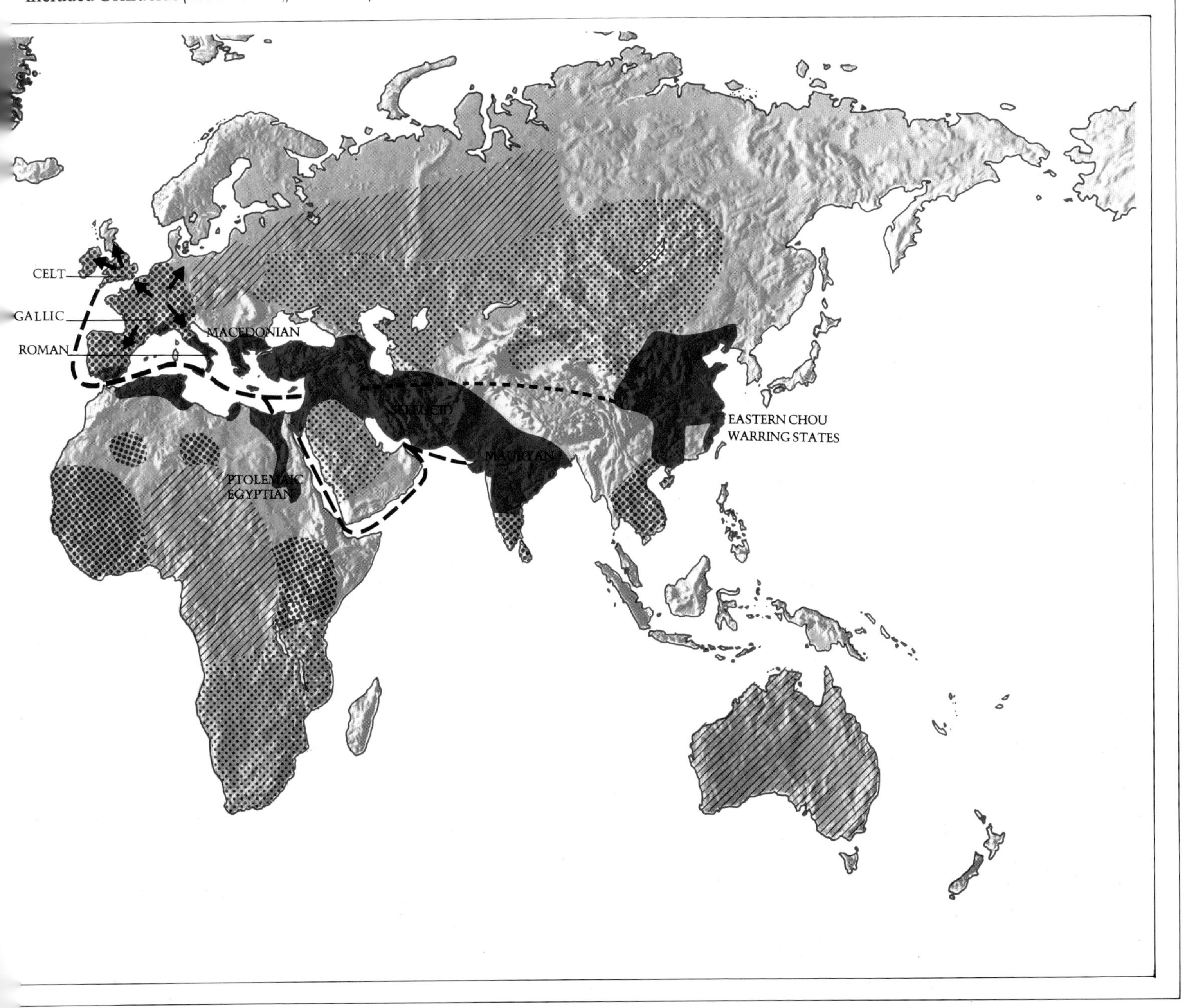

Yahweh's Temple Restored

The Hebrews returned from exile about 538 BC to rebuild their Temple and city in Jerusalem. When the community's morale was particularly low, Nehemiah rallied it with strong administrative measures. Later Ezra supplied a more positive and permanent inspiration — the official laws by which the Jews were to live.

RIGHT **The 'Star of David', here shown carved as part of the decoration of the synagogue at Capernaum, became a symbol of the new Jewish nation after the exile in Babylon. By that time the Hebrew kings had been replaced by the rule of the priests of the Temple in Jerusalem, but King David remained the ideal Jewish leader. He had given his people victory over their enemies and made Jerusalem the central symbol of Hebrew solidarity. The interlocking star became an expression of hope in God, who would restore the glories of King David's time and give the Jews as great a leader.**

By 538 BC the Persians were in firm control of the former Babylonian Empire, including Palestine, and King Cyrus turned his attention to the various national groups which had been exiled by the Babylonians. Among them were the Hebrews exiled from Judah and Jerusalem in 598 and 587 BC, although after a period of some 50 years, they must have consisted mainly of the descendants of the original exiles. In accordance with Persian policy, Cyrus authorized their return to Palestine, with the Temple treasures looted by the Babylonians and the support of funds from the Persian treasury. Some certainly returned, but many remained to become part of the Jewish Diaspora, the Jews living outside Palestine, who would from now always be more numerous than the Palestinian Jews. The Book of Ezra gives a detailed list of the Jews who returned to Jerusalem, but it may reflect the desires of later Jews to have ancestors involved with the return (Ezr 2:1-67).

The Jewish leader, Sheshbazzar, immediately began to organize the rebuilding of the Temple (Ezr 5:14-16), but he disappears from the record and his place is taken by his nephew, Zerubbabel, who was a direct descendant of David. If the Persians intended to restore the Hebrew monarchy it came to nothing, and the new Jewish community was eventually ruled by high priests. The pioneers of restoration brought back the sacrificial worship, practised before the exile, even before the foundations of the new Temple were laid, but the returning Hebrews made a diplomatic blunder which had far-reaching effects. The Samaritans, who were descended from the people brought into the old northern Hebrew kingdom by the Assyrians when they destroyed it in 721 BC, and the people from Judah who had been spared the Babylonian exile, asked to help with the work of rebuilding the Temple. Their help was refused. This was the first step in the long process of withdrawal and isolation, the cultural and political effects of which can still be detected today.

The people whose help had been refused began to oppose the work, a series of poor harvests added to the troubles of the returned exiles, and they felt that they had to devote all their efforts to building houses for themselves and to raising food. At the death of King Cyrus's son and successor Cambyses I in 522 BC, Darius I (522-486 BC) only gained control of the empire after a year of disorder. The prophet Haggai urged the Jewish community to give their attention to rebuilding the Temple, for he warned them that the poor harvest would continue until the work was finished. The disorders in the empire inspired other predictions of an intervention by the Hebrew God, Yahweh (Zech 1-8), in images drawn from the Persian army and through obscure symbolism. The same passages point to Zerubbabel being displaced as joint leader of the community, and control passing into the hands of Joshua, the high priest, alone. The Temple was completed and dedicated in 515 BC.

With the Temple restored, all should have been well, but the neighbouring peoples, especially those from north of the city, managed to prevent work on

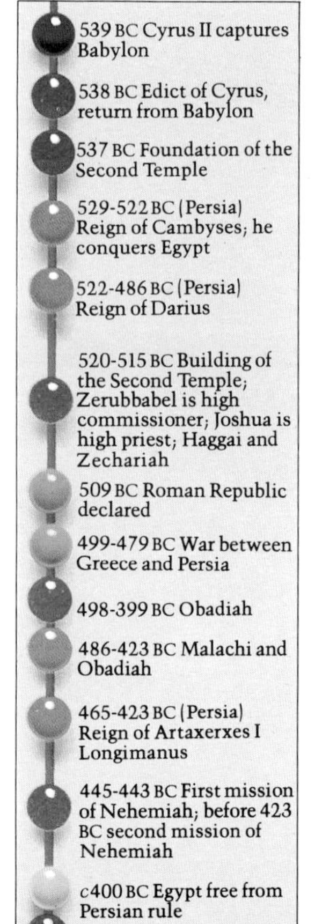

539 BC Cyrus II captures Babylon
538 BC Edict of Cyrus, return from Babylon
537 BC Foundation of the Second Temple
529-522 BC (Persia) Reign of Cambyses; he conquers Egypt
522-486 BC (Persia) Reign of Darius
520-515 BC Building of the Second Temple; Zerubbabel is high commissioner; Joshua is high priest; Haggai and Zechariah
509 BC Roman Republic declared
499-479 BC War between Greece and Persia
498-399 BC Obadiah
486-423 BC Malachi and Obadiah
465-423 BC (Persia) Reign of Artaxerxes I Longimanus
445-443 BC First mission of Nehemiah; before 423 BC second mission of Nehemiah
c400 BC Egypt free from Persian rule
398 BC Ezra's mission

INSETS The beliefs and way of life of the ancient nomadic shepherds was idealized by later Hebrews. All the main traditions and laws of the nation were collected together, in the first five books of the Bible. However, the people quickly adopted the farming methods of the area they conquered, and the new nation of Jews which emerged from the exile in Babylon was deeply influenced by all the changes going on around it. But the ancient traditions were still a centre of stability, and nothing was accepted if it contradicted the religious truths handed down. The Jews welcomed Persian, Greek and Roman ideas, but rejected polytheism and emperor worship.

Ezr, Neh, Isa 56-66, Hag, Zech 1-8, Mal, Obad, 1 and 2 Chr, Ps.

Arise, shine out, for your light has come,
the glory of Yahweh is rising on you,
though night still covers the earth
and darkness the peoples.
Above you Yahweh now rises
and above you his glory appears.
The nations come to your light
and kings to your dawning brightness.
Lift up your eyes and look round:
all are assembling and coming towards you,
your sons from far away
and your daughters being tenderly carried. (Isa 60: 1-4)

restoring the fortifications of Jerusalem, while the new central Persian government found ample evidence in its archives to confirm the Hebrew reputation for sedition. There was real danger that the small Jewish community in Jerusalem would succumb to Persian suspicions and lose its sense of identity. Had this occurred, the Jews of the Diaspora could have had little hope of maintaining the unique religious insights of the Hebrews.

Two men – Nehemiah and Ezra – saved the Jewish community as it struggled to rebuild the shattered Jerusalem. Both of the books in the Old Testament which bear their names were written long after the events they describe, and although they quote documents contemporary with the events themselves, the order in which they are presented is probably not the way things actually happened. For example, it is probable that Nehemiah's two visits to Jerusalem took place before Ezra went there. Nehemiah was a Jew with a position of authority in the court of the Persian king, Artaxerxes I (465-423 BC), to whom he had access. He heard of the low morale of the Jerusalem community and obtained permission from the king to visit the city with an escort of troops, and encourage its people to finish the rebuilding of the city walls. Despite opposition from the Samaritans and the Persian governor of the province, Nehemiah was able to see the walls rebuilt and was then appointed governor of the Jewish area around Jerusalem. He served for 12 years, reformed the taxation system and made Jerusalem a city which would attract more Jews to return to it. During a second term of office, Nehemiah took strong action to protect the worship in the Temple and the observation of the Sabbath. He also legislated against mixed marriages between Jews and non-Jews which had tended to dilute loyalty to the Hebrew religion during the period of the monarchy.

However, any lasting reform of the Jewish community in Jerusalem needed a more positive and permanent form of inspiration than could be provided by administrative measures. Such a transformation was provided by Ezra, who arrived in Jerusalem in 398 BC from the Babylonian Jewish community, armed with Persian royal authority to direct the religious practices of anyone who wished to be recognized as a Jew in the area controlled from Jerusalem. Ezra provided the Jerusalem Jews with the official law by which they were to live. It is not possible to be absolutely certain about the contents of this law, but it was probably the first five books of the Old Testament in their present form.

These books are given the general title of 'the law' in the Hebrew Bible, not merely because they contain the whole body of Hebrew law – religious, civil and criminal – but because their historical sections record the saving acts of God in the creation of the universe, in the escape from Egypt and the covenant. Thus they show the power which lies behind the law, explaining the means by which people can relate effectively to God. The main pattern of these books had been established during the Babylonian exile, under the inspiration of the prophetic teaching about a new covenant which would be available to restore the nation (Jer 31:31-34; Ezek 36-37).

The law was read to the people and explained, with a solemn renewal of the covenant. Ezra then went beyond Nehemiah's regulations about mixed marriages, forcing Jews who had married non-Jewish women to divorce them and renounce the children of the marriage. The new community of the pure law was to be strictly exclusive. This set the pattern for the subsequent exclusiveness of some forms of Judaism.

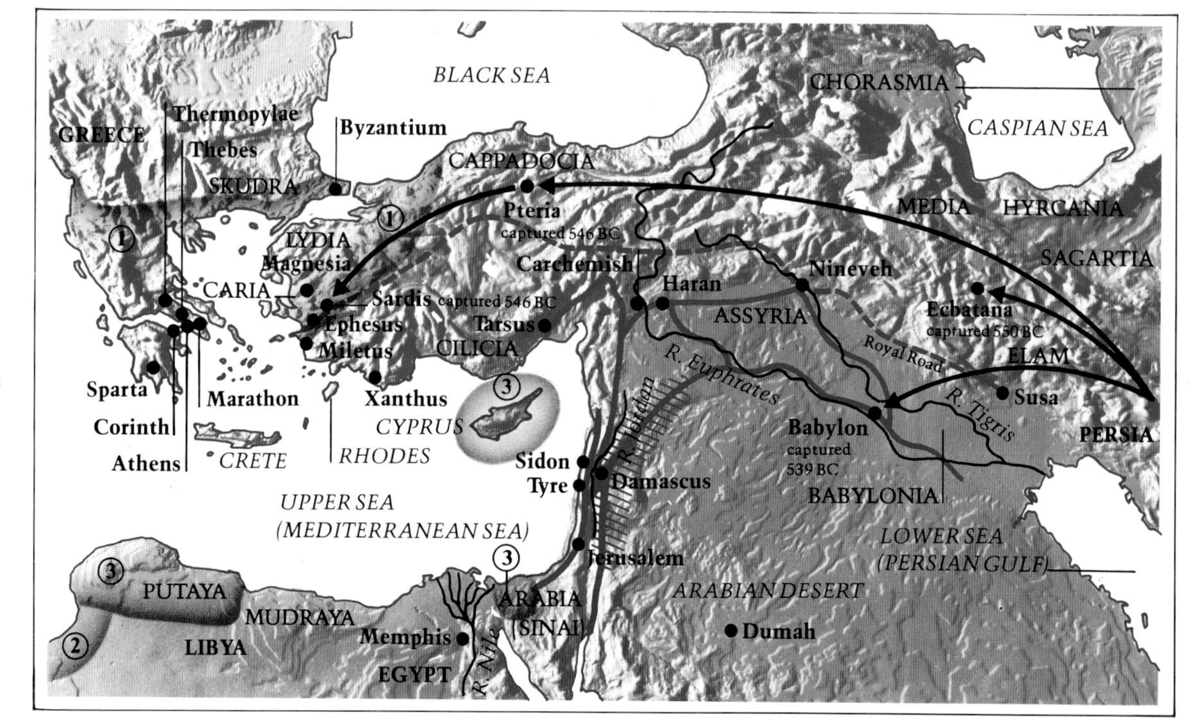

CYRUS AND THE JEWS **The Persian Empire under Cyrus was split into provinces, each ruled by a satrap – 'Beyond the River' was one of the most important. The Persians respected the rights of minorities and the Jews of the Diaspora were able to live according to their own Hebrew law.**

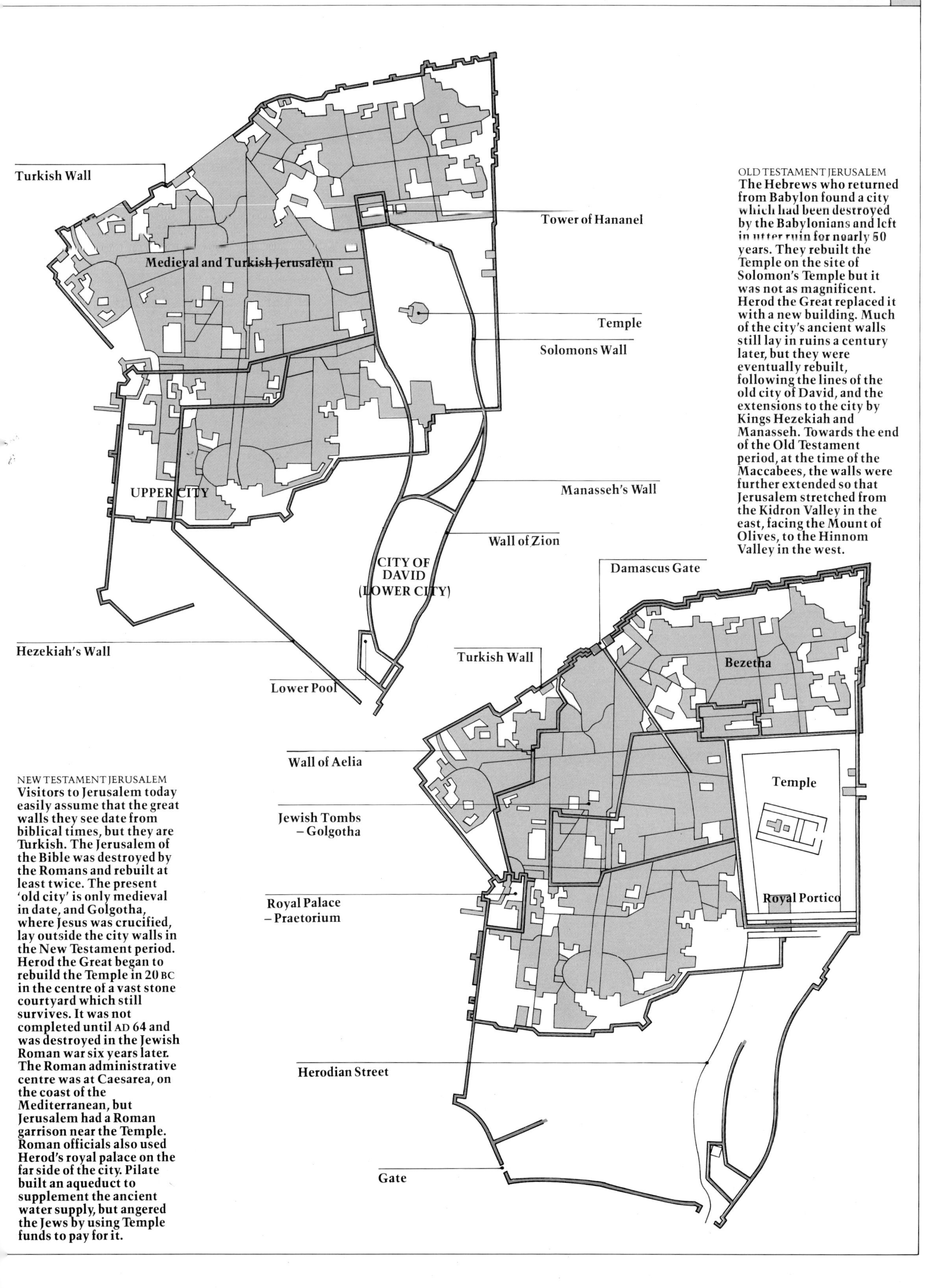

OLD TESTAMENT JERUSALEM

The Hebrews who returned from Babylon found a city which had been destroyed by the Babylonians and left in utter ruin for nearly 50 years. They rebuilt the Temple on the site of Solomon's Temple but it was not as magnificent. Herod the Great replaced it with a new building. Much of the city's ancient walls still lay in ruins a century later, but they were eventually rebuilt, following the lines of the old city of David, and the extensions to the city by Kings Hezekiah and Manasseh. Towards the end of the Old Testament period, at the time of the Maccabees, the walls were further extended so that Jerusalem stretched from the Kidron Valley in the east, facing the Mount of Olives, to the Hinnom Valley in the west.

NEW TESTAMENT JERUSALEM

Visitors to Jerusalem today easily assume that the great walls they see date from biblical times, but they are Turkish. The Jerusalem of the Bible was destroyed by the Romans and rebuilt at least twice. The present 'old city' is only medieval in date, and Golgotha, where Jesus was crucified, lay outside the city walls in the New Testament period. Herod the Great began to rebuild the Temple in 20 BC in the centre of a vast stone courtyard which still survives. It was not completed until AD 64 and was destroyed in the Jewish Roman war six years later. The Roman administrative centre was at Caesarea, on the coast of the Mediterranean, but Jerusalem had a Roman garrison near the Temple. Roman officials also used Herod's royal palace on the far side of the city. Pilate built an aqueduct to supplement the ancient water supply, but angered the Jews by using Temple funds to pay for it.

Greek Influence in the Bible

The Greeks were essentially observers, critically analyzing the world and humanity as they saw it. The influence of the Hellenistic approach can be seen in the collection of biblical material called the 'wisdom literature' – in particular, the Books of Proverbs, Wisdom and Ecclesiasticus.

BELOW **The fashion for things Greek was so powerful that even the Jews of Palestine embraced it enthusiastically. Many of the cities were rebuilt in the Greek style, and in some parts of the area Greek colonies were established. Eventually, the Old Testament had to be translated into Greek, for Hebrew was no longer in everyday use.**
INSET **Theatres and gymnasiums transformed the tastes and habits of the more fashionable Jews, and were to be found all through the country.**

Alexander the Great and his Greek army conquered Palestine between his victory over the main Persian army at Issus in Cilicia in south-east Turkey in 333 BC, and his occupation of Egypt in 332 BC. Little reliable evidence is available about his actions in Palestine, but it suggests that the people north of Jerusalem, the Samaritans, first welcomed him and then rebelled and killed the official left in charge of the area by Alexander. Alexander destroyed Samaria, the chief city, killed most of its citizens as they were escaping, rebuilt the city along Greek lines and settled Macedonians in the area. From the Jewish point of view, another foreign element had been added to the mixture of peoples in Samaria, making Samaritans even less acceptable to strict Jews.

In the aftermath of Alexander, Palestine came under the rule of the Ptolemy kings of Egypt from 304-200 BC, who were descended from one of Alexander's generals. Ptolemy I had taken Alexander's body to Alexandria in the Nile Delta of Egypt, the first of the many new cities to which Alexander had given his own name, and the act symbolizes the enthusiasm with which the Ptolemies introduced the Greek way of life into Egypt. There would have been little clash with traditional Egyptian ideas, for Alexander had been declared a god near Egypt and Egyptian kings had long claimed divinity. Moreover, Alexandria was a new city which the Ptolemies proceeded to make immensely wealthy and develop into the greatest port in the Mediterranean.

The actions of the Ptolemies during the century following Alexander's death in 323 BC were only an extreme example of what was happening in other parts of Alexander's divided empire. The new Greek colonies Alexander had founded attracted Greek immigrants in great numbers, who themselves founded new cities or rebuilt existing ones, and everywhere brought with them the Greek way of life – in architecture, the theatre and gymnasium, poetry, philosophy, historical writings and Greek attitudes towards citizenship. By the time of Alexander there had been at least three centuries of high Greek civilization, and the impetus continued. Alexander himself had been tutored by Aristotle, and Greek traditions in science and philosophy were

Prov 1-9, Eccles, Wis, S of Songs, Job, Eccles, Ezek 38-39.

For within her is a spirit intelligent, holy
unique, manifold, subtle,
active, incisive, unsullied,
lucid, invulnerable,
benevolent, sharp,
irresistible, beneficent,
loving to man,
steadfast, dependable,
unperturbed,
almighty, all-surveying,
penetrating all intelligent,
pure
and most subtle spirits;
for Wisdom is quicker to move than any motion;
she is so pure, she pervades and permeates all things.
She is a breath of the power of God,
pure emanation of the glory of the Almighty;
hence nothing impure can find a way into her.
She is a reflection of the eternal light,
untarnished mirror of God's active power,
image of his goodness.
(Wis 7: 22-26)

BELOW **Greek and Roman theatres developed from the dancing areas surrounding altars, by building tiers of seats up a hillside. By the end of the first millenium BC they were elaborate and large structures with a stage backed by a stone screen containing windows and doorways. The stage was separated from the tiers of seats by a flat semi-circular area which was the only reminder of the original design. Plays were normally performed in association with the regular festivals of the gods.**

RIGHT **As sacrifices could only be performed in the Temple in Jerusalem, the many synagogues of Jews in other places did not have priests. Each synagogue had an elected chairman.**

336-323 BC (Greece) Reign of Alexander the Great; 333 BC he conquers Syria; 332 BC he captures Tyre and Gaza; 332 BC he enters Egypt, 331 BC foundation of Alexandria; 331 BC he ends the Persian Empire; 330-326 BC he conquers the eastern satrapies and India; 323 BC he dies in Babylon

c305-125 BC Seleucid Dynasty

304-200 BC Judea is ruled by Ptolemies

continued in cities such as Alexandria which could boast of such great figures as Zeno, Epicurus and Archimedes.

The Jews in Palestine were deeply influenced both by growth in Greek culture within Palestine itself and by their close involvement with Egypt. Palestinian cities were rebuilt as Greek colonies and some changed their names to signify their new character. Beth-shan became Scythopolis, while Acco was renamed Ptolemais. Little from this period has survived subsequent rebuilding, but it is significant that even later builders developed Greek themes.

Palestine lay on the Egyptian frontier, and both land and sea communications were good. The Jewish population of Egypt, and particularly of Alexandria, grew considerably until Jews constituted the largest foreign element in the city with their own quarter and permission to manage their own affairs. Alexandria became the main source of Greek influence on Jewish ways of thought, but the same process was going on throughout the Diaspora. The Jews dispersed through the ancient world had now become deeply influenced by the Greek way of life.

The effects of this influence on the Hebrews can be seen in many ways. The clearest indication was the need to translate the Hebrew sacred books into Greek, and Alexandria, with its large Jewish community and its official support for scholars, was the obvious place for it to be done. Under the Ptolemies the translation work proceeded during the third century BC, eventually to produce the Greek version of the Old Testament known as the Septuagint. It is an important witness to

BELOW **The influence of Greek dramatic traditions may be seen in the structure of the Old Testament's Book of Job. Job's sufferings, the speeches of his 'friends' and God's intervention would have been familiar theatre.**

the actual contents of the books of the Old Testament at the time when the translation was made, and was also, of course, the version normally used by New Testament authors when quoting from the Old Testament. Most Jews, whether in Palestine or elsewhere, no longer used Hebrew, and for very many of them Greek was their native tongue.

Greek attitudes may be seen in more subtle ways in the Hebrew books of the Old Testament and its associated books, which were written or edited at this time. The Greeks were essentially observers and recorders of the world and humanity as they actually saw them, and they tried to establish the principles which would help explain what they observed. They hoped that such a process of critical analysis would provide a firm foundation for life. Hebrew authors, influenced by this Hellenistic approach, adopted a similar attitude and applied it to the traditional Hebrew understanding of life in relationship with God. The result was the collection of biblical material usually called the 'wisdom literature'. The heart of such writings consists of collections of wise sayings – proverbs – which can be found from the earliest times in Egypt, while the wisdom is the practical knowledge of what is needed for stable government and a satisfying life. Among the Hebrews, King Solomon had a reputation for such knowledge, and much of the Hebrew wisdom literature was attributed to him.

Traditional proverbs and guides for correct conduct predominate in three of the biblical wisdom books: Proverbs, Wisdom and Ecclesiasticus, but even in these there are passages which reflect characteristically Greek ideas about the nature of the world (for example, Prov 8:22-31). The books also contain delightful, well observed and vividly related glimpses into the seamier side of Hebrew life, (as in Prov 7.6-20), and such famous passages as the description in Proverbs of the perfect wife (Prov 31:10-31). One of the books, the Song of Songs, is a collection of love poems, certainly secular in origin, which implies that this is a glimpse of the consummation of man's relationship with God.

The beauty and grandeur of the natural world is another prominent theme in the wisdom books, which delight in the sheer variety and richness of the world as evidence of the creative power of God (Job 28:1-12). But there is also a deeper theme running through them. This is the realization that enquiry exposes the limits of human reason, and yet the questions have to be asked relentlessly. Two books, Job and Ecclesiastes, pursue this theme in their different ways. The Book of Job is a persistent enquiry into the problem of innocent suffering. Earlier Hebrew writings tended to deny this question as suffering was seen as evidence of guilt. It provides no answer except an agnosticism in the presence of the omniscience of God. Ecclesiastes examines a wide range of human endeavours, and can find nothing of lasting value in them. Only the final chapter (Eccles 12) gives a glimpse of a divine plan beneath the transitory state of the world. Many of the themes in the wisdom writings can be found in the Psalms, which gives a clear indication of their popular appeal. Although tradition attributed the Psalms to King David, they evolved over many centuries of use, particularly by worshippers in the Temple.

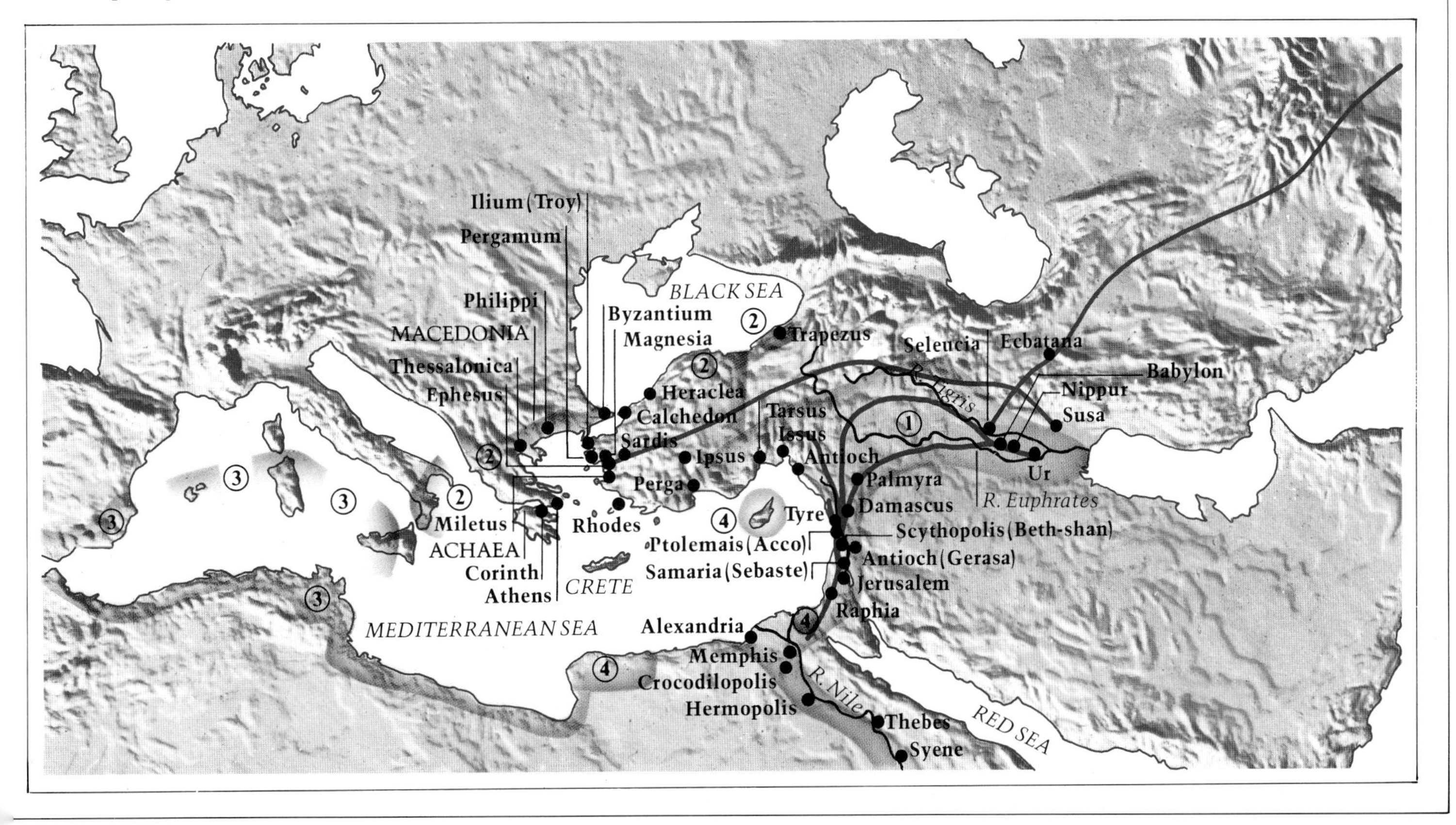

Main trade routes

① Areas of Jewish settlement before 500BC

② Extension of Jewish settlement after Alexander

Movement of the Diaspora:

③ Carthaginian Jews

④ Jewish settlements established under supervision of Egypt

EXTENDING THE DIASPORA
Traders, craftspeople and scholars, many of them Jews, were attracted to the new cities built by Alexander. Alexandria in Egypt had the largest Jewish colony.

The Struggle for Independence

The Seleucids gained control of Palestine from the Ptolemies in 200 BC, at a time when the Jerusalem Jews were themselves divided into two bitterly opposed factions. Civil war broke out, followed by the Maccabean war against the Seleucids, which eventually led to a brief period of Jewish independence.

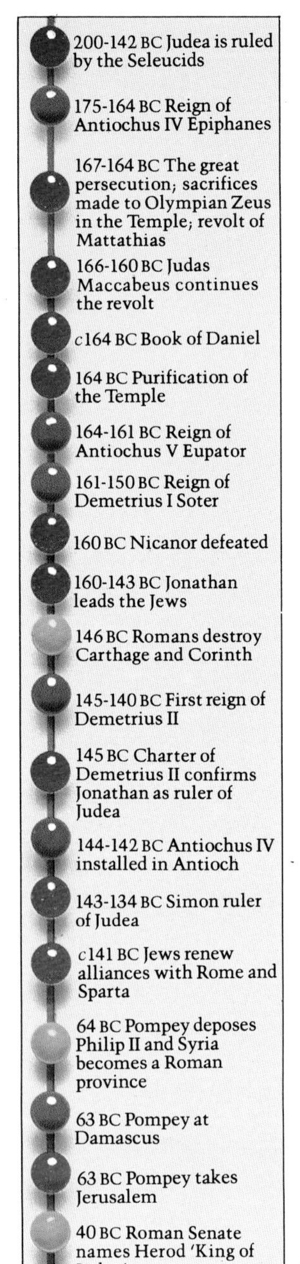

200-142 BC Judea is ruled by the Seleucids
175-164 BC Reign of Antiochus IV Epiphanes
167-164 BC The great persecution; sacrifices made to Olympian Zeus in the Temple; revolt of Mattathias
166-160 BC Judas Maccabeus continues the revolt
c164 BC Book of Daniel
164 BC Purification of the Temple
164-161 BC Reign of Antiochus V Eupator
161-150 BC Reign of Demetrius I Soter
160 BC Nicanor defeated
160-143 BC Jonathan leads the Jews
146 BC Romans destroy Carthage and Corinth
145-140 BC First reign of Demetrius II
145 BC Charter of Demetrius II confirms Jonathan as ruler of Judea
144-142 BC Antiochus IV installed in Antioch
143-134 BC Simon ruler of Judea
c141 BC Jews renew alliances with Rome and Sparta
64 BC Pompey deposes Philip II and Syria becomes a Roman province
63 BC Pompey at Damascus
63 BC Pompey takes Jerusalem
40 BC Roman Senate names Herod 'King of Judea'

In the course of an upheaval typical of the ancient Near East, control of Palestine changed hands yet again in 198 BC, following the defeat of the Ptolemaic ruler of Egypt by the Seleucid King Antiochus III (223-187 BC) at Panion near one of the sources of the River Jordan in the southern foothills of Mount Hermon. It was an exchange of one Hellenistic ruler for another, for the Seleucids, like the Ptolemies, were also descended from a general of Alexander the Great, but it broke the comfortable relationship which had developed between the influential Jews of Jerusalem and their Egyptian rulers. Jews had been allowed to live by the Hebrew laws and practise their religion without interference. Like Egyptian priests and temples, the priests of Jerusalem and all the revenues of the Temple were exempt from tax; the Temple worship was subsidized from Egyptian state funds, and funds were given for the maintenance of the buildings. All this was threatened by the change of rule.

At first, the Seleucids continued to allow the Palestinian Hebrews to continue their traditional way of life unhindered. But Rome was just beginning to exert its influence on the area, and this was to have radical effects on the Seleucid kings as their vast empire disintegrated under pressure from the Romans in the west and the Parthians in the east. The Jews of Palestine experienced the results in the form first of increased taxation, and then of direct interference with the Hebrew religion.

Rome had defeated its old enemy Carthage in 201 BC, and the Carthaginian general, Hannibal, fled to the Seleucids. King Antiochus of Seleucia foolishly invaded Greece as the protector of Hellenism, the Greek culture of the Near East. He was driven back by the Romans and defeated in western Asia Minor in 190 BC. Antiochus was forced to abandon Asia Minor to Roman protection and to pay a great sum of money as indemnity. From then on, the Seleucid kings always had the threat of Rome hanging over them and were always in need of financial support.

Antiochus himself was killed in 187 BC while taking treasures from a temple in the eastern part of the empire, and his successor, Seleucus IV (187-175 BC), tried to gain possession of funds in the Temple in Jerusalem, with the help of a dissident Jewish faction. Both aspects of this incident – only resolved by the Jewish high priest taking the matter to the royal court – were significant, for it highlighted the deep tensions among Jerusalem Jews between those who supported Hellenism and those who rejected it as a danger to traditional Hebrew religion. It also shows that the Temple itself was vulnerable to the financial needs of the Seleucid kings.

When Seleucus IV was assassinated in 175 BC, his brother succeeded him as Antiochus IV (175-164 BC). He had the title Epiphanes, meaning 'god manifest'. Antiochus had been a hostage in Rome as security for Seleucid conformity to Roman policy, and found his empire on the verge of disintegration. He mounted a vigorous campaign to unite his people, successfully invaded Egypt to neutralize Egyptian attempts to take

BELOW The small Jewish state gained independence for about 95 years after the Maccabean war, but it was soon torn by bitter internal divisions. Such strongholds as Masada were a refuge for Jewish rulers from the anger of their own people, as well as being defensive against national enemies. INSET Greek forms were still the main force in Jewish art and architecture even after they had won freedom from Greek rule.

Joel, Zech 9-14, Isa 24-27, Dan, 1 and 2 Macc, Ruth, Jon, Esth, Judith, Tobit, Bar.

'I gazed into the visions of the night.
And I saw, coming on the clouds of heaven,
one like a son of man.
He came to the one of great age
and was led into his presence.
On him was conferred sovereignty,
glory and kingship,
and men of all peoples, nations and languages became his servants.
His sovereignty is an eternal sovereignty
which shall never pass away,
nor will his empire ever be destroyed. (Dan 7: 13-14)

control of Palestine again, and encouraged Hellenism as a common bond among his varied subjects. He did nothing to stop other expressions of religion and ways of life, so at first there was no direct suppression of the Hebrew religion or even interference with it. But the situation was ripe for a bitter explosion among the rival factions within the Jewish client state, which was ruled by the high priests of Jerusalem. Actions of Antiochus Epiphanes sparked these tensions into civil war.

In the second century BC Jerusalem housed a strange mixture of attitudes. At one extreme were Jews who enthusiastically embraced the Hellenistic way of life. They fostered every expression of it in architecture, dress, drama, and naked athletics took place at a gymnasium erected by Jews within Jerusalem itself. At the other extreme were Jews who maintained the strictest interpretation of the Hebrew law, as it had been imposed by Nehemiah and Ezra two centuries earlier on the basis of the most sacred of the Hebrew religious books: the opening five books of the Old Testament. Surprisingly, the various religious parties were not divided between religious officials and laity, indeed, some of the most extreme expressions of Hellenism were fostered by one of the high priests and the priests of the Hebrew Temple itself.

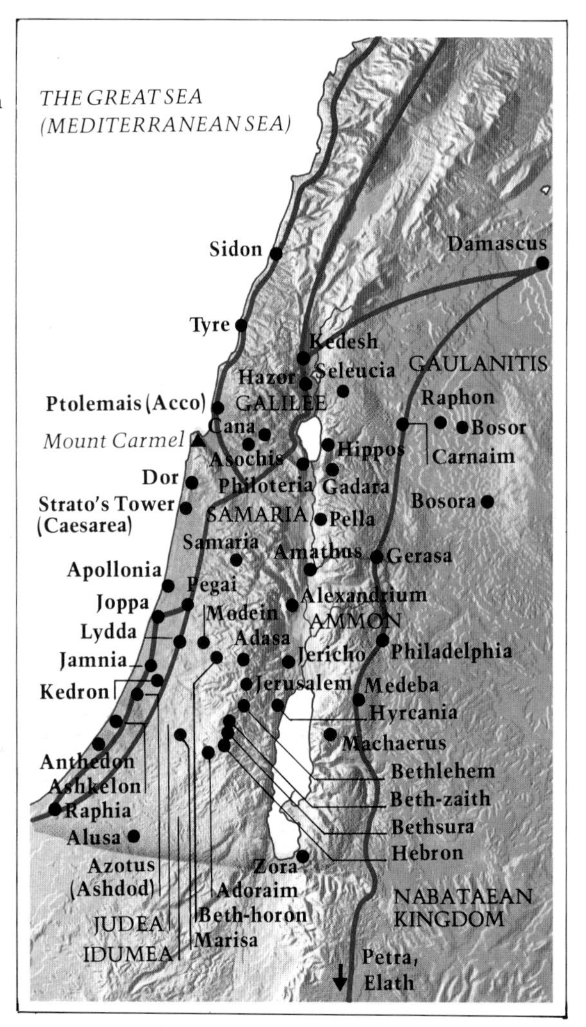

Main trade routes

Extent of the Maccabean kingdom

THE MACCABEAN WARS
After Alexander the Great, Greek rulers controlled the Near and Middle East for more than 200 years. Palestine was ruled first by the Ptolemies of Egypt and then by the Seleucids of Syria, until the Jews won their freedom by the Maccabean rebellion. The rising was provoked by Greek interference with the Temple in Jerusalem and with Jewish rites, coupled with demands by the Seleucid king that he be worshipped as a god. Although some Jews accepted Greek religious claims, a small group resisted fiercly to keep the purity of the Hebrew faith. Fierce persecution provoked a full war, in which the Jews were at first defeated. When the Jews at last gained their independence, the Maccabean dynasty ruled from Jerusalem as high priests. The ancient sanctuaries of Dan and Beer-sheba became the national boundaries for a time. Although other sanctuaries were in use, the Temple in Jerusalem was the only official place of sacrifice. The newly won freedom soon foundered in civil war.

In the convoluted politics of Jerusalem, the high priest – the head of what was in effect a puppet kingdom – was appointed by the Seleucid emperor, always provided that the Hebrew legal requirements for the office were fulfilled. In 174 BC Antiochus IV deposed the high priest Onias in favour of Onias's brother Jason, a fervent Hellenist who could pay Antiochus well for the office. Jason in turn was outbid and deposed in 171 BC in favour of Menalaus, who sold the Temple vessels to pay Antiochus's bribe. Onias, deposed three years earlier, protested and was assassinated. Civil war broke out, and when the high priest Menelaus was driven from Jerusalem, Antiochus treated it as a sign of rebellion against Seleucid rule, and plundered the Temple. Conservative Jews now began to see Antiochus as an enemy of the Hebrew religion.

The final provocation came in 167 BC when a royal commissioner, appointed by Antiochus to help the high priest with his policy of Hellenization, found that he did not have sufficient troops to keep order in Jerusalem. A large force of Greek mercenaries was despatched to Jerusalem by Antiochus. They slaughtered many of the people and built a fortress, called the Acra, near the Temple to house a Greek garrison. This fortress was given the status of a self-governing city-state, and its members treated the Temple as their shrine. The Hebrew God, Yahweh, was regarded as Zeus, the main Greek god, while Antiochus himself would have been worshipped there.

Naturally, all this provoked further opposition from conservative Jews, which Antiochus met by stopping all the privileges enjoyed by the Hebrew religion, forbidding the sacrifices, observation of the Sabbath and the traditional festivals, stopping circumcision and ordering the Hebrew sacred law books to be destroyed. An altar of Zeus was erected in the Temple and pigs were sacrificed on it. Jews throughout Palestine were forced to take part in what they regarded as idolatrous and pagan worship. Some Jews found no objection to much of this, for it was normal in the Hellenic world to identify local, national gods with the Indo-European gods of Greek religion. Others accepted it unwillingly, but some took to arms to resist the decrees of Antiochus. He reacted ruthlessly against any Jews who tried to resist his commands. There were massacres and Jews were executed by the cruellest means. In some cases they refused to defend themselves because they were observing the Sabbath.

The persecution – for such it had become – produced a Jewish leader, a priest from the village of Modein near Lod, who in 167 BC killed a conforming Jew and a royal officer, and fled to the hills with his five sons. When he died in the following year, his son Judas Maccabeus led an organized rebellion which marks the beginning of the Maccabean War, which eventually led to Jewish independence. The rebels sought to restore the ancient purity of the Hebrew religion, but at first they only represented a minority of Jews. Other Jews were content to accept Hellenistic culture as fully compatible with traditional Hebrew ideals about God.

The Maccabean War of the Jews against the Seleucids is recorded in the two Books of Maccabees. The first is a reasonably convincing account of the compaigns which ended with the defeat of the Seleucids and it also contains a fascinating account of the impression Rome made on the Jews at this time, and of the treaty of friendship (1 Macc 8). The second book is more concerned with two popular Jewish feasts which originated in the Maccabean rebellion.

The Seleucid king Antiochus Epiphanes was committed to a campaign against the Parthians in the eastern part of his empire, so the guerrilla forces of Judas Maccabeus were able to win a series of victories against Seleucid armies, and his successes attracted more Jews to join him. The rebellion gained momentum, and, after further victories against more formidable Seleucid armies, Judas Maccabeus was able to take Jerusalem in 164 BC, besiege the Seleucid garrison in its fortress, clear the Temple of all its non-Hebrew worship and rededicate it to the Hebrew God, Yahweh. This achievement is still commemorated by the Jewish Feast of the Dedication. The rebellion had already proved successful beyond all expectations.

The Maccabees then extended the rebellion to help Jewish groups in the rest of Palestine and the surrounding areas. But their fortunes changed in 163 BC when Judas was defeated by Lysias, the regent of the young Antiochus V (164-161 BC) who became Seleucid king at the death of Antiochus. Lysias and Antiochus V had to return to Antioch, where they were both murdered, and the Hellenistic Jews appealed to the new Seleucid king, Demetrius I (161-150 BC), for help against the Maccabee brothers and their supporters. Judas Maccabeus defeated and killed the Seleucid general Nicanor near Upper Beth-horon and Adasa in 160 BC. This feat is commemorated by the Jewish festival 'The Day of Nicanor'. Later in the same year Judas himself was defeated and killed by another Seleucid army led by Bacchides in a battle near the site of Nicanor's defeat.

Judas's brother Jonathan took over the leadership and held it from 160 to 143 BC. Jonathan was able to take advantage of the shifting politics of Seleucid royal power, as the throne changed hands three times in quick succession. He was high priest from 152 to 143 BC, but he was imprisoned and murdered at the end of that period. Another Maccabee brother, Simon, stepped into the leadership, and in exchange for his support of King Demetrius II (145-140 and 129-125 BC) was made high priest and ruler of the Jews. This marks the beginning of control by Jews over their own affairs. Despite further attempts by Seleucid kings to impose their rule over the Jews, pressure from Rome put restraints on the Seleucid efforts. Yet this was far from being a peaceful period. The different parties within the Jewish state fought each other bitterly for power, and although Jewish control was extended to the boundaries of the old Davidic empire and the Greek cities were forced to accept some form of Judaism, internal tensions reached a state of civil war in which both sides appealed to Rome for help. The Roman general Pompey (106-48 BC) entered Jerusalem in 63 BC, captured the Temple, which was being defended by the current king and high priest, and made Palestine part of the Roman province of Syria. The brief period of Jewish independence had not even lasted 100 years.

The religious groups and parties familiar from New Testament times emerged during the rebellion against Greek rule and the period of independence under the Maccabees. The Sadducees were mainly the priests and their supporters while Pharisees were mainly lay people, possibly originating with the Hasideans of the early Maccabean rebellion who were particularly strict towards the Hebrew law. The Essenes, who formed the community at Qumran near the north-western end of the Dead Sea, may also have originated with the Hasideans.

The apocalyptic biblical writings, such as Zechariah 9-14 and the Book of Daniel, are best seen against the background of political protest and rebellion which characterized the period of Seleucid rule. This kind of literature employs deliberately obscure symbolism to reassure its readers – who would understand the allusions – that God would triumph over their persecutors. The Hebrew writings had reached their final stage, and would soon be formed into the collection of material which Christians call the Old Testament. It reflects the experiences and religious insights of the Hebrew people through 2,000 years of their history, and it would inspire people worldwide through future centuries – Jews, Christians and Muslims – who would revere it as a major source of religious truth.

BELOW **Under the rule of the Maccabees, the Jews entered into a defensive alliance with Rome, to protect their newly won independence. When the Jewish state collapsed in civil war, both sides called for the Romans to restore peace. From 65 BC onwards Palestine was ruled by Rome, which appointed native kings under a Roman governor. Herod the Great was the first such puppet king of the Jews, and retained his throne until his death in 4 BC. Herod and his family ruled ruthlessly and held their power, with Roman help, from five great fortresses: Masada (BELOW), Herodium, Machaerus, Alexandrium and Hyrcania. During this period groups formed with names familiar from the New Testament, such as Pharisees, Sadducees and Zealots. The religious life of Jews, and much of their secular life was well, was under the control of the high priest of the Temple in Jerusalem, who presided over the Sanhedrin, a council of 71 members.**

BELOW Despite its great beauty, the Dead Sea and its shores are inhospitable and sterile, except for places where fresh water springs make farming possible. But it was an area of strategic importance, as the mountains to the east harboured some of the Hebrews' most bitter enemies, and the Hebrews themselves had conquered Palestine from these parts after the escape from Egypt. During the period of independence, and in the early years of Roman protection, the Jews fortified two natural strongholds, Machaerus and Masada, on either side of the Dead Sea. They commanded the important roads through the region. The garrison of Masada would have had this view across the Dead Sea. During the Jewish-Roman war (AD 66-70), Masada became a powerful symbol of Jewish resistance to foreign rule.

INSETS The enormous water cisterns built into the rock on the top of Masada, had to be filled from springs more than 1000 feet (300 metres) below. The fortress was maintained by slaves.

5 · *ORIGINS OF*

CHRISTIANITY

When the evening came he arrived with the Twelve. And while they were at table eating, Jesus said, 'I tell you solemnly, one of you is about to betray me, one of you eating with me'. They were distressed and asked him, one after another, 'Not I, surely?'
(Mark 14:17-19)

The Witnesses of Jesus

The New Testament records the life and work of Jesus, through the sermons and writings of the disciples who had been with him during his public life and had witnessed his crucifixion and resurrection. They regarded themselves as the new chosen people, through whom God was offering salvation to the whole world.

The most widely accepted date for the crucifixion and resurrection of Jesus Christ is AD 30, and the New Testament as it now exists began to be written about 15 years afterwards. During the years before anything was written, the new Christian faith was transmitted by word of mouth. Information about Jesus was obtained by contact with people who had known him personally, passing information to others who became his followers.

The men and women who had been with Jesus throughout his public life, and who had been witnesses of his crucifixion and resurrection – the disciples – were convinced that, by receiving the Holy Spirit, they had been given a share in the risen life of Jesus and in his freedom as Son of God. Consequently, they looked on themselves as the new chosen people, through whom God was offering salvation to the whole world. This conviction was confirmed for them by the experience of trying to live as Jesus had lived. They continued to worship in the temples and synagogues of the Jewish religion, but their experience of Jesus led them to a new interpretation of the Jewish Passover – the eucharist – based on the actions and words of Jesus at the meal he ate with his disciples before his arrest and death.

This is the background for the apostles' preaching which was reported in the early chapters of the Acts of the Apostles. The general structure and contents of the apostles' sermons and speeches are reflected in the Letters of the New Testament, which emphasize the significance of Jesus's life. Eventually this material became the basis of the four Gospels.

Those who listened to the apostles heard that God's revelations during the Old Testament period had reached their climax and fulfilment in the life, death and resurrection of Jesus. He was the Messiah, the Christ. He had come from God and had now returned to him to be 'Lord of the whole creation', as both man and God. Through the Holy Spirit, Jesus Christ now shared his powers with the members of the Christian community, which was open to all who were prepared to turn to God, to accept Jesus as Lord, and to receive baptism. They were told to act swiftly because God would soon bring his whole plan of salvation to its completion with the second coming of Jesus and a general judgement of all people.

The apostles supported their preaching and teaching with recollections of Jesus' life as they had witnessed it. They told of the things he did and said, particularly details of his final days in Jerusalem, leading up to his crucifixion and resurrection. Christianity was still based on word of mouth, but the people who knew Jesus personally began to die or be killed. The Gospels were then written down to record the apostles' experiences of Jesus. Some of this material may have been preserved in written form at an earlier date, but it was not until about AD 65 that the first of the Gospels was written in the form that is familiar today. This was some 35 years after the death of Jesus. During the next 20 years the other three Gospels were written. The New Testament Letters date from about AD 45 to the end of the first century.

BELOW Seen from the Mount of Olives, the Temple area dominates Jerusalem. The main feature is the great stone platform for the Temple courtyards, built by Herod the Great. The Temple itself stood on the site of the domed building, a Muslim shrine which protects the bare rock of the hill sacred to Jews and Muslims. The Jerusalem of King David's time lay to the left of the present Temple area, and the city spread beyond the Temple, where modern Jerusalem has continued the expansion.

The Strength of Judaism

Rome's power was at a peak during New Testament times. Until the Jewish war in AD 66-70, Jews throughout the empire enjoyed special privileges, including the freedom to practise their religion. But they still regarded Jerusalem as the true Hebrew centre and only there could the full rites be practised.

Almost everywhere in Europe, and throughout the Mediterranean area, there is still visible evidence of Roman civilization from nearly 2,000 years ago. During New Testament times the empire was reaching its greatest extent and Rome was at the peak of its power. Palestine was incorporated into a Roman province by Pompey (106-48 BC), who deposed the last of the Seleucid kings in 64 BC, and in the following year captured Jerusalem. He was in the Near East by authority of the Roman Senate, but the years which followed his return to Rome saw the end of the old political balances in the Roman state, civil war, and the transition from republic to dictatorship.

In 27 BC, Octavian became emperor and took the name Augustus. By this time, Julius Caesar had defeated Pompey and in his turn been assassinated in the Senate. In addition, Antony had committed suicide after defeat by Octavian in the naval battle at Actium in 31 BC. After these events the people of Rome were glad to be ruled by a man who was strong enough to end the civil wars which had raged for a century. Although in theory the emperor ruled by authority of the Senate, his real power lay in control of the army and the elite praetorian guard responsible for his personal safety. In all, there were about 300,000 men, organized in 25 legions and nine cohorts of praetorians. A legion contained between 3,000 and 6,000 soldiers and a cohort a tenth of that number. However, exact numbers are not really relevant, for there were also auxiliary troops, and, in any case, the Roman army's military superiority rested on its efficiency, training and ruthless discipline, rather than on numerical strength. Its routine discipline was in the hands of long serving centurions, who were theoretically in charge of groups of 100 men, but junior and higher command fell to members of the senatorial aristocracy as normal stages in political advancement. Thanks to the good roads it had constructed, Rome could move troops swiftly throughout the empire.

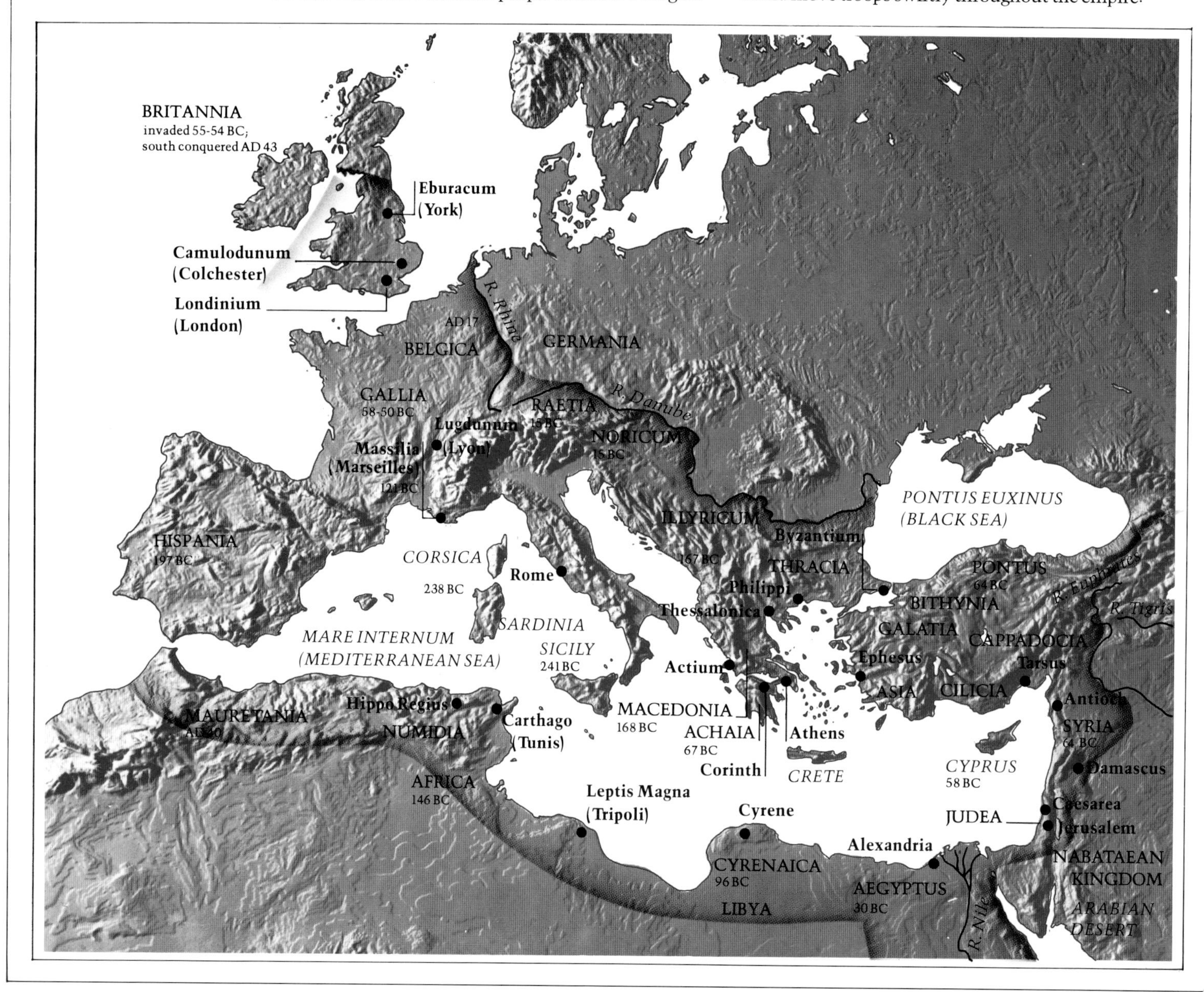

THE SUPREMACY OF ROME **The power of the Romans was at its zenith under the early emperors. Their vast empire extended over western Europe, Asia Minor, the Near and Middle East, and included most of the north coast of Africa.**

Extent of Roman Empire, 1st century AD

Augustus took control of the empire's financial structure. This was administered by a competent civil service created by extending the imperial household, and sustained by direct and indirect taxation. Law was administered by tribunals, and, in theory, rested on written laws constitutionally enacted, but Augustus could reverse any decision, give rulings which became law, and control the way the law was administered. In effect, he and subsequent emperors were law-makers who were themselves above the law. This was to have important effects when the army grew to such power that it could depose and create emperors.

The successes of Roman armies flooded Rome and the empire with slaves, who outnumbered free Romans long before the days of the emperors. Slaves constituted the lowest layer of Roman society which embraced incredible extremes of wealth and poverty, privilege and oppression. Roman citizenship, which was gradually extended to other parts of the empire by purchase or for services to the Roman state, gave much valued protection to those who possessed it. For example, Paul was to benefit greatly from his Roman citizenship (Acts 22:25-29). Slavery also had serious effects on politics and on the economy, as free tradesmen were driven out of business by the use of slaves, increasing the numbers of those dependent on support from the state itself or prominent citizens.

Within the Roman Empire, Jews enjoyed special status and privileges, reached by agreement with successive emperors until the Jewish war in AD 66-70. This complicated their position but even then payment of a special tax gave them freedom to practise their exclusive religion. Jews living outside Palestine had outnumbered Palestinian Jews from at least the time of the Babylonian exile in the sixth century BC. By New Testament times Jewish communities were to be found all over the empire. They occupied many trades and professions, being prominent among farmers, traders, merchants, and mercenaries. For example, the Egyptian ruler Ptolemy II (285-246 BC) settled 30,000 Jews as a frontier defence force on the Sinai border of Egypt in 270 BC. The tradition of Jewish mercenaries dated back at least to the Persians.

When the Romans established their supremacy over the other Mediterranean peoples, Jews were already living throughout the area, and were absorbed into Roman rule like everyone else. They had no cause to resist it. Indeed, the Roman emphasis on developing good, safe communications throughout the empire would have appealed to Jewish communities which were dependent on travel and trade.

When Egypt became a Roman province in 30 BC, Jews constituted the largest and most important foreign community in Alexandria, which was essentially a Hellenic city and the great port of the Hellenistic world. Egypt was now the chief source of Rome's essential

c7 BC Birth of Jesus

4 BC Death of Herod

4 BC-AD 39 Herod Antipas is tetrarch of Galilee and Peraea; Philip is tetrarch of Gaulanitis, Batanaea, Trachonitis and Auranitis

AD 6-41 Judea is a prefectorial province of Rome

AD 14-37 (Rome) Emperor Tiberius

AD 17 Romans conquer north Germany

c AD 26-36 Pontius Pilate is procurator

AD 37-41 (Rome) Emperor Caligula

AD 37 Caligula gives Agrippa I the tetrarchies of Philip and Lysanias

AD 39 Caligula exiles Antipas and gives his tetrarchy to Agrippa I

AD 41 Agrippa I is given tetrarchies of Judea and Samaria

AD 44-46 Judea again a prefectorial province of Rome

AD 53 Claudius gives Agrippa II the tetrarchies of Philip and Lysanias

AD 54-68 (Rome) Emperor Nero

AD 66-70 Jewish war against Romans

AD 66 Jerusalem attacked by Cestius Gallius; Christians take refuge in Pella

AD 70 Judea an imperial province of Rome

LEFT Jews at the Western Wall in Jerusalem continue the tradition of praying at the foundation stones of the Temple platform, the only part of the Temple to have survived. As the Temple was the only place where the Jewish religious laws allowed sacrifices, these ceased when the Temple was destroyed in AD 70. Since then Judaism has been a religion led by lay people, not priests, who traditionally can hold services whenever 10 men are gathered together. If a descendant of the old Hebrew priesthood is present he gives a special blessing.

BELOW Herod the Great restored the Temple in Jerusalem, but only the foundation stones of the platform on which it was built have survived. As the Western Wall these old Temple foundations are the most sacred shrine of modern Judaism. Strict Jews will not go onto the Temple site itself because only the high priest was allowed by sacred law to enter the holiest part of the Temple. The site is also sacred to Muslims.
INSET Jews from all parts made the journey to Jerusalem to sacrifice in the Temple, and the Western Wall now attracts many thousands of pilgrims, who queue to pray at it.

BELOW **People gather for informal discussion at the Western Wall, as well as for prayer, just as they did in the Temple courts and in the synagogues in biblical times. Jesus and his disciples would have been able to 'teach' like this near the Temple.**

grain supplies, which were carried in ships from Alexandria, and the Jews there supported the Romans when the Alexandrians tried to rebel against outside rule and government.

Jews lived in Rome itself from at least the first century BC, according to contemporary authors such as Horace and Cicero. In the first century AD, the Jewish historian Josephus recorded that after the death of Herod the Great in 4 BC, there were at least 8,000 Jews in Rome who supported a deputation of Palestinian Jews who had come to plead to Augustus for the autonomy of their nation.

For such dispersed Jews, as for Palestinian Jews too, the local synagogue was the centre of worship and unity. The word means 'assembly' in Greek, and it refers to the place where Jews assembled for worship and discussion. Because sacrifice could only be offered officially at the Temple in Jerusalem from 622 BC, communities of Jews outside Jerusalem had to develop their own meeting places for non-sacrificial worship if they observed the law. Synagogue remains dating from the third century AD have been found near Alexandria, and Paul's letters and the Acts of the Apostles indicate that there was a synagogue in every town with a sizeable Jewish community.

In each synagogue scrolls of the Hebrew sacred scriptures, particularly the law, the opening five books of the Bible, were kept in a special chest and treated with great reverence, but it is significant that the Old Testament books were translated into Greek in Alexandria during the second century BC. By then, Hebrew was becoming a language as unfamiliar to Jews as Latin is to most people today. But wherever they lived, Jews looked to Jerusalem as the true focus of their religion, for Jerusalem contained the Temple, the only place on earth where the full rites of the Jewish religion could be celebrated.

In 22 BC, the eighteenth year of his bloody reign, Herod the Great (37-4 BC) decided to rebuild the Temple of Jerusalem on an even more magnificent scale than before. Work started two years later and continued for 80 years, organized so that the Temple services could continue without interruption throughout the period. Six years after the work was completed the new Temple was destroyed at the climax of the Jewish war with Rome (AD 66-70). Its site is now occupied by the Dome of the Rock, the Muslim shrine built in AD 691, but the great platform for Herod's Temple still remains,

BELOW **On the lower slopes of the Mount of Olives lies the Garden of Gethsemane where Jesus prayed while awaiting his arrest. In the first part of the garden today is the Russian Orthodox Church of Mary Magdelene which has gilded domes.**

dominating the eastern side of Jerusalem and separated from the Mount of Olives by the Kidron Valley. The Temple itself was a comparatively small building surrounded by walled areas. Immediately surrounding the Temple was the court of the priests. This housed the great altar of burnt offerings and only priests could enter. Beyond that lay first the court of Israel, restricted to men, and then the court of women. Furthest from the Temple lay the court of Gentiles (non-Jews), which anyone could enter.

Inside the Temple building was the porch, entered by a doorway 30 feet (10 metres) high and twice as wide. Then came the holy place, with a doorway half the size and containing another altar, a table and the seven-branched lampstand. Finally came the 'most holy place', empty, dark, and veiled by a curtain, which only the high priest could enter once a year, on the Day of Atonement. The Ark of the Covenant, for which the original Temple had been built by Solomon, is heard of no more after the destruction of Solomon's Temple by the Babylonians in 587 BC. The Temple was a place of unique religious importance for Jews throughout the world, for it was the only place where sacrifices could be offered, and the many different kinds of sacrifice were the supreme expression of Hebrew religion. It made Jerusalem the main centre of pilgrimage for all Jews.

A complex hierarchy of priests of various grades and families administered the activities associated with the Temple, maintained the structure and controlled its use. They ranged from the high priest to doorkeepers and singers. Together with all the other costs of the Temple, priests were maintained by a tax levied on Jews throughout the empire, gifts, a proportion of everything produced, and they ate parts of the sacrifices.

A lamb was sacrificed every morning and afternoon, and the ritual of sacrifice increased, both in complexity and in the number and kinds of offerings, according to the importance of the festivals, which ranged from the weekly Sabbath, to the great pilgrimage feasts and the Passover. Compared with the Temple services, other expressions of religion by Jews in the home and the local synagogue may seem unimportant. However, for most Jews, the synagogue services and domestic expressions of their religion on the Sabbath and at Passover time would have been their normal forms of worship. Their importance is demonstrated by the survival and strength of Judaism after the destruction of the Temple in AD 70.

BELOW **Goats have always been valued for both their milk and skins. Today they can still be seen making their way through the backstreets of Jerusalem. Often they are in the charge of a child, as they would have been in biblical times.**

The Dead Sea Scrolls and Qumran

The excavated ruins of Khirbet Qumran have revealed an extensive complex of buildings and caves occupied by a strict Jewish sect during the early years of Christianity. Biblical manuscripts and scrolls which throw light on contemporary religious attitudes in Palestine were also discovered there.

The Bible sometimes gives the impression that Jewish religion was uniform in practice, closely controlled and strictly regulated by the priests of Jerusalem. However, actual evidence suggests otherwise – and nowhere more than at Qumran. The discovery in 1948 of ancient biblical manuscripts and other Hebrew writings in caves near the northern end of the Dead Sea, changed modern knowledge about religion in Palestine during the first centuries BC and AD. Within the next 10 years hundreds of complete scrolls and fragments of scrolls came to light, and the ruins of Khirbet Qumran nearby were thoroughly excavated.

The excavations and the evidence of the scrolls revealed a Jewish community occupying an extensive complex of buildings on a spur overlooking the Dead Sea and 25 caves in the steep sides of the cliffs nearby. The buildings with their eight courtyards, included a refectory, kitchen, assembly rooms, a laundry, two potteries, and eight water cisterns of various sizes, some of them with steps leading down into them. There was evidence of a dam in a large gully in the cliffs, and channels to lead water from the dam to the cisterns. Stone writing tablets which had fallen from an upper storey were also discovered. Objects found in the excavations, especially coins, made it possible to date the occupation periods accurately. The community started at Qumran in the early part of the first century BC and abandoned the site after an earthquake in 31 BC. Herod the Great ruled at the time, and this may be why the community did not return to the site until after his death in 4 BC. It continued there until the summer of AD 68, when the community hid its manuscripts in caves and fled before the Roman general Vespasian (AD 9-79) and the Tenth Legion, who destroyed most of the buildings.

The vast collection of writings unearthed at Qumran included books or fragments from the whole Hebrew Bible (except for Esther), other religious writings similar to parts of the Bible, and documents about the organization and life of the community itself. The discoveries provided biblical manuscripts many centuries earlier than any that had previously survived, but they differed in many places from the ones authorized by the main Jewish authorities.

The community lived a strict life with joint ownership of all possessions, rituals of purification by water, public prayers and religious meals. It kept a calendar of religious festivals different from the official calendar of the Jerusalem Temple. The members believed that the real meaning of the scriptures had been revealed by a 'Teacher of Righteousness' at the beginning of the community's existence, and that they were chosen by God to be 'Sons of Light' in the conflict with all 'Sons of Darkness' until God finally sent a Prophet and two Messiahs to bring victory and judgement. It seems certain that the members of the community were Essenes, a strict Jewish sect. Their beliefs and practices are of first importance for the light they throw on religious attitudes in Palestine during the early years of Christianity.

BELOW **The scrolls made at the Qumran community settlement were stored in pottery jars. The jars, and the extremely dry climate of the area, ensured that the scrolls were still in perfect condition after 2,000 years.**

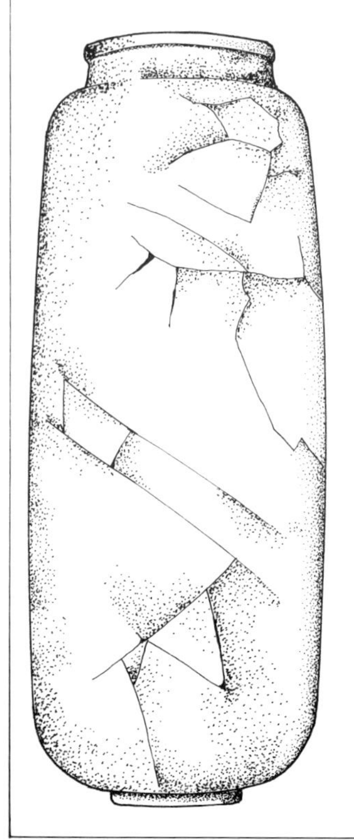

BELOW The community of the 'Dead Sea scrolls' in the deep valley east of Jerusalem rejected the worship in the Temple and followed their own form of the Hebrew religion. It became famous in 1947 when its library was found hidden in caves near the ruins of the community buildings, where it had lain since the site was abandoned during the Jewish-Roman war of 66-70 AD. The members of the community led a strict life, with an elaborate water system for ritual purifications.

INSET This is the mouth of one of the 25 caves where the scrolls were found by a young shepherd.

Herodian Rule in Palestine

King Herod the Great ruled Palestine on behalf of Rome from 40 BC, and his family remained a major force in the area for the next 130 years. Although there were deep differences between Jewish factions during the whole of this period, eventually, in AD 66 they rebelled against the Romans.

The politics of Palestine in the first century AD form a complex and changing pattern as different groups manoeuvred and fought for control. The Romans imposed an uneasy peace on the warring factions, having first entered the arena at the request of two groups of Jews locked in civil war, with one group besieging the other in Jerusalem. When Pompey (106-48 BC) captured Jerusalem in 63 BC, he made Palestine part of the Roman province of Syria, ruled by a Roman legate, and limited the religious authority of the high priest to the parts of Palestine where the Jews recognized the Temple in Jerusalem. Some parts of Palestine, such as Samaria, observed a different form of Hebrew religion.

The brief period of peace was short lived, as Rome itself slid into civil war again and consequently its rule over Palestine weakened. But then the Roman Senate named the politically astute Herod, who was probably half Jewish, King of Judea in 40 BC. Herod conquered his kingdom three years later with the aid of Roman soldiers and ruled it for the next 31 years as a puppet king of Rome. He subdued his unruly kingdom and his own treacherous family with ruthless cruelty, backed by his own army, and established fortresses in many parts of his kingdom, where he could find security in times of trouble.

During his uneasy period of peace, Herod built new cities, and provided buildings for every kind of different civic need, from baths, theatres and gymnasiums to a temple for emperor worship and, above all, a magnificent rebuilding of the Temple itself, the central symbol of Hebrew religion. It was all done through forced labour and extortionate taxation. The diversity of buildings points to the deep differences between Jewish groups during the whole New Testament period. The Herods, and their supporters, the Herodians, remained a

major force in Palestinian politics until the Jewish war of AD 66-70, but most of Hebrew Palestine, Judea and Samaria, was put under the direct rule of Roman procurators in AD 6.

The other main groups, who were normally at variance with each other, were the Pharisees, Sadducees and the Essenes. At the extreme of fanatical nationalism were the Zealots, called 'sicarii' (stabbers) by the Romans because of their reputation for stealthy assassination. The Pharisees believed in meticulous obedience to Hebrew law, which brought every detail of daily life within the province of religion, but they took account of changing circumstances and oral traditions of interpreting the law, which made them more flexible than the other main group, the Sadducees. Paul was a Pharisee before becoming a Christian, and this flexibility can be seen in his approach to problems. The Sadducees were violently opposed to the Pharisees and rejected any attempt to adapt the written law to new situations, but their opposition was intensified by their political stance and their religious privileges. Most of the Jerusalem priests belonged to this party, which tended to support occupying powers such as the Romans for the sake of political stability. Although the high priest of the Temple had to be chosen from certain priestly families, the appointment was made by whoever ruled Palestine at the time, whether a Herod or a Roman procurator. There is no mention of the Essenes in the New Testament, because they played no part in mainstream Hebrew religious practices or politics. Similarly, the Samaritans, in the hilly area north of Jerusalem, practised their own form of the Hebrew religion and kept to themselves. After the Jewish war (AD 66-70) the synagogues and their rabbis became more prominent but the mould of Jewish politics in Palestine had been broken.

BELOW **In New Testament times Palestine was able to support a large population. Parts of the country were very fertile, and it was farmed intensively. The Jews also benefited from the great trading routes which passed through the region, and from the many pilgrims to the Temple in Jerusalem. Some of the richest provinces of the Roman Empire lay to the north and south of Palestine. The region was of great importance as a frontier marking the easternmost limits of Roman rule.**

Festivals of the Hebrews

The great annual Hebrew feasts, mostly agricultural in origin, were adapted from the old Canaanite festivals and timed according to the ancient calendar. Each has its own ritual and variations in the sacrifices offered to mark it, but Passover remains the most important.

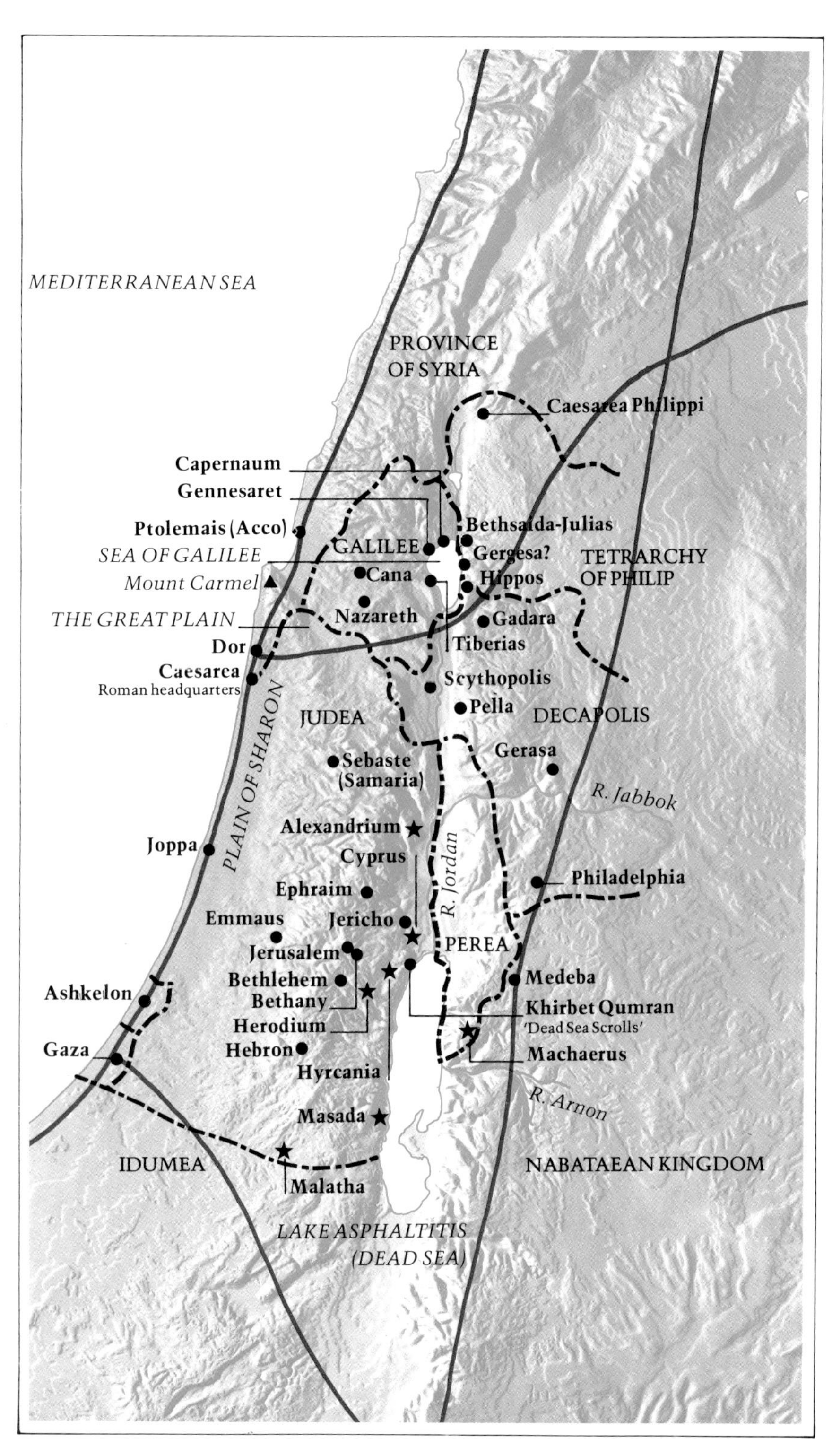

Main trade routes

★ Fortresses

INDEPENDENT RULE ENDS

Herod the Great was made puppet king from Galilee to Gaza in 40 BC, and reigned until his death 36 years later. Palestine was then divided between three of his sons. In AD 6, Archelaus was deposed as ruler of Judea and Samaria, and the area put under the control of Roman officials responsible to the emperor in Rome. The Roman administrative centre was Caesarea, with a lesser base and garrison in Jerusalem. A Jewish council of 71, presided over by the high priest, had limited authority. After the Jewish-Roman war of AD 66-70, the Roman emperor Vespasian took Judea as his private property, let out to tenant farmers. The Khirbet Qumran settlement, and the 'Dead Sea Scrolls' found there, dates from this period.

The New Testament is full of technical expressions used for various kinds of measurement, which mean little today, even though some of them – such as 'talent' – have entered modern language. However, even a word like 'day' can be confusing, for by New Testament times, Jews reckoned the day from sunset to the following sunset. By this reckoning, the Last Supper took place on the same 'day' that Jesus was crucified. Smaller divisions of time could be measured by water clocks and the passage of the sun's shadow, and the night was divided into four 'watches'. Months consisted of 29 and 30 days alternately, beginning with each new moon and celebrated with sacrifices. All the major Hebrew festivals were timed in relation to the cycle of months, starting with Nisan, which falls in the March-April period in the modern calender. Passover was held halfway through that month at the full moon.

The week created its own cycle of seven day periods, in which each seventh day was a Sabbath when no work was allowed. Whatever the origins of this may have been, it became a symbol of the covenant (Deut 5:14) and of the creation of the world by God (Gen 2:2-3; Exod 20:11). The Hebrew Sabbath was – and still is – the seventh day of the week, but early in New Testament times Christians began to observe the first day of the week in commemoration of the resurrection (Acts 20:7; 1 Cor 16:2). The twelve month year occasionally had an extra month added to keep the solar and lunar cycles synchronized, and originally began in spring with the month of Nisan. Just before the Babylonian exile, in the sixth century BC, the Hebrews changed to the Babylonian New Year in the autumn, where it is still observed, and particular years were identified by reference to prominent events or a particular ruler (Luke 3:1).

Two quite different economic needs are skilfully combined in the great annual festivals. Passover is a pastoral festival, with symbolism meaningful to shepherds, and it especially commemorates the escape of the Hebrew people from Egypt and the covenant with God when they were still shepherds. Three other main festivals – Unleavened Bread, Weeks (Pentecost) and Tabernacles – are agricultural in origin. The first two fell at the beginning and end of the grain harvest, and the last one marked the end of the whole harvest season when everything had been gathered in. When the Hebrews became predominantly agricultural people they adopted these old Canaanite agricultural festivals. They were made festivals of the Hebrew God of the covenant, not the Canaanite fertility gods, by attaching the first feast, Unleavened Bread, to the Passover. Lesser festivals were the New Year, the Dedication of the Temple, and the Day of Nicanor and Purim – both of which commemorated Jewish victories in battle. Each festival had its own ritual and variations in the sacrifices offered to mark it, but Passover remained the most important. As Jesus was crucified at Passover time, it became the Christian Easter, and its significance was transferred to his death and resurrection from the grave.

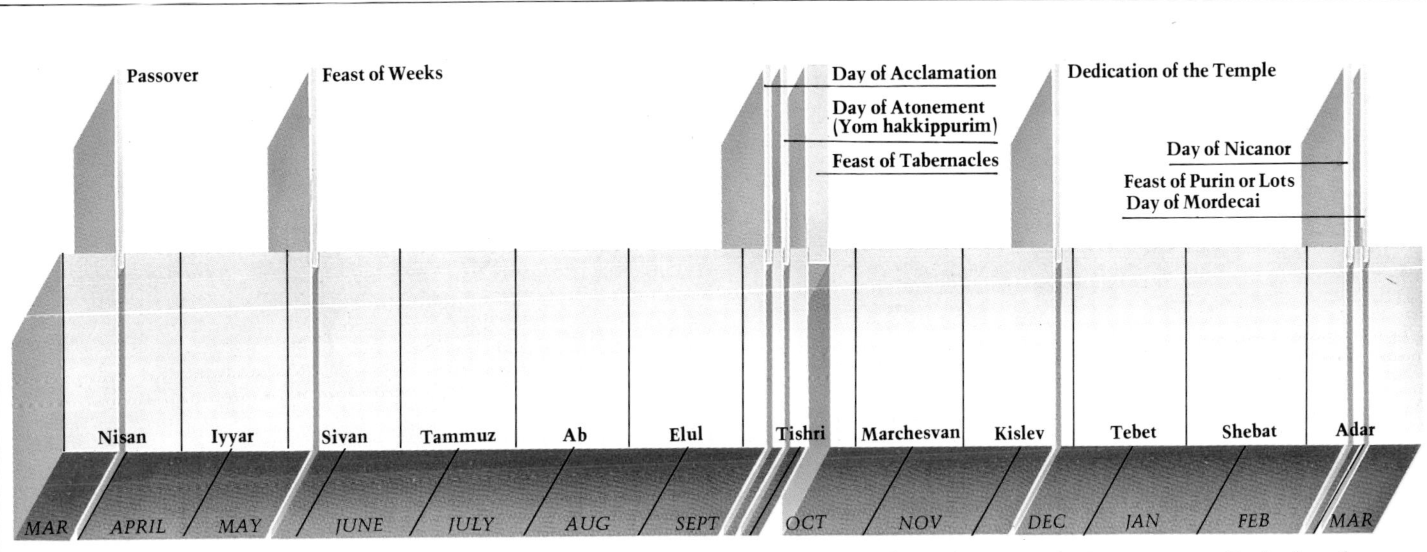

ABOVE Although later Hebrews believed that all their main feasts were given to Moses by God at the escape from Egypt, it is more probable that they were adopted over the years, to meet new needs. Passover is the oldest feast, dating from the nomadic shepherds. To this were added three harvest feasts when the Hebrews settled in Canaan: Unleavened Bread (which continued the Passover), Weeks or Pentecost, and Tabernacles. By linking these directly or indirectly with Passover, the Hebrews made the harvests an expression of the same divine power which had saved them from slavery in Egypt. The Day of Acclamation was an old New Year festival, and the Day of Atonement an old purification rite. Other feasts commemorate victories over the Greeks.

BELOW Barley has always been grown in the Palestinian region. Where possible, infertile land is irrigated so that cereals and other crops may be cultivated for food.

The Classical Influence

In a deeply corrupt and insecure world, salvation was a real need and religion provided saviour gods. The Romans, as previous conquering powers had done, greatly influenced other peoples' beliefs and ways of living, by spreading their own brand of Hellenistic religion and culture.

Ancient Palestine lay across some of the most important strategic and trading routes of the world. Where desert and sea squeezed these routes into a narrow corridor of land, Palestine provided a pass between two great cradles of civilization. Consequently, its inhabitants were exposed to all the cultural and religious influences of the ancient Near and Middle East. Traders and troops from many lands passed through the area, while the settlers were mobile and borrowed freely from the cultures of the places where they traded or fought. Successive conquering powers – Egypt, Assyria, Babylon, Persia, Greece and Rome – needed to control Palestine for their own strategic needs and left behind their patterns of life, thought and worship. The Romans were themselves greatly influenced by other peoples' religions and philosophies, particularly those of the Greeks, and introduced their own brand of Hellenistic beliefs and ways of living throughout the empire.

The bewildering array of faiths and gods worshipped in the Roman Empire reflected the many different needs people felt in an age when famine, disease and war were normal experiences. Polytheism, belief in many gods, reflected many different needs as well as localities which each had its own divinity, and rulers themselves were often declared divine. The gods were not jealous when their adherents worshipped other gods as well, provided always that there was no threat to political power. Despite the Bible's fierce assertion of exclusive monotheism, belief in a single god, the Hebrews were deeply influenced by other religions and borrowed freely from them, sometimes for political reasons. Salvation was a real need in a deeply corrupt and insecure world, and religion provided saviour gods. Some were heroes

RIGHT **The Classical world was full of poets, lawyers and scholars travelling from town to town, ready to perform or teach for a fee. Some of them had acquired a doubtful reputation as dishonest practitioners who would teach people how to sway a jury without regard for the justice of the case. Others were seen as false philosophers only concerned with the impression they made. Such teachers were at times criticized by such philosophers as Plato and Aristotle for their emphasis on the skills of rhetoric and oratory rather than knowledge. Paul was at pains to reassure the Christians of Corinth that he had no such motives when he brought the gospel to them. In an age when books were expensive to produce and few people could read, the travelling scholars were the main source of information and of instruction. Great events were recounted in epic form, particularly at the main festivals of the gods, and entered popular oral tradition. The life of Jesus, with the kind of things he taught, was recounted in a similar way by the disciples and Paul on their missionary visits. Eventually such teaching became the basis for the written Gospels.**

who were born of a union between gods and humans; others were manifestations of gods who temporarily disguised themselves as humans to intervene in human affairs. In many minds, this accounted for the success of an Alexander or an Augustus Caesar, and worship of such great rulers reinforced the stability of the state.

Sometimes the sacredness of the gods was protected by secrecy and rites which expressed the worshippers' sense of awe in the presence of the powers which could save them. Just how those powers could help was explained in stories about the gods' own experiences, which showed how they related to human needs, or to the fertility pattern of the agricultural year. These mystery religions were practised throughout the Roman Empire and had vivid rites of initiation with symbolism which admitted members to salvation. Blood was an obvious symbol of life and shared relationships, and, in some 'mysteries', worshippers were drenched in the blood of sacrificial bulls dedicated to the divine power.

The powers of nature and the 'heavenly' bodies – the sun, moon, stars and planets – were worshipped through animal or human forms which symbolized their influence on the world of humans. Drama played a large part not only in the theatre, but in religion, in rites of worship. In a world where most people were illiterate, religious attitudes were communicated and expressed in visual form, particularly through temple architecture and representations of the gods. The sheer number and range of small statues of gods which have been unearthed on domestic sites shows that miniatures of the great temple statues were used in the home. Producing sacred images of Diana was an important industry at Ephesus.

BELOW **Every town had its open area, such as this one at Beth-shan, adjacent to its main temple. A travelling teacher could be sure that he would be able to attract an audience there, and if people were interested he could continue in a more private place. In many places Christianity spread in this way, as well as through the Jewish synagogues.**

The World in the 1st Century AD

Although most of the Roman provinces were self-supporting, trading links – over land and sea – were strengthened with India and China. Recent excavations have revealed the magnificence of this period in Han-ruled China, as well as the technical skills of the highly-organized Paracas in South America.

Although the Romans had conquered the whole of the Mediterranean coastal countries by the end of the first century AD, with Europe to the River Rhine and all but the northern parts of Britain, it was not a self-contained Roman world. Most of the provinces were self-supporting, and all basic needs could be met from within the empire itself, but there was still a ready market for luxury goods.

Roman trade with the East developed strongly after the collapse of Alexander's empire and as the Romans expanded into the eastern seaboard of the Mediterranean. This strengthened their trading links with India and China, particularly after the second century BC when Greeks from the powerful commercial centre of Bactria, in what is now Afghanistan, crossed the Hindu Kush mountains into the northern Indus Valley. They were followed by the Parthians, and in the first century AD by Kushans who controlled the Punjab for the next two centuries.

The Mauryan Empire, which since 305 BC had controlled all India except the deep south, had been destroyed. The newcomers developed trading routes into central Asia, and sea routes to Arabia and Persia. Along these routes from the east flowed spices, incense, precious stones, and silk for the togas which were the status symbol of wealthy Romans. In exchange the Roman world sent gold, and slaves with special skills such as dancing and acrobatics.

The Han Dynasty of China (206 BC – AD 220) extended their control throughout China during the first hundred years of their rule, and secured the silk route to the far western city of Kashgar, where the route skirted the Indian Kush to reach the Parthian capital, Ecbatana, and on into the Roman Empire. The Parthians had defeated a Roman army in 53 BC, and resisted successive invasions, so the Romans turned to sea routes from the Red Sea to the Persian Gulf, India and China itself. At the beginning of the first century AD as many as 120 Roman galleys a year sailed to the Middle and Far East, where they were met by Chinese trading ships. Gold was exchanged for silk and spices.

In China, recent excavations of Han Dynasty tombs have revealed the magnificence of this period, with burial vestments constructed of over 2,000 pieces of jade linked together with gold and diagrams of mechanical silk looms capable of weaving a damask or polychrome cloth with 3,000 warps.

In Central America, the man-jaguar cult had spread into the valley where Mexico City now stands, and developed into the beginnings of the first known city in the Americas – Teotihuacán. Eventually it produced the great complex of pyramid-type buildings to the north-east of Mexico City. The Mayan civilization in the Yucatan Peninsula also began during this period. Where the border between Peru and Chile now runs, excavated Paracas burial sites have yielded brilliantly embroidered shrouds, clothing, food, weapons, gold ornaments and vessels, which confirm that the people lived in highly organized society which had knowledge of advanced technology.

Developed cultures
Nomadic pastoralists
Hunter-gatherers
Farmers
Main trade routes
Silk route

AT THE TIME OF CHRIST **The Romans were firmly in control of the whole Mediterranean area. Their influence is still felt today, through laws, administrative methods, and the road system which linked all parts of the empire. But the Romans themselves were deeply influenced by the ideas and religions they found in provinces of the empire, and Rome became totally dependent on provinces such as Egypt for food. Under the Han emperors the process of Chinese unification, begun in the 3rd century BC by the short-lived Ch'in Dynasty, was carried further. The Americas remained unknown, but the well-worn trading routes – both land and sea – with India and China were further developed.**

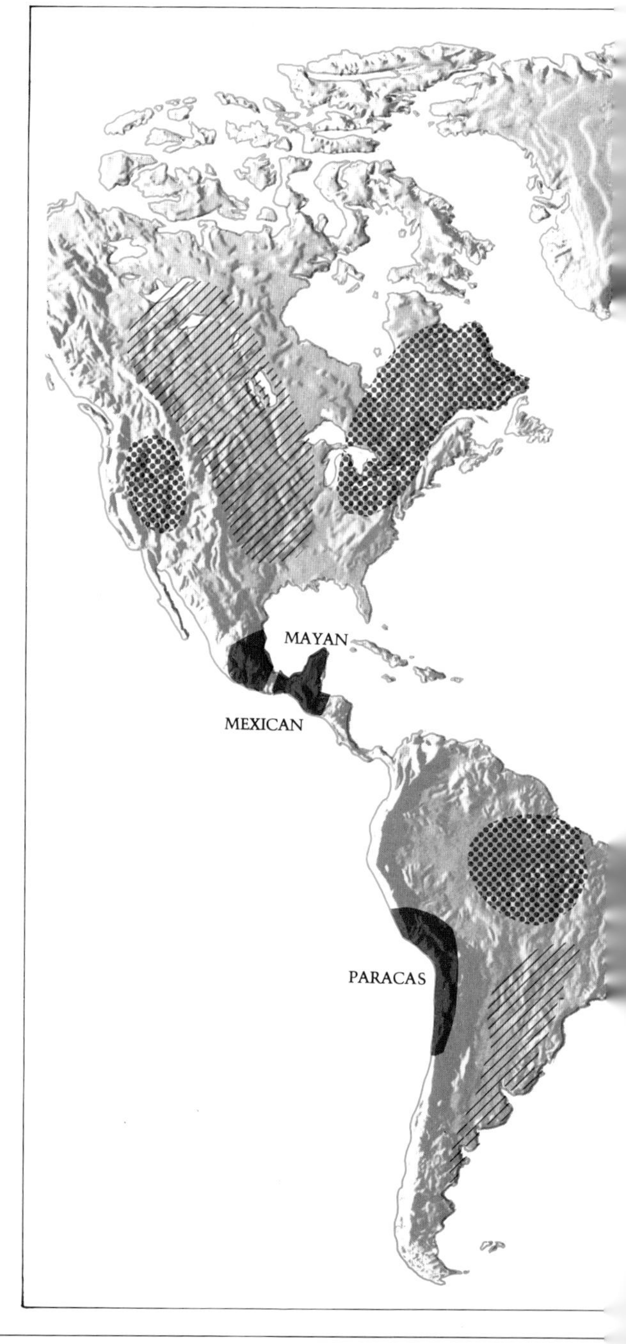

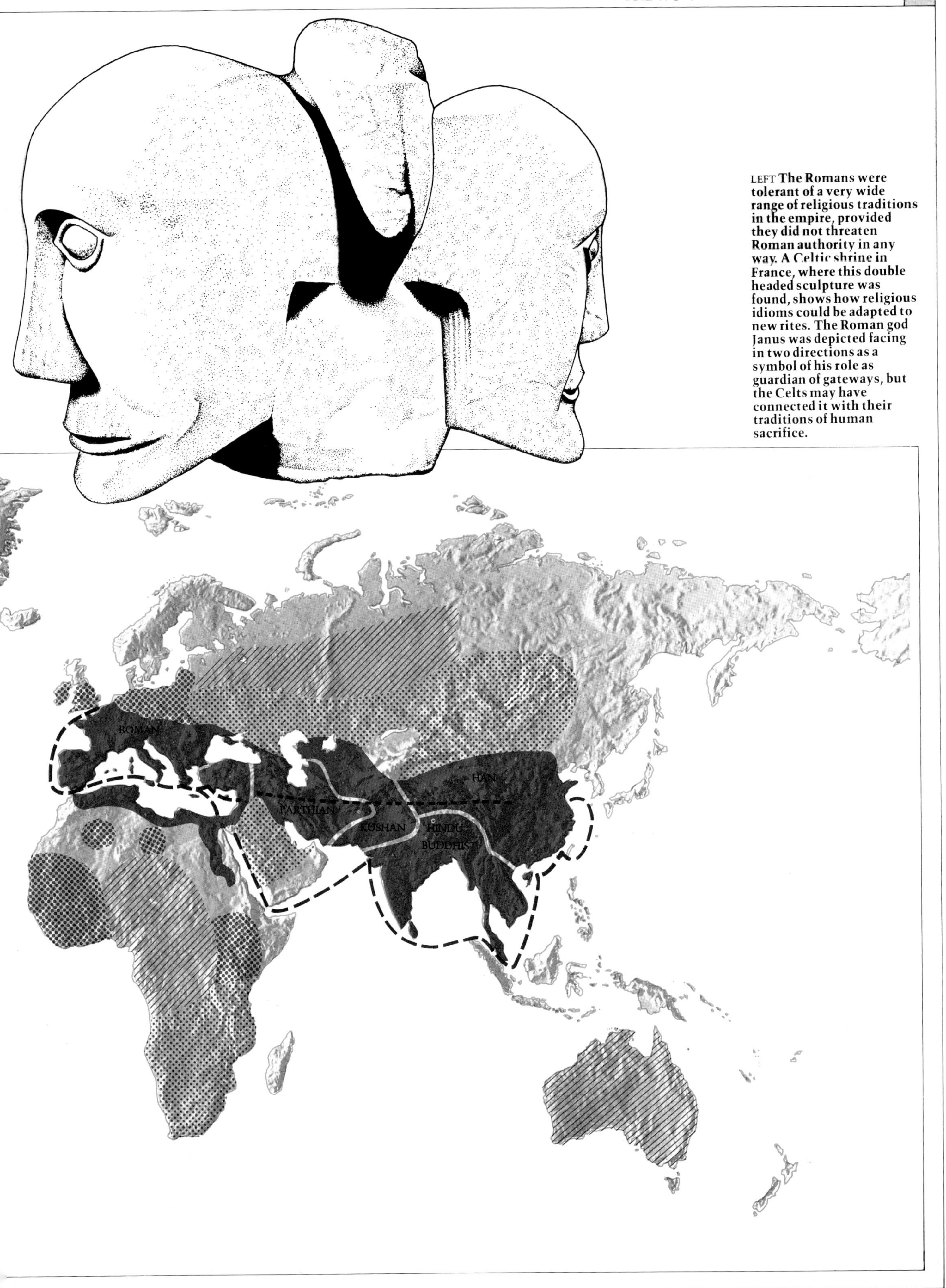

LEFT **The Romans were tolerant of a very wide range of religious traditions in the empire, provided they did not threaten Roman authority in any way. A Celtic shrine in France, where this double headed sculpture was found, shows how religious idioms could be adapted to new rites. The Roman god Janus was depicted facing in two directions as a symbol of his role as guardian of gateways, but the Celts may have connected it with their traditions of human sacrifice.**

The First Christians

It was assumed by the first Christians that the new beliefs were compatible with their native Judaism: a view shared by Paul, but he felt the two were not tied, and despite much opposition, supported non-Jews who wanted to become Christians. Meanwhile, claims made about Jesus incensed the Jewish authorities.

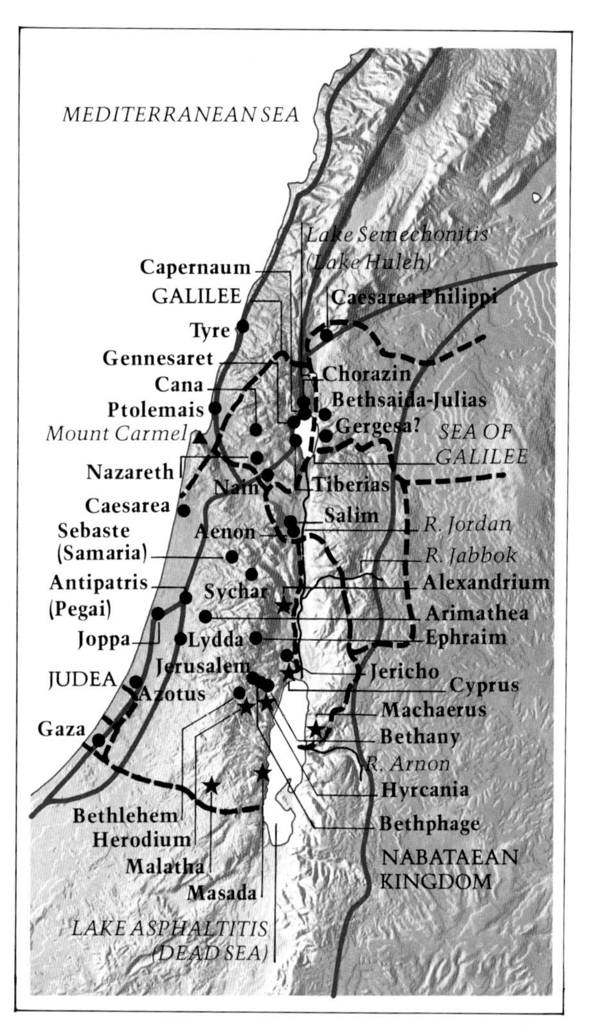

★ Fortresses

- - - Political boundaries

—— Main trade routes

THE HERODS IN PALESTINE **To keep the country in submission, Herod the Great strengthened a number of strategically-placed fortresses, which he also used as palaces. In many places in Israel and Jordan today, the massive remains of Herodian buildings – the Romans destroyed them all in AD 73 – can be seen (there is a good example in the hill of Masada). At Herod's death, Palestine was divided among three of his sons and Rome only intervened in the administration when public security was threatened.**

Gospel materials and beliefs transmitted orally, Acts 1-15, Ja.

For this is what I received from the Lord, and in turn passed on to you: that on the same night that he was betrayed, the Lord Jesus took some bread, and thanked God for it and broke it, and he said, 'This is my body, which is for you; do this as a memorial of me'. (1 Cor 11: 23-26)

RIGHT **The synagogue at Capernaum was excavated by Franciscan monks after the First World War. It was probably constructed on the site of the one Jesus visited, and built in the third century AD.**

Jesus Christ, the person from whom Christianity takes its name, was born in Bethlehem, about 5 miles (8 km) south of Jerusalem, shortly before Herod the Great died in 4 BC. Strictly speaking, 'Christ' is a title, the Greek translation of the Hebrew 'messiah', but came into use as a surname for Jesus soon after his death, and replaced the older 'Jesus of Nazareth'. Nazareth, in Galilee, was the home town of Jesus during his childhood. Bethlehem, in Judea, was the administrative centre for the Hebrew tribe of Judah, to which Jesus belonged. It had also been the birthplace of David, the greatest of the Hebrew kings. So Bethlehem symbolized the Hebrew hope that God would send another liberator like David – a messiah with royal authority – to restore their former glories and their freedom. Thus the Galilean Jesus was also the 'Christ' of Bethlehem.

To say that Jesus was born some time BC seems confusing, but a mistake was made in the sixth century AD when the Roman system of numbering years was changed for the Christian system which uses the birth of Jesus as a reference point. However, historical documents ensure that the date of King Herod's death is known with certainty. Herod ruled Palestine from 37-4 BC as a puppet king answerable only to the Roman emperor. His slaughter of the children of Bethlehem after the birth of Jesus there is entirely in character. Throughout his reign he ruthlessly killed anyone who threatened his power. The report that Joseph and Mary fled to Egypt with the young Jesus, staying there until Herod's death, is completely consistent with Herod's reputation as someone to be feared.

After the death of Herod the Great, his kingdom was divided among three of his sons. Two northern areas went to Philip. Galilee was given to Herod Antipas, the Herod who later beheaded John the Baptist. Archelaus received Judea, but 10 years later he was deposed by the emperor Augustus. Roman procurators were put over Judea, and made responsible for keeping order and for Roman taxation.

With Herod the Great dead, Joseph and Mary risked returning to their home in Nazareth with the young Jesus. Apart from a visit to Jerusalem at the age of 12, nothing further is known about Jesus until he began his public ministry when he was 'about thirty years old' (Luke 3:23). His public life lasted no more than three years, and centred on Galilee and Judea.

Jesus was arrested in Jerusalem by order of the Jewish high priest just before Passover. The most probable date was AD 30. The Romans allowed local peoples of the provinces to administer most of their own laws, but serious charges had to be tried in Roman courts by Roman magistrates. As Jesus was charged with capital offences, he was first tried under Hebrew law before the supreme Jewish religious council, the Sanhedrin, and then by the Roman procurator, Pontius Pilate. Crucifixion was a normal method of execution for condemned criminals. The resurrection of Jesus, on the third day after his death, is the most distinctive belief held by Christians. Followers of Jesus after the resurrection wrote the New Testament after this event.

BELOW **The altar screen in the Church of the Nativity stands over the cave where tradition holds that Jesus was born. As the birthplace of King David, Bethlehem helped Christians to identify Jesus as the Messiah, the 'Son of David'.**

The first Christians were Jews, who continued to practise their Jewish religion while they waited for the risen and ascended Jesus to return in glory. In private they expressed their new faith by prayers and 'the breaking of bread' (Acts 2:42), but they continued to worship in the Temple in Jerusalem and in the synagogues. It did not occur to them that they might have to separate from their native Judaism. For example, according to the Acts of the Apostles (Acts 3: 11-26), Peter's first public statement was made to people who came from many places in the Near East, who were all Jews on pilgrimage to Jerusalem for the Jewish feast of Pentecost.

Several factors helped to change this situation. The claims made about Jesus aroused indignation, and then official opposition from the religious authorities. Five or six years later the stoning of Stephen, the first Christian martyr, by a lynch mob increased the tension. Many of the Jerusalem Christians fled to other towns, particularly Antioch, where they came into closer contact with Greek and Roman ways of thinking and living. Non-Jews began to ask to be received into the Christian communities and it was hard to ask such people to accept traditional Judaism as well.

The whole question was brought to a head by the conversion of Saul (Acts 9:1-19), and his subsequent missionary achievements as Paul. As a young and intensely loyal Pharisee trained in the Jewish law school at Jerusalem, Saul had been made responsible for arresting Jewish followers of Jesus, and taking them to Jerusalem for trial by the supreme Jewish religious court. Saul, the lawyer, was convinced that the new beliefs were incompatible with traditional Judaism. When he became a Christian himself, the same thinking showed him that non-Jews need not accept Judaism along with Christianity. The experience of the people of the Old Testament had been a preparation for the coming of the Christ. If Jesus was Christ, the preparation period was over. Those who followed Jesus did not need the Mosaic law and the religion of the Temple and the synagogue. Paul was prepared to oppose anyone, even Peter, on this point.

The first of Paul's missionary journeys, into Asia Minor, brought in groups of people for whom a clear decision had to be made. In his missionary work Paul nearly always began in the local synagogue, where his ideas would be understood even if they were rejected. But he attracted many non-Jews as well. That first journey took him and his helpers from Antioch to Cyprus and across to Asia Minor, where he visited towns in Pamphylia and southern Galatia before returning to Antioch again.

After that journey Paul raised the whole matter of non-Jewish converts to Christianity, at a meeting with the Christian leaders in Jerusalem. They decided that such people should only be required to abstain from practices associated with the religions they were leaving. The way was now clear for Christianity to make a universal appeal, free from the restrictions of the Judaism in which it had been born.

BELOW **The baptism of Jesus in the River Jordan marks the beginning of his public work, normally thought to have lasted nearly three years until his crucifixion in about AD 30. The traditional site is an attraction for pilgrims, even though it is near a sensitive military area now.**
BELOW LEFT **The mother and child theme in Christian worship comes from the unique status accorded to Jesus's mother, Mary, in the early chapters of Matthew and Luke's Gospels.**
BELOW RIGHT **The Mount of Olives looks across to the Temple area from the eastern side of the Kidron Valley. The Garden of Gethsemane, where Jesus was arrested, is near the foot of the hill.**

Paul's 1st journey

Egnatian Way

PAUL'S CRUSADE **Christianity began as a Jewish movement and spread from Palestine itself through the Hebrew groups dispersed in the main cities of the Roman Empire. Paul was largely instrumental in this success: on his first missionary journey, he concentrated on Cyprus and the area of Asia Minor to the north of the island. He did not reach the Egnatian Way – a Roman road linking the Bosphorus with the Adriatic Sea – until his next journey which he started in AD 49.**

Spreading the New Faith

Soon there were Christian churches in Asia Minor and Greece, where Paul had concentrated his missionary efforts between about AD 49 and 58. His letters to his converts were generally in response to specific problems and he variously chided, praised, showed anger and even engaged in self-analysis.

Acts 15-20, 1 and 2 Thess, Gal, 1 and 2 Cor, Rom.

Paul waited for them in Athens and there his whole soul was revolted at the sight of a city given over to idolatry. In the synagogue he held debates with the Jews and the God-fearing, but in the market place he had debates every day with anyone who would face him. Even a few Epicurean and Stoic philosophers argued with him. Some said, 'Does this parrot know what he's talking about?' And, because he was preaching about Jesus and the resurrection, others said, 'He sounds like a propagandist for some outlandish gods'.
(Acts 17: 16-18)

The meeting of church leaders in Jerusalem, which thrashed out the difficulties of non-Jews who became Christians, took place in AD 48, 18 years after the death of Jesus. Almost all the available information in the New Testament now concentrates on the journeys of Paul into Asia Minor and Europe, until he reached Rome in AD 61. Undoubtedly there was much Christian activity before the war between the Jews and the Romans from AD 66 to 70, which led to the destruction of Jerusalem. By then, there were Christian churches in many places in the Near East and in Rome, only some of which had been founded by Paul. The traditional belief that Peter started the church in Rome should be seen in this context.

Paul set out on his second missionary journey in AD 49, only intending to revisit the places where he had founded churches on the first journey. He and his companions travelled by land into Galatia again, where Paul changed his plans by going on to Troas, the busy port near the old site of Troy. From Troas, Paul and his party – including Luke – sailed to Neapolis, on the main land route from Italy to the east, and began their dramatic mission through Macedonia and Greece. Paul's letters show that he succeeded in forming small Christian groups in the towns he visited, but the reception he and his companions received was mixed, and occasionally violent.

At Philippi, where they went after Neapolis, Paul's party ran into trouble which reveals much about the political problems of provincial towns in the Roman Empire. Paul and Silas were arrested, flogged and imprisoned to await trial on a charge of advocating practices unlawful for Romans. But the two men were Roman citizens, a status which should have protected them from such treatment, and they were released. Citizenship was an honour which could be given by the Roman state or purchased; Paul had inherited his.

Thessalonica, a later stop, was a free city, where the Romans allowed locally elected magistrates to control affairs. Any hint of disloyalty to Rome would have ended such privileges, and Paul's party fled from the city when his new converts were accused of treason. They were again opposed in the next town, Beroea. As more trouble erupted, Paul went to Athens while the rest of his companions later left for Corinth. In Athens, Paul changed his methods and presented Christianity in terms of Greek philosophy, but the resurrection of Jesus was too much for most of his listeners, and Paul moved on to Corinth.

As a great port, capital of the Roman province controlling southern Greece, and centre of the Aphrodite religion, Corinth was a large and cosmopolitan city. There Paul and his helpers found the more positive response they had hoped for and they stayed for 18 months. Paul's two Letters to the Thessalonians, probably written during this stay in Corinth, show that the Christian church he founded there had a hard time after he left. His Letter to the Galatians reveals a different problem. That church was insisting that Christians had to keep the Jewish laws as well. Paul feared that all his work among them would be undone. His letter – or epistle – to them is the angriest of all the letters he wrote.

Paul returned to Caesarea, the main Roman administrative centre for Judea, by way of Ephesus. It was a logical route to use for the safest sailing, with busy sea routes available across the Aegean to Ephesus, and round the coast of Asia Minor to Palestine. Paul established contacts amongst the Jews of Ephesus, and promised to return.

He kept his promise quickly, after a short time at his home church of Antioch. Paul set off again and took the overland route through Galatia and Phrygia once more, but Ephesus was his main destination, and when he reached it he stayed for more than two years. According to Acts (19) Paul met with great success both in Ephesus and among the people of the surrounding area. So great, indeed, was Paul's success that it threatened the trade in silver copies of the famous statue of Diana of the Ephesians, to whom the city's main temple was dedicated. Rioting broke out, and Paul decided to leave for Macedonia, by way of Troas again.

While in Ephesus, Paul had written to the church he had founded on the other side of the Aegean at Corinth. The consequences also contributed to his decision to move on. Paul's First Letter to the Corinthians starts with a series of rebukes for various matters which had been told him about his Corinthian Christians. There were factions in the church there, law suits, a case of incest and members of the church who were still worshipping at the Temple of Aphrodite. The letter continues with comments on various questions raised in a letter he has received from Corinth. It reveals concern about marriage, social relationships with non-Christian friends, details of church order, and the resurrection. Both the rebukes and the worries throw light on the experience of being a Christian in such a varied and busy city as ancient Corinth. But Paul's response to the situation in Corinth had startling

BELOW **A Jerusalem tomb of New Testament times, with its circular stone door to seal the entrance, is typical of the place where Jesus was buried after his crucifixion. The empty tomb of Jesus three days later, and his repeated appearances to his followers, convinced them that he had risen from death and gave them the confidence to spread their beliefs throughout the Roman world.**

BELOW **Jewish tombs from every period face the Temple area of Jerusalem, in the belief that the Messiah will proclaim his rule from the Temple. When Christianity spread to Europe, Christians still regarded Jerusalem as the centre of the Church.**

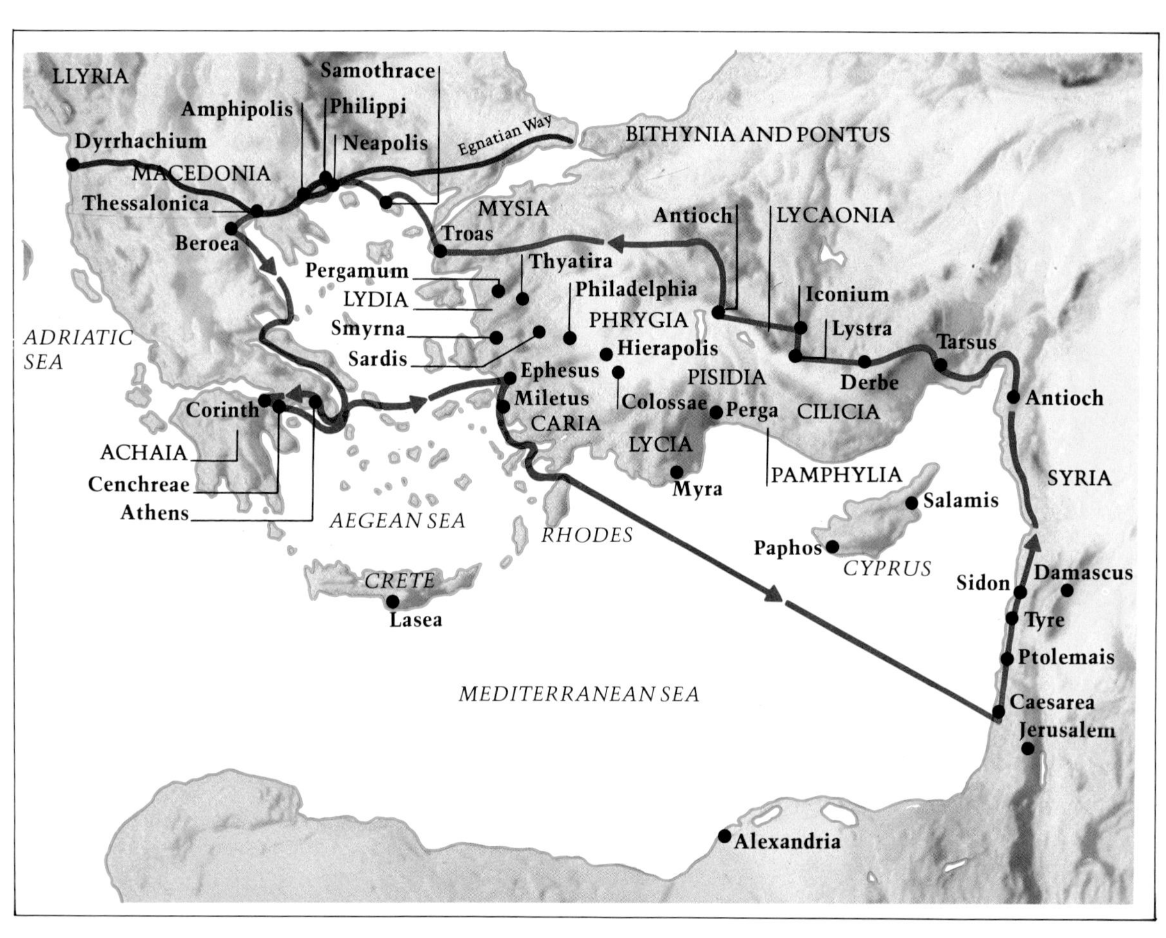

—— Paul's 2nd journey

THE CONTINUING MISSION
The second was possibly the most significant of Paul's journeys, for he travelled west through Asia Minor, as far as the Aegean area, where he first preached the gospel on the continent of Europe. On his way to Corinth, where he stayed for nearly two years, he founded many Christian communities.

- AD 45-49 First mission of Paul
- cAD 48 Famine in Judea; the Council of Jerusalem
- AD 49-52 Second mission of Paul
- AD 50-52 Letters to the Thessalonians
- AD 52-60 Antonius Felix is prefect
- AD 53 Claudius gives Agrippa II the tetrarchies of Philip and Lysanias
- AD 53-58 Third mission of Paul
- AD 54-68 (Rome) Emperor Nero
- cAD 57 First Letter to the Corinthians; AD 57 second Letter to the Corinthians; Letter to the Galatians; Letter to the Romans
- AD 58 Paul arrested in the Temple
- AD 58-60 Paul held at Caesarea

repercussions for him. The Corinthian Christians were so angry that they came near to rejecting him. This may be the deeper reason for Paul leaving Ephesus. The sequence of events is not clear. He may have written another letter and paid a swift visit by sea which only made matters worse. In the end, he sent his companion Titus to heal the breach, and was then so anxious that he crossed from Troas to Macedonia to meet Titus on his way back from Corinth.

Titus had succeeded, and Paul wrote his Second Letter to the Corinthians to send on ahead as he made his way there. It is a very different letter from the first one, full of self-analyzing on the experience of preaching Christianity. It reveals more about Paul than anything else he wrote, and about the experience of commitment to Jesus Christ. The three months Paul now spent in Corinth were the occasion for his most systematic exposition of his beliefs – his Letter to the Romans, in which he sets out his understanding of the Christian faith. He intended to make Rome the base for the next phase of his work, and this letter formed his personal introduction to the Christians who were living in Rome.

Paul and at least six companions retraced their steps through Macedonia to Philippi, and so by stages back to Jerusalem. He little knew that his next major journey would be to Rome, but under arrest with a guard of Roman soldiers to stand trial before Nero.

BELOW LEFT **Monuments from the biblical period on the outskirts of Jerusalem show how deeply Roman and Greek styles had penetrated into even the most conservative expressions of ancient Jewish culture.**

BELOW **The basic means of travel remained unchanged throughout the biblical period, and is still very much in use. The donkey or ass was specially useful because of its adaptability for many different tasks as a pack animal, for riding, or even drawing a plough.**

Paul: Disciple in Captivity

In the eyes of orthodox Jews, Paul broke Hebrew law twice while in Jerusalem in AD 58. To subdue the resulting riot, he was arrested and eventually sent to Rome under heavy escort. There he was in custody – probably for about two years – and he continued writing to the churches he had established.

Acts 20-28, Philem, Phil, Col, Eph.

This, then, is what I pray, kneeling before the Father, from whom every family, whether spiritual or natural, takes its name: Out of his infinite glory, may he give you the power through his Spirit for your hidden self to grow strong, so that Christ may live in your hearts through faith, and then, planted in love and built on love, you will with all the saints have strength to grasp the breadth and the length, the height and the depth; until, knowing the love of Christ, which is beyond all knowledge, you are filled with the utter fullness of God. (Eph 3: 14-19)

The Jerusalem to which Paul returned in AD 58 was in ferment. Eight years later it erupted into the disastrous war between Jews and Romans in which Jerusalem was destroyed. Some of this turmoil can be seen in the events which led to Paul's arrest, his long wait for his case to be heard, and his demand to be tried by the emperor in Rome. Innocently enough, Paul went to the great Jewish Temple in Jersalem to pray and to show that he did not encourage Jewish Christians to abandon their traditions. Rumour had it that he had taken a non-Jew into the Temple with him. Such desecration of the Temple carried the death penalty in Hebrew law, recognised by the Romans, and a crowd quickly gathered to lynch him.

Immediately alongside the wall of the Temple area stood the main guard tower of Jerusalem, which had been enlarged by Herod the Great and was now used by the Roman garrison. That, too, was an offence to strictly orthodox Jews. The Roman guard stopped the riot by arresting Paul, and he would have been interrogated under the lash if he had not told them that he held the privileges of Roman citizenship. The next move was a request for Paul, as a Jew, to be tried before the Sanhedrin, the main religious council, but word reached him that there was a plot to assassinate him on the way. The senior Roman officer in Jerusalem decided to move Paul to the safety of Caesarea, the main Roman administrative centre, which was well away from Jerusalem. They sent him there with a strong escort. At Caesarea, Paul could be tried by Felix, the procurator of Palestine, whose harshness towards the Jews under his rule was a major cause of the coming rebellion.

If Paul had been tried by Felix the charges against him would certainly have been dismissed, but Felix kept him waiting two years and then was replaced by a new procurator, Festus. By this time, Paul had had enough. Although Festus was cast in a different mould from Felix, Paul exercised his rights as a Roman citizen to have his case transferred to Rome itself. Perhaps Paul was influenced by the actions of the current King Herod, Agrippa II (AD 50-*c*100), – who had had James executed and imprisoned Peter. Even a Roman citizen might be sacrificed in the jungle of Palestinian politics.

Paul's voyage to Rome, in the charge of a centurion and a detachment of Roman soldiers, took the best part of a year. A coastal vessel took the group to Myra, where they joined one of the great grain ships which sailed regularly between Egypt and Italy. Headwinds delayed progress and forced the ship down to Crete, then a storm drove them westwards for a fortnight until they ran aground on Malta where the ship broke up. It was three months before the voyage could be resumed in another Egyptian corn ship, which called at Syracuse in Sicily and Rhegium on the toe of Italy, before finally reaching Puteoli near Neapolis (Naples). Paul found there were Christians at Puteoli, and stayed a week there, then travelled with his escort and guard along the Appian Way to Nero's Rome. It was AD 61, three years before the great fire of Rome and the beginning of Nero's persecution of Roman Christians.

When Paul first reached Rome there were no signs of hostility from any Roman officials towards Christians. Paul himself looked to the Roman administration for protection, so that he could be free to spread his beliefs, and in his Letter to the Romans he even wrote that '... since all government comes from God, the civil authorities were appointed by God' (Rom 13:1). The Roman Empire was near the height of its power with control over the whole Mediterranean area, Spain, most of Europe, southern Britain and Egypt. Rome itself was a tightly knit maze of narrow streets and lanes, contrasting with large open spaces and imposing state buildings and temples. Nearly a million people lived in the city, for the distribution of free food, the public amusements provided by prominent citizens or the state, and the wealth of the city attracted people from many parts of the empire. The final chapter of Romans shows that Paul already knew many of the Christians in Rome when he first arrived there.

The Acts of the Apostles ends with Paul's arrival in Rome, and meetings he arranged with leading members of the Jewish community. It says that he spent 'the whole of the two years in his own rented lodging' (Acts 28:30), where he would be under custody while waiting for his case to be heard, but says neither whether he gained a hearing nor what happened to him. Later Christian writings, some of them very near to New Testament times, say that he was freed at the end of the two years mentioned in Acts. If this was the case, he could have carried out his plan to extend his missionary work into the western parts of the Roman Empire, particularly Spain.

Four of Paul's letters mention that he was imprisoned when he wrote them. Even at the time of his Second Letter to the Corinthians, he wrote that he had often been imprisoned, so it is far from certain that his 'captivity letters' were all written from Rome. One of them, Philemon, written to a fellow Christian, gives a vivid glimpse of the change Christianity could bring to human values and social differences. The letter urges Philemon to receive back an escaped slave, whatever wrongs he may have committed. At this time there was no legal restraint on an owner's treatment of his slaves, but Paul urges the slave to be received 'as a brother in the Lord' and to 'welcome him as you would me' (Philem 16f). Philippians was written to the Christians in Philippi, which Paul first visited 11 years before his arrival in Rome, and the contents of the letter suggest that it belongs to an earlier stage of Paul's thinking. Colossians and Ephesians, on the other hand, deal with the problems arising from a new philosophical and religious movement which was attracting Christians. Evidence suggests that Ephesians was written to a number of Christian churches around Ephesus, so the whole area may have been influenced.

The new religion of these many different churches formed a patchwork of beliefs and practices taken from a wide range of religions and philosophies. However, Paul remained steadfast in his insistence that only Jesus Christ could give full salvation.

LEFT **The main religion of the ancient Near East was a polytheism of many gods and goddesses, expressing an implicit pantheism. Although the names of the divinities differed from place to place, the same themes are found in the representations of the divine, as here in the ancient coastal city of Ashkelon.**

- AD 58 Paul arrested in the Temple
- AD 58-60 Paul held at Caesarea
- AD 60 Paul appears before Festus and appeals to Caesar; he starts his voyage to Rome
- AD 61-63 Paul in Rome; Letters to Colossians, Ephesians, Philemon, and Philippians(?)
- AD 62 James, brother of John, stoned to death
- *c*AD 63 Paul set free (?); Gospel of Mark and 1 Peter; Letter of James, 1 Timothy; Letter to Titus (?)
- AD 64 Burning of Rome, persecution of Christians
- *c*AD 64-67 Martyrdom of Peter at Rome
- AD 66 Florus crucifies some Jews in Jerusalem; troubles in Caesarea and throughout the country
- AD 66-70 Jewish war against Romans
- AD 66-67 Nero in Greece; he appoints Vespasian and Titus to restore order in Palestine
- AD 66 Jerusalem attacked by Cestius Gallius; Christians take refuge in Pella
- AD 67 Vespasian reconquers Galilee
- *c*AD 67 Paul a prisoner in Rome; 2 Timothy; Paul is beheaded; Letter to the Hebrews
- AD 67-68 The Zealots are masters of Jerusalem
- AD 70 Titus lays siege to Jerusalem, burning of the Temple, capture of the Upper City and the Palace of Herod
- AD 70 Judea an imperial province of Rome

The Colosseum, the great elliptical amphitheatre in Rome, is the most impressive surviving monument of imperial Rome. The present ruins (LEFT AND BELOW) are of the stage the building had reached by AD 217, when the wooden uppermost storey was replaced by stone, but it was begun in the first century AD by the emperors Vespasian and Titus. Many spectacles were staged there, ranging from the gladiatorial contests to the reenactment of naval battles in a flooded arena. The enormous crowds it could contain were controlled by a complex of passageways beneath the tiers of seats, shown in the section (ABOVE), which directed people to the exit arches all round the building. Ancient authors claimed that it could seat nearly 100,000 people.

Records of Jesus' Life

The Gospels are arrangements of material drawn from the life of Jesus, which the first Christians used to help them to understand their beliefs and to explain them to others. Mark's Gospel, with its description of Hebrew customs, was written for non-Jewish Christians who were being persecuted.

I Pet, Mark.

Then they took the colt to Jesus and threw their cloaks on its back, and he sat on it. Many people spread their cloaks on the road, others greenery which they had cut in the fields. And those who went in front and those who followed were all shouting, 'Hosanna! Blessings on him who comes in the name of the Lord! Blessings on the coming kingdom of our father David! Hosanna in the highest heavens!' He entered Jerusalem and went into the Temple.
(Mark 11: 7-11)

- AD 30 Death of Jesus
- cAD 34-35 Martyrdom of Stephen; conversion of Paul
- AD 37-41 (Rome) Emperor Caligula
- cAD 39 Peter in Samaria
- AD 41-54 (Rome) Emperor Claudius
- AD 44 Agrippa orders the beheading of James, brother of John
- AD 45-49 First mission of Paul
- cAD 48 Famine in Judea; the Council of Jerusalem
- AD 49-52 Second mission of Paul
- AD 50-52 Letters to the Thessalonians
- AD 53-58 Third mission of Paul
- AD 54-68 (Rome) Emperor Nero
- cAD 57 First Letter to the Corinthians; AD 57 second Letter to the Corinthians; Letter to the Galatians; Letter to the Romans
- AD 58 Paul arrested in the Temple
- AD 58-60 Paul held at Caesarea
- AD 61-63 Paul held in Rome; Letters to Colossians, Ephesians, Philemon, and Philippians (?)
- cAD 63 Paul set free (?); Gospel of Mark and 1 Peter; Letter of James; 1 Timothy; Letter to Titus (?)
- cAD 64-67 Martyrdom of Peter at Rome

The early Letters of Paul were the first parts of the New Testament to be written. Their advice to the early churches differs in emphasis from the material of the Gospels, which give details of the life of Jesus. Although the Gospels precede the Letters in the New Testament, they were certainly written later than the early Letters and in a different order to the one in which they appear in Bibles today.

The first letter of Peter is written to non-Jewish Christians in Pontus, Galatia, Cappadocia, Asia and Bithynia. Paul also worked in some of these places. These areas cover most of what is now Turkey. The Christians there were under pressure, but not the kind of official, state persecution which developed later in the century. Although there is nothing about it in the New Testament, early sources and very strong tradition assert that Peter was executed in Rome during Nero's reign, which would put this letter before AD 68, and also, perhaps, give an indication of when Mark's Gospel was written. Peter's letter lays stress on baptism as the assurance that his readers have been saved by Jesus Christ and have received the Holy Spirit, so they cannot be hurt, even by suffering. Early Christian tradition links Mark's Gospel with the kind of teaching Peter gave in Rome.

None of the Gospels are biographies of Jesus, in the modern sense, but are arrangements of the material used by the first Christians to help them to understand their beliefs about Jesus and to explain those beliefs to others. They are selections of information, obtained from the people who had direct contact with Jesus throughout his public life and from his family. The raw material consists of actions and encounters from the life of Jesus, together with examples of the things he taught, all carefully arranged to point towards the full significance of his death and resurrection. The people who used this material in this way believed that baptism was a symbolic representation of the death, resurrection and ascension of Jesus, by which those who held these beliefs about Jesus could share in his risen life. Seen in this way, all the Gospels build on the experience of baptism and the Christian way of life into which it leads.

Mark's Gospel, the earliest, was written around AD 63-68, at a time when the church's first leaders were being executed, and there were fears that the unique witness of the people who had actually known Jesus would be lost. Its contents had already been shaped by more than 30 years of preaching and teaching about Jesus, but it is very probably the first Gospel to come down to us as it was written. If there were earlier written collections of material about Jesus, they have not survived, and Matthew and Luke seem to have started from Mark's Gospel when they wrote their Gospels some 10 years later.

Mark's Gospel was written for non-Jewish Christians who needed to have Jewish customs explained to them, and who were experiencing persecution. These could have been Christians in Rome at the end of Nero's reign or the Christians of Asia Minor to whom Peter wrote.

BELOW **Baptism, here shown in the River Jordan, was already practised by groups of Jews, such as the Essenes who lived at Qumran near the entry of the Jordan into the Dead Sea, but it was unusual in Judaism. John the Baptist baptised Jesus in the River Jordan after Jesus insisted that it was the appropriate symbol for the beginning of his public work. Jesus himself baptised people and taught that it is a sign of being born again and of accepting his way of life. Since then it has been the normal initiation for Christians.**

Christian Persecution

A series of natural and military disasters in Italy and the empire aroused suspicions that Nero was out of favour with the gods. In about AD 65, needing scapegoats, he had many Roman Christians put to death with sadistic cruelty. This created a precedent for widespread persecution of Christians.

- *c* AD 64 Burning of Rome, persecution of Christians
- *c* AD 64-67 Martyrdom of Peter at Rome
- AD 66-70 Jewish war against Romans
- AD 66-67 Nero in Greece
- AD 66 Jerusalem attacked by Cestius Gallius; Christians take refuge in Pella
- AD 67 Vespasian reconquers Galilee
- *c* AD 67 Paul a prisoner in Rome; 2 Timothy; Paul is beheaded; Letter to the Hebrews
- AD 67-68 The Zealots are masters of Jerusalem
- AD 68 (Rome) Galba is emperor; Nero commits suicide
- AD 69-79 (Rome) Emperor Vespasian
- AD 70 Titus captures Jerusalem
- AD 70 Judea an imperial province of Rome
- AD 71 Triumph of Vespasian and Titus in Rome
- AD 73 Capture of Masada
- *c* AD 75 Gospel of Matthew; Gospel of Luke; Acts of Apostles; the Letter of Jude
- AD 79-81 (Rome) Emperor Titus
- AD 81-96 (Rome) Emperor Domitian
- *c* AD 95 2 Peter; Gospel of John; 1 John (3 John and 2 John possibly earlier); Revelation
- AD 96-98 (Rome) Emperor Nerva

Nero, the Roman emperor to whom Paul appealed, began his 14 year reign in AD 54 with assassinations and executions to secure his power and finance his extravagances, but there was no attempt to discredit or suppress Christians. Nero's predecessors had centralized power and increased the efficiency of the Roman civil service until the emperor's actions were beyond any control – provided the army remained loyal to him. Emperors began to be honoured as divine, and the 16 year old Nero encouraged the cult. Such absolute power could only be sustained by strong rulers, and Nero was not cast in that mould. A series of natural disasters in Italy, and military crises on the borders of the empire, aroused the suspicion that Nero was out of favour with the gods. In Britain, a rebellion led by Queen Boadicea very nearly drove the Romans out of the province they had only conquered some 18 years earlier. At the other extreme of the empire, in the east, the Parthians inflicted a decisive defeat on a Roman army, and Nero had to agree to peace terms. In AD 63 an earthquake destroyed most of Pompeii, anticipating its final destruction 16 years later.

Fire broke out in Rome itself near the Circus Maximus in the summer of AD 64. The congested city was familiar with fires, but this one spread rapidly for six days until all the southern part of the city had been

RIGHT **The strength of Rome's military power can be appreciated from the number of great fortresses it captured. In many cases provincial kings drew their inspiration for their strongholds from the Romans themselves, only to discover to their cost that the strength of Rome lay in the iron discipline of its troops rather than in fortified positions.**

BELOW From the top of the Masada fortress, on the shores of the Dead Sea, the Roman siege camp can still be seen. The Romans applied siege tactics wherever they fought, and relied on the mobility of their armies to meet rebellion wherever it arose in the empire. Soon the army became the most powerful political force in the empire, able to make or depose emperors.
INSET The two royal palaces on the top of Masada housed a main Jewish administrative centre.

destroyed as far as the Tiber and the Servian wall, then it broke out again and spread through the northern districts. By the time it finally died down it had burned through 10 of the city's 14 wards. Nero was widely blamed for the fire, which was said to have been started on his orders, and even the rebuilding of the city caused unpopularity, as the rest of Italy and the provinces were squeezed to pay for the work. A plague in the following year added to the misery. The Christians in Rome were convenient scapegoats, and Nero had as many as could be found put to death with sadistic cruelty, not only for the fire but also on the charge that they were 'haters of the human race' who refused to take part in other religious activities.

The persecutions of Christians under Nero seem to have been confined to Rome, as a distraction from the suspicions about his own involvement in the fire and other disasters, but it did create a precedent for Roman officials in other parts of the empire and it ended any possibility of the Christian church coming to a similar agreement with Rome as that enjoyed by Jews, whose exclusive religion was recognized by the state and respected, without any suggestion that it smacked of treason. There could be no hope of that for Christianity in the foreseeable future, especially as Jesus himself had been condemned by a Roman magistrate on a treason charge, and executed. It would no longer be possible for Christians such as Paul to hope that Roman citizenship would provide protection from trouble. This formed the background to the last years of Paul and Peter.

Paul's three Letters to Timothy and Titus are usually called the pastoral letters, because they are addressed to individual leaders of local churches, and contain advice about church organization and worship. Timothy was in Ephesus and Titus in Crete. These are the last letters attributed to Paul and show that two of the earlier threats to Christian beliefs had now combined – an insistence that all Christians must express their Christianity in Jewish form, and belief in a system of secret knowledge which guaranteed salvation and allocated a subordinate role to Jesus. This belief, called gnosticism, from the Greek *gnosis* meaning 'knowledge', dogged Christianity throughout the rest of the New Testament period and beyond.

Information about Paul's last years and death is very sparse, in contrast to the wealth of detail provided by Acts about his arrest in Jerusalem and his struggles to have his case tried properly. Acts ends with Paul staying two years in Rome under house arrest, but does not say what happened to him then. It was still only about AD 63, before Nero began his attacks on Christians, and the charges against him would certainly have been dismissed at that time if he received a fair trial.

If Paul was in fact released, he probably went back to Macedonia, and to Asia Minor and Crete where his old companions Timothy and Titus were in charge of churches. He then returned – or was taken – to Rome again after the great fire to a more severe form of imprisonment and to death. This would account for passages in the pastoral letters about Paul's movements and his expectation of death. They would have been written during the second imprisonment in Rome, which ended with Paul's execution near the end of Nero's reign.

Alternatively Paul might have been executed after the two years imprisonment described in Acts, and someone else wrote these three final letters to give the kind of teaching and advice Paul would have given to leaders of local churches. So it seems likely that Paul was executed before Nero committed suicide in AD 68. He was taken outside the southern walls of the city of Rome and beheaded, as befitted a Roman citizen. Early church tradition asserts that Peter was crucified during the same period in the Vaticanum, an area west of the River Tiber.

Nero's reign ended in chaos, amidst events which created a totally new situation for the Christian churches. His death marked the end of a dynasty and resulted in a year of civil war in Rome. Whatever the Roman constitution said, real power lay with the military – the praetorian guard in Rome and the great armies guarding the frontiers of the empire. During the bloody struggle for political power, Rome itself was stormed by Roman troops, the Capitol was burned, three emperors were proclaimed and overthrown, and finally Vespasian emerged as victor. He reigned as emperor from AD 69-79.

In this period the situation in Palestine deteriorated swiftly. Even before the death of Nero, war had broken out between Rome and the Jews of Palestine and this was to have disastrous effects on the privileges Jews enjoyed throughout the empire, on their economic and political power, and on their cultural influence.

BELOW **Masada survived the frequent destruction and rebuilding which more accessible sites in Palestine experienced during the Roman occupation and afterwards. Consequently, it provides valuable evidence for the wealth and prosperity of distant provinces of the Roman Empire. Provided they kept their people loyal to Rome, and saw that Roman taxes were gathered efficiently, the native rulers could survive the bloody battles for power in Rome itself.**

Under the corrupt rule of the last of the Roman procurators, Florus, a comparatively small protest grew to open rebellion when Jerusalem Jews compelled Florus and his soldiers to retreat to Caesarea, the Roman administrative centre for Judea. The governor of Syria, Gallius, then marched on Jerusalem with the Roman Twelfth Legion, and was in turn repulsed with heavy losses at the end of AD 66. The rebellion had turned into a war, and Nero sent one of his most able generals, the future emperor, Vespasian, with 60,000 men.

Vespasian began a systematic campaign to subdue Palestine, beginning with Galilee. He drove the Zealots before him to take refuge in Jerusalem, where they murdered Jewish opponents and moderates. By the end of AD 68 all Judea and Idumea had been subdued, and only such strongholds as Jerusalem and Masada held out. It was at this time that the Jewish community at Qumran hid its library in caves and fled to Masada.

When Vespasian was proclaimed emperor in AD 69, his son Titus carried on in his place, and began the full siege of Jerusalem early in AD 70. That part of the war was over by September, with the city and its Temple destroyed, and the Jews of Jerusalem killed or sold into slavery. Titus celebrated his victory with sacrifices to the standards of the Roman Legion in front of the ruins of the Temple. The following year Vespasian and Titus had their victory proclaimed by a 'triumph', a huge procession in Rome in which treasures from the Jerusalem Temple were carried and Jewish captives walked in chains. The occasion is vividly portrayed in the carvings of the Arch of Titus.

Further strongholds fell one by one during the years AD 70-73. These included the Herodium, south of Jerusalem, Machaerus, east of Lake Asphaltitis (Dead Sea), and, finally, the massive fortress of Masada, where Jewish slaves built a ramp to its summit, more than 1,000 feet (300 metres) above the shore of Lake Asphaltitis. On the night before the final assault the defenders killed their families and themselves. This marked the end of the war.

The Christians of Jerusalem had fled the city before the siege closed, and settled at Pella in the Jordan Valley. This had a wide ranging effect on the early Christian church as the Christians of Jerusalem could no longer be a centre of authority and stability for the growing number of Christians elsewhere in the Roman Empire. The Jewish Christians who had left Jerusalem came under fire from both Jews and Romans, but the only time anything like a serious persecution occurred was later in the reign of Domitian (AD 81-96).

In the New Testament three letters which are difficult to date may best be understood as belonging to the period of radical rethinking for Christians which followed the destruction of Jerusalem. The Second Letter of Peter was probably written after Peter's death to show how he would have guided Christians in the new situation, and it has many similarities to the Letter of Jude, which deals with problems of false teachers and worries about the delay in the expected return of Jesus. The long and remarkable Letter to the Hebrews differs radically from anything else ascribed to Paul, and his authorship has been questioned from very early times. It presents the work of Jesus in terms of the Hebrew priesthood and sacrifices. These are ways which would particularly appeal to Jewish Christians after the destruction of the Temple.

1 and 2 Tim, Tit, Jude, 2 Pet, Heb.

With so many witnesses in a great cloud on every side of us, we too, then, should throw off everything that hinders us, especially the sin that clings so easily, and keep running steadily in the race we have started. Let us not lose sight of Jesus, who leads us in our faith and brings it to perfection: for the sake of the joy which was still in the future, he endured the cross, disregarding the shamefulness of it, and from now on has taken his place at the right of God's throne. Think of the way he stood such opposition from sinners and then you will not give up for want of courage. In the fight against sin, you have not yet had to keep fighting to the point of death.
(Heb 12: 1-2)

LEFT **The scale of the building works on the top of Masada, which had very difficult access, suggest the power rulers such as the Herods had over their own people, even under Roman occupation. The massive water system would have needed an army of slaves to build it and keep it filled.**

BELOW The Zealots took over the royal stronghold of Masada as their place for a last stand against the Romans, and held it for nearly six years before it fell in AD 73. By then the Romans had used slave labour to build a great ramp to the fortifications on the top of the sheer, isolated crag, to take it by assault. In the final attack the Roman troops met with no resistance and found that the Zealot defenders had killed their own families and committed suicide.

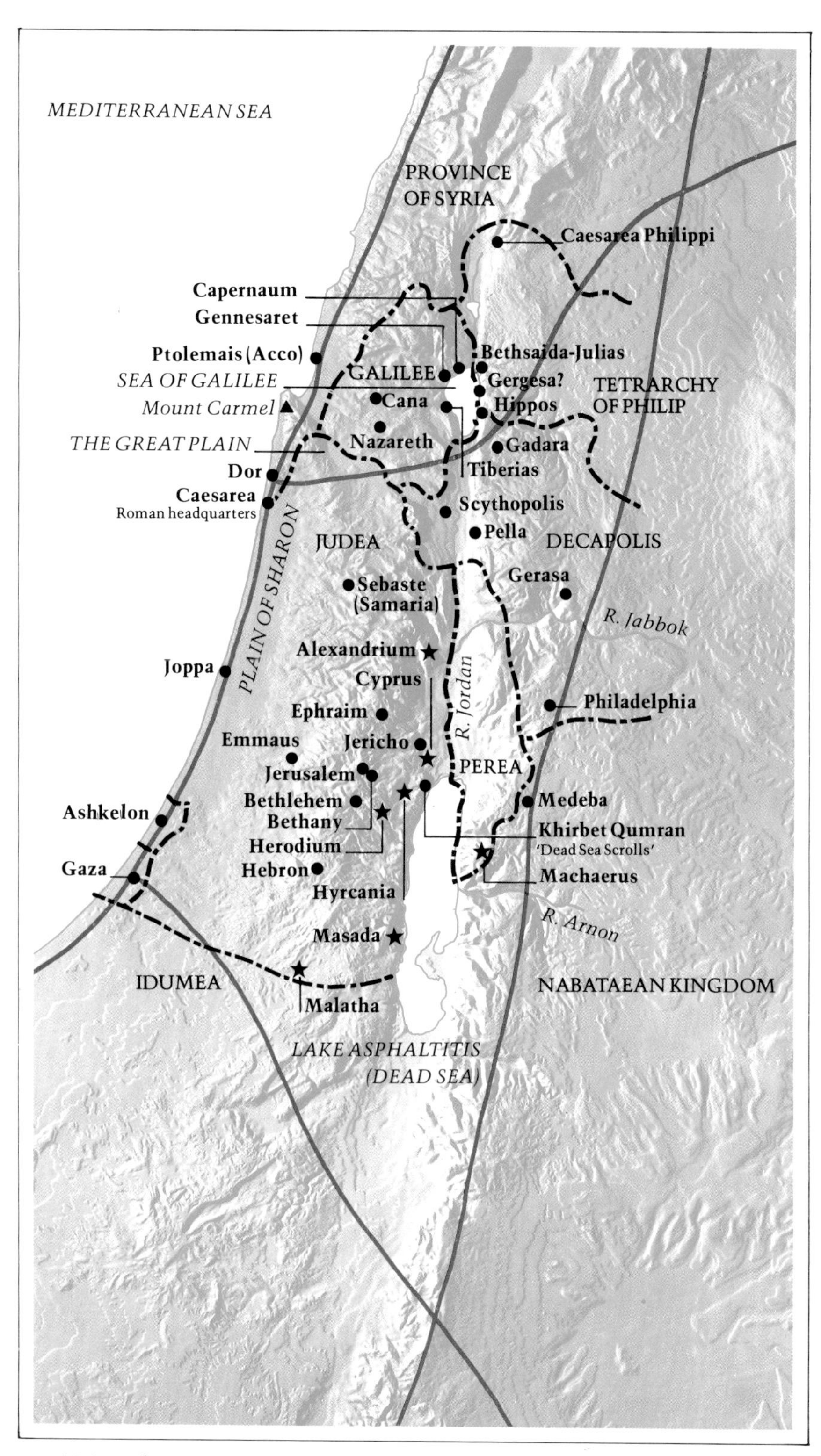

THE JEWISH-ROMAN WAR Roman occupation of Palestine was severely tested in the Jewish-Roman war of AD 66-70; isolated pockets of resistance held out for three more years. The war began with disturbances near the Roman administrative headquarters in Caesarea, and spread throughout the country. Such extreme patriotic groups as the Zealots provided the main Jewish resistance to Roman occupation, and were ready to commit suicide – as at Masada – rather than submit. The war reached its climax in the Roman siege of Jerusalem, which they captured in stages until only the Temple held out, defended by Zealots. The siege ended with the burning of the Temple, and the destruction of Jerusalem.

BELOW **The triumphal arch of Titus in Rome, the victor of the Jewish-Roman war, commemorates his victory with carvings of Roman soldiers carrying the treasures of the Temple of Jerusalem, including the seven branched lamp.**

BOTTOM **Whether seen from the shores of the Dead Sea, where it towers against the cliffs behind it, or used as a vantage point looking across to the mountains of Jordan, Masada is a vivid reminder of the violent background to Palestine in biblical times.**

Matthew and Luke

Matthew presented Jesus as an interpreter of the old Jewish law who was greater than Moses, and who replaced the old covenant with a new one. The emphasis in Luke's Gospel is on the Holy Spirit, as the means by which all Christians share in the life and power of the risen Jesus.

Matt, Luke, Acts.

But the angel spoke; and he said to the women, 'There is no need for you to be afraid. I know you are looking for Jesus, who was crucified. He is not here, for he has risen, as he said he would. Come and see the place where he lay, then go quickly and tell his disciples, "He has risen from the dead and now he is going before you to Galilee; it is there you will see him". Now I have told you.' Filled with awe and great joy the women came quickly away from the tomb and ran to tell the disciples. (Matt 28: 5-8)

In the aftermath of the destruction of Jerusalem, the Christians of the Roman Empire might have been expected to turn their back on the Hebrew origins of their religion. The New Testament shows that the central message of Christianity was expressed in different ways to meet the needs and attitudes of the various groups of people. Inevitably, the main differences tend to be between Christian groups with Jewish backgrounds, and people with more Hellenistic ways of thinking. These two main attitudes were to be found all over the empire, for Judaism had been dispersed throughout the ancient world from at least the time of the Babylonian exile, five centuries before the beginnings of Christianity; the Roman world was permeated by Greek cultural influences. The Gospels themselves reflect these differences.

More importantly, the central Christian tradition, expressed throughout the New Testament, rejected both the exclusiveness of Judaism and the compromises of Hellenism by keeping a firm hold on the actions and sayings of Jesus himself during his public life. Christianity could not deteriorate into a philosophy while it kept alive the personality of Jesus. Although incidents and sayings were detached from their original context and combined together in different ways by Christian teachers, they were never separated from the life of Jesus as he moved towards death and resurrection.

Collections of sayings, perhaps arranged in a simple chronological sequence, existed during the early years of preaching and teaching, and may even have circulated in written form. None of them seems to have survived in their original forms. Matthew's Gospel contains five such collections of Jesus's teachings on various topics, of which the most famous is the Sermon on the Mount (Matt 5-7). But the whole work is best understood as an expansion and adaptation of Mark's Gospel, which was written for Jewish Christians after the destruction of Jerusalem in AD 70. It presents Jesus as a teacher and interpreter of the Jewish law greater than Moses, and traces his descent from Abraham and David in a form which emphasizes the replacement of the old covenant by the new one of Jesus. He is the new Moses, the new Israel, the fulfilment of numerous Old Testament prophecies about the messiah.

The whole of Matthew's Gospel breathes the atmosphere of Jewish rabbinical thought but without for a moment implying that non-Jewish Christians are lesser citizens of the Kingdom of God. It has been suggested that it presents Jesus in ways which Jewish

Christians could use in their discussions with orthodox Jews during the terrible years after the Jewish war with the Romans. Matthew shows that the Hebrew experience of God had not been destroyed, for it had already been fulfilled and all its potential realized in Jesus.

Luke's Gospel also uses material from Mark, and expands and rearranges it, but it does so for a quite different audience than Matthew's. The New Testament contains a sequel also written or inspired by Luke, and longer than the Gospel itself. This is the Acts of the Apostles, which develops the same themes of the Gospel covering the 30 years following the death, resurrection and ascension of Jesus. Acts uses a number of sources including Luke's own personal experience. Luke was a close companion of Paul and is mentioned in three of Paul's letters, those to Philemon, Colossians and the second of his letters to Timothy. These references to Luke are consistent with an unusual literary feature of Acts, in which four passages change from the normal third person singular or plural to the first person plural – from 'he' or 'they', to 'we' – in a way which suggests that Luke was with Paul and his companions at the times being discussed. The passages refer to part of the second missionary journey, from Troas to Philippi (Acts 16:10-17); part of the third missionary journey, from Philippi to Jerusalem (Acts 20:5-15; 21:1-18); and the whole of the journey from Caesarea to Rome when Paul was under guard, including the shipwreck (Acts 27:1 – 28:16).

This close association with Paul, and particularly with Asia Minor, helps explain the special features of Luke's Gospel. While it never denies or understates the Hebrew origins of Christianity, nor the importance of Hebrew religious symbolism for the significance of Jesus, it presents Jesus as the saviour sent by God to all mankind. It emphasizes the aspects of Christianity which would appeal particularly to the non-Jewish, Hellenistic Christians reached by Paul in his missionary journeys. The structure both of Luke's Gospel and of Acts is designed to help make this message clear. The two works are mainly arranged in a series of Jesus's journeys – from Nazareth to Bethlehem and Jerusalem at his birth; from Nazareth to the Temple in Jerusalem when he was 12 years old; and the final journey from the far north of Palestine to Jerusalem, into which Luke packs so many of the incidents and teachings from the ministry of Jesus which are not found in Mark's Gospel. Acts uses a similar method to show how the church expanded from its origins in Jerusalem through Asia Minor and eastern Europe to the centre of the Roman Empire in Rome itself.

Luke gives particular emphasis to the Holy Spirit as the key to Jesus's own life, and as the means by which Christians share in the life and power of the risen Jesus. Such a precious gift is open to all people, Jew and non-Jew alike, and all people are equally pardoned by Jesus when they turn to him. Disadvantaged people of all kinds – including, for the world of Luke's time, women – are given special consideration. This Gospel presents Christianity in a way which would have special appeal to the diverse peoples of the Roman world, which combined, on the one hand, vast social differences and, on the other, a sincere desire for a practical way of realizing Greek ideals about the value and equality of all.

BELOW **The road across the Mount of Olives is the most dramatic approach to Jerusalem, which suddenly opens out to travellers approaching from the east, with the Temple area in the foreground. It was the route chosen by Jesus for his final entry into Jerusalem, and for his agonized prayer in the Garden of Gethsemane, where he awaited his arrest after Judas had left the Upper Room to tell the authorities where he could be found.**

Paul's 3rd journey

Paul's journey to Rome under arrest

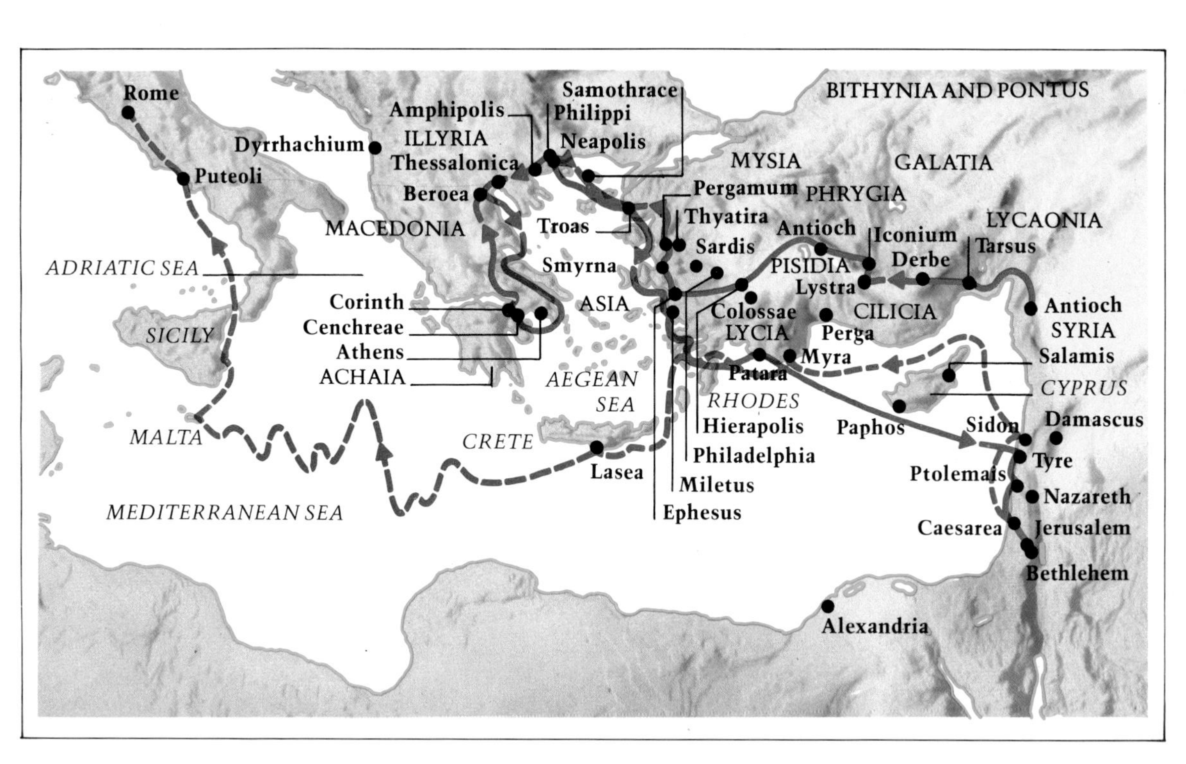

PREACHING AND PRISON **The third of Paul's missionary journeys saw the disciple based in Ephesus, from which he wrote the First Letter to the Corinthians, and perhaps Galatians. A crisis among the Christians of Corinth made him write his distressed Second Letter to them which he followed with a visit. From there Paul wrote his most famous letter, to the Romans. He had intended to make Rome his base for further missionary work, but he went under arrest appealing as a Roman citizen to the emperor Nero to hear charges brought against him by the Jewish religious authorities.**

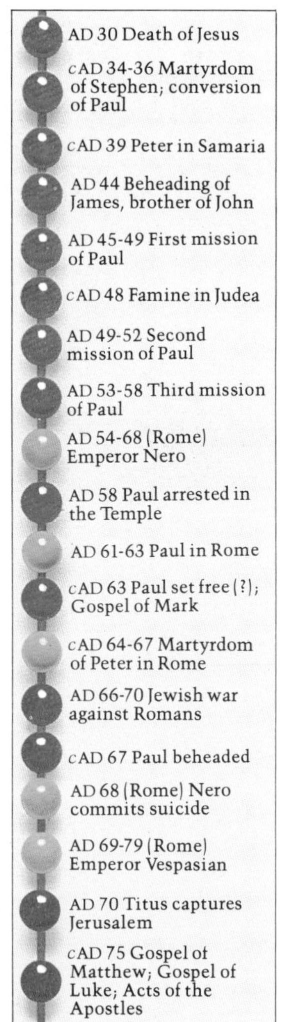

LEFT Women harvesting vegetables near Capernaum show the kind of familiar scene used by Jesus when teaching in this area. His parables subtly connect deep truths to everyday experience, and also make the hearers draw the conclusions themselves.

BELOW Capernaum was the centre for the earlier part of the public work of Jesus, not far from his home town, but near the main route to the north. The mixed population of Galilee may have been more ready to listen to new ideas than Jerusalem Jews.

John's Gospel and Revelation

John's Gospel uses details of seven miracles, or 'signs', as the key to understanding the work of Jesus. The Book of Revelations – possibly by the same author – is in a cryptic 'apocalyptic' style, but its teaching is clear: whatever forces seem to rule the world, God cannot be defeated by them.

1, 2 and 3 John, John, Rev.

As the Father has loved me,
so I have loved you.
Remain in my love.
If you keep my commandments
you will remain in my love,
just as I have kept my Father's commandments
and remain in his love.
I have told you this
so that my own joy may be in you
and your joy be complete.
This is my commandment:
love one another,
as I have loved you.
A man can have no greater love
than to lay down his life for his friends. (John 15: 9-13)

As the numbers of Christians grew outside Palestine, main centres of Christian influence developed to which lesser churches looked for advice and security. When Jerusalem was still the heart of Christianity, even Christians as independently minded as Paul went there to make sure that their teaching was true to the main tradition. But in AD 70 Jerusalem was destroyed by the Romans and its Christians had fled. Its place was taken by Antioch, Ephesus and Rome, and by cities such as Alexandria, which are, however, little mentioned in the New Testament. Although Jerusalem was rebuilt, its Christians never regained the influence which they had held earlier.

The earliest church historians link the John of John's Gospel and Letters with Asia Minor. The area had already been a thriving centre for Christianity during Paul's missionary work, as his letters show, and it is the most probable location for John's writings during the third generation after Jesus towards the end of the first century AD. Its main Christian church was at Ephesus, but other traditions link John with Antioch, and even Palestine itself.

At first sight, John's Gospel is completely different from the other three. It uses a different chronology which seems to place some incidents differently from the first three Gospels. It only gives details about seven miracles, but states that there were many more. It calls them 'signs' and uses them as the key to understanding the work of Jesus. In addition the whole style of language distinguishes this Gospel from the other accounts of Jesus. These differences all point to a very precise purpose in the author's mind, and to a time when Christians had been able to reflect on the significance of Jesus over many years. The religious movements which flourished in the Greek speaking world of Asia Minor towards the end of the first century AD form a possible audience. John's Gospel presents the Jewish background of Jesus in ways which would appeal to Hellenistic Christians attracted by religions which offered secret knowledge of the real powers which control the universe.

Thus John starts his Gospel with a deliberate reminder of the opening chapter of the Book of Genesis, but here Jesus is the 'word', God's agent of creation whose life and teachings provide the key to the pattern of the universe. The design of the whole creation was revealed in the things that Jesus did and said, particularly in his love. He was a real person who could be seen and touched, not a remote power only accessible through special knowledge. Most important of all, the crucifixion and resurrection of Jesus were real expressions of God's love and power, in which all could now share. The Son of God really did become a human being, who suffered, died and rose again, to free all people from the fear that they were cut off from God by powers which could destroy them.

The first and longest of John's Letters has the same theme as the Gospel, emphasizing the goodness of Jesus, his power over evil, his love, and the convincing reality of the fellowship his disciples had with him. The other two Letters are brief appeals, written to individual Christians exhorting them to love one another and to beware of false teachers.

The Book of Revelation states who wrote it, where it

BELOW **John's description of Jesus as the 'word' draws on many associations. One was the permanence and authority of inscriptions, particularly legal codes setting out the pattern of life for a nation. Such a code carved in stone was the Ten Commandments, which were the foundation of Hebrew law and were called 'ten words'. The Gospels present Jesus as the fulfilment of this law.**

was written, and for whom it was written. The author is 'John', who was 'on the island of Patmos for having preached God's word and witnessed for Jesus' (Rev 1:9). The book is addressed to 'the seven churches of Asia' (Rev 1:4). These were at Ephesus, Smyrna, Pergamum, Thyatira, Sardis, Philadelphia and Laodicea. Patmos was a Roman prison island off the west coast of Asia Minor, and the seven churches named all lie within about 100 miles (160 km) of the port of Ephesus.

The fact that Patmos was a prison island is a useful clue to the purpose of the book, and even to the author's identity and the peculiar style in which the book is written. The main problem of authorship is raised by the differences in style and vocabulary between John's Gospel and Revelation, but these differences could easily be deliberate on the author's part. It belongs to a style of Hebrew literature called 'apocalyptic', which flourished in times of persecution when it was necessary to give encouragement and hope without providing an excuse for even further persecution.

The situation is referred to in terms which are deliberately obscure. The persecuted group would know what the allusions really meant, and that the people and places named were really a code for the powers that were oppressing them. In this example of apocalyptic writing, 'Babylon' symbolizes Rome, the seven heads of the beast are Rome's seven hills, and the 10 horns are 10 subject kings within the Roman Empire who were persecuting Christians. If such a piece of writing fell into the hands of the Roman authorities or their puppets, it could not be used as evidence of treason. The John who wrote it had wide authority over Christian churches, and was already being punished for his pastoral and evangelistic activities. There is no reason why this should not be the same John who wrote the Gospel, and who knew Jesus personally, but it is impossible to say with certainty whether they were one and the same.

Dating the book is also difficult. The persecution of Christian, by Nero in the final years of his reign, AD 64-68, concentrated on Christians in Rome, but local kings and officials might have followed his example in other parts of the empire. There is no evidence of any further trouble for Christians until the reign of Domitian (AD 81-96), who proclaimed himself 'lord and god', and demanded public worship of himself. The main evidence points to suffering by some of the Christians of Rome, but any group in the empire which refused to join in such worship would be suspect, even at this early stage in the development of emperor worship. From the time of the Jewish war in the reigns of Nero and Vespasian, it was easy for religious nonconformity to be interpreted as treason.

The Book of Revelation is so cryptic that it is impossible to identify the precise circumstances for which it was written, but its teaching is clear. Whatever forces may seem to rule the world, God cannot be defeated by them. Their oppressive powers are illusory and transitory and there can be no doubt about the outcome of their fight against God and his people. The heavenly Jerusalem, which Revelation foretells, will become the capital of a new world, and all faithful Christians will be citizens of it. Even the might of Rome itself, at the height of its glory, cannot prevent that.

BELOW **Jerusalem is one of th most powerful symbols used by the author of the Book of Revelation. God's final victory over all his people's enemies results in a 'new Jerusalem', open to the world and with God as its ruler (Rev 21).**

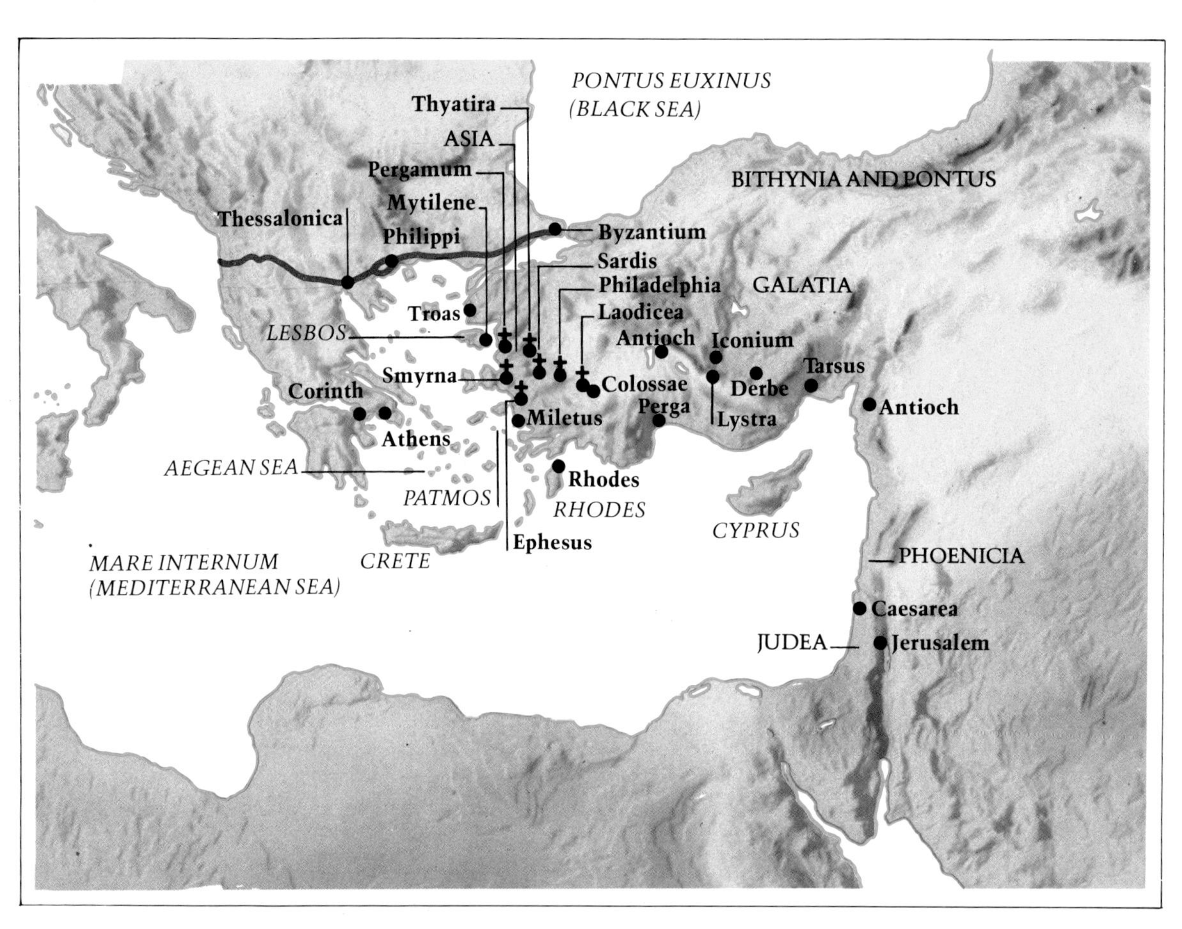

A MESSAGE FOR THE ASIAN CHURCHES **It is far from certain that the author of the Book of Revelation is the same 'John' as the author of John's Gospel, but he applied the same basic truths of the Christian faith to the needs of a persecuted group of Christians in Asia Minor. The churches mentioned in the book (which is written - from the prison island of Patmos, off the coast of Asia Minor - in the form of a letter) all lie around the port of Ephesus. The cryptic language used is a carefully disguised code, which refers to the Roman state in terms of ancient Babylon and would have been easily recognized by the Christians with their knowledge of the Old Testament. It would have been difficult to have proved that it was critical of the ruling power, if it fell into Roman hands.**

RIGHT **Growing grain, harvesting and bread are all main themes in the teaching of Jesus, who drew his illustrations from the everyday lives of his listeners. He told them he was 'the bread of life' sent by God.**

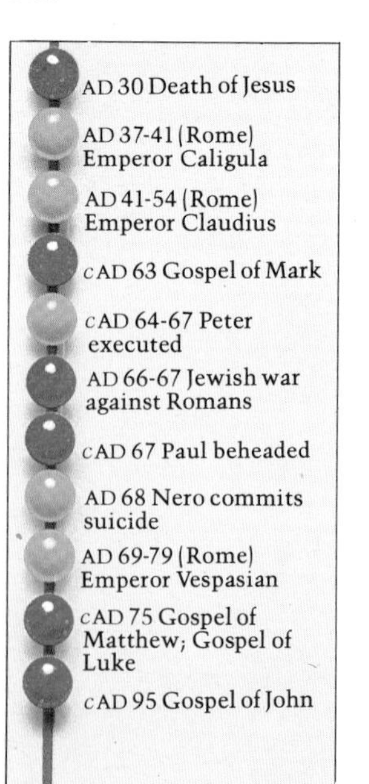

BELOW **John's Gospel emphasizes that all creation is part of God's love, and shares in the redemptive power of Jesus. This theme is found in many parts of the Old Testament, for God created everything in one ordered whole.**

Religious Expansionism

Despite intermittent periods of persecution, Christianity expanded rapidly, was given Roman legal status in 313, and was helped by the monastic movement. However by about 750, Mohammed's Islamic religion which recognized Allah as the only god, controlled some Mediterranean areas and the east as far as India.

During the early days of Christianity, the authors of the New Testament saw the rapid spread of the new faith as miraculous. It provided direct evidence of the divinity of Jesus. The final phase of God's plans to save the world must have begun, clearly shown by the Christian groups which sprang up and survived in the towns of the eastern Mediterranean area from Palestine to Rome. The movement was helped by a number of factors, particularly the peace imposed by Rome on her empire, which by now included all the peoples of the Mediterranean and Black Sea areas, the whole of Europe as far east as the River Rhine, and most of Britain. Wherever the Romans gained control they created safe, efficient communications by both land and sea, in order to move administrators and troops swiftly, and to supply the needs of Rome's teeming population.

The official religions of the empire were extensions of Roman power which tended to confirm and justify their rule and the divine authority of the emperor. Christianity, on the other hand, offered its members a sense of freedom, equality and community which transcended all differences of race, social class and legal status. The destruction of Jerusalem by the Romans in AD 70 helped to free Christianity from its Jewish origins so that it could make a more universal appeal and meet the needs of non-Jewish converts without the restrictions of the Hebrew religious laws.

From the time of Alexander the Great's triumphant reign (336-323 BC), Greek culture and language had dominated the eastern Mediterranean region, and this also assisted the spread of Christianity beyond the confines of Palestine. The scattered Jewish communities in towns throughout the Near East spoke Greek, had a Greek translation of the Old Testament, and provided the first Christian missionaries with convenient points of contact with the population. The first, rapid expansion of Christianity during New Testament times was northwards into the Greek world of Syria, Asia Minor and Greece, and into the Greek speaking areas of northern Africa, particularly Alexandria and Cyrene. The lists of the early bishops of Rome show that until the end of the second century, they were all Greek-speaking and, indeed, the New Testament was originally written in Greek.

Edessa in Syria was the gateway for Christianity to reach beyond the borders of the Roman Empire into Mesopotamia, where Syriac became the language of Christian worship and devotion, and from there Christianity spread slowly into Persia and India. Once it had penetrated effectively into the western, Latin speaking areas of Roman rule, Christianity made rapid advances. By the third century AD there were more than a hundred bishoprics in Italy, and Christianity was firmly established in Gaul and Spain. In the following century, when the Romans gave Christianity official recognition, there were at least three bishoprics in Britain (London, York, and either Colchester or Lincoln), while St Patrick's mission to Ireland began about 432.

Persecution of Christians by the Roman authorities was usually spasmodic and localized, typified by Nero's notorious cruelty against them in Rome following the great fire of AD 64. However, the martyrdoms at Lyons in 177, during the reign of the Emperor Marcus Aurelius (161-180), show how intense such local persecutions could be. There are records of two more universal persecutions – the Emperor Decius (249-251) mounted a systematic attack on Christianity in 250, and a subsequent period of tolerance ended abruptly in 303 when the Emperor Diocletian (284-305) ordered all churches and Christian books to be destroyed, and followed this with the execution of Christians during the next eight years. The first main phase of Christian expansion ended with the Edict of Milan in 313, when the joint Emperors Constantine (*c*306-337) and Licinius (308-314) gave Christianity legal recognition. From that date, Constantine, as senior emperor, forged close links between Christianity and the Roman state.

In granting recognition to Christianity in 313, the Emperor Constantine hoped that Christianity would unite all his subjects in a common faith, and help withstand the barbarian incursions, for the Roman Empire was beginning to disintegrate. In 331 Constantine moved the capital of the empire from Rome to Constantinople (Istanbul), the new city he had built to command the sea passage from the Mediterranean to the Black Sea. As the western parts of the empire crumbled, so too the cultural differences between the eastern, Greek speaking Christians, and the western, Latin speakers became more obvious. The uncertainties of intermittent persecution and toleration had helped unite Christians, but the new period of official recognition brought differences out into the open.

Freedom from fear of official interference allowed resentments to surface against Christians who had

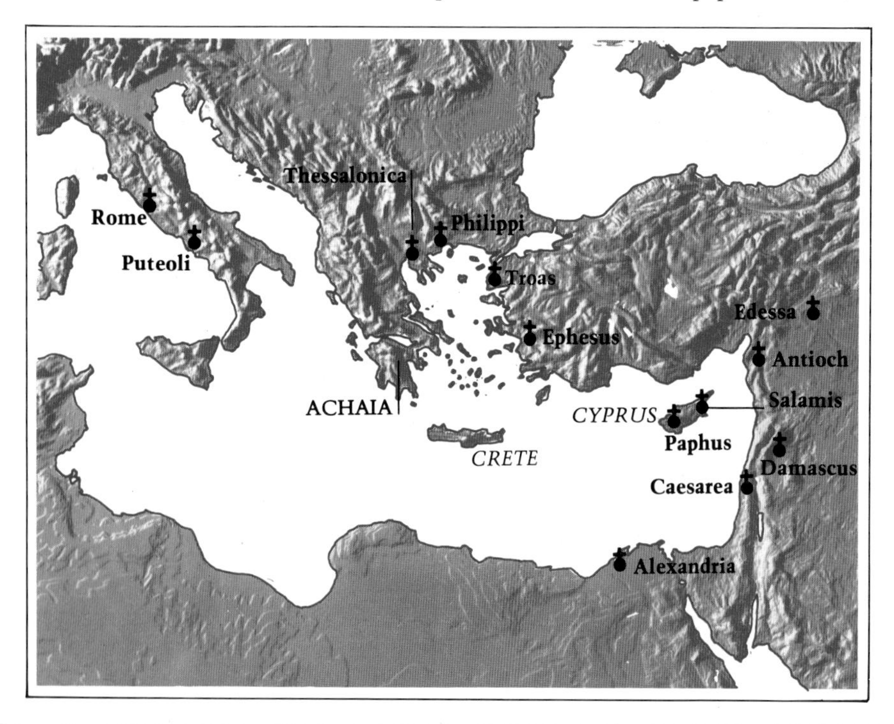

THE FIRST CHURCHES
Jewish opposition to the new religious movement, together with the number of non-Jewish converts, soon forced the first Christians to break from their strict Jewish roots. Main centres of Judaism, such as Alexandria, soon had established Christian groups, and Paul's three journeys added churches in Asia Minor, Macedonia and Greece. There was already a Christian church in Rome when Paul went there in about AD 61. Despite sporadic persecutions, the new religion spread widely in the empire and beyond.

submitted to the Roman laws against Christianity, even though a church synod ruled that there should be no rejection of the lapsed who wished to return. A more serious split amongst Christians developed from Alexandria, where a controversy raged about the exact status of Jesus Christ as God, and spread throughout the eastern churches. The Emperor Constantine convened a council at Nicea in 325, which set out the basic beliefs of Christianity in a creed for universal acceptance. Nicea was followed by six more 'ecumenical' councils during the following four and a half centuries to try to settle further controversies and establish a form of Christianity agreed by all Christians. They met at Constantinople (381), Ephesus (431), Chalcedon (451), Constantinople again (553 and 680), and Nicea (787).

Inevitably, the Christians adopted much of the administrative organization of the Roman Empire, if only because it provided convenient and natural geographical divisions, and symbols of authority – even in such matters as ceremonial dress familiar to all. A 'diocese' was originally a larger administrative region of secular government within the Roman Empire, containing a number of provinces. In time the term was applied to the larger areas of ecclesiatical jurisdiction, containing a number of bishoprics, and finally to the smaller area ruled by each bishop. An important stage in the recognition of special influence by the Bishop of Rome was reached at the time of the Council of Chalcedon (451), when the Bishop of Constantinople appealed to Leo, Bishop of Rome, for help and received a summary of the Christian faith, 'the Tome of Leo', which was given official status by the Council.

Even before the recognition of Christianity by Constantine, a new movement developed first in Egypt and then in other places which was to have lasting effects on the spread of Christianity. Christian hermits, who had withdrawn to the desert in Egypt, became so numerous that they organized themselves into communities with a common rule which recognized the individualism of the hermits' ideals but provided for shared worship. The movement, monasticism, spread in modified forms to Arabia, Asia Minor, north Africa, Spain, and Britain, where Patrick made it the means of consolidating Christianity in Ireland. In the following century, Columba took monasticism from Ireland to Scotland, establishing a monastery at what was then a centre of communications on the island of Iona, and consolidated the work begun by Ninian nearly two centuries earlier.

The form of monasticism most familiar in the west stems from Benedict, who transformed the hermit type of monasticism in Italy into a thoroughly integrated and organized form of community life controlled by his famous Rule. Benedict's twin principles of 'stability', commitment to the community for life, and 'obedience', to the head of the community and to the Rule, rapidly gained followers. The Benedictine form of monasticism spread rapidly within Italy, and was introduced into Britain by Augustine of Canterbury in 597. Eventually, it became the normal form of monasticism in the west and one of the main means of extending the influence of Rome within Christianity.

With the collapse of the western parts of the Roman Empire under barbarian attacks, and the gradual conversion of the invading peoples, it might have seemed that Christianity would prove to be a unifying force to replace the old military might of Rome. However, an important setback to such an ideal came from an unexpected area in the Arabian Desert to the east of the Red Sea.

A large proportion of the people Christian

A smaller proportion of the people Christian

OFFICIAL RECOGNITION **The Roman motive for recognizing the Christians was not, in fact, one of benevolent tolerance. Rather, it was a desperate attempt to encourage their subjects in a common faith and, hence, a coherent political unity.**

IONA
Derry
Armagh
Clogher
Clonard
Kells
Clanmacnoise
Durrow
Ardagh
Cashel
Cloyne
Ardmore
Kildare
Monasterboice
Bardsey
CALDEY ISLAND
Candida Casa (Whithorn)
Lindisfarne
Jarrow
Wearmouth
Bangor Fawr
Eboracum (York)
Lindum (Lincoln)
Bangor Iscoed
Roffa (Rochester)
Cantuaria (Canterbury)
Tornacum
Colonia
Camaracum
Laudunum
Rotomagus
Paris
Senones
Turones
Luxovium (Luxeuil)
Vesontio
S.Galli
Lauriacum
Santones
Burdigala
Elusa
Iria
Britonia
Aurensis
Dumium
Portus Cale
Pallentia
Viseum
Salamantica
Conimbriga
Caurium
Ebora
Emerita
Ossonoba
Hispalis
Caziona
Elberris
Moors
Carteia
Basiania
Bigastrium
Cartennae
Caesarea
Tipasa
Hippo Regius
Carthage
Thagaste
Theveste
Ammaedera
Sicca Veneria
Cercina
Arelate
Massilia (Marseilles)
Lerinum
CAPRARIA
Pisa
Florence
Monza
Aquileia
Grado
Parentium
Ravenna
Nursia
Farfa
Rome
Subiacense (Subiaco)
Capua
Casinense
Nola
ACHAIA

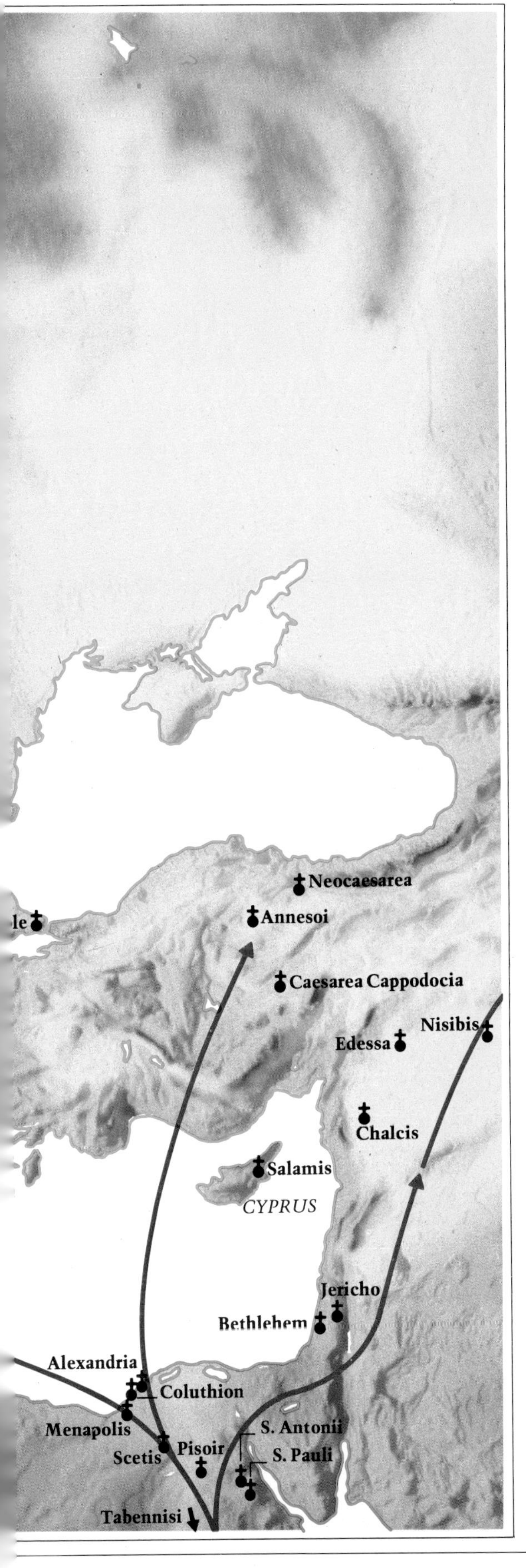

The main religion of the nomads of the Arabian Desert, and the people of the isolated towns on the main caravan routes, was a polytheism of many gods associated with particular localities or various aspects of nature and of human need. All that was changed dramatically by Mohammed, who was born into a prominent family in Mecca about 570. The first 40 years of his life were in no way extraordinary. Mohammed travelled with the caravans from Mecca as far as Syria as a merchant, and married. His call as a prophet came to him at the age of 40, and he began his preaching some three years later in Mecca.

Both Judaism and Christianity had penetrated into Arabia, and the caravans came into contact with them at the great trading centres in Syria and Mesopotamia, but Mohammed preached a monotheism which identified Allah, the chief god of Mecca, as the sole God of the universe who alone must be worshipped. The main practical consequence for believers was acceptance of the equality of all people before God, and the duty of all to care for the less fortunate. Mohammed claimed that he was only the last of a line of prophets sent by God, which included Abraham, Moses and Jesus, but, to Mohammed God dictated a sacred book through an angel, which contains all that is needed for belief, the regulation of personal life and the organization of society. This book, the Koran or Qu'ran, is in Arabic and is divided into 114 chapters or suras. It is so sacred for Islam that strict Muslims will not recognize any translation of it. The pattern of life derived from the Koran is expressed in five 'pillars of faith' – belief in Allah as the only God, and Mohammed as his prophet; prayer five times each day; almsgiving; fasting during daylight hours in the month of Ramadan; and a pilgrimage to Mecca.

From the beginning, Mohammed had to assert the supremacy of his teaching by force, to overcome the antagonism of the families which controlled western Arabia, particularly Mecca. War remained a legitimate means of spreading God's revelation if people would not accept it peacefully. But the religion preached by Mohammed and perpetuated through the Koran would never have achieved such remarkable success if it had not been so attractive. To the believer, it provides a simple, systematic and coherent way of life.

With remarkable speed, the new religion embarked on a great campaign of conquest, first within Arabia itself and then into the surrounding areas of Syria, Palestine, Mesopotamia, Egypt and northern Africa. By the middle of the eighth century it had expanded into India and had control of most of Spain. Much of this was achieved within 20 years of the death of Mohammed in 632. Breathtakingly beautiful shrines were erected, such as the Dome of the Rock in Jerusalem. It was built in 691 over the place where Muslims believe that Mohammed began his 'night journey' in which the glories of heaven were revealed to him. Traditionally, this is also the place where Abraham was prepared to sacrifice Isaac (Gen 22), and the site of the Hebrew Temple before its destruction by the Romans in AD 70.

Egyptian monasticism

Benedictine monasticism

THE SPIRITUAL LIFE **The Christians of the fourth century found a new method of testifying their allegiance to God. Monasticism was born among hermits in Egypt and it gradually developed into a communal existence. The spiritual lives of the monks were filled with prayer, fasting and vigil. In the early sixth century, a young Roman nobleman named Benedict used the Egyptian model to Latinize the monastic code. His followers soon spread throughout Europe and Asia Minor, preaching Christianity wherever they went.**

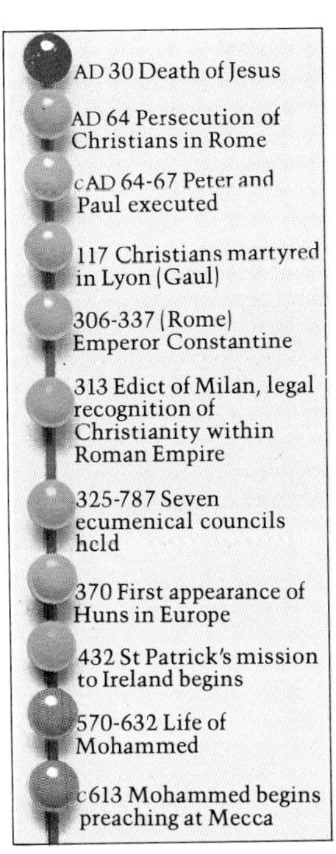

Lands of Conflict

Today the lands of the Bible are of vital importance to the rest of the world – not only because the vast quantities of oil which have been found in the region are essential to the industrialized nations, but, tragically, because of the long bloody conflicts still taking place there.

 Disputed areas occupied by Israel

 Unstable area

----- Pre-1967 borders

AN ETERNAL WAR ZONE?
Bitter hatreds and violent passions continue to ravage the biblical lands. At the end of last century, Jews tried to recreate a state of their own in a land occupied for centuries by Arabs. Their plan was on the point of floundering in the 1930s as every year many more Jews were leaving the area than were migrating to it. But that changed after the Second World War. When the extent of Jewish persecution became known, support for the Israeli ideal was almost universal, and the nation became a reality. But there have been five major Arab-Israel conflicts since then, while in 1982 Lebanon erupted into a bloody and tragic battlefield. Lasting peace for the Palestinian region seems even more remote than ever.

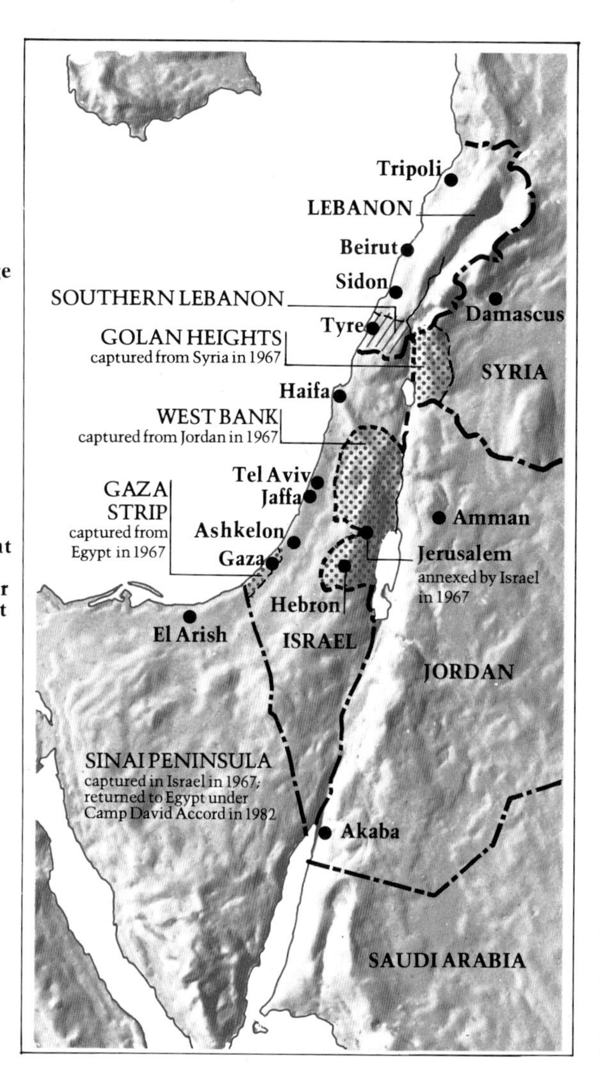

The lands of the Bible have never been at peace for long. Even today the area is being fought over almost constantly with periods of uneasy peace intervening. The same place names occur in news reports of incidents today as featured in the biblical accounts, and it is evident that Palestine is still a key area in the Near and Middle East. Jerusalem contains sacred sites of central importance for three world religions – Judaism, Christianity and Islam. The Palestine area from north of the Sea of Galilee to the desert, south of the Dead Sea, is all sacred to Jews as the 'Holy Land' and the ancient homeland of the Hebrew people, but even in New Testament times the Jews were losing control of the area. Effective Jewish rule was not regained until the establishment of the modern state of Israel by the war of 1948. Jerusalem was divided between Israel and the kingdom of Jordan from 1948 to 1967. Israel occupied the area from Jerusalem to the River Jordan (the West Bank), the Sinai Desert, the Gaza Strip and the the Golan Heights. Since then the Sinai Desert has been handed back to Egypt. At its greatest extent, in 1967, modern Israel controlled nearly 27,000 sq miles (70,000 sq km) of territory, of which Judea and Samaria comprised less than 2,300 sq miles (6,000 sq km).

With the exception of Israel, the Near and Middle East is still predominantly Muslim with pockets of Christianity, and Israel itself has a large Islamic population. Palestine, Lebanon and western Syria remain vitally important corridor areas along the eastern coast of the Mediterranean – not as links between Egypt and Mesopotamia, as in biblical times, but because areas nearby produce most of the world's oil. The pipelines across the Arabian Desert have taken the place of the old caravan routes. And the Suez Canal has been an important link though today many ships no longer use it, since its long closure during war and the advent of super tankers, some of which are too large to pass through the canal.

Irrigation remains as important as ever it was throughout the biblical lands, from Egypt to Mesopotamia, and the diversion of water for irrigation purposes is one of the main points of political sensitivity. In Egypt the Aswan High Dam helps control the waters of the River Nile on which Egyptian agriculture still depends, while in Palestine modern methods of irrigation and new agricultural techniques have enabled Israel to extend its agriculture into parts of the country previously thought useless for cultivation.

The Arabian Desert is still an area where nomadic herding preserves a way of life little changed over the centuries. The brief period of lush growth after rain, followed by months of sparse scrub, supports herds of camels, whose milk and meat provide for the desert nomads. But the great transformation in the area has come through the discovery of oil in vast quantities in the Persian Gulf and northern Mesopotamia. Not only has it brought great wealth to the area, but it has made the countries of the Gulf and Mesopotamia regions of vital interest for the world's industrial powers who depend on oil. The politics of Saudi Arabia, Iraq, Iran and the smaller oil states of the Gulf are of central importance for the prosperity of the rest of the world, for they set the price of the world's oil even for countries which they do not themselves supply.

While biblical writings are no longer studied for the light they throw on the politics of the peoples of the Near and Middle East, they have much to say about ultimate values and human relationships – both at international and personal levels. Today political and geographical factors are as closely connected with the way the values are identified and expressed as they were in biblical times.

ABOVE **In all parts of the biblical lands there are place names and features which bring back the foundation events of great religions. But equally important are the basic human activities, such as a woman pricking out plants, which have remained unchanged.**

LEFT **The way new generations respond to the religious traditions they inherit may shock their elders, as modern Israel has discovered. However, they also reach new insights which apply old truths more effectively to the problems of today.**

Abandoned tanks litter the Middle East and are a stark reminder of how this troubled region is dominated by the threat of war. The plastic binding the barrel of the tank (BELOW) **indicates it is disarmed, but in fact the raised barrel is pointing towards the Syrian border.** INSET CENTRE **The 17-year-old Israeli soldier guarding the entrance to a kibbutz was only recruited three weeks previously.** INSET RIGHT **Even when off-duty, these Israeli troops exploring the ruins of Masada carry their weapons.**

· APPEN

DICES ·

The Bible in Context

There cannot be certainty about when the biblical material was written as it was so long ago and has been edited by a number of people. However, there is broad agreement about when the books were finally edited. This chart shows how the Bible developed under the stimulus of contemporary events.

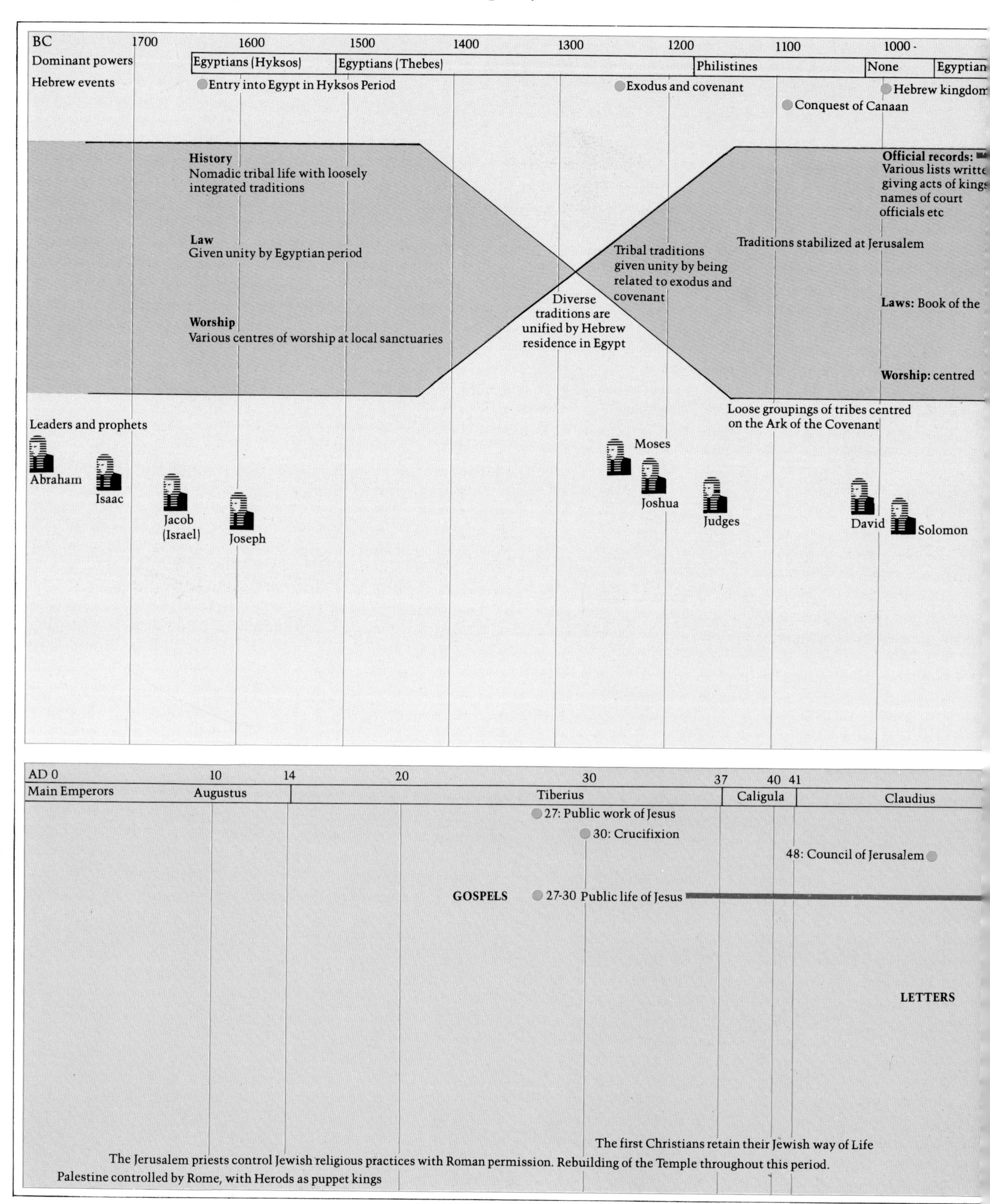

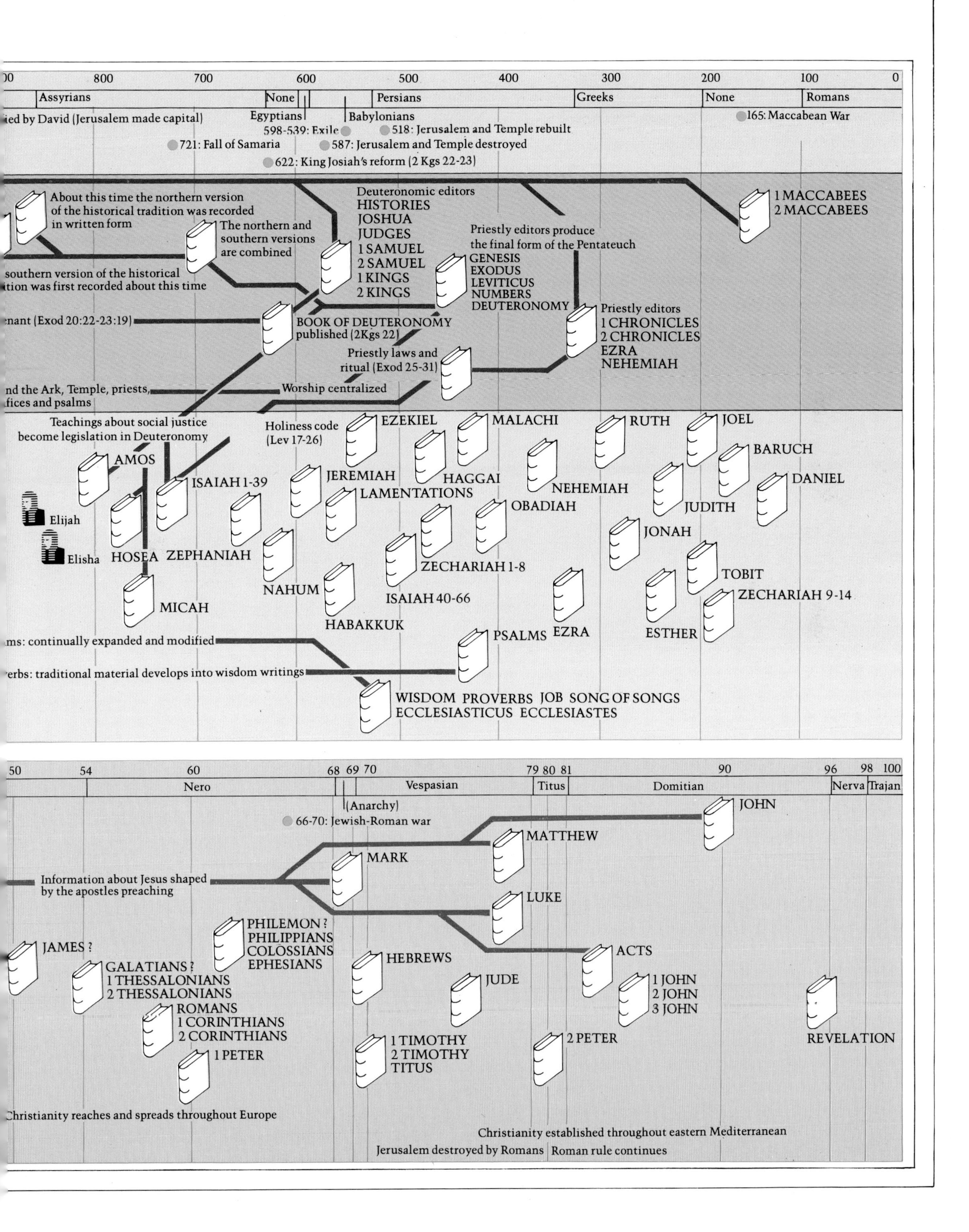

00 800 700 600 500 400 300 200 100 0
Assyrians
None
Persians
Greeks
None
Romans
Egyptians
Babylonians
ied by David (Jerusalem made capital)
598-539: Exile
518: Jerusalem and Temple rebuilt
165: Maccabean War
721: Fall of Samaria
587: Jerusalem and Temple destroyed
622: King Josiah's reform (2 Kgs 22-23)
About this time the northern version of the historical tradition was recorded in written form
The northern and southern versions are combined
southern version of the historical
ition was first recorded about this time
Deuteronomic editors
HISTORIES
JOSHUA
JUDGES
1 SAMUEL
2 SAMUEL
1 KINGS
2 KINGS
Priestly editors produce the final form of the Pentateuch
GENESIS
EXODUS
LEVITICUS
NUMBERS
DEUTERONOMY
1 MACCABEES
2 MACCABEES
nant (Exod 20:22-23:19)
BOOK OF DEUTERONOMY published (2Kgs 22)
Priestly editors
1 CHRONICLES
2 CHRONICLES
EZRA
NEHEMIAH
Priestly laws and ritual (Exod 25-31)
nd the Ark, Temple, priests,
fices and psalms
Worship centralized
Teachings about social justice become legislation in Deuteronomy
Holiness code (Lev 17-26)
EZEKIEL
MALACHI
RUTH
JOEL
BARUCH
AMOS
ISAIAH 1-39
JEREMIAH
HAGGAI
NEHEMIAH
DANIEL
LAMENTATIONS
Elijah
OBADIAH
JUDITH
Elisha
HOSEA
ZEPHANIAH
JONAH
ZECHARIAH 1-8
TOBIT
NAHUM
ISAIAH 40-66
ZECHARIAH 9-14
MICAH
HABAKKUK
PSALMS
EZRA
ESTHER
ms: continually expanded and modified
erbs: traditional material develops into wisdom writings
WISDOM PROVERBS JOB SONG OF SONGS
ECCLESIASTICUS ECCLESIASTES
50 54 60 68 69 70 79 80 81 90 96 98 100
Nero
Vespasian
Titus
Domitian
Nerva
Trajan
(Anarchy)
66-70: Jewish-Roman war
JOHN
MATTHEW
MARK
Information about Jesus shaped by the apostles preaching
LUKE
PHILEMON ?
PHILIPPIANS
COLOSSIANS
EPHESIANS
JAMES ?
GALATIANS ?
1 THESSALONIANS
2 THESSALONIANS
HEBREWS
ACTS
JUDE
1 JOHN
2 JOHN
3 JOHN
ROMANS
1 CORINTHIANS
2 CORINTHIANS
1 PETER
1 TIMOTHY
2 TIMOTHY
TITUS
2 PETER
REVELATION
Christianity reaches and spreads throughout Europe
Christianity established throughout eastern Mediterranean
Jerusalem destroyed by Romans
Roman rule continues

Chronology

3000

2500

MESOPOTAMIA

3000-2600 BC Semitic shepherds in Mesopotamia and Arabian desert

2600-2130 BC Sumerian

2130-

EGYPT

3000-2600 BC 1st-3rd Dynasties

2600-2130 BC Old King

2130-203

Hyksos rulers expelled; Egypt united; wars with Mitan

PALESTINE

3100-2100 BC Canaanites

2130-

2000 | 1500 | 1000

n south-east; Akkadians begin to dominate from Babylon

030 BC Sumerian revival; Amorites in west; Assyria briefly dominant

c1724-1595 BC Old Babylonian Empire; Hurrians in north; Persians in east

c1724-1686 BC Reign of Hammurabi

c1720 BC Code of Hammurabi

c1595-1360 BC Mitanni in north, Hurrians under Aryan rulers; Assyria controls central Mesopotamia; Kassites overthrow Babylon

Assyria dominant under Tiglath-pileser I c1100 BC

21st Dynasty, capital: Tanis 1070-945 BC

h-8th Dynasties, capital: Memphis; first completed pyramids

t Intermediate Period, 9th-11th Dynasties, capitals: Heracleopolis and Thebes

2030-1640 BC Middle Kingdom, 11th-14th Dynasties, capitals: Memphis and Thebes

1640-1530 BC 2nd Intermediate Period; 15th-16th Dynasties, Hyksos kings, capital: Avaris (Tanis); 17th Dynasty, capital: Thebes; Hittites in Asia Minor

New Kingdom, 18th-20th Dynasties, capital: Thebes; 1550-1070 BC

c1358-1349 BC Reign of Tut'ankhamun

Akhnaton tries to impose monotheism; capital: Tell el-Amarna 1360 BC

Reign of Rameses II, capital: Pi-Rameses 1290-1224 BC

20th Dynasty 1194-1070 BC

Reign of Rameses III 1194-1163 BC

Victory over the 'Sea Peoples' 1175 BC

30 BC Canaanites; Amorites in north; Egypt controls coastal region

c1800-1600 BC Abraham, Isaac and Jacob

1640-1530 BC Hebrew groups settle in Egypt on borders of Canaan

Canaanites under Egyptian control 1550-1070 BC

Hebrew groups settle in northern, central and southern Canaan c1360 BC

Battle of Kadesh, narrow Egyptian victory over Hittites 1285 BC

Hebrew escape from Egypt (the exodus) 1250 BC

Hebrew domination of Canaan begins under Joshua 1220-1200 BC

Philistines occupy the Palestinian coast 1200-900 BC

The Judges c1200-1025 BC

Reign of David c1010-970 BC

Reign of Saul c1030-1010 BC

Samuel c1040 BC

YRIA

Victory of the Philistines at Aphek c1050 BC

OME AND GREECE

Aramaean kingdoms of Damascus, Zobah, Hamath etc c1100 BC

SIA MINOR AND BEYOND

Trojan War 1194-1184 BC

1000 | 900 | 800

MESOPOTAMIA

EGYPT

945-924 BC Reign of Sheshonk I, his campaign in Palestine

945-725 BC 22nd Dynasty, capital: Bubastis

PALESTINE

841-835 BC (Judah) Reign of Athaliah

● c1000 BC Capture of Jerusalem

835-796 BC (Judah) Reign of Jo

c970-931 BC Reign of Solomon

814-798 BC (Israel) Reign of Jeho

931-910 BC (Israel) Reign of Jeroboam I

798-783 BC (Israel) Reig

931-913 BC (Judah) Reign of Rehoboam

796-781 BC (Judah) Re

913-911 BC (Judah) Reign of Abijah

841-814 BC (Israel) Reign of Jehu

911-870 BC (Judah) Reign of Asa

910-909 BC (Israel) Reign of Nadab

909-886 BC (Israel) Reign of Baasha

886-885 BC (Israel) Reign of Elah

● 885 BC (Israel) Zimri rules for seven days

885-874 BC (Israel) Reign of Omri; founding of Samaria

874-853 BC (Israel) Reign of Ahab; Elijah

870-848 BC (Judah) Reign of Jehoshaphat

853-852 BC (Israel) Reign of Ochozias

852-841 BC (Israel) Reign of Jehoram; Elisha

848-841 BC (Judah) Reign of Jehoram

Captur

SYRIA

Hazael, king of Damascus, defeated by Shalmaneser III 841 BC ●

Tiglath-pileser III receives tribute from Rezin, king of Damascus

ROME AND GREECE

● c75

ASIA MINOR AND BEYOND

● 841 BC (Assyria) Shalmaneser III reaches the sea

883-859 BC Revival of Assyria, reign of Ashurnasirpal

858-824 BC (Assyria) Reign of Shalmaneser III

● 853 BC Battle at Qarqar

700 600 500

704-681 BC Reign of Sennacherib
701 BC Sennacherib defeats Egyptians at Eltekeh and captures Lachish
680-669 BC Reign of Esarhaddon
626-539 BC Neo-Babylonian Dynasty
626-605 BC Reign of Nebupolassar
609 BC Nebupolassar repulses the army of Necho II
605 BC Crown prince Nebuchadnezzar defeats Necho's armies at Carchemish
c750 BC Rivalry between 22nd Dynasty (capital: Bubastis) and 23rd Dynasty (capital: Thebes)
669-630 BC Reign of Ashurbanipal
556-539 BC Reign of Nabonidus
Cyrus II captures Babylon 539 BC
724-715 BC 24th Dynasty, capital: Sais
605-562 BC Reign of Nebuchadnezzar
715-663 BC 25th Dynasty, capital: Nubia
685-664 BC Reign of Tirhakah
c671 BC Esarhaddon takes control of Lower Egypt
750 BC (Israel) Amos and Hosea
668 BC Ashurbanipal pushes Tirhakah back beyond Thebes
743 BC (Israel) Reign of Shallum
663 BC The sacking of Thebes
Joash
740 BC (Judah) Isaiah
663-525 BC 26th Dynasty, capital: Sais
Amaziah
663-609 BC Reign of Psammetichus I
781-740 BC (Israel) Reign of Uzziah
c650 BC Psammetichus I drives the Assyrians out of Egypt
743 BC (Israel) Reign of Zechariah
609-594 BC Reign of Necho II
743-738 BC (Israel) Reign of Menahem
601 BC Nebuchadnezzar is defeated in Egypt
740-736 BC (Judah) Reign of Jotham; Micah
c 630 BC Zephaniah
594-589 BC Reign of Psammetichus II
738-737 BC (Israel) Reign of Pekahiah
642-640 BC Reign of Amon
589-570 BC Reign of Apries (Hophra)
737-732 BC (Israel) Reign of Pekah
Beginning of reign of Psammetichus III 525 BC
735-715 BC (Judah) Reign of Ahaz; Rezin and Pekah besiege Jerusalem; Isaiah's prophecy of Emmanuel
c734 BC Tiglath-pileser III captures part of Galilee
640-609 BC Reign of Josiah
732-724 BC (Israel) Reign of Hoshea
627 BC Call of Jeremiah
582-581 BC Further exile to Babylon
724-722 BC Samaria besieged by Shalmaneser V
622 BC Religious reform
715-687 BC Reign of Hezekiah
c612 BC Nahum
711 BC Sargon captures Ashdod
609 BC Reign of Jehoahaz
c704 BC Hezekiah pays tribute to Sennacherib
609-598 BC Reign of Jehoiakim
687-642 BC Reign of Manasseh
588 BC Diversion by Apries
604-587 BC Nebuchadnezzar conquers Palestine
600 BC Revolt of Jehoiakim; Habukkuk
598-597 BC Reign of Jehoiachin
597-587 BC Reign of Zedekiah
589 BC Revolt of Zedekiah, siege of Jerusalem
destruction of Jerusalem, exile to Babylon; assassination of the governor of Judah, Gedaliah 587 BC
c732 BC Tiglath-pileser III leads campaign against Rezin
Foundation of the Second Temple 537 BC
738 BC
c732 BC End of independence of Damascus
The Edict of Cyrus, return from Babylon 538 BC
Building of the Second Temple; Zerubbabel is high commissioner; Joshua is high priest; Haggai and Zechariah 520-515 BC
ounding of Rome
(Greece) Life of Pythagoras 570-497 BC
Roman Republic declared 509 BC
721-705 BC (Assyria) Reign of Sargon II; 721 BC he captures Samaria, inhabitants deported; he defeats Sibe, of Egypt
Nebupolassar and Cyaxares, king of Medes, take and destroy Nineveh 612 BC
606 BC Nebupolassar ends the Assyrian Empire
(Persia) Reign of Cyrus II 555-529 BC
783-745 BC Assyria weak
Cyrus II captures Ecbatana 550 BC
754-727 BC (Assyria) Reign of Tiglath-pileser III
Cyrus II captures Sardis and Pteria 546 BC
726-722 BC (Assyria) Reign of Shalmaneser V
(Persia) Reign of Cambyses' 529-522 BC

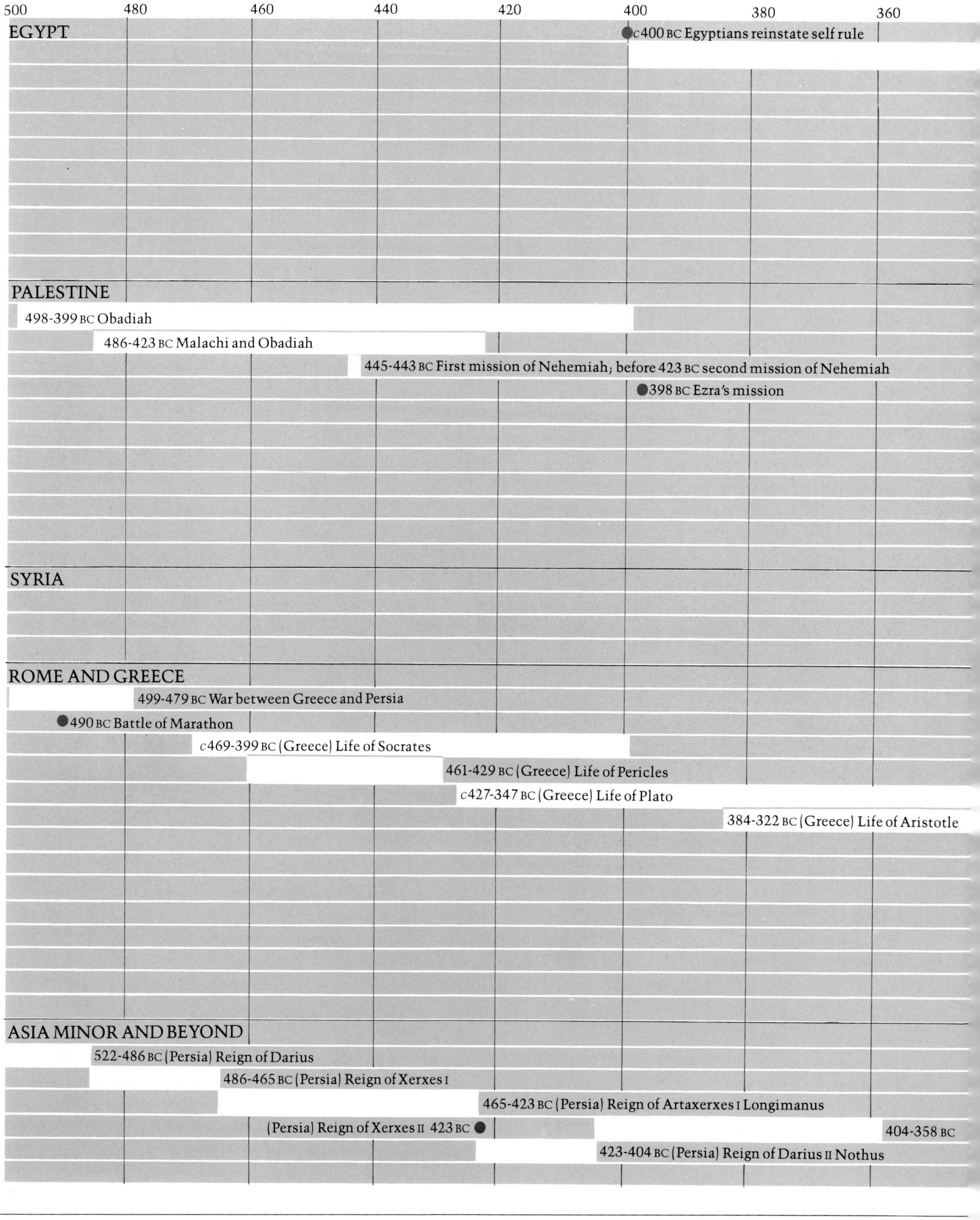

500 480 460 440 420 400 380 360

EGYPT

- c400 BC Egyptians reinstate self rule

PALESTINE

- 498-399 BC Obadiah
- 486-423 BC Malachi and Obadiah
- 445-443 BC First mission of Nehemiah; before 423 BC second mission of Nehemiah
- 398 BC Ezra's mission

SYRIA

ROME AND GREECE

- 499-479 BC War between Greece and Persia
- 490 BC Battle of Marathon
- c469-399 BC (Greece) Life of Socrates
- 461-429 BC (Greece) Life of Pericles
- c427-347 BC (Greece) Life of Plato
- 384-322 BC (Greece) Life of Aristotle

ASIA MINOR AND BEYOND

- 522-486 BC (Persia) Reign of Darius
- 486-465 BC (Persia) Reign of Xerxes I
- 465-423 BC (Persia) Reign of Artaxerxes I Longimanus
- (Persia) Reign of Xerxes II 423 BC
- 404-358 BC
- 423-404 BC (Persia) Reign of Darius II Nothus

340 320 300 280 260 240 220 200

400-343 BC 28th-30th Dynasties
Reign of Ptolemy V Epiphanes 204-180 BC
● 331 BC Foundation of Alexandria
304-30 BC Egypt is ruled by Ptolemies
304-284 BC Reign of Ptolemy I Soter
285-246 BC Reign of Ptolemy II Philadelphus
276-273 BC Egypt at war with Syria
Reign of Ptolemy III Euergetes 246-221 BC
Reign of Ptolemy IV Philopator 221-205 BC

Before 336 BC Joel; Chronicles; Ezra-Nehemiah
c336-331 BC Jonah; Tobit
● 332 BC Alexander captures Tyre and Gaza; he enters Egypt
304-200 BC Judea is ruled by Ptolemies
● c246 BC Esther and Ecclesiastes
Egyptian victory over Antiochus III at Raphia 217 BC ●
Antiochus III reconquers Palestine 202-200 BC

c305-125 BC Seleucid Dynasty
c305-281 BC Reign of Seleucus I Nicator
281-261 BC Reign of Antiochus I Soter
● 333 BC Alexander conquers Syria
261-246 BC Reign of Antiochus II Theos
Reign of Seleucus II Callinicos 246-226 BC
Reign of Seleucus III Ceraunus 226-223 BC
Reign of Antiochus III the Great 223-187 BC

336-323 BC (Greece) Reign of Alexander the Great
333-63 BC The Hellenist Period
● 323 BC Alexander dies in Babylon
● c305 BC (Greece) Foundation of the Epicurean and Stoic schools
First Punic War between Rome and Carthage 264-241 BC
● 241 BC Romans conquer Sicily
Romans conquer Sardinia and Corsica 238 BC ●
Hannibal's land campaigns against Rome 219-202 BC
Second Punic War between Rome and Carthage 218-201 BC
Hannibal's land campaigns against Rome 209-207 BC

ersia) Reign of Artaxerxes II Mnemon
● 301 BC Battle of Ipsus
● 331 BC Alexander ends the Persian Empire
330-326 BC Alexander conquers the eastern satrapies and India

200 | 180 | 160 | 140 | 120

MESOPOTAMIA

171-138 BC Reign of Mithridates I Arsaces I, king of the Parthi

● 141 BC Mithridates takes Seleucia (on the Tigris) and Babylon

EGYPT

PALESTINE

200-142 BC Judea ruled by the Seleucids; Antiochus III confirms

c189-175 BC Simon II (the Just) is high priest; then Onias III is high priest

174-171 BC Jason is high priest

● 171 BC Menelaus is high priest, he has Onias III killed

167-164 BC The great persecution; sacrifices made to Olympian Zeus in the Temple; revolt of

166-160 BC Judas Maccabeus continues the revolt

104-10

● c164 BC Book of Daniel

103-76

● 164 BC Purification of the Temple

● c1

● c162 BC Judas Maccabeus allied with Rome

● 160 BC Nicanor defeated

160-143 BC Jonathan leads the Jews

● 152 BC Jonathan is made high priest

● 145 BC Charter of Demetrius II confirms Jonathan as ruler of Judea

143-134 BC Simon ruler of Judea

● c141 BC Renewal of alliances with Rome and Sparta

● c130 BC Formation of the Essene community a

SYRIA

● 190 BC Antiochus III defeated at Magnesia

187-175 BC Reign of Seleucus IV Philopator

175-164 BC Reign of Antiochus IV Epiphanes

164-161 BC Reign of Antiochus V Eupator

161-150 BC Reign of Demetrius I Soter

145-140 BC First reign of Demetrius II

144-142 BC Antiochus IV installed in Antioch

142-138 BC Tryphon succeeds Antiochus VI in Antioch

129-125 BC Second reign of Demetrius II

● 197 BC Flaminius of Rome defeats Philip V of Macedonia; Spain conquered by Rome

ROME AND GREECE

149-146 BC Third Punic War between Rome and Carthage

● 148 BC Macedonia becomes a Roman province

● 146 BC Romans destroy Carthage and Corinth

● 133 BC Attalus III, king of Pergamum, bequeaths his

ASIA MINOR AND BEYOND

● c150 BC Mithridates is ruler of almost all Persia

100 80 60 40 20 0

40 BC Parthians in Syria and Palestine

38 BC Parthians driven from Syria and Palestine

51-30 BC Reign of Cleopatra VII

30 BC Suicide of Antony and Cleopatra, Egypt becomes a Roman province

he theocratic status of the Jews

Mattathias

Reign of Aristobulus I

Reign of Alexander Jannaeus

50 BC Judith

76-67 BC Reign of Alexandra

67-63 BC Reign of Aristobulus II, he is also high priest

63 BC Pompey takes Jerusalem; Idumaean Antipator is real ruler of Judea

54 BC Crassus pillages the Temple

c50 BC Wisdom

47 BC Herod is named strategos of Galilee

Qumran

41 BC Herod and Phasael are made tetrarchs

37 BC Capture of Jerusalem by Herod and Sosius

37-4 BC Reign of Herod the Great

Rebuilding of the Temple begins 20 BC

Birth of Jesus c7 BC

Death of Herod 4 BC

95-88 BC Reign of Demetrius III (at Damascus)

63 BC Pompey at Damascus

state to Rome

67 BC Crete and Cyrenaica become a Roman province

66-62 BC Pompey in the east; Pontus and Bithynia become Roman provinces

64 BC Pompey deposes Philip II and Syria becomes a Roman province

55 BC Romans invade Britain

48 BC (Rome) Julius Caesar defeats Pompey

44 BC (Rome) Caesar assassinated

40 BC Roman senate names Herod 'King of Judea'

(Rome) Octavian defeats Antony at Actium 31 BC

Octavian is made Imperator of Rome for life 29 BC

Octavian is made emperor and named Augustus Caesar 27 BC

Galatia becomes a Roman province 25 BC

70 BC Tigranes, king of Armenia, dominates Syria

0 20 40 60 80 100 120 140 160 180 20

EGYPT

AD 38 Persecution of Jews in Alexandria

PALESTINE

4 BC-AD 39 Herod Antipas is tetrarch of Galilee and Perea; Philip is tetrarch of Gaulanitis, Batanaca, Trachonitis and Auranit

AD 6-14 Judea is a prefectorial province of Rome

c AD 26-36 Pontius Pilate is procurator

AD 27 John the Baptist preaching and the beginning of the ministry of Jesus

AD 30 Death of Jesus; outpouring of the Spirit of the Church

c AD 34-36 Martyrdom of Stephen; conversion of Paul

AD 53-58 Third mission of Paul

AD 58-60 Paul held at Caesarea

AD 67-68 The Zealots are masters of Jerusalem

c AD 39 Peter in Samaria

c AD 75 Gospel of Matthew; Gospel of Luke; Acts of Apostles; the Letter of Jude

AD 41-48 Herod becomes king of Chalcis

AD 44-46 Judea again a prefectorial province of Rome

AD 70 Judea an imperial province of Rome

AD 45-49 First mission of Paul

c AD 95 2 Peter; Gospel of John; 1 John (3 John and 2 John possibly earlier); Revel

c AD 48 Famine in Judea; the Council of Jerusalem

AD 49-52 Second mission of Paul

116 Rebellion against Romans leads to dispersion of Jews

AD 50-52 Letters to the Thessalonians

AD 66 Jerusalem attacked by Cestius Gallius; Christians take refuge in Pella

AD 66-70 Jewish war against Romans

AD 67 Vespasian reconquers Galilee

c AD 67 Paul a prisoner in Rome; 2 Timothy; Paul is beheaded; Letter to the Hebrews

c AD 57 First Letter to the Corinthians; AD 57 second Letter to the Corinthians; Letter to the Galatians; Lette

AD 58 James's Letter to the Jews of the Dispersion; Paul arrested in the Temple

AD 69 Vespasian subdues Judea but the Zealots hold out in Jerusalem, Herodium, Masada and Macha

AD 60 Paul appears before Festus and appeals to Caesar; he starts his voyage to Rome

AD 61-63 Paul in Rome; Letters to Colossians, Ephesians, Philemon, and Philippians(?)

AD 70 Titus lays siege to Jerusalem, burning of the Temple, capture of the Upper City and the Palace

c AD 63 Paul set free(?); Gospel of Mark and 1 Peter; Letter of James; 1 Timothy; Letter to Titus?

AD 66 Florus crucifies some Jews in Jerusalem; troubles in Caesarea and throughout country

ROME AND GREECE

AD 14-37 (Rome) Emperor Tiberius

AD 37-41 (Rome) Emperor Caligula

AD 41-54 (Rome) Emperor Claudius

AD 54-68 (Rome) Emperor Nero

AD 64 Burning of Rome, persecution of Christians

AD 64-67 Martyrdom of Peter at Rome

AD 66-67 Nero in Greece; he appoints Vespasian and Titus to restore order in Palestine

AD 68 (Rome) Galba is emperor; Nero commits suicide

AD 69 (Rome) Otho proclaimed emperor by the Praetorians, Vitellius proclaimed emperor by the legi

AD 69-79 (Rome) Emperor Vespasian

AD 79-81 (Rome) Emperor Titus

AD 96-98 (Rome) Emperor Nerva

AD 98-117 (Rome) Emperor Trajan

AD 81-96 (Rome) Emperor Domitian

117 The Roman Empire reaches its greatest extent

117 Christians martyred in Lyon (Gaul)

300 400 500 600 700

306-337 (Rome) Emperor Constantine

● 313 Edict of Milan, legal recognition of Christianity within the Roman Empire

the Romans

● 325 First ecumenical council held at Nicea

● 331 Capital of Roman Empire moved to Constantinople

● 370 First appearance of Huns in Europe

of Herod

381-787 Further six ecumenical councils

ROME AND GREECE

● 432 St Patrick's mission to Ireland begins

in Germany

ASIA MINOR AND BEYOND

● *c*350 Huns invade Persia and India

Life of Mohammed 570-632

Mohammed begins preaching at Mecca *c*613 ●

Glossary

Altar A place of sacrifice, usually a heap of earth or stones, a single stone or a stone table, standing before a temple.

Akkadian An ancient language spoken in Mesopotamia from *c* 3000 BC until the time of Christ. Assyrian and Babylonian were two dialect forms. The Akkadians adopted the cuneiform system of writing. *See Cuneiform.*

Amalekites A nomadic shepherd tribe of southern Palestine and the Sinai Peninsula.

Ammonites An Aramaean tribe settled east of the Jordan Valley.

Anoint To pour oil on people or objects to show they are dedicated to sacred purposes, particularly kings or priests. *See Christ and Messiah.*

Apostle From Greek, the word means 'one who is sent with authority'. In the New Testament it usually refers to one of Jesus' 12 disciples. *See Disciple.*

Apocalyptic writing Deliberately cryptical works, written to encourage persecuted groups.

Aramaeans Nomadic tribes of Syria and Mesopotamia related to the Hebrews.

Aramaic The Semitic language of the Aramaeans widely used for 1,000 years from the time of the Persian Empire. This was native language of Jesus.

Ark of the Covenant The small, sacred box, containing the Ten Commandments, carried to Canaan by the Hebrews, for which the Temple in Jerusulem was built.

Aryans Nomadic tribes who invaded Asia Minor and Mesopotamia from southern Russia and Turkistan during the 2nd millenium BC.

Asherah A Canaanite fertility goddess, consort of Baal.

Asia Most of the western part of what is now Asia Minor.

Assyrians The Mesopotamians who conquered the Near and Middle East early in the 1st millenium BC. Their main capital was Nineveh on the River Tigris.

Baal Literally 'overlord' in Hebrew; the title of the main Canaanite fertility god.

Babylonians The Mesopotamians of the River Euphrates who overthrew the Assyrians and took the Hebrews into exile.

Blood The life principle released by sacrifice.

Bronze An alloy of copper and tin, strong and easily worked, in common use before iron. The Bronze Age was *c* 3200-1200 BC.

Buddhism One of the main Asian religions, founded in the sixth to fifth century BC by Siddhartha Gautama, the Buddha.

Canaan The older (2nd millenium BC) name for the general region of Palestine.

Cataract A stretch of rapids interrupting the flow of the River Nile. There are six main cataracts and they were sometimes used to mark political frontiers.

Chaldeans A Semitic tribe of southern Mesopotamia.

Christ Literally 'the anointed one' in Greek, and thus God's chosen servant. *See Messiah.*

City-state A self-governing city which was also a state and often had dependencies, mainly found in ancient Greece.

Council The supreme Jewish religious council during New Testament times.

Covenant The solemn agreement in which the Hebrews believed God had chosen them.

Crucifixion Execution by nailing or tying to a wooden cross.

Cuneiform From the Latin word for 'wedge', Mesopotamian writing which had wedge-shaped letters. It was written on clay tablets with a stylus.

Desert Marginal pasture areas supporting nomadic pastoral tribes.

Diaspora Jewish communities outside Palestine.

Dynasty A line of rulers who usually come from the same family. The rulers in ancient Egypt and China belonged to dynasties.

Edomites People living from the Dead Sea southwards to the Gulf of Aqaba.

Egyptians People of the Nile Valley from the First Cataract to the Mediterranean.

Essenes An unorthodox Jewish monastic movement of New Testament times, now famous for the 'Dead Sea Scrolls'. *See Scrolls.*

Ethiopians People of the Nile Valley above the First Cataract living in Cush (modern Sudan). They were also called Nubians.

Eucharist Literally 'thanksgiving' in Greek. *See Last Supper.*

Evangelist A teacher of the 'gospel'; more usually the author of a Gospel.

Exile The deportation of Hebrews to Babylonia in 598 BC and 587-539 BC.

Exodus The escape of the Hebrews from Egypt in *c* 1250 BC.

'Fertile crescent' The agricultural area from Upper Egypt, through Palestine and Syria, to Mesopotamia and the Persian Gulf.

Fertility gods The deities worshipped in fertility rites performed by primitive agricultural communities to ensure an abundance of crops and the successful birth of children.

Gentile Anyone who is not a Jew.

Gnosticism Derived from the Greek meaning 'pertaining to knowledge'; a religious movement which offered salvation by secret knowledge.

Gospel Literally 'good news'; the message of salvation associated with Jesus Christ.

Greeks All who spoke the Greek language and adopted the Greek way of life. *See Hellenism.*

Hebrews The descendants of Abraham; the origins of the word are obscure and may have designated a mercenary warrior class associated with nomadic Semitic tribesmen.

Hebrew language A Canaanite dialect, replaced by Aramaic but surviving in sacred writings and worship.

Hellenism The culture which spread from the Greek mainland and its colonies.

Herod Usually Herod the Great, king of Judea under the Romans 37-4 BC, but also several of his descendants.

Hieroglyph A pictorial symbol used in ancient writing particularly by the Egyptians.

High place Essentially an open air sanctuary where a primitive cult was practised.

Hinduism A main religion of India which developed gradually over 4,000 years and is unique as it has no founder.

Hittites A people who ruled Syria from Turkey before the time of the Israelites and Arameans. They narrowly lost the Battle of Kadesh against the Egyptians in 1285 BC.Their empire disappeared when the 'Sea Peoples' invaded in *c* 1200 BC.

Hurrians A group of people who formed part of the Hittite Empire. They date from 2500 BC and were settled throughout the 'fertile crescent'. Mitanni in Upper Mesopotamia was an influential Hurrian state.

Hyksos The Asiatic people who invaded Egypt in the Second Intermediate Period between the Middle Kingdom and the New Kingdom. It is likely that the Israelites settled in Egypt during the Hyksos period.

Incense Aromatic gums burned in worship, especially during sacrifices.

Iron The more common metal from *c* 1200 BC, hence 'Iron Age'.

Islam The main religion of

much of Asia in which Mohammed is the prophet. Followers of the Islamic religion are called Moslems. They are devoted to the Koran, a book written in Arabic, which is believed to be the revelation of God to Mohammed.

Israelites Confusingly, all Hebrews, or members of the northern Hebrew kingdom from the split into two kingdoms (931 BC) until its destruction in 721 BC. Their capital was Samaria.

Jehovah *See Yahweh.*

Jew Strictly, a member of the tribe of Judah, but after the exile any Hebrew.

Judea Southern Palestine in Greek and Roman times.

Judah One of the 12 tribes, and the southern Hebrew kingdom after the split of 931 BC until its destruction in 587 BC; the capital was Jerusalem. *See Exile.*

Judaism The modern name given to the religious beliefs, practices and way of life of the Jews. The term is not used in the Bible.

Kassites A people who ruled in Babylon from the eighteenth century until the twelfth century BC. They were probably Indo-Europeans.

Law In a special sense, the first five books of the Bible.

Last Supper Also called the Lord's Supper, the final meal of Jesus and the disciples before his arrest. The Christian commemorative meal, the eucharist, derived from it.

Maccabee Literally 'hammer' in Hebrew; the nickname of the leaders of the successful Jewish rebellion against Greek rule in 165 BC.

Magi Persian priests.

Marduk The chief god of Babylon.

Mesopotamia The land area from the Persian Gulf northwards, drained by the Tigris and Euphrates rivers.

Messiah Literally 'the anointed one' in Hebrew. *See Christ.*

Midianites A nomadic tribe closely associated with the Israelites who lived along the coast of the Red Sea to the south of Edom. Moses married a Midianite wife. The Midianites were the first to domesticate the camel.

Millenium A period of 100 years.

Mitanni The name of a state in Mesopotamia powerful betwen 1500 and 1370 BC. It supported a large Hurrian population. Mitanni was eventually conquered by the Hittites early in the fourteenth century BC.

Moabites A people who lived to the east of the Dead Sea on the River Arnon. Although they were related to them through Lot, they frequently fought against the Israelites during the Old Testament period.

Monotheism A belief in the existence of only one god and the exclusive worship of that god.

Mosaic covenant The covenant made with Moses on Mount Sinai in which the Ten Commandments were given to the people. *See Covenant.*

Mystery religion A type of religion in which its members are sworn to secrecy.

Nomads Tented tribes who herd sheep and goats across sparse pastures.

Nubians *See Ethiopians*

Obelisk A four-sided tapering shaft of stone with a small pyramid at the top. Obelisks were associated with sun worship and were often placed in pairs outside the entrances of Egyptian temples and tombs.

Oil Invariably, olive oil used in cooking, medicine, cosmetics, lamps and religious rites. *See Anoint.*

Palestine Strictly the coastal strip northeast of Egypt settled by Philistines, but extended to refer to the land from Lebanon to the Sinai Desert.

Panathenea A Greek religious festival held annually in Athens in honour of their goddess Athena.

Pantheon Originally, the term applied to the temple at Rome built in 27 BC to all the gods. It is also used to describe all the gods as a group.

Pantheism From the Greek words for 'all' and 'god', any religion or belief which holds that 'God is all and all is God' so identifying God and the whole universe with each other.

Parthians A people, famous for their archers and horsemen, whose empire was at its height in the first century BC. It extended from the River Euphrates as far as the Indus and the Indian Ocean. The empire fell into decline when the Persians conquered the Parthians in AD 226.

Passion The sufferings of Jesus from his arrest to his crucifixion.

Passover The oldest Hebrew festival commemorating the exodus.

Patriarchs The main Hebrew ancestors from Adam to Joseph.

Pentateuch Literally 'five books' in Greek; the first five books of the Old Testament.

Pentecost From the Greek meaning 50th; a harvest festival 50 days after that of Unleavened Bread.

Persians A people east of the Persian Gulf who overthrew the Babylonians in 540 BC, themselves overthrown by Alexander the Great in 331 BC.

Pharisees A lay Jewish group committed to a strict interpretation of the law.

Philistines The people who occupied the Palestinian coastal plain between the sea and the Shephelah. The name 'Palestine' is a derivative of Philistine. Some of the 'Sea Peoples' who invaded Egypt in the late 19th and early 20th dynasties were Philistines.

Polytheism The belief in many or more than one god.

Prefectorial province A district administered by a prefect appointed by the authorities in ancient Rome.

Priest The class responsible for oracles, law and performing sacrifices, eventually exclusive and hereditary.

Procurator A Roman official directly responsible to the emperor.

Prophet A person claiming to speak in God's name.

Psalm A song used in worship.

Puppet kingdom A kingdom which is more or less completely governed by and is answerable to a more powerful kingdom or state.

Qumran Site of an Essene community near the northwest shore of the Dead Sea.

Rabbi Literally 'my master' in Aramaic; a teacher, especially a scribe.

Satrap A governor of a province (or satrapy) in ancient Persia.

Scroll A rolled book usually written on a long strip of papyrus or sheepskin. The 'Dead Sea Scrolls' are the recently discovered Essene library from Qumran.

'Sea Peoples' *See Philistines.*

Semites Peoples from the Arabian Desert, including Hebrews, with related languages.

Septuagint The ancient translation of the Old Testament into Greek.

Sumerians People controlling southern Mesopotamia in the 3rd millenium BC.

Synagogue Literally 'assembly place' derived from Greek; a Jewish meeting place for worship, teaching and discussion.

Tabernacle The tent shrine of the Ark of the Covenant before the Temple was built.

Tabernacles The third harvest festival, named after the tents harvesters used in the fields.

Tell An artificial mound indicating an abandoned settlement.

Temple Any building dedicated to gods and associated with their presence. In this book, temple with a capital 'T' refers to the one in Jerusalem.

Testament Another translation of the words for 'covenant'. *See Covenant.*

Tetrarchy In the Roman Empire, a fourth part of a country or province. Each was ruled by a tetrarch.

Theocracy A form of government in which a god is recognized as supreme ruler and his laws are carried out by priests.

Unleavened Bread Bread made without yeast, offered as a pure harvest sacrifice, hence the name of the first harvest festival attached to the Passover.

Vulgate The ancient Latin translation of the Bible.

Wadi A watercourse which is dry except during periods of rainfall, found in places such as Egypt.

Yahweh The modern transliteration of the Hebrew personal name of God.

Zeus The chief god of the ancient Greeks, identified as Jupiter by the Romans.

Ziggurat A Mesopotamian tower-like temple.

Zion The ancient Davidic citadel of Jerusalem. The exact location is not certain.

Zealots A fanatical Jewish sect who rebelled against the Romans and were not accepted by other Jews. They carried out many assassinations and were responsible for numerous revolts. They were the main initiators of the Jewish-Roman war in AD 66.

Index

Italic page numbers refer to the illustrations.
Bold numbers refer to the maps.